Participation in Public Policy-Making

Editor: Tiziano Treu

Participation in Public Policy-Making

The Role of Trade Unions and Employers' Associations

Editor: Tiziano Treu

A Publication of the International Industrial Relations Association

Walter de Gruyter · Berlin · New York 1992

Tiziano Treu is Professor of Labour Law at the Catholic University of Milan and President of the Italian Section of IIRA.

(International Industrial Relations Association) and Member of the Executive Committee of IIRA.

With 11 figures, 5 charts and 23 tables

∞ Printed on acid-free paper which falls within the guidelines of the ANSI to ensure permanence and durability

Library of Congress Cataloging-in-publication Data

Participation in public-policy: the role of trade unions and employer's associations/editor, Tiziano Treu.
XIV, 282p. 15,5 × 23 cm.
"A publication of the International Industrial Relations Association."
Includes bibliographical references and index.
ISBN 3-11-012913-2 (alk. paper)
1. Trade-Unions—Political activity. 2. Employers' associations—Political activity. 3. Industrial relations. I. Treu, Tiziano. II. International Industrial Relations Association.
HD8031.P37 1992 91-46453
322'.2—dc20 CIP

Deutsche Bibliothek Cataloging-in-Publication Data

Participation in public policy-making: the role of trade unions and employers' association / a publ. of the International Industrial Relations Association. Ed.: Tiziano Treu.—Berlin; New York: de Gruyter, 1992
ISBN 3-11-012913-2
NE: Treu, Tiziano [Hrsg.]; International Industrial Relations Association

Printed in Germany
Typesetting: Wyvern Typesetting Ltd, Bristol, GB—Printing: WB-Druck GmbH, Rieden a/Forggensee—Binding: Lüderitz & Bauer GmbH, 1000 Berlin 61—Cover design: Johannes Rother, 1000 Berlin 21.

To Ezio Tarantelli
in memory and affection

Editors' Preface

The issues presented in this volume have been repeatedly discussed in the study group set up at the Kyoto Congress of the IIRA (International Industrial Relations Association) in September 1984 by Ezio Tarantelli and myself on "Tripartism and concerted actions and economic policies".
Most of the papers were formally presented at the last session of the study group during the 8th Congress of the IIRA (Bruxelles, September 1989) which was organized in memory of Ezio Tarantelli; to him most of the writers are still bound by strong memories and affection.
I am grateful to Roger Blanpain, Past Presidento of the IIRA, and to Alan Gladstone, Secretary of the same Association, for their advice and support in the preparation of this volume.

Milan, October 1991 Tiziano Treu

Table of Contents

1 Tripartite Social Policy-Making: An Overview

Tiziano Treu

1.1 Content and Purpose of a Comparative Analysis

The issues presented in this volume have a long tradition in social science research and were at the center of intense discussion during the 1970s. During that decade recurrent criticism was directed at the poor functioning of the pluralistic models of industrial relations, particularly in those European countries where they originated and developed.

This criticism had previous and wider origins: In many respects it anticipated the specific analysis of the economic and (social) shortcomings of the pluralistic industrial relations systems. Some of the most penetrating analysis denounced the political "inconsistencies" and distortions of this system whereby its features appeared considerably altered with respect to the model and to its assumptions.

Competition between pluralistic groups and their voluntaristic character was being reduced; the relations of these groups with the state, on the contrary, intensified (in both directions) accounting for an ambivalent mixture of functions; the *pluralistic* interaction of the groups did not guarantee rational distribution of resources nor social peace, contrary to the optimistic theories of the 1960s which had forecast a peaceful convergence of developed societies toward the same model favored by a balanced composition of distributive conflicts.

Not only was the "*destabilizing*" potentials of conflict among organized groups underestimated, but also *their negative* impact on labor and price/wage flexibility. In fact the negative effects of these systems on (national) economic performances came to be under attack in coincidence with the severe oil and inflationary "shock" suffered by Western economies during that period.

Precisely as a reaction to these shortcomings, in the 1970s a large part of the European systems introduced significant corrections to the pluralistic model. They were directed essentially at increasing the institutional *involvement* of interest groups (unions and employers in the first place) in economic and social decision-making, through concerted action supported by state action toward what came to be commonly (re)named the neocorporatist model.

Social research and political debate during that period devoted considerable attention to the innovation introduced in the practice of industrial relations and to their implication for the structure and functioning of the pre-existing systems, to the elements of continuity and discontinuity with the past. Some basic concepts of the pluralistic system were re-examined, beginning with the distinction between collective bargaining, consultation, and participation; and between bipartism and tripartism in industrial relations. But the very notion of neocorporatism maintained a substantial degree of uncertainty and ambiguity in spite of its long history and of the great analytical efforts made to clarify it.

These conceptual controversies are far from settled, as evidenced in the paper by Dell'Aringa and Samek, where the authors review the different constructions of "neocorporatism" and consequently the different implications for the measurement of the degree of corporatism of different national systems (and in fact we have used also for this reason a different terminology to indicate our object of analysis).

More important for our purpose is to note that during the 1970s analysis was largely theoretical and only to a limited extent supported by empirical evidence. Empirical research was scarcely developed and conducted on national cases with analytical tools hardly sufficient to draw comparative inferences based on a complete or significant set of variables.[1] Moreover, it was concentrated predominantly on specific and partial applications of the corporatist model – those developed in central European countries. On the other hand, it was directed toward analyzing the centralized aspects of these corporatist practices, namely social concertation, aimed at controlling inflation and economic crisis. In this respect it was clearly influenced by the critical issues of the decade. Accordingly, income policies came to be considered as "the heart of neocorporatism", which in itself is questionable.

The rather narrow approach of empirical research, to some extent more limited than the practice itself, may have been influential in emphasizing some conceptual and political polemics on the issue. It has contributed to obscure the elements of continuity and to exacerbate those of opposition between neocorporatist practices (or similar forms of tripartite policy-making) and the pluralistic formulas, and between their basic components (in particular collective bargaining and consultation participation; bilateral and trilateral exchange); to emphasize centralization as a typical or inevitable feature of social concertation; and to present these practices as responding to a monolithic model instead of a "multidimensional concept and formula susceptible of being applied on different scales and degrees".[2]

At the beginning of the 1980s drastic changes in the economic and labor

[1] See Lehmbruch, G. (1982), Introduction. In: *Patterns of Corporatist Policy-Making*. Lehmbruch, G. and P. Schmitter (eds.). London: Sage, p. 8.

[2] Lehmbruch, G., l.c., p. 12.

relations scenario came to alter most of these assumptions and consequently the focus of social research, even among some of the observers most convinced of the importance of concertation.

The episodes of social concertations which were reiterated in some Mediterranean countries like Italy and Spain in those years were not considered significant enough to change these judgements. In spite of their relative success, and of some specific traits which differentiated them from the middle European prototypes, they appeared to many observers as relics of the past linked to the specific characters of these nations as "latecomers" in the neocorporatist club (and indeed among the systems provided with pluralistic industrial relations).

Attention was focused on the developments of labor relations that responded to a *neoliberal* political and ideological inspiration with the intention of curing the evils of pluralism with a medicine opposed to that of neocorporatism and quite divergent from the pluralistic tradition, namely by restoring the role of market forces through a parallel reduction of the constraints imposed by organized groups, in particular labor confederations, and of the support given to them by the state.

In the following years the research on social concertation has been deeply influenced but not cancelled by these changes; some opinions presented here seem to indicate that the same is true with the practice of concertation.

This volume does not claim to fully reproduce and update the international debate concerning concertative policy-making and prospects in the 1980s, but it analyzes concertative practices from different disciplinary and methodological viewpoints, and also with different evaluations on the prospects of concertation.

Some papers are based on recent national experiences of concertative practice. This is a rather traditional approach but it still seems necessary, particularly given the relative delay and difficulty of empirical research.

The others have a comparative outlook. Most of them analyze general aspects and prospects of concertative practices with respect to the new challenges facing all models of labor relations in different national and regional contexts; they point to revisions (some even to denial) of the assumptions common to the 1980s.

The need for revision emerges from the very terminology adopted, not only in these papers: The concept of neocorporatism, always much discussed, is slowly drifting toward and being equated with that of concertation.[3] Concertation is seen more and more as a technique of labor relations applicable to

[3] According to P. Schmitter (In: *Patterns of Corporatist Practise*, l.c., ch. IX) the term "concertation" would mainly refer to a mode of socio-political decision-making (output) to some extent broader than the term neocorporatism (which implies a specific mode of interest-representation and organization: input).

areas and objects well beyond those considered in the decade of neocorporatist studies.

Two characteristics of this collection deserve to be mentioned:

1. An attempt has been made to extend the analysis beyond the traditional groups of countries still prevailing in comparative labor relations research (i.e. Europe, US, and lately Japan), and to include other areas as different as Australia and South America which have a long (even though *heterogeneous*) tradition of concertative practices.
2. Specific attention has been devoted to correlate concertative practices with economic policies in many respects: On one side by discussing the economic factors which challenge their effectiveness and even the usefulness of these practices, or request their revision (see the papers by Mitchell and Zaidi, and Streeck).

On the other, by reviewing the long debated but unsettled question of the impact of the same practices on the economic performance of the various national systems (see the paper by Dell'Aringa and Samek).

1.2 The Factors Undermining Concertative Tripartite Policy-Making in the 1980s

The factors undermining the neocorporatist practices during the 1980s have been identified with the decline of the basic features of industrial relations prevailing in the 1970s. This decade is seen, in this respect more than in others, as the "last decade" of traditional, industrialist-style labor relations.

The first relevant feature is the *centralization* of industrial relations in general, and of collective bargaining in particular. In fact centralization has always played a major role in sustaining neocorporatist (or more loosely cooperative) arrangements through the double function of controlling wage claims at the lower levels of the industrial relations system and of obtaining resources on the political market in exchange for bargaining moderation.

A *second* common characteristic of the 1970s, although in different degrees, was the increase in the institutionalization of the labor relations system, that is, of state intervention in labor management relations with a combination of supportive and regulatory roles.

Both *the centralization and institutionalization* of labor relations were reinforced in most countries by a parallel intra-organizational control by the peak interest organizations (labor unions and employers' associations) on their constituents, favored in turn by the (still) compact representative cohesiveness of these organizations.

The 1980s have often been described in terms (almost) opposite to the 1970s with respect to these features.

Centralization was substituted with decentralization not only in collective bargaining but also in most aspects of social and economic life, although with different intensity in the various systems. Significantly, the push toward decentralization of bargaining – favored by technological change – came predominantly from employers who began to take the initiative in industrial relations as never before. Decentralization went along with a trend toward fragmentation of collective bargaining and of collective organizations, toward the reopening of wage differentials and toward the increasing differentiation of industrial relations patterns.[4]

"Deregulation" becomes a dominant theme, polemically used against the inflexibility of all regulatory approaches, again not only in industrial relations but also in social life as well.

All these phenomena are finalized toward a greater "flexibility" of most dimensions of labor relations; the need for "control" seems to drift away, beginning with that for "income" control, which was the core of concerted action in the past.

At the basis of these trends a complex set of structural factors is underlined and often considered "preclusive" to the continuation of neocorporatist practices (see the paper by Streeck): *changed conditions of product market* (mainly greater variability and unpredictability of demand in a context of increasing international competition); *decline of national markets* and of state powers as a consequence of the internationalization of the economy; *increased differentiation of the labor force* and fragmentation of labor markets; and *technological innovations* and consequent innovation in organization and production (flexible specialization and the like).[5]

1.3 Their Uneven Impact on Different Industrial Relations Systems: Centralization, Institutionalization, and Unionization

While these observations have attracted wide attention and polemics they, too, appear far more general both in merit and in their implication for our issue. The evidence accumulated in recent years, as suggested in most of the papers presented here as well, outlines a less simplistic picture of the past decade and more problematic prospects for the 1990s.

On the one hand, variation must be *introduced* among the national systems, and within them, according to the periods and to specific aspects of the issue. *On the other hand*, concertative practices have proved on some occasions to be more articulated and adaptable than the picture offered by the mere analysis of concerted income policies.

Variations are already visible in the general trends mentioned so far:

[4] See Treu, T. (1985), Centralization/Decentralization in Collective Bargaining. In: *International Journal of Comparative Labor Law and Industrial Relations*, Vol. I, p. 41.

[5] See, among others, OECD (1986), *Flexibility and Labor Markets*. Paris; Piore, M. and C. Sabel (1984), *The Second Industrial Divide*. New York, Basic Books.

centralization, institutionalization of labor relations, and position of labor unions.

In many respects the various labor relations systems have reacted not uniformly but quite differently to the new realities of the 1980s beginning with the trends toward decentralization. Attempts to break central bargaining have, by and large, been rejected in countries such as Sweden, Austria, Australia (see the paper by Brown; but a more skeptical view on Sweden in the paper by Pestoff), and the Federal Republic of Germany (FRG). Nor have they been really successful even in Italy (see the papers by Brunetta and Tronti, and Negrelli), France, or Spain, although they have resulted in increased divisions, particularly on the employees' side, from the top to the bottom of the bargaining structure, as well as in greater freedom of action for employers at company level.

More drastic changes have been introduced in the United States and the United Kingdom, which were already inclined to stronger decentralization. But, on the whole, for the majority of countries it seems misleading to refer to decentralization as an absolutely dominant trend for the present, and, possibly, for the future.

Even in Japan, which traditionally has a decentralized system of bargaining, the practice of setting wage guidelines at national level in line with economic prospects continues to be followed. Matters like tax reform have been the object of national concern, if not of concerted action with national trade unions; and tripartite systems of representation are organized at the levels of industry and region (see the paper by Shimada).

A recent comparative analysis on collective bargaining practices in IMEC countries, organized by the ILO, confirms that there is not enough evidence to hold that these countries have abandoned all kinds of central control on bargaining, nor some sort of agreement among the parties with state intervention or indirect support in this direction (see also the paper by Slomp).

But the control of highly diversified systems has become more problematic than in the past; indeed it is a critical issue which cannot be solved with traditional neocorporatist practices. A more "articulated" set of answers is needed to explain (evaluate) the relations between centralization and decentralization, as suggested by some papers (Slomp, Negrelli, and also Mitchell and Zaidi).

A comparative evaluation is particularly difficult with respect to the trends toward deregulation and flexibility. Both are multidimensional concepts, given the different areas where they can be applied and the different "techniques" in which they can be implemented.

More than an outright "deregulation", that is, abolition of norms, the practice implemented in many European nations is "flexible re-regulation". The norms tend to become adaptable to the different situations, usually under (some sort of) bilateral agreement between the collective parties, often with public monitoring or support: It is also, for example, in the areas of fixed-term contracts, of atypical labor contracts, and of working-time regulation.

The intensity of collective and public control varies not only in the various countries but also according to different regions and dimensions of productive units: It is more realistic to speak of deregulation in connection with small units where unions are absent or weak.

The degree of institutionalization in labor relations also differs, following parallel lines. In some countries (UK, US) state action has supported market forces in dismantling some of the institutions which had been "keeping the system together". But in other countries of Europe and South America (see the paper by Morgado), as in Australia and Canada, the institutionalization of collective bargaining is a stable reality and sometimes even on the increase, at the initiative either of the parties themselves, or, more often, of the legislator.

It is worth noticing instead that the forms of state and public intervention in labor relations are spurred to change, at least in two respects:

1. The rigid regulatory intervention typical of labor law and of directive income policies has been challenged by the need for decentralization and flexibility. Often it is being substituted by more flexible intervention, for example, in the form of supportive fiscal and labor market policies (see the papers by Brunetta and Tronti, Negrelli, O'Kelly, Zapata, and Morgado).
2. State resources available to support concertative practices have become scarce.

Concerted action itself has contributed to this "shortage", particularly in some countries (the Latin Mediterranean and the South American). It has consumed more public resources than expected and this has resulted in large public deficits. One of the reasons for such consumption is the very weakness of the experiments of social pact in those countries: scarce control of central organizations on their periphery; little capacity on the part of public administration to implement long-term reformist policies; and political polarization.

These elements of weakness increase the tendency, already present in tripartite macro arrangements, to "fiscalize" social conflict, that is, to reduce its effects and promote consensus at public expense, in particular to compensate with welfare provisions the lack of trust among the various social parties and the long-term inconsistency of state policies.

Reducing welfare costs is a major problem, especially in those countries where social concertation – or solidarity – is less firmly established and where sectorial interest groups are less controlled by political authorities.

Here again the the alternative is more complex than the sheer substitution of state action with market forces; a more complex interaction is needed and in some cases visible.

The evidence is equally complex with respect to the position and role of labor unions. It indicates that the challenges to this position both at the national and workplace level are not transitory; at the same time it has not confirmed the forecasts of "no future" for unionism which attracted much attention at the beginning of the 1980s.

Significant differences are visible in the trends of union density, a good indicator of health of the collective action. The scenario varies from cases of dramatic decline (US and, to some extent, UK – even though British unions seem to have somehow stabilized), to cases of slow shrinking (Italy) and of relative stability (FRG, Austria, and Australia), or even relative growth (Scandinavian countries and Canada).

Equally interesting is that these trends do not follow a uniform logic. The explanatory value of typical indicators, such as those of the business cycle, the demographic profile of the labor force, the influence of public institution, and political parties, has to be relativized.

The various types of union have showed different capacity of adjustment to the representative crisis of the 1980s in the various countries according to a complex set of variables.[6] The most widely considered are: the mix of centralization/decentralization of the industrial relations system; union alliance and influence with respect to political actions; and, in general, the scope of their initiative with respect both to the employers and the political system.

The unions which have adjusted best are those which have expanded their action beyond traditional economic and normative negotiation in more than one direction: toward political action, including concertation with the state; and toward some sort of participation within the enterprise and in the labor market (to manage the process of manpower reconversion and labor mobility through tripartite action).

This type of "multifunctional" unionism has been favored in its performance when operating within systems of industrial relations which have undergone at least some experience of central control of bargaining and of concerted action at various levels. The widening of functions has helped the unions go beyond the traditional negative motivation for organizing blue-collar industrial workers and to offer a positive agenda to the expectations of the differentiated and sophisticated working population of the "service society", thereby counteracting the declining appeal of traditional collective bargaining.

At the same time it may favor working relations with the state and with

[6] See Visser, J. (1988), Trade Unionism in Western Europe: Present Situation and Prospects. In: *Labour and Society*, p. 125; Kochan, T., The Future of Worker Representation: An American Perspective, l.c., p. 183; Cella, G. P. and T. Treu (1990), National Labor Movements. In: *Comparative Labour Law and Industrial Relations* (4th edn). Blanpain, R. (ed.). Kluwer, ch. X.

employers by widening the grounds for possible collaboration and trade-off: Industrial adjustment, smooth introduction of technological innovation, active manpower policies, stabilization of welfare, and fiscal policies are some of the grounds where multifunctional unionism can be a valuable partner for both states and employers.

The structural position and ideological orientation of labor unions are so different in other countries, for example Latin-American, that no simple parallel is possible with Europe (see the papers by Cella and Morgado). The relative pros and cons of the various solutions are to be evaluated differently. However, a strategy of social concertation in the broad sense, which can be meaningful in these countries, has appeared to be for labor movements the major or only alternative to a role of sheer radical opposition. This is particularly the case in those countries where governments are committed to the democratization and modernization of the system.

1.4 The Attitudes of the Actors in Industrial Relations toward Concertation

The analysis of these general indicators suggests caution in drawing general conclusions with respect to the possible adjustment of the various models experienced in the past.

While the pressures toward decentralization and diversification of the "once" monolithic models are clear, even in the "strong" systems like the Scandinavian (see the paper by Pestoff), the reactions and outcomes are far from uniformly determined, according to fixed factors which include those mentioned at the beginning (technology and international competition).

The complexity of the picture is confirmed if one considers the strategy of the social and political actors in this respect, which is particularly relevant since the scenario presented here is not *deterministic.*

Rather clear-cut indications can be drawn from the position of the labor movement: The majority of established national unions in developed countries, and also most unions in Latin America, are still supporters of some sort of *concerted action* including *central* control on industrial relations, which, to some extent, is sustained by public powers.

Criticism has been recurrently addresed to specific forms of central concerted action and to their results, which in many countries (both the Mediterranean and Latin American) have been much less beneficial for the workers than for the national economy. But no other alternative is considered and the attempts are directed to better *articulate* and finalize concertative practices rather than to abandon them, in order to rely on traditional collective bargaining at the plant/sectorial level only.

Concertation is resisted by business unionism and on the other side by left-wing, communist-oriented labor movements.

But these types of unionism are the most exposed to decline among the established unions, as shown by comparative analysis, while the most convinced supporters of concertation have been more effective in maintaining their position.

This trend is particularly clear in Europe where a concerted approach to national and European labor policies is supported by the strongest reformistic labor unions while the collapse of Eastern regimes has dramatically accelerated the crisis of even the powerful Italian communist confederation.

A major threat to the position of established unionism in developed countries comes from the new forms of independent, sectorial organization which denounce (among other aspects) the excessive "generalist" and centralistic policies of the confederations. This is indeed a critical challenge to traditional unionism and specifically to the strategy of concertation, which calls both for profound adaptation of labor unions' strategies and concertative practices if they want to persuade the working population and the other actors of their usefulness.

Employers' strategies are more difficult to generalize also with respect to these problems.

It is well known that the pressure toward decentralization and deregulation has come predominantly from the employers, even in countries like the Scandinavian with highly centralized systems (see the paper by Pestoff). This is a reaction to the economic factors mentioned above and to some aspects of labor relations dominant in the 1970s, beginning with excessive rigidity stemming from centralization among other factors. But it does not necessarily imply a rejection of all forms of labor management cooperation and of concertation. The importance of some types of central bargaining in quite a few European countries is being reasserted by employers' associations, which seem to appreciate their value against the excessive fragmentation of labor relations. The state itself is still recognized as an important part of the industrial relations system.

The countries analyzed in this volume confirm the persisting importance of publication in governing labor relations and on the whole a positive attitude of public powers toward some kind of tripartism.

The possibility of pursuing economic stabilization and adjustment without or against labor union consensus in exclusive agreement with employers' associations is hardly considered in most European countries, in Australia, and even in many South American systems. Here the scope of public action and of the social pact is so broad as to coincide with that of national survival and democracy (see the papers by Cella and Morgado).

At the same time the strategies of public powers are becoming more problematic and more diversified than in the past. An objective difficulty is the consumption of resources indicated above. Moreover, the increasing need for flexibility and efficiency expressed by employers and acknowledged more and more widely by public opinion, including employees, has convinced even pro-labor governments and political parties to take a more balanced position, to reduce generalized "protection" of traditional unions' practices; the pressure is clear, if not to favor the employers' position, to shift the emphasis of state action toward more articulated and production-oriented forms of tripartism.

The same need is also apparent in some areas of the South American context, even though concertation and public action is still "overloaded" due to emergency situations. Said overload is one of the indicators of the historically rooted fragility of concertation practices in that continent (see the paper by Cella).

1.5 The Differentiation of Concertative Policy-Making and Levels

The general trends of industrial relations and the actors' strategies converge in indicating growing differentiation (also) in concertative practices.

The decline of one specific formula of neocorporatism, namely the centralized tripartite income policies experienced mainly in middle European countries during the 1970s, however, does not allow – in my opinion – general conclusions on the outcome of the practices which have been experienced in other countries nor on the decline of the functions and needs that these practices may fulfill.

Organizational as well as institutional variables have to be combined in dynamic models in order to account for the different capacities of the various industrial relations systems and their forms of action, in particular concertative practices, to adjust to the new potentially adverse conditions of the 1990s.

More specifically distinction must be made when analyzing the position and functions of concertative policy-making according to their actors, levels, and object.

Indeed, concertation and neocorporatism do not identify themselves necessarily with specific institutional arrangements prevalent in the 1970s, even though they may be historically most significant and closer to some "ideal type" of neocorporatism. The variety of institutional arrangements, objects, and level of corporatist practices is not unknown to comparative analysis, even though it has been obscured in the immediate past by the prevalence of "one model" of corporatism.

These practices have a common feature which is not necessarily linked with too specific objects and institutional rules: It relates to the objectives of the action, to the actors and interests involved, and consequently to the output.

In this respect concertative practices may be considered part of a wider category including all *solidaristic* or *participative* systems in so far as they imply action in view of the "common interests" of the actors and are opposed to other systems of action which pursue different (opposed) interests of the individual actors. Within this broader category concertative practices still maintain specific traits which justify the analytical utility of the concept: In particular the *tripartite* character of the arrangements, whereby the social parts collaborate with public actors in the economic decision-making process and accordingly public/private authorities are combined in the regulation of various aspects of labor relations.

Some hierarchy among the various levels of concertative practices tends to be maintained by the tripartite actors as a guarantee of a *balanced* pursuance of their common interests.

We will return on that, but this is a tendency which may be actually implemented in different degrees according to different variables (economic and political).

According to the same variables the objects of tripartite concertation may vary from the traditional *distributive* items centered around income policies to "productive" and organizational issues.

These variations are analyzed in this volume and have significant examples in the practice of quite a few countries.

The analysis does not rule out the importance of concertation directed to stabilize macroeconomic policies as indicated in the papers on Australia, Ireland, Latin Mediterranean, and Latin American countries.

The need to *control inflation*, which was the main push toward the income policies of the 1970s, has decreased in the following decade, even in some countries where concerted income policies appeared particularly difficult for structural reasons. Such a result shows the effectiveness, at least contributory, of macro concertation as an "emergency" remedy. But inflation still needs to be kept under control, as recent events of 1990–1991 dramatically confirm. The techniques most effective to this end are controversial. Mitchell's and Zaidi's paper suggests that "wage setting is moving toward a greater responsiveness to labor market conditions" and that "given reasonable monetary politics" economic stability can be obtained even without social concertation.

But even admitting that control of inflation, given certain circumstances, may amount to less than explicit tripartite concertation, most experiences still indicate that it may require something more than the absence or indifference of industrial relations practice at macroeconomic level, which is typical of the traditional pluralism (and business unionism). In most developing countries the need to cope with inflation and to organize some sort of income policy continues to be of primary importance. If this has to be done through consensus and not through authoritarian state intervention, social concertation may be the most likely solution.

Some papers (in particular Negrelli) indicate, furthermore, that tripartite arrangements can be decentralized, at least at three levels below the *central* all-economy level typical of traditional income policies.

The level of the economic sectors has a long tradition, not only in collective bargaining where it is dominant in most European countries, but also in handling issues of common interest for the parties (e.g. industrial policies) through tripartite formal or informal arrangements by the sectorial organizations supported by the public powers.

The territorial level of concertation is also quite well established, particularly in countries with the longest practice of neocorporatism such as the Scandinavian ones, the FRG, but also in Italy. Its main focus is on critical economic adjustment areas such as labor market policies, vocational training, and reconversion connected with industrial restructuring (but also consumer policy and housing; see the paper by Pestoff). These concertation practices at the meso level have been important in implementing a controlled flexibilization of the labor market, often along the lines decided by centralized tripartite decision.

For this reason the "meso" level of labor relations has contributed both to reduce the overload of the central tripartism of the 1970s and to increase the reassuring effects of public policies, particularly *vis-à-vis* the trade unions, which in these countries are present within many public institutions. The experience acquired in this way by thousands of union representatives is spreading the practice of tripartite involvement in new areas, not merely distributive. It has contributed to reduce their reaction toward the excesses of centralization of the 1970s, to accept the risky process of the flexibilization of manpower, and of decentralization. It has also helped the unions not to loose complete control over the vital network of small firms which are almost unreachable by direct organizational efforts. The network of tripartite institutions and practices has been decisive in some industrial districts in sustaining new forms of "flexible specialized" production.[7]

Finally, the *level* of the enterprise and of the enterprise group as a developed form of entrepreneurial organization has proved very significant in the experimentation of concerted action and participation which go beyond traditional collective bargaining, particularly in matters like labor mobility and restructuring policies.

This has been true also in the Mediterrenean and South American countries with no tradition of this kind, that is, mostly characterized by labor management confrontation.

Negrelli indicates all these levels and objects of concertative practices, even when they are formally bilateral, receive decisive contributions by state actions such as supportive legislation and financial subsidies, and gives appropriate examples concerning Italy, France, and Spain.

All these levels of concertation share the common trait of handling not distributive, but productive and organizational issues mainly. Such a trait

[7] References in: Piore, M. and C. Sabel, *The Second Industrial Divide*, l.c.

induced W. Streeck to consider this concertation as a sort of supply-side decentralized corporatism[8] and Negrelli to stress that it has promoted flexibility and at the same time reduced its social cost favoring both an efficient and solidaristic use of flexibility, while Mitchell and Zaidi underline the importance of social concertation in responding to micro-level employee concerns related to labor market instability.

These remarks and experiences indicate – in my opinion – the possibility of a multilevel/multidimensional type of concertation, and its potential for a socially controlled process of economic growth and adjustment (a more skeptical view is presented in the paper by Streeck).

The importance of these practices for the *performance* of the national systems is analyzed in the paper by Dell'Aringa and Samek, although they indicate that the evidence is less clear-cut in the last years (1983–1987) analyzed than in the previous ones (1974–1982 and in the whole period 1974–1987).

A recent research by D. Soskice has confirmed even more clearly the positive correlation between micro and meso forms of cooperation and coordination between the actors in social and economic matters and economic performance of the various countries.[9]

These indications, however, are not definitive and the evidence itself is partial.

1.6 Problems and Alternatives

The most obvious doubts concern the *conditions* for these concertative practices to operate successfully, and prevail over the possible alternatives, at all centralized and decentralized levels. Central direction of economic adjustment might be implemented by public authorities without significant union contribution, possibly with the support of employers and public opinion, directly represented (also in this respect) by political parties. Similarly, employee involvement in enterprise affairs may be obtained outside union channels, with or without state support. While these possibilities cannot be ruled out, they meet with difficulties where collective industrial relations and labor movements are solidly entrenched. In countries as different as Italy, the FRG, and also Canada, Australia and even the United Kingdom, employers (particularly the large ones) consider the policy of union exclusion and of individual participation too risky; and state action does not favor this choice (apart from the UK). Among other reasons the alternative to collective par-

[8] Streeck, W. (1987), *Skills and Limits of Neoliberalism.* Paper presented at Turin Conference, Nov. 27–28.

[9] See the paper by Soskice, D. (1990). In: *Labour Relations and Economic Performance.* Brunetta, R. and C. Dell'Aringa (eds.). London: Macmillan.

ticipation is not necessarily individual management-controlled participation in the development of the enterprise; it may be conflictual bargaining with aggressive and loosely organized groups of employees, out of union control as well. The aggressiveness of newly organized groups of key employees has already caused serious difficulties to management in some areas of the private and public services. In quite a few countries the end of the destructive phase of industrial restructuring, coupled with the relatively good economic prospects of the second half of the 1980s, has contributed to strengthen employee bargaining power at the enterprise level, which again increased management willingness to accept union involvement (at least as a second-best choice).

If pure liberalistic options appear unlikely in European countries and even more so neointerventionist policies, a more likely prospect is the development of a strictly *micro* version of labor management cooperation at the enterprise level as a key element of economic coordination.

This possibility, traditionally discarded in the European tradition, has been considered by some commentators (Dore) as the "real" alternative to both neoliberalism and neocorporatism.[10] According to these analyses the basis of new labor relations and social arrangement will be the development of "community-type" commitments within the firm fostering functional flexibility, productivity, and security for the members (only) of this community (outside broader solidarity and social cooperation).

The implications are wide ranging not only for the industrial relations systems, but also for the general organization of society and of the welfare state. If the focus of loyalty and solidarity shifts from central entities – nation, region (or class) – to the enterprise, social and political control over most organizations could be reduced or lost; the unions would change from being an actor involved in this control to "junior members of the various firms' communities".[11]

This hypothesis would also have drastic consequences on the balance and equality within the various social systems. More precisely it would push toward "dualistic social systems" since it rules out a major force, political and social cohesion or – if you prefer – solidarity, which could prevent excessive social "dualisms" and promote the collective action necessary to control centrifugal factors. Indeed, some commentators seem to believe that such a development is not necessary. They suggest that micro-corporatism arrangements based on collaboration between social and economic actors could develop harmoniously beyond the enterprise and be somehow coordinated and stabilized by broader communitarian and solidaristic values if not at

[10] Dore, R. (1986), Flexible Rigidities: Industrial Policies and Structural Adjustment. In: *The Japanese Economy*. London: Athlone Press.

[11] Salvati, M. (1989), A Long Cycle in Industrial Relations or: Regulatory Theory and Political Economy. In: *Labour*, Vol. I, p. 57.

a central (like in the neocorporatism of the 1970s), at least at a regional or territorial, level.[12]

From these suggestions it is unclear how this coordination could come about: What factors or social-political forces could implement it? It is hardly possible to imagine that such a result could develop by way of some automatism attributed not to market forces but to community integration.

On the contrary, all recent developments seem to indicate increasing pressure against integration and toward the "diversification" of social and industrial relations systems, not only across countries, but within the same nation or even within the same enterprise.

This phenomenon reflects broader trends in the economy and society (diversification of the working population, segmentation or miniaturization of markets, and of productive structures), and possibly even more general trends in value and culture: The collapse of models and general rules in the so-called "centerless society". For these reasons also, the interplay of the various factors analyzed above might well lead not to definite trends but to different solutions with respect to the alternatives: centralization/decentralization; concertation/conflict; and collective/individual participation. The interplay of these factors might favor "multiple dualism" among various countries, sectors of the market, and groups of actors, following different axes: not only northern/southern regions; skilled/unskilled labor; high/low technology production; but also large/small firms; protected/non-protected sectors; and private/public services. Collectively regulated areas of labor relations might develop side by side with non-regulated or individually regulated areas; and share the ground with different forms of institutional participation; publicly controlled incomes policies might be compatible with areas of *laissez-faire* and total deregulation (or possibly made tolerable by them). The multiplication of dualism is already visible in some respects.

These multiple dualisms might be favored, not contrasted, by the actual implementation of the single European market (see the paper by Streeck).

The hypothesis proposed by Dore, therefore, cannot be easily discarded, even though it, too, may be influenced by observation of the Japanese model (and of Japanese values?). I find myself hard put, particularly in relation to Western developed countries, "to think of a society which sticks together only on a basis of an unconstrained adhesion of its members to rat-race values and/or to micro-corporative loyalty to their own productive organization".[13]

But it is also illusory, as Negrelli reminds us, to rely on a possible revival of general identity values, such as class and nation. Monolithic patterns of social

[12] Some suggestions along these lines seem to come from the works quoted of Piore, M., C. Sabel, and W. Streeck (footnotes 7 and 8).

[13] Salvati, M., l.c., *A Long Cycle*, p. 66.

and industrial relations can hardly be a sufficient answer to the present problems.

The growing complexity of productive organizations and the pressure toward flexibility cannot be controlled or regulated by monolithic and centralized systems of rules and values.

That is why the challenge for concerted action as a method of social governance is to adapt itself: To combine and not to oppose *central* concertation on income policies to *micro* concertation on labor policies and flexibility; more, in general, to diversify its levels (macro and micro), techniques (regulatory, supportive, incentive), and functions (not only distributional but "productive") in order to provide different adaptable answers to variable needs without accepting dualism and fragmentation as inevitable.

The institutions of industrial relations – like other socio-economic institutions of our times – have to face, particularly in this respect, a task more difficult than ever before – that of coordinating a complex and variable set of segments (i.e. adapting to diversification) without losing some identifiable and shared design of social interests. The need for coordination and control over (excessive) centrifugal pressure is still important (see the paper by Slomp) for most systems and for their basic institutions including industrial relations. New techniques of coordination, softer than the traditional ones, may be possible; they might be facilitated by the same new technologies which are spurring decentralization. Many researches on the "network firm" show the possibility offered by telematics to select specific levels of centralization/decentralization of functions according to the circumstances, to reduce costs, and differentiate methods of coordination and quasi-integration among semi-autonomous units.

Some attempts to fulfill this task of adaptation of concertative policy-making are being made in various countries. Evidence of success has been found in the recent past (but not necessarily conclusive; see the paper by Pestoff) in systems such as the Scandinavian, and in the FRG, which have particularly "favorable" preconditions: relative autonomy and competitiveness of national economic systems; tradition of collaboration between the social parties at various levels; and social and political cohesion.

Some evidence emerges also from the countries presented in this *volume*. To what extent progress in this direction can also be made in other countries with less favorable conditions is open to question. A better knowledge of recent evolutions in different countries is necessary to formulate more precise hypotheses. As indicated above, no deterministic approach is justified to reduce the importance of policy options and actors' strategies.

1.7 Tripartite Policy-Making and Regional Integration of Industrial Relations

A final issue can appropriately be raised here: Whether these problems can be analyzed only or predominantly at the national level, as has been true so far for concerted action and in general for industrial relations systems. It seems more and more unlikely.

Indeed, the internationalization of the economy is probably the most serious challenge to the prevailing practices of tripartism and social pacts. Up to now this challenge has been underestimated in comparative analyses of concertation.[14] But it is now clearly analyzed by Streeck. Concertation has been so far essentially a national phenomenon supported by national states, and in some cases during the 1970s an alternative to international responses. Now internationalization tends to put pressure on the national states to reduce deficit spending and indeed it reduces their "effective sovereignty"; consequently it weakens the basic ingredients of traditional tripartism. These trends challenge the possibility of social tripartite arrangements even in those countries where it has been most firmly established (Northern European). The very effectiveness of social pacts could indeed allow them to continue to exploit international market niches: A major factor which has renewed the need of collaboration between the social parties at enterprise and central level is precisely the need to coordinate national efforts with minimum cost and maximum productivity in order to meet international competition.

The very prospects of internationalization may favor *joint efforts* of national actors in meeting this competition that in the *short run* maintain or strengthen the relative importance of national systems. But even here the prospects are judged differently (see the paper by Pestoff).

The chances of success of these efforts will be reduced far more for the countries more exposed to international turbulence; for them an exclusively national approach to tripartite collaboration, and to other socio-economic problems, will be more and more inadequate to face the international scenario of the 1990s.

A reaction to these international pressures is the acceleration of economic integration among various countries at a regional level. The European move toward a unitary market in 1992, at a pace which was unexpected until a few years ago, is a most significant example.

Similar, although less wide-ranging moves can be noticed in other regional areas: See the closer cooperation which is already in place between the United States and Canada; that which is planned between the United States and Mexico; and the attempts, so far not very successful, to coordinate the economies of South American states.

While economic integration is rapidly becoming a reality in Europe and

[14] See Schmitter, P., l.c.

might accelerate also in other areas, the pace of social integration is much slower. The ultimate impact of an economically united Europe on the various labor relations systems and working conditions itself is uncertain.

According to some analysis – see here the paper by Streeck – European entrepreneurs in this respect supported by national elites have accepted a united Europe as an opportunity or necessary step to operate on a wider and less regulated market. This implies a reduced regulatory capacity of the European authorities and a reduction of pre-existing national limitation to competition. In spite of official pledges to social Europe this *deregulatory* trend would apply specifically to national and community regulation of the labor market.

The growing competition among different social regimes and the possibility allowed by the principle of "mutual recognition" for individual enterprises to engage in "regime shopping", that is, choosing less costly and more flexible social regimes, might result in a sharp reduction of labor protection and influence on the labor market, and in a corresponding freedom of choice by international managers.

In this perspective the reduction of influence of national states will not be compensated by any sort of transnational coordination of labor and industrial policies nor by the formation of "regional governments" within the emerging complex European system of governance (Streeck). Consequently global competition will be more than ever regulated by the markets; or to put it more realistically led by giant multinational enterprises which act as international economic powers. This process would relaunch at international level the chances of market and enterprise efficiency which have been hindered in the 1970s by national political and social rigidities, and inaugurate what has been called a new phase of "international Fordism".[15]

According to Streeck the "evolutionary alternative to Thatcherism as a model for the European political economy is not (German or Scandinavian) neocorporatism. An American trajectory is more likely: A political system of disjointed pluralism", or "competitive federalism" organized at no less than three levels – regions, nation-state, and "Brussels'.

Social policies at European or supranational level would at best *maintain* some minimum *redistributive* functions directed to assist the weakest areas of the community. A different outcome would be the construction of a European social dimension endowed with a productive – as distinguished from merely redistributive – purpose, that is, with effective responsibilities in those critical areas (labor market and industrial policies) which have represented the core of social welfare in most European states but which are

[15] Such a possibility is presented by Piore, M. and C. Sabel (In: *The New Industrial Divide*) as the alternative to another possible development – that of "flexible specialization" (more desirable for the authors).

now being taken from the national actors precisely by the internationalization process.

The possible positive effects of this approach also on European economic performance are indicated in the papers by Dell'Aringa and Samek, and Slomp.

The transfer of *social policies initiative* and institutions from the national to a supranational level (even relatively homogeneous like Europe) is an extremely difficult process without precedent in history. One can assume that the potential actors of the process are the same three known to national histories because they represent basically the same interests of organized labor and capital, and the "general interest of the public as expressed by democratic political institutions, and that the two *methods* of *bargaining* and *concertation* are technically applicable also beyond state borders.

One can also point at some initial experiences of European social concertation which move in the directions indicated above: Social dialogue at top level between the European organization of unions and employers assisted by the Community, stating broad guidelines for Community policies in the field of manpower policies and safety; tripartite dialogue conducted by the same parties in a few sectors (textile, agriculture) where the pursuance of common interests is most needed, particularly to meet foreign competition; some experiments of concerted action to develop depressed areas with Community funds; and the first examples of transnational bargaining among unions and the large enterprise group which are still bilateral and limited to procedural matters, but which might claim Community support (e.g. fiscal benefits for enterprises willing to adopt the status of social Europe and to accept worker participation or financial assistance in, for example, a restructuring process or transnational labor mobility).

But the weakness of the first experiments is evident. As Slomp puts it: "Tripartism at the community level is only in an infant stage. This weakness reflects also the uncertain or contractory attitudes of the actors of the process. The majority of European employers are either opposed or very hesitant to accept effective transfer of social policy decision-making to supranational level for the reason indicated above. This is not to exclude that part of them might accept a greater involvement on social concerted action as they have accepted it at national level. The positive effects of concertation on economic performance has been experienced on quite a few occasions. But that would presuppose a strong initiative in this direction by the two other actors, labor union and public powers, and adequate 'rewards', as has been the case for national concertation."

In any event this would require long-term investment, because the positive effects of concertative practices are typically visible in the long run.

At present the European labor unions, which would appear the obvious promoter of an effective social policy of Europe, are not equipped to sustain any significant initiative in this respect. The weakness of their Brussels headquarters is not an "organizational" coincidence, but it reflects divergent national interests and the underlying national imbalances, in particular among weaker and stronger member states (see the paper by Streeck). While it is possible to argue that common social standards and policies might favor union positions and improve working conditions in weak areas more than they threaten the conditions of the stronger areas, the control of this delicate process is very difficult and open to uncertain results.

On the other hand, the power of Community authorities to support the process is far from the level which enabled the national states to sustain the labor movement in social concertation: to correct temporary imbalances among various subsectors of the working class; and to compensate and reassure the employers.

The need of a unanimous vote to approve EEC directives in labor matters is indicative of such a political weakness.

That is why the overcoming of this rule with an acceleration of the political dimension of Europe and of political rights of European citizens is indicated as a precondition by those who advocate an active role of Community authorities in European social policies and concertation (as it was the creation of national political rights, and Parliament in the creation of national welfare).

1.8 Concluding Remarks

Many authors, including some of those published in this volume, have indicated a set of factors which undermined during the 1980s the traditional neocorporatist or concertative practices prevailing in the 1970s, that is, changed conditions of product markets, mainly greater unpredictability of demand in a context of increasing international competitiveness; decline of state powers and national markets as a consequence of the internationalization of the economy; new decentralized and flexible forms of production and organization pushed by the above-mentioned factors; and increased differentiation of the labor force and fragmentation of the labor markets.

The evidence accumulated by recent research shows, however, that the various industrial relations systems have reacted differently to those factors in many aspects: in the degree of decentralization; in the forms of flexibilization and deregulation of existing practices; in the position and influence of labor unions; and in the very role of public intervention in labor relations.

This evidence confirms that the decline of a particular formula of social concertation, that is, of centralized incomes policies, does not imply the disappearance of all forms of tripartite concertative practices directed to shape social and economic policies.

In many countries, reviewed in this volume, some sort of central control over excessive centrifugal pressures is still held important by the factors of industrial relations, in spite of the growing, often prevailing, emphasis on decentralized forms of concerted action at various levels (sectorial, territorial, enterprise).

The increased "freedom" left to the pluralistic market in many areas of labor relations has not cancelled the role of public action in regulating those relations and even less in supporting and controlling the various forms and techniques of self-regulation by the social parties.

Control of inflation by social concertation has appeared less urgent in the 1980s; but this is really the case only in some developed countries under specific circumstances of monetary and economic policies, and the balance has been revealed to be rather precarious at the beginning of the 1990s in an increasingly turbulent international scenario. Other non-distributive, productive, and organizational decisions important for the economic performance are still being handled by tripartite concertation or what has been called supply-side decentralization corporatism.

The same experience has not obscured the possible advantages of concerted action and its impact in pursuing collective objectives. The economic performance and social balance of national systems, as measured by various indicators, still reveal positive correlations with the practices of cooperation between public and private actors of industrial relations in policy-making.

These practices have contributed to reach an acceptable balance between economic efficiency and social solidarity; to reduce the social costs of the intensive productive reorganization, which have gone through the last decades, to respond to employees' concerns related to the flexible use of manpower and to labor market instability; and this has promoted a better commitment of the same employees to productivity. At the political level the various forms of social concertation which have supported and strengthened in the industrial countries the institutions of pluralism, particularly in periods of crisis, are being used to supplement the weakness of pluralism in less developed societies like those of Latin America, particularly during the transition stage to democracy.

They could be put to a similar test in the Eastern European states: Their transition from "real socialism to liberal democratic" order takes place in a context different from all the others known to Western history, but characterized by a similar shortage of societal support to political and economic regulation.

The chances that these potentials of concertative practices may be in fact exploited with success cannot be overestimated. The hindering factors inherited from the 1980s will not disappear in the 1990s. These chances are unevenly distributed among the various countries, depending on their social and economic preconditions, including previous successful experience of concertation itself. The chances might initially be greater in those countries where the practice of social tripartite agreements has been most firmly established than in the newcomers, regardless of the possible needs and advantages of these practices. The impact of the factors mentioned above, unless corrected by some sort of transnational concertation, might result in increasing divergences among the various national systems.

A polarization might develop around the strongest alternatives to concertative patterns of labor relations: The relaunching at international level of the chances of markets in which has been defined a new phase of international Fordism. On the other hand, there is the development of strictly micro versions of labor management cooperation at the enterprise level (a sheer return to authoritarian forms of social regulations seems unlikely at least in developed countries).

The capacity of concertative arrangements to compete with these alternatives are clearly linked to the basic features of the various systems but require in any event a profound adaptation of actors, objectives, and techniques.

It seems illusory that *micro-corporative* policy-making may spontaneously develop beyond the enterprise level so as to guarantee acceptable levels of social integration, but the attraction of micro corporatism cannot be counteracted simply by appeals to general identity values (such as class and nation), nor controlled by centralized systems of rules.

In this respect the challenge for concerted action as a method of social governance and policy-making is to combine, not to oppose, central concertation on income policies to micro concertation on labor policies and flexibility; more, in general, to diversify its levels (macro and micro), techniques (regulatory, supportive, incentive), and functions (not only distributional but also productive) in order to provide different adaptable answers to variable needs without accepting dualism and fragmentation as inevitable. The present forms of concerted action must be so diversified and structured as to coordinate a complex and variable set of segments without losing some identifiable and shared design of social interest.

On the opposite side, the internationalization of the economy tends to reduce the influence of national states and their propensity/capacity to use deficit spending as a social resource thereby weakening a basic ingredient of traditional, that is, national, tripartism (again in different degrees according to the exposure of the individual states to international pressures).

Internationalization of markets and authorities will be the most serious challenge to all nationally institutionalized patterns of labor relations, particularly to the existing forms of tripartism and, in general, of pluralism organized with (national) state support.

It is surprising that this challenge has greatly been underestimated both in its practical and also theoretical implication. A reconsideration from both points of view is needed: This is particularly true for the adaptation and success of concertative practices. Other models, such as those mentioned above of *international Fordism* or *disjointed pluralism*, may benefit from the international dimension of economic action for the (simple) *absence* of countervailing social and political forces.

The basic structures of labor relations patterns are affected by internationalization, beginning with the social actors.

The challenges of internationalization to the present status of concertative practices where they are established and *a fortiori* where they are most precarious can be met only by international (social and political) actors at international levels. This is clearly the case for labor unions and public institutions: If they are to remain agents of social and political transformation capable of promoting economic arrangements both efficiently and socially acceptable, they have to develop adequate supranational strategies and eventually forms of organization.

Enterprises, particularly large ones, are already by themselves international actors: But whether their performance will benefit or lose in the long run from the absence of social and political institutions at the international level is far from certain.

The relevance of centralized interest organizations for concertative practices at national level cannot be reproduced at international level simply by prolonging their organizations and power across the border.

Even admitting a fast reorganization of trade unions along these lines, which is far from being easy, the objects of bilateral and trilateral activities at international level will be different from those common to national collective bargaining and political exchanges. And this is bound to alter the very substance of collective powers and authorities.

The initial and still obscure debate on European collective bargaining is indicative of these difficulties.

Forms and grounds of workers' participation to the enterprise are equally changing and possibly evanescent, even in a continent like Europe which has a relatively long tradition of participative practices.

A similar rather unpredictable alteration can be envisaged for the forms and techniques of collective conflicts, already altered by the "tertiarization" of strikes.

The "extension" of national public institutions at the international or even regional level meets with no less serious obstacles. It can hardly follow established patterns including those which have brought about in the past the major federal states.

Here, too, the techniques and objects of public interventions do not reproduce those available at national level: Major examples can be found in the basic components of the welfare state, which have been determinant in sustaining tripartism and which so far have not found even initial application beyond national borders.

The international dimension by itself requires a reconsideration of the essence of government powers as well as of the strategies of social actors.

Indeed, it confirms the "relativity" of basic analytical tools used in comparative analyses such as that of centralization/decentralization; collaboration/conflict, and possibly regulation/deregulation (at least in so far as the sources and effectiveness of regulations are affected).

2 Industrial Relations and Economic Performance

Carlo Dell'Aringa and Manuela Samek Lodovici

2.1 Introduction

As a consequence of the oil shocks in the early 1970s and 1980s, all industrialized countries experienced slowing economic growth rates and rising inflation along with increasing unemployment.

However, the degree of deterioration differed greatly from country to country, especially regarding trends in inflation and unemployment (Table 1). Member countries of the European Economic Community (EEC) registered the worst performances, while those with the best performances in terms of employment growth and lower inflation were the Scandinavian countries, Austria, Switzerland, Japan, the United States, and Canada. Excluding the two North American nations, these countries also show the lowest levels of unemployment.

The characteristics of the labor market and system of industrial relations in these countries offer an important explanation for these diverse trends, and particularly for the ability of these systems to maintain wage moderation throughout the 1970s, along with lower inflation and unemployment.

Most scholars concerned with the relationship between industrial relations and economic performance interpret the economic results of the 1970s and early 1980s as a sign of the success of highly corporatist economies (Bruno and Sachs 1985; Crouch 1985; Tarantelli 1986; Newell and Symons 1987, to cite a few). Others, however, associate success with flexible and decentralized markets (Klau and Mittelstadt 1986), while some include both kinds of markets (Calmfors and Driffill 1988; Freeman 1988).

Wage moderation can be achieved in both types of labor markets. In neocorporatist markets, characterized by large interest groups representing substantial segments of society, there are usually institutional structures (committees, joint committees) that serve in tripartite consultation and mediating interests, allowing an effective application of income policies based on consensus. Conflict is generally low, and negotiations occur primarily at a centralized level.

Table 1: Growth, Unemployment and Inflation 1974–1987. An International Comparison.
(percentage changes from previous year-average over period)

	Real GNP	Standardized Unemployed rates	Consumer prices
Japan	3.78	2.27	5.94
Switzerland	1.06	0.49	3.71
Austria	2.19	2.86	5.13
Norway	3.94	2.16	8.88
Sweden	1.79	2.35	8.99
Germany	1.86	4.83	3.79
Denmark	1.90	7.42	8.87
Finland	2.90	4.86	9.90
Netherlands	2.05	7.81	5.00
Belgium	1.84	9.15	6.82
Australia	2.77	6.57	10.16
United Kingdom	1.71	8.15	11.14
Italy	2.85	8.30	14.10
France	2.16	7.01	9.41
United States	2.49	7.22	6.98
Canada	3.47	8.61	7.96

Source: OECD, Economic Outlook, No. 44, 1988 (Dec.).

The advantages associated with these systems of industrial relations can be summarized as follows:

1. There is a higher likelihood that large interest coalitions internalize effects of their own behavior. Trade unions and employers are, therefore, sensitive to macroeconomic constraints stemming from wage increases.
2. Centralized bargaining allows for simultaneous negotiations, thereby reducing the risk of upward wage spirals.

This system is typical of the Scandinavian countries and Austria: In these countries the main worker and employer organizations collaborate with the government in defining income policies. The main associations represent wide segments of society and all social groups, which enables the typical problems of this type of negotiating (prisoner dilemma and free-riding) to be overcome, and cooperative agreements to be reached.

Important aspects that permit these systems to operate include the size of the coalitions, the proportion of costs of each action that is supported by each coalition (Olson 1982), and the degree of centralization of industrial relations.

The second system which allows for real wage moderation is the complete opposite of that described above, and is characterized by competitive markets, weak interest groups, and fragmented wage negotiations and industrial relations that take place primarily at the individual firm level. In these countries, wage moderation is imposed by market mechanisms. In the 1970s and 1980s, the United States and Canada show wage moderation and relatively good performances regarding inflation and employment growth, even if somewhat less positive than the corporatist countries with respect to unemployment.

Countries with intermediary types of industrial relations systems such as Italy, France, and the United Kingdom are in the worst situation: Interest organizations are strong enough to impose their conditions in the negotiating process, but are not encompassing enough to significantly sustain the social costs of their actions.

After reviewing the most recent literature on the relationship between industrial relations systems and economic performance, this paper will examine the stability of these relations under changing economic conditions. In particular, we shall see if neocorporatist systems maintain their supremacy in different economic conditions from those of the 1970s, and how they function when structural changes occur in the workforce and labor market.

2.2 Corporatism and Economic Performance: A Review of the Most Recent Literature

The interdisciplinary analysis of existing interdependencies between industrial relations and the functioning of macroeconomic systems has kept researchers busy in the areas of economics, law, and political science for quite a while. The stagflation of the 1970s and early 1980s made this subject timely, particularly among the neocorporatist theorists. According to this line of analysis, there is a positive relationship between economic performance and the degree of corporatism in the industrial relations system that passes through a "political exchange" mechanism between a labor union ready to slow wage demands and employers and government willing to keep employment levels high and to maintain fiscal equity.

The most common methodology used in empirical analysis is to correlate rankings of the various countries according to economic performance indicators and indicators of the level of corporatism and/or centralization of industrial relations. In the most recent works, theoretical models have been developed which clarify and analyze the mechanisms that link the bargaining system or industrial relations system to the outcome in terms of wage increases. Price and/or wage equations that include industrial relations or institutional indicators are estimated on the basis of these models.

Performance indicators used by most scholars are inflation, unemployment, and trade-off indicators between the two variables, such as their sum (OKUN index). However, international comparison based on indicators such as unemployment rate could be misleading, due to the great differences in measuring methods. In Japan and Switzerland, for example, the high cyclical behavior of the secondary labor force (mainly women and the elderly) makes the unemployment rate a misleading indicator of the degree to which resources are underutilized. In Austria, Germany, Finland, and Switzerland the outmigration of foreign workers hides a part of the decline in employment starting in 1973. In Sweden, the official unemployment statistics do not count unemployed workers enrolled in professional training programs. For this reason, in the most recent works, other performance indicators are used: growth in gross domestic product (GDP), productivity growth, fixed capital investments (Bruno and Sachs 1987; Jackman 1989); economic policy indicators (Calmfors and Driffill 1988); indicators of wage flexibility (Bruno and Sachs 1985), and wage dispersion among sectors and/or occupations (Freeman 1988).

The indicators and issues used by the various authors to determine the degree of corporatism are very similar, even though the importance given to each may differ from author to author. Some highlight the significance of the level of centralized bargaining and union strength, while others (especially political scientists) underline the importance of the consensus system and of social cohesion and integration among workers, employers, and government. For example, Switzerland and Japan are characterized by a rather decentralized system of industrial relations and negotiation; nevertheless, they are systems in which, as Lehner (1987) indicates, there is a high level of "concordance" or agreement: Social cohesion and stability are representative of the political system.

The level of centralization is generally measured on the basis of four principal indicators:

1. The level at which bargaining (national, industrial, or regional as opposed to local or plant level) takes place, and the power of national organizations compared to local ones.
2. The number of labor and employer organizations and the degree of cooperation and coordination among, and within, themselves (national, sectorial, firm, or professional).
3. The level of synchronization in which contracts are stipulated, and the existence of key contracts which influence all others.
4. The degree of coverage of collective bargaining compared to local bargaining.

The concept of "corporatism" includes other important aspects of the workings of the industrial relations system and the socio-political system. Some variables, used especially by political scientists, try to measure the way in which wage bargaining is influenced by more general motivations and interests, such as government involvement in wage negotiations, the existence of consensus between labor and firms and, thus, low levels of conflict (Soskice

1983; McCallum 1983), and the existence of political and ideological similarity between unions and governments (Schmidt 1986; Lehner 1987; Paloheimo 1988).

The reference period is important in defining the rankings because, as will be seen further on, different periods can be identified in each country characterized by different levels of corporatism and/or centralization of industrial relations. For example, developments in Australia beginning in 1983 would suggest including the country among those with a high level of corporatism. The same can be said for Finland. However, Sweden, Norway, Denmark, and Germany have experienced a weakening in the corporatist system in recent years. The United Kingdom is the most evident case of a radical change in the industrial relations system beginning in 1979, even if before it was not considered to have a high degree of corporatism.

Table 2 shows several rankings of countries based on the level of corporatism and centralization according to different authors. The orderings differ according to the use of a centralization or corporatism indicator. The biggest differences concern the position of Japan, Switzerland, Germany, and the Netherlands, which show high rankings in the area of consensus systems (corporatism), but only intermediate positions regarding centralization. The position of these countries in the corporatism ranking depends on the relative weight each author gives to components linked to consensus and centralization.

Many authors find a positive relationship between the degree of corporatism and economic performance in the 1970s. The countries with the highest degree of corporatism show a lower growth in unemployment and a greater control over inflation during the crisis years; they did not suffer too much in terms of growth either, as took place in the pluralistic countries (US, Canada). The explanation lies in the structure of the labor market: For example, Bruno and Sachs show that the most corporatist countries exhibit a more moderate rate of growth in real wages after the first oil shock.[1]

Nevertheless, even very decentralized industrial relations systems, as in the United States and Canada, achieve wage moderation due to the low sensitivity of nominal wages to inflation. Compared to the 1960s, however, the corporatist countries register better performances regarding rates of inflation, unemployment, and growth.

In the most recent works, which analyze the impact of different aspects of corporatism on performance, more complex relationships are found.

Calmfors and Driffill (1988) concentrate on the degree of centralized bargaining, which is thought to be an indicator more objectively measurable

[1] Using a wage-gap measure (given by the ratio between wage growth and labor productivity growth), these authors find that highly corporatist countries display an average wage-gap of 0.2 in the 1973–1979 period, while countries with a low level of corporatism showed an average of 5.1.

and more directly and analytically linked to wage trends. Their findings show a non-monotonic relationship ("U"-shaped) between the degree of centralized bargaining and economic performance: The best performances regarding inflation and unemployment trade-off are registered both in countries with a high degree of centralized bargaining (Austria, Norway, Sweden, Denmark, Finland), and in countries with decentralized industrial relations systems (France, UK, Italy, Japan, Switzerland, US, Canada). The great dissimilarity between the industrial relations and the institutional systems regulating the labor market in those countries with decentralized bargaining makes this finding difficult to interpret. In fact, if Japan and Switzerland were dropped from the group of decentralized countries (since they have different socio-institutional characteristics than the European and North American countries), the performance of decentralized countries in the 1974–1985 period worsens considerably, and we see a monotonic relationship. However, if one considers the variations in the unemployment and employment rates in the years after the oil shocks compared to 1963–1973, the relationship is a "U"-type; but this will be addressed in the following section.

Estimates of wage equations carried out on time-series data for each country (Bean, Layard, and Nickell 1986; Newell and Symons 1987; OECD 1987) show that nominal wages in corporatist countries are highly sensitive to unemployment, and thus lower increases in unemployment are necessary to attain a certain downward adjustment in wages.

Econometric tests of the wage determination models used by most of the authors cited are not able to differentiate between the possible causes of why the unemployment rate has such a profound impact on wages. This impact can be explained by both a greater speed in nominal wage adjustment to variations in the unemployment level, and by the corporatist economies' greater ability to maintain high employment levels while adjusting to external shocks without incurring excessive wage increases. Such employment rigidity is permitted by the use of various tools, such as "active" labor market policies exchanged in the social contract for wage moderation, and policies designed to increase employment in the public sector (Jackman 1989).

OECD estimates show that corporatist countries have displayed greater employment inelasticity compared to GDP performance (Table 3), and higher public sector employment growth than that of other countries (Table 4).

This type of policy in the 1970s and early 1980s did not lead to growing wage demands from labor unions, since centralized wage negotiations considered the prevailing conditions in the private sector exposed to international competition rather than the general unemployment rate. As we will see later on, this policy has worked well during the crisis years, but appears to have been less effective in the 1980s.

In studies undertaken by political scientists, analysis is progressing toward

Table 2: Rank Orderings of Countries According to their Degree of Corporatism and Centralization.

Centralization						
Tarantelli	Schmitter	Cameron	Bruno/Sachs	Calmfors/Driffill	Blyth	Ours
Austria	Austria	Sweden	Austria	Austria	Austria	Austria
Japan	Norway	Norway	Germany	Norway	Norway	Norway
Germany	Sweden	Austria	Netherlands	Sweden	Sweden	Sweden
Denmark	Denmark	Belgium	Norway	Denmark	Denmark	Denmark
Finland	Finland	Finland	Sweden	Finland	Finland	Finland
Norway	Netherlands	Denmark	Switzerland	Germany	New Zealand	Germany
Sweden	Belgium	Netherlands	Denmark	Netherlands	Australia	Netherlands
Netherlands	Germany	Germany	Finland	Belgium	Germany	Belgium
Belgium	Switzerland	United Kingdom	Belgium	New Zealand	Belgium	Switzerland
France	United States	Australia	Japan	Australia	Netherlands	Australia
Australia	Canada	Switzerland	New Zealand	France	Japan	Japan
Italy	France	Italy	United Kingdom	United Kingdom	France	France
United Kingdom	United Kingdom	Canada	France	Italy	United Kingdom	United Kingdom
Canada	Italy	United States	Italy	Japan	Italy	Italy
United States		France	Australia	Switzerland	United States	Canada
		Japan	Canada	United States	Canada	United States
			United States	Canada		

Corporatism

Tarantelli	Schmitter	Cameron	Bruno/Sachs	Lehner	Ours
Austria	Austria	Sweden	Austria	Japan	Japan
Germany	Norway	Norway	Germany	Switzerland	Switzerland
Japan	Sweden	Austria	Netherlands	Austria	Austria
Sweden	Finland	Belgium	Norway	Sweden	Norway
Norway	Denmark	Finland	Sweden	Norway	Sweden
Denmark	Netherlands	Denmark	Switzerland	Netherlands	Denmark
Australia	Belgium	Netherlands	Denmark	Belgium	Germany
Netherlands	Germany	Germany	Finland	Germany	Finland
Finland	Canada	United Kingdom	Belgium	Denmark	Netherlands
Belgium	France	Switzerland	Japan	Finland	Belgium
Canada	United Kingdom	Australia	New Zealand	Australia	Australia
United States	Switzerland	Italy	United Kingdom	United Kingdom	United Kingdom
France	Italy	Canada	France	Italy	France
United Kingdom		United States	Italy	United States	Italy
Switzerland		France	Australia	Canada	United Kingdom
Italy		Japan	Canada	France	Canada
			United States		

Table 3: Employment Rigidity and Real Wage Flexibility.
(business sector)

	Employment rigidity[1]	Long run wage flexibility[2]
Austria	0.80	−0.83
Italy	0.99	−0.60
Japan	0.91	−1.66
Sweden	0.78	−1.40
United Kingdom	0.77	−0.15
France	0.75	−0.33
Belgium	0.73	−0.49
Germany	0.68	−0.14
Finland	0.67	−0.49
Australia	0.60	−0.39
United States	0.58	−0.60
Canada	0.44	−0.50
Average (unweighted)	0.72	−0.55

1. Employment rigidity is measured by the output coefficient b in the equation:
$(Q/L) = a + b\ Qt + cQt - 1$
where Q is output growth, L is employment and Q/L is labour productivity growth. The observation period is 1960–1986. If the b co-efficient is low, employment is elastic and vice versa.
2. Wage flexibility is measured by the elasticity of nominal wage changes with respect to the rate of unemployment.
Source: OECD, Economic Survey, Austria, 1988.

defining models which underline the importance of the government's role and relations between government and labor organizations. These interrelationships influence the effectiveness of acceptable macroeconomic policies in each country. Many authors argue that in countries with a centralized bargaining framework, better results are obtained when a leftist government is in power; the opposite is true in decentralized countries.

In a study which combines both cross-country and time-series analyses,[2] Paloheimo (1988) identifies four different politico-institutional systems. The first system is exemplified by the Scandinavian countries, which are characterized by highly unionized and centralized bargaining systems, and by stable social democratic political systems; there is, as well, a close interdependence between unions and social democratic governments. During the crisis of the 1970s, these countries registered relatively good performances in terms of growth, employment, and price stability. The second system is that of countries with centralized wage negotiating systems, but with centrist or

[2] Each observation is a country/time-period coupling according to the level of corporatism reached in each period.

Table 4: Employment in the Private and in the Public Sector: Percentage change 1973–1982.

	Private sector	Public sector
Australia	5	31
Austria	−3	30
Belgium	−9	29
Canada	21	22
Finland	1	25
France	−1	13
Germany	−8	19
Italy	5	23
Japan	7	16
Netherlands	4	22
Norway	15	46
Sweden	−3	45
Switzerland	−7	16
United Kingdom	−8	9
United States	17	13

Source: Schmidt, 1987: 16.

conservative governments. Several examples include Belgium, Sweden between 1976 and 1982, and Norway between 1981 and 1985. These countries/periods performed more poorly than those in the first group, particularly regarding economic growth and unemployment, due to the greater difficulty of coordinating macroeconomic policies and wage policies. A third group of countries is made up of decentralized industrial relations systems, low levels of unionization, and center-rightist governments. Examples include Canada, France before 1981, Ireland, Japan, Switzerland, the United States, and the United Kingdom after 1979. In these countries the role of market forces is very important. Finally, there are those countries with decentralized structures and leftist or center-leftist governments (France after 1981, Italy). Attempts to create corporatist-like relations between the government and unions in these countries have frequently failed, and stabilization policies have not had much success. Performances in these countries were worse than those of decentralized countries with conservative governments.

Lehner (1987) and Schmidt (1987) produce similar analyses, which are centered on the political system of government and the interdependence between interest groups and government. Schmidt identifies two possible paths toward full employment: The first is called "labor dominated" as found in corporatist countries (Austria, Sweden, Norway), with leftist governments and mostly Keynesian policies. The second is called "conservative-reformist", as found in Japan and Switzerland; it is characterized by conservative governments and greater freedom for market mechanisms.

Tarantelli (1986), is the economist most able to integrate the different aspects of analysis: The economic features of the relationship between bargaining system, wage flexibility and economic policies, and the institutional features of interaction between politico-institutional systems and government, labor, and employers, which is so important in forming the expectations and behavior of the different actors. How politico-institutional systems and industrial relations systems regulate the conflict of interests has an influence on the "reliability curve", and thus the credibility of the contractual exchange and the effectiveness of income policies. The degree of neocorporatism does not only depend on how centralized negotiations are, but also on how involved interest organizations (labor unions and employers) are in administering macroeconomic policies, and on the means used to regulate industrial conflicts.

2.3 Corporatism and Performance: The Empirical Evidence

In order to estimate the relative importance of all the elements of corporatism, compared to the one element represented by the centralization of industrial relations in permitting wage moderation and positive economic performance, two rank orderings of countries have been constructed.

The first (CORP) reflects both the degree of social consensus existing in each country and the level of centralization of industrial relations. It was constructed mainly on the basis of the corporatism rankings of Tarantelli (1986) and Lehner (1987).[3] Japan and Switzerland are in the first positions: They show a rather decentralized industrial relations system and low levels of unionization; however, the informal system of coordinating and managing consensus is highly articulated, and as such, interest groups are integrated at the central level.

The more truly neocorporatist countries make up the next group: Austria, Norway, and Sweden. Those of a more intermediate degree of corporatism are: Germany, Denmark, Finland, Australia, the Netherlands, and Belgium. In some of these countries unionization is high, though unions are generally divided between themselves for linguistic or religious reasons (Belgium, Netherlands) or for ideological reasons (Finland), and negotiations occur primarily at a sectorial level. In Australia, the low level of centralized collective bargaining is offset by an obligatory federal system of settlement and arbitration, which has substituted collective bargaining as the main means of resolving legal disputes and conflicts of interest. Germany has a low level of

[3] The correlation coefficient between our ranking and that of Lehner is 0.93, and between our ranking and that of Tarantelli is 0.63. The relative position of different countries within each group depends on partly subjective evaluations of the industrial relations and socio-political systems in each country. As mentioned, this also depends on the reference period.

unionization and a more decentralized bargaining system than the Scandinavian and Austrian versions: Most negotiating takes place at the industry level, while work councils have an important role in bargaining at the firm level. On the contrary, the level of centralization and coordination of the National Employers Association (BDA) is very high.

The countries with a weak level of corporatism are Italy, France, and the United Kingdom; they are characterized by a fragmented and unstable system of industrial relations, a relatively high level of unionization (with the exception of France) and many unions that were powerful in the 1970s, but are divided along ideological and political lines, making coordination and cooption on effective income policies very difficult to implement. In these countries, bargaining occurs at various uncoordinated levels; systems for regulating conflict settlement do not exist, nor do formal or informal controls over the bargaining process.

Finally, there are the North American countries (US and Canada) which have pluralistic systems with low levels of unionization, extremely decentralized bargaining at the firm level, and a lack of cooption and involvement mechanisms between government and unions. Given the absence of a highly centralized strong labor movement, not even a main employers' federation exists.[4] In Canada, the greater autonomy of the provinces has led to the development of sixteen different industrial relations systems around the country. Canada also shows a higher level of political conflict than the United States. One characteristic of these countries is the importance of labor legislation in regulating bargaining and the low level of institutional protection of trade unions.

The ranking according to the degree of centralization of industrial relations (CENTR) differs from the previous one basically due to the fact that Japan and Switzerland are now in intermediate positions.[5] The simple correlation coefficient between the two rankings is 0.75.

Tables 5a and 5b show several performance indicators for these groups of countries in the two periods following the oil crisis of 1973: The stagflation period (1974–1982) and the economic recovery period (1983–1987). Tables 6a and 6b show the correlation coefficients among these indicators and the rankings in terms of corporatism and centralization.

The performance indicators used here are those most frequently commented on and used: unemployment rates (standardized), inflation rates, the sum of inflation and unemployment (OKUN index), and rates of change in the gross domestic product (GDP).

[4] The AFL-CIO in the United States and the Canadian Labor Congress do not include all the national or local unions among their associated organizations. In addition, the AFL-CIO cannot intervene in collective bargaining.

[5] The ranking according to the level of centralization was constructed as an average of the rankings of Calmfors and Driffill, Tarantelli, Schmitter, Cameron, Bruno and Sachs, and Blyth. The greatest similarity is with Calmfors and Driffill's ranking ($r=0.94$).

Table 5a: Corporatism and Economic Performance.

	Average annual percentage changes				Average levels				
	Real GNP		Consumer prices		Unemployment rates[1]		Okun Index[2]		
	74–82	83–87	74–82	83–87	74–82	83–87	74–82	83–87	74–83[3]
Concordance	2.01	3.16	6.50	1.80	1.17	1.75	7.67	3.55	2.70
High Corporatism	2.58	2.75	8.80	5.61	2.03	3.23	10.83	8.84	7.32
Medium Corporatism	2.04	2.55	9.15	4.32	5.70	8.70	14.85	13.02	10.17
Weak Corporatism	2.10	2.48	14.38	6.47	6.31	10.53	20.69	17.00	12.82
Pluralism	2.34	4.13	9.44	3.93	7.38	8.87	16.82	12.80	11.53
Japan	3.67	3.98	8.52	1.28	2.03	2.70	10.56	3.98	3.04
Switzerland	0.34	2.34	4.48	2.32	0.31	0.80	4.79	3.12	2.36
Austria	2.41	1.80	6.29	3.04	2.07	4.28	8.36	7.32	4.96
Norway	3.87	4.06	9.79	7.24	1.91	2.60	11.70	9.84	9.36
Sweden	1.46	2.40	10.33	6.56	2.10	2.80	12.43	9.36	7.65
Germany	1.66	2.24	5.01	1.58	3.63	6.98	8.64	8.56	5.56
Denmark	1.47	2.68	10.97	5.10	6.53	9.02	17.50	14.12	11.52
Finland	2.74	3.18	12.26	5.66	4.68	5.18	16.93	10.84	9.16
Netherlands	2.03	2.08	6.92	1.54	6.14	10.80	13.07	12.34	8.34
Belgium	2.04	1.48	8.19	4.36	7.79	11.60	15.98	15.96	11.75
Australia	2.28	3.66	11.54	7.68	5.43	8.62	16.98	16.30	14.67
United Kingdom	0.78	3.38	14.74	4.66	6.37	11.36	21.11	16.02	12.72
Italy	3.07	2.44	16.92	9.02	7.13	10.40	24.06	19.42	14.87
France	2.46	1.62	11.47	5.72	5.44	9.84	16.91	15.56	10.88
USA	1.64	0.04	9.01	3.32	7.12	7.40	16.13	10.72	10.25
Canada	3.03	4.26	9.87	4.54	7.64	10.34	17.51	14.88	12.81

1. Standardized unemployment rates, with the exception of Switzerland and Denmark.
2. Okun Index = sum of the period average inflation rate and the period average standardized unemployment rate.
3. The Okun Index for the 1974–1987 period is given by the sum of the average unemployment rate in the period 1974–1987 and of the average inflation rate in the period 1985–1987.

Source: OECD, Economic Outlook, n. 44 and OECD, Historical Statistics, 1960–1986.

Table 5b: Corporatism and Economic Performance. Differences in Average Percentage Changes.

	Okun				GNP			Consumer prices		
	(74–82)– (60–73)	(83–87)– (74–82)	(74–87)– (60–73)	(74–87)– (60–73)*	(74–82)– (60–73)	(83–87)– (74–82)	(74–87)– (60–73)	(74–82)– (60–73)	(83–87)– (74–82)	(74–87)– (60–73)
Concordance	1.65	−4.12	0.17	−3.33	−4.89	1.15	−4.48	1.08	−4.70	−0.60
High Corporatism	4.16	−1.99	3.45	0.65	−1.67	0.18	−1.61	3.90	−3.19	2.76
Medium Corporatism	8.50	−1.83	7.85	3.82	−3.06	0.52	−2.88	4.38	−4.83	2.66
Weak Corporatism	12.08	−3.69	10.76	4.21	−2.44	0.38	−2.30	9.28	−7.91	6.45
Pluralism	8.80	−4.02	7.36	3.50	−1.99	1.79	−1.35	5.94	−5.51	3.97
Japan	3.01	−6.58	0.66	−4.51	−5.82	0.31	−5.70	2.17	−7.24	−0.41
Switzerland	0.29	−1.67	−0.31	−2.15	−3.97	2.00	−3.26	−0.02	−2.16	−0.79
Austria	0.26	−1.04	1.89	−1.14	−2.96	−0.61	−3.17	1.89	−3.25	0.73
Norway	4.60	−1.86	3.94	2.26	0.08	0.19	0.15	4.39	−2.55	3.48
Sweden	5.63	−3.07	4.54	0.85	−2.14	0.94	−1.81	5.43	−3.77	4.09
Germany	4.19	−0.08	4.16	1.11	−3.38	0.58	−3.17	1.36	−3.43	0.14
Denmark	9.95	−3.38	8.74	3.97	−2.52	1.21	−2.08	4.72	−5.87	2.62
Finland	9.03	−6.09	6.86	1.26	−3.21	0.44	−3.05	6.56	−6.60	4.20
Netherlands	6.67	−0.73	6.41	1.94	−2.85	0.05	−2.83	1.67	−5.38	0.25
Belgium	9.88	−0.02	9.87	5.65	−3.19	−0.56	−3.39	4.34	−3.83	2.97
Australia	11.28	−0.68	11.04	8.97	−3.24	1.38	−2.75	7.64	−3.86	6.26
United Kingdom	12.66	−5.09	10.84	4.27	−2.62	2.60	−1.69	9.19	−10.08	5.59
Italy	13.76	−4.64	12.10	4.25	−1.88	−0.63	−2.11	12.02	−7.90	9.20
France	9.81	−1.35	9.33	4.57	−2.81	−0.84	−3.11	6.62	−5.75	4.56
USA	8.23	−5.41	6.30	3.78	−1.57	2.36	−0.73	5.51	−5.69	3.48
Canada	9.36	−2.63	8.42	2.35	−2.40	1.23	−1.96	6.37	−5.33	4.46
				4.66						

* (Average unemployment rate 1974–1987+average inflation rate 1985–1987) less (average unemployment rate 1960–1973+average inflation rate 1960–1973).
Source: See Table 5a.

Table 6a: Performance and Corporatism/Centralization Ranking: Correlation Coefficients

		Corporatism	Centralization
GNP	1974–82	0.01	−0.03
	1983–87	0.18	0.34
	1974–87	0.08	0.12
Standardization	1974–82	0.82	0.52
Unemployment	1983–87	0.77	0.46
Rate	1974–87	0.81*	0.50
Inflation	1974–82	0.59	0.39
Rate	1983–87	0.40	0.05
	1974–87	0.57	0.31
Okun	1974–82	0.80*	0.51
Index	1983–87	0.80*	0.38
	1974–87	0.82*	0.48

* Significant at the .001 level
Source: Table 5a.

Table 6b: Changes in Performance and Corporatism/Centralization Ranking: Correlation Coefficients

		Corporatism	Centralization
GNP	74–82/60–73	0.28	−0.18
	83–87/74–82	0.22	0.41
	74–87/60–73	0.35	−0.03
Standardization	74–82/60–73	0.46	0.24
Unemployment	83–87/74–82	0.47	0.24
Rate	74–87/60–73	0.50	0.23
Inflation	74–82/60–73	0.74	0.48
Rate	83–87/74–82	−0.49	−0.55
	74–87/60–73	0.72*	0.40
Okun	74–82/60–73	0.82	0.49
Index	83–87/74–82	−0.12	−0.35
	74–8760–73	0.82*	0.43
Adjusted Okun Index**	74–87/60–73	0.73*	0.28

* Significant at the 0.001 level.
** Okun 74–87 = average unemployment rate 1974–1987+average inflation rate 1985–1987.
Source: Table 5b.

The indicators in Tables 5a and 5b are quoted both as levels (annual averages of the periods under consideration), and as variations between the annual average of a given period and the annual average of the preceding period. In fact, it is interesting to study the relationship between the degree of corporatism and/or centralization and the levels of these indicators in the critical periods of the 1970s and 1980s, as well as the variations that these indicators underwent in the critical periods compared to the previous periods.

The aim is to understand whether or not the degree of corporatism can explain the performance of those years, as well as the worsening in performance compared to the 1960s stemming from the oil crisis. Finally, it could be interesting to see if the relative improvement of performance in the 1980s over the 1970s can be explained according to the level of corporatism. Thus, in Tables 5a and 5b, the annual average variables of the different performance indicators have been grouped for the various countries according to the degree of corporatism.

The rankings are similar both for the variations in the OKUN indices for the whole 1974–1987 period compared to the base period 1960–1973, and for the crucial period of 1974–1982 compared to the same base period. The relative worsening in performance is similar as well: modest deterioration in the "concordance" countries; and increasingly worse performances in the countries with strong, average, and weak corporatism.

The pluralistic countries do not display the largest increase in the OKUN index as they are placed at the level of countries with average corporatism and, thus, prior to those with weak corporatism (i.e. France, UK, and Italy). Therefore, we find a "U"-relationship similar to that of Calmfors and Driffill (1988), but only among countries that do not have high levels of social cohesion. Among these, the worst performances are registered by countries with a low level of corporatism (Figure 1).

The ranking does not change substantially if instead of using the traditional OKUN index, a "corrected" index is used which takes into consideration the increase in unemployment for the whole 1974–1987 period, but that gives less weight to inflation, especially in the past[6] (Figure 2).

A "U"-relationship is also found by examining GDP growth rates in the periods following the oil crisis, and examining the changes in growth rates compared to the period prior to the oil crisis. However, Japan and Switzerland's performances are worse than those registered in the other countries under examination. As we shall see presently, this is an indication of the different ways in which these countries faced the crisis, and of how greatly they differ from the strongly corporatist countries (Austria, Norway, and Sweden).

Tables 6a and 6b show some descriptive statistics that draw the same

[6] The corrected OKUN index is given by the sum of the average rate of unemployment in the 1974–1987 period and the average inflation rate in the three years of 1985–1987.

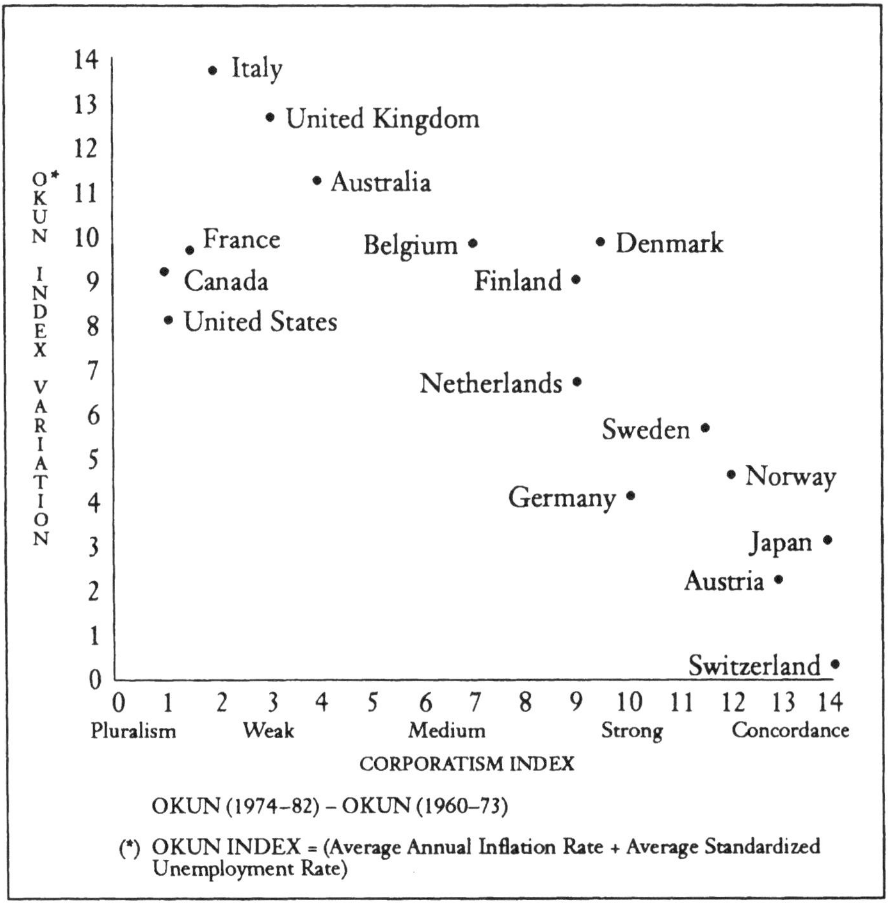

Figure 1: Corporatism and Performance in the Years of Stagnation: 16 Countries

conclusions. These tables indicate the Pearson correlation coefficients between corporatism and centralization rankings and performance indicators. For inflation, unemployment, and OKUN indicators, the positive coefficient shows that the higher the level of corporatism or centralization, the better the performance.

For the entire 1974–1987 period, or else for the first critical period of 1974–1982, the correlation coefficients are positive and the coefficients are high. The coefficients are higher for the corporatism ranking than for the centralization one: It is clear that concordance countries play a crucial role since they exhibit a very good performance in terms of unemployment and inflation, and are placed at the top of the corporatism ranking.

The results are different for the 1983–1987 period, especially if perform-

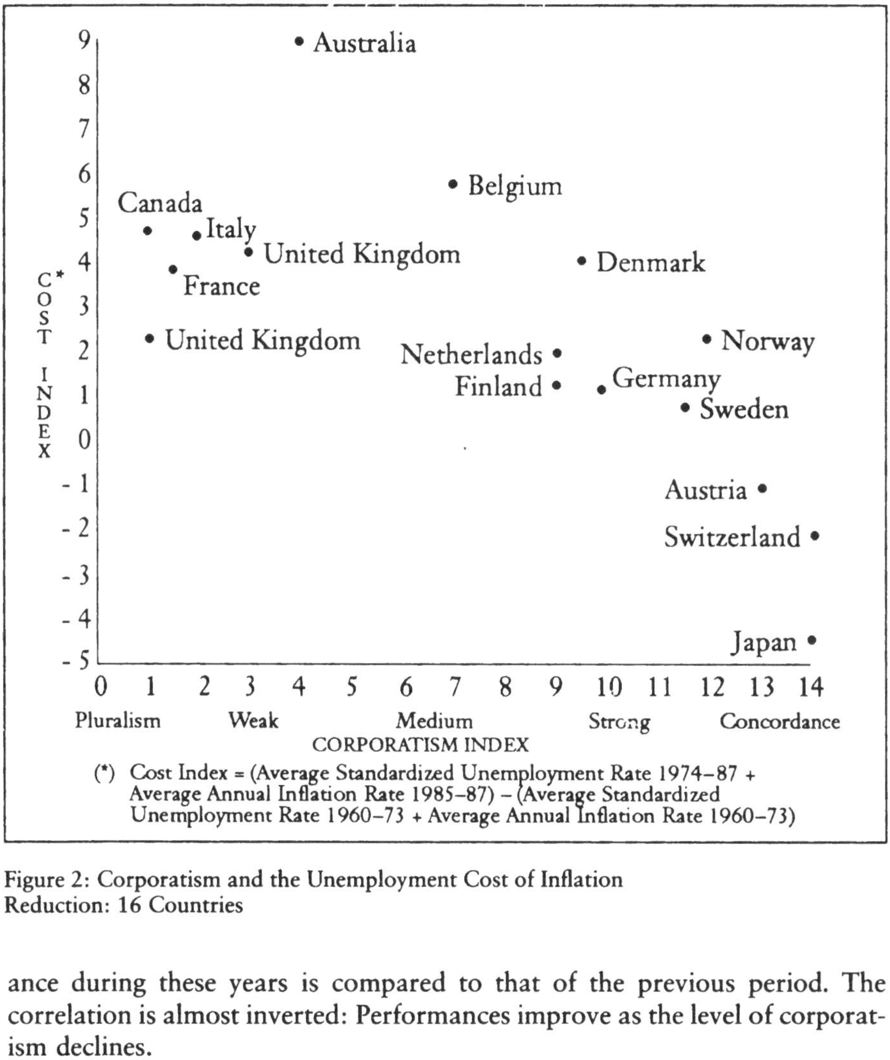

Figure 2: Corporatism and the Unemployment Cost of Inflation Reduction: 16 Countries

ance during these years is compared to that of the previous period. The correlation is almost inverted: Performances improve as the level of corporatism declines.

The same conclusions can be reached by looking at the results of several linear regressions presented in Table 7. The estimates, based on cross-country data, consider the impact of the level of corporatism and centralization on variations in the OKUN index. Other corporatism rankings have been tried besides the one presented in Table 2 (which ranks the countries in descending order) in an effort to capture the "U"-relationship between the industrial relations system and performance. The "U"-corporatism rankings (CORPU) places groups of countries in an alternating sequence in order to have both concordance countries and pluralistic countries in the top places, countries with strong and weak corporatism in the secondary places, with the

Table 7: Corporatism, Centralization, Conflict and Performance: Regression Analysis.
Dependent variable: Changes in Okun index between period averages. Cross-countries OLS, 16 countries (t-statistics in parentheses).

	(1974–1987)–(1960–1973)					(1974–1982)–(1960–1973)					(1983–1987)–(1974–1982)				
	A	B	C	D	E	A	B	C	D	E	A	B	C	D	E
COSTANT	1.79 (1.67)	3.41 (1.72)	−1.74 (−1.08)	−1.84 (−1.07)	2.67 (1.79)	2.64 (2.45)	3.87 (1.98)	−1.70 (−1.29)	−1.77 (−1.26)	4.10 (2.49)	−2.38 (2.25)	−1.28 (−1.08)	−0.52 (−0.34)	−0.20 (−0.13)	−4.74 (−4.61)
CORP	0.64 (5.25)					0.66 (5.36)					−0.05 (−0.43)				
CENTR		0.35 (1.76)		0.03 (0.23)			0.41 (2.09)		0.28 (0.22)			−0.17 (−1.4)		−0.10 (−0.75)	
L(GPS)			1.77 (4.99)	1.72 (4.56)				1.94 (7.37)	1.90 (5.89)				−0.48 (−1.58)	−0.35 (−1.01)	
CORPU					0.51 (3.02)					0.45 (2.43)					0.23 (2.18)
R2 corr.	0.63	0.12	0.66	0.64	0.35	0.64	0.18	0.79	0.78	0.25	−0.06	0.06	0.09	0.6	0.20
F	27.60	3.11	30.29	14.10	9.10	28.70	4.37	54.35	25.20	5.92	0.19	−1.96	2.50	1.49	4.77

Variables: CORP, CENTR = corporatism and centralization rankings (see Table 3).
L(GPS) = logarithm of the average days lost to strikes in the 1965–1986 period. For the group of regressions relative to the (1974–1982)–(1960–1973) period, the strike variable relates to the log of days lost during the period 1965–1982.
CORPU = "u"-shaped corporatism ranking Japan, Switzerland, United States, Canada, Austria, Norway, Sweden, Italy, France, United Kingdom, Germany, Denmark, Finland, The Netherlands, Belgium, Australia.
For the group of regressions relative to the latest period, CORPU is constructed placing pluralist countries at the top of the ranking: United States, Canada, Japan, Switzerland, United Kingdom, Italy, France, Austria, Norway, Sweden, Germany, Denmark, Finland, Australia, Belgium, The Netherlands.

last positions going to those countries with an intermediate level of corporatism.[7]

The degree of corporatism, in its monotonic specification, is the explanatory variable that statistically shows the best results in producing changes in the OKUN index, both in the 1974–1987 period compared to the period preceding the oil crisis, and in the 1974–1982 period. The level of centralization, on the contrary, appears to be of little significance. The importance of the consensus system in bringing about the best performances in terms of variations in the OKUN index is emphasized by including an indicator of the level of conflict in each country among the explanatory variables. Following McCallum (1986), this indicator is measured by the logarithm of the average number of days lost to strikes in the given period. The equation containing this social consensus indicator gives better results than the equation with the level of centralization as the explanatory variable.

The explanatory ability of both the corporatism and consensus indicators is cancelled if one considers the variation in the OKUN index in the 1983–1987 period compared to 1974–1982.[8]

Before examining this important change, it is necessary to comment on the results registered in the most critical period, that is, between the beginning of the 1970s and the early 1980s.

2.3.1 The Stagnation Years

In the 1974–1982 period, unemployment rates increase steadily moving from the concordance countries to the pluralistic ones: The highly corporatist and the concordance countries are able to keep unemployment levels very low even during the stagflation years.

The ability to maintain full employment despite the crisis was due to

[7] Two "U"-rankings were constructed. The first begins with the concordance countries, followed by the pluralist countries, then the highly corporatist countries, and so on: Japan, Switzerland, the United States, Canada, Austria, Norway, Sweden, Italy, France, the United Kingdom, Germany, Denmark, Finland, the Netherlands, Belgium, and Australia.

The second ranking places at the top the pluralist countries and shows a different rotation: the United States, Canada, Japan, Switzerland, the United Kingdom, Italy, France, Austria, Norway, Sweden, Germany, Denmark, Finland, Australia, Belgium, and the Netherlands.

For similar methodology in constructing "U"-rankings, see Calmfors and Driffill (1988).

[8] Regression estimates that have a different indicator of the decline in macroeconomic performance as the dependent variable (given by the sum of the slowdown rate of GDP growth and the rising inflation rate (Misery Index), give results similar to those reported for the OKUN index. However, the sharp decline of productive performance in Japan, and especially Switzerland, reduces the explanatory capacity of the corporatism index, as it reduces the correlation between corporatism and centralization rankings and GDP growth.

different factors in the two groups of countries. In the concordance countries, this situation was permitted by keeping the strongest groups among the labor force employed, while the adjustment process fell almost entirely on the marginal labor force (women, the elderly, and small business employees in Japan; foreign workers and women in Switzerland). On the other hand, maintaining full employment in the corporatist countries was achieved primarily through employment growth in the public sector (Table 4), efficient employment policies (especially in Sweden), and moderately expansive fiscal and monetary policies (in Austria and Norway especially).

The different methods with which the concordance countries and highly corporatist countries were able to curb unemployment can be seen in employment and GDP trends. Compared to the other countries under examination, Japan and Switzerland display the sharpest slowdown in employment and GDP growth rates, while Austria, Norway, and Sweden see employment increase at rates higher than those in the preceding period (Table 8), and show among the mildest slowdowns in GDP growth rates.

Pursuing full employment policies during these years was not accompanied by rising inflation. The average annual rate of inflation is lower in these countries than the others, even if the differential in relation to countries with a medium level of corporatism or pluralistic countries is not as high as the differential for the unemployment rate.

The regression results, relative to the deterioration in the OKUN index in this period as compared to the years preceding the oil shocks (1960–1973), show the importance of the economic and social consensus system in explaining the economic performance of different countries. The best results are given by the specification of the equation that displays as explanatory variable the average level of conflict (measured by number of days lost to strikes) from the mid-1960s until 1982. The assumption of a non-monotonic relationship, indeed a "U"-type, between corporatism and the OKUN index is confirmed by estimates (the coefficient of the CORPU variable is statistically significant and of the expected sign), but the monotonic specification of the corporatism ranking (CORP variable) presents a decidedly better explanatory capacity. In this period, the economic performance of concordance countries and highly corporatist countries is better than that of the pluralist countries.

Therefore, the empirical evidence concerning this period underlines the existence of an important link between performance, consensus, and corporatism. Countries with higher social consensus were able to better confront the period of stagflation than other countries, since it allowed employment preservation policies to be carried out without incurring upward wage spirals and rising inflation. How these consensus levels are reached is a different topic: In some countries, a system of very centralized industrial relations and high-level political exchanges between labor unions and government are necessary; in others, integrating interests occurs through more informal and

Table 8: Corporatism and Employment.

	Average annual percentage rate of change		Differences between period averages		
	74–82	83–87	(74–82)–(60–73)	(83–87)–(74–82)	(74–87)–(60–73)
Concordance	0.24	0.70	−1.08	0.46	−0.92
High Corporatism	0.95	0.93	0.54	−0.03	0.53
Medium Corporatism	0.11	0.83	−0.91	0.72	−0.65
Weak Corporatism	0.13	0.53	−0.06	0.40	0.09
Pluralism	0.2	2.41	−0.38	0.41	−0.23
Japan	0.77	0.96	−0.43	0.19	−0.36
Switzerland	−0.28	0.44	−1.73	0.72	−1.47
Austria	−0.21	0.24	0.11	0.03	0.12
Norway	1.81	1.84	1.26	0.03	1.27
Sweden	0.83	0.70	0.23	−0.13	0.19
Germany	−0.49	0.20	−0.79	0.69	−0.54
Denmark	0.07	1.66	−1.13	1.59	−0.56
Finland	0.56	0.42	0.21	−0.14	0.16
Netherlands	−0.18	0.52	−0.98	0.70	−0.73
Belgium	−0.37	0.14	−1.22	0.51	−1.04
Australia	1.09	2.06	−1.56	0.97	−1.21
United Kingdom	−0.57	1.24	−0.82	1.81	−0.17
Italy	0.76	0.58	1.21	−0.18	1.14
France	0.19	−0.24	−0.56	−0.43	−0.71
USA	1.79	2.46	−0.16	0.67	0.08
Canada	2.21	2.36	−0.59	0.15	−0.54

Source: See Table 5a.

less regulated mechanisms that do not directly go through the industrial relations system.

The causal links are probably interrelated: Neocorporatist systems are possible where cultural and political homogeneity already exist, and by themselves direct and foster this similarity, carrying it along higher development paths.[9] On the other hand, it is possible that the same positive economic performance generates a higher level of consensus in the labor market; thus, the cause/effect link is difficult to interpret.

[9] In the Scandinavian countries, values concerning solidarity and egalitarian income distribution are deeply rooted in society, and make the political system and interest groups politically homogeneous.

2.3.2 Corporatism in Crisis? Industrial Relations and Economic Performance in the 1980s

The 1980s brought great changes in the economic conditions of the countries examined here. Inflation has returned to pre-oil crisis levels in all countries, while unemployment is high and increasing in most European nations.

Many structural aspects of the labor market are changing in all the countries as well: Tertiarization of Western economies has increased the importance of white-collar and professional employment compared to blue-collar labor; the weight of secondary sectors of the workforce (women and young adults) is growing compared to the primary sector (men of working age). In several important countries, the rate of unionization is declining considerably. Technological innovation and increasing internationalization of firms encourages research in internal collaboration and arrangement systems between workers and the firm, and make "national" interests ever less binding.

Thus, it is interesting to see if highly corporatist systems can maintain consensus and show better performances than more fragmented structures, despite changing economic conditions and labor markets.

The data concerning performance indicators used until now show a certain decline in the performance of highly corporatist systems significant enough to worsen the less corporatist countries over other countries. This observation is valid for the years of disinflation (1983–87), considering the variations of most variables with regard to the preceding period (table 5). While Japan and Switzerland display rather positive performances, the Scandinavian countries and Austria did not do as well as the more fragmented systems.

Whether considering variations in the OKUN index or changes in the GDP growth rate between the period 1983–87 and the preceding period (1974–82), one observes a ranking that is almost the inverse of the one examined for the stagnation years. Excluding the concordance countries, improvements in performance (variations in the OKUN index are, in fact, negative) are greater as the level of corporatism decreases.

Even the correlations in table 6b show that there is no longer a relationship between the degree of corporatism and the OKUN index for the most recent period (compared to the preceding one): The correlation, in fact, changes its sign. This fact is even more evident for the inflation rate, where the correlation is inversed with regard to the degree of both corporatism and centralization. This finding may be due to the fact that the less corporatist countries had very high inflation towards the end of the 1970s, making the decrease that took place during the 1980s more significant. In any case, this sharp drop in inflation was not achieved through unemployment increases significant enough to worsen the less corporatist countries' OKUN index more than that of the corporatist nations.

Rather, as seen in Table 5, the OKUN index improved more in the countries with weak corporatism than in highly corporatist countries. In this case the relationship is even more of a "U"-shape than for the previous period: The most consistent improvements in performance are registered at the ends of the ranking. Finally, Japan and the United States appear to have the most consistent improvements in recent years, along with two countries traditionally weak in terms of corporatism: Italy and the United Kingdom.

The regressions concerning this period (Table 7) confirm what we have seen up to now: The explanatory capacity of the level of corporatism and the conflict indicator (logarithm of the days lost to strikes) is cancelled out and the sign of the coefficient changes. Only if the "U"-ranking of corporatism (which puts the pluralist countries in first place) is considered as the explanatory variable are moderately significant results obtained: Both concordance countries and especially pluralistic and weakly corporatist countries are those that show the best performances in terms of re-entry in the OKUN index.

What are the factors that explain this partial deterioration in the position of the neocorporatist countries?

The main factor lies in the intrinsic instability of highly centralized systems, such as the Scandinavian and Austro-German types.[10] Contrary to the forecasts of early neocorporatist theorists, the 1980s witness a trend toward more decentralized and fragmented industrial relations and socio-political systems, even if the evidence is rather contradictory.

The highly corporatist countries displayed a weakening in the neocorporatist model. In Sweden and Norway, social democratic governments were substituted by conservative regimes for a certain number of years. Changes in the labor market weakened the fundamental structures on which the neocorporatist consensus and agreement system of the 1960s and 1970s was based.

The neocorporatist system functions with a high level of unionization and centralized control by labor organizations. In order for the model to function, it is necessary to maintain a high level of consensus. This consensus is often achieved through a series of political exchanges between government, labor, and employers that can lead to high costs in terms of public spending, to distortions in the wage structure, employment and production, and to bureaucratic and institutional rigidities.

The factors which have corroded the consensus system in the 1980s are tied to an ever smaller maneuvering space resulting from slowing growth rates, increasingly unbearable public deficit levels, and growing international competition. As Table 9 shows, the Scandinavian countries and Austria reached high levels of public and foreign deficit throughout the 1970s and 1980s.

[10] The intrinsic instability of the neocorporatist model is discussed in Newell and Symons (1987).

Table 9: Public Spending and Current Balances as a Percentage of GNP/GDP. Period averages.

	Total outlays of government as percentage of GDP			Current balances as a percentage of GNP/GDP		
	60–73	74–82	83–87	60–73	74–82	83–87
Concordance	20.05	29.64	32.10	0.96	1.84	3.98
High Corporatism	38.58	51.99	55.20	1.30	2.69	0.31
Medium Corporatism	33.83	45.78	50.19	0.19	−1.34	−0.48
Weak Corporatism	36.48	44.57	49.61	0.43	0.39	0.29
Pluralism	30.85	36.89	41.73	0.20	0.71	1.68
Japan	19.60	30.04	33.28	1.43	0.22	3.26
Switzerland	20.50	29.24	30.93	0.50	3.46	4.70
Austria	38.90	47.82	51.35	−0.70	−1.59	−0.02
Norway	37.30	50.50	49.80	−2.13	−4.41	0.56
Sweden	39.55	57.66	64.45	1.08	−2.06	−0.34
Germany	37.75	47.97	47.58	0.73	0.52	2.68
Denmark	34.60	52.42	59.30	−1.98	−3.43	−3.56
Finland	30.50	36.78	40.90	−1.95	−2.24	−1.32
Netherlands	41.30	55.07	60.55	1.20	1.76	3.22
Belgium	34.55	48.26	54.30	2.90	−1.47	0.96
Australia	24.25	34.18	38.53	0.25	−3.17	−4.88
United Kingdom	37.30	45.13	47.05	0.58	−0.04	0.42
Italy	33.95	43.57	49.90	0.45	−0.78	−0.16
France	38.20	45.01	51.88	0.25	−0.33	−0.28
USA	29.65	33.33	36.58	0.03	0.00	−2.76
Canada	32.05	40.44	46.88	0.38	−1.41	−0.60

Source: See Table 5a.

These factors reduced the maneuvering spaces for the distribution of benefits, and forced labor unions to lower their expectations. In addition, the increasing importance of new groups of workers (white-collar and public employees) has reduced the capacity of the central labor organizations to present unified demand packages and to control members' reaction to central agreements.[11] An important element of instability stems from the flattening of wage differentials between skilled and unskilled workers that coherent and centralized policies often entail. Each group of workers could certainly do better by getting out of the central agreement (free riding), and even employer associations may disagree with the narrowing of wage differentials since it could distort the internal labor markets. Thus, corporatism crisis periods are usually accompanied by spreading wage differentials, as observed in Table 10 taken from Freeman (1988).

[11] Crouch (1988) underlines the importance of a union being led by its own industrial component in guaranteeing social and economic stability, due to the industrial sector's greater exposure to international competition.

Table 10: Dispersion of Industry Earnings Within OECD Countries, 1970–1986 (variance of logarithm of earnings by industry, multiplied by 100).

	UN		EUROSTAT		CEE		ILO		BLS	
Earnings dispersion	73	83	72	81	70	83	75	84	75	86
High And Increasing										
United States	23	28			28	33	25	26	25	28
Japan	25	26			25	28	24	25	26	29
Canada	21	25					24	26	22	26
Austria	21	27					21	22	21	25
Increasing										
New Zealand	17	21					14	20		
United Kingdom	20	27	16	16				17	19	19
Australia	21	24								
Norway	19	25					10	12		
Moderate And Stable										
Belgium	25	24	18	17	24	30	19	16	19	20
Ireland	22	21	16	16			19	22	19	20
Germany	19	20	12	13	23	23	14	14	17	19
Netherlands			13	11	29	23	13	14	15	16
Switzerland									19	17
Decreasing										
Italy	32	19	24	13	48	37	19	10	22	13
France			16	13	34	34	13	14	15	14
Low										
Denmark	15	14	11	9	26	16	12	12	10	10
Sweden	12	13			9	8	9	9	9	10
Finland	17	15					14	14		

Notes: BLS data for Belgium and Netherlands refers to 1985. ILO data for Italy refers to 1982 and are based on smaller number of industries.
Source: Freeman 1988, Table 2.

Since firms need cooperative relations with the more qualified and specialized workforce, there is a greater pressure to adopt industrial relations and bargaining systems that are more decentralized and individualized. For example, in Sweden in 1983, the Federation of Employers in the Metal and Mechanical Industries (VF) decided to bargain directly with the union of metal and mechanical workers, separating itself from the central SAF/LO accords in order to reach special agreements with the most qualified workers. In both Sweden and Norway, the mid-1970s saw an increase in the number of different union federations, both for employers and workers, as well as growing competition among the federations; the new union associations represent the white-collar and professional groups of workers.

In Norway, added to the LO (which represents the largest union federation) were the Federation of Vocational Unions (YS) and the Federation of Professional Associations (AF). Among employer associations, the strength of the NAF (which primarily includes the tertiary sector) has decreased, while that of the other federations has increased.

In 1973, Sweden saw the formation of the Federation of Salaried Workers in Services and Industry (PTK), which negotiates for TCO (the union that gathers some 70% of white-collar workers) and SACO-SR (Central Organization for High-level Employees). They are all union federations that have opposed the unifying policies of the LO (the federation which represents primarily industrial laborers). All this has brought about several contract renewals in the 1980s (those of 1981–1982 and 1985–1986 in Norway, and that of 1983–1984 in Sweden) that took place completely outside the central federations.

Due to these factors, corporatist countries are experiencing declining levels of corporatism and centralized bargaining in the 1980s. Conflict is increasing, as is the unionization rate (Table 11), especially in the public sector which is characterized by unions that are more "corporative" than corporatist; however, membership in industrial unions is declining (partly because employment in industry is declining). Among other things, these changes have led to a partial abandonment of the traditional bargaining mechanisms in the Scandinavian countries, where the industrial sectors exposed to international competition had the role of wage leaders, followed by the protected sectors. In several recent wage rounds (e.g. Sweden in 1980) the public sector has assumed the role of wage leader. The result is lower wage flexibility with regard to productivity and international prices, and an increase in wage dispersion.

On the other hand, some countries with fragmented industrial relations systems such as Italy, or that are intermediately corporatist such as Finland and Australia, experience phases of increased agreement between labor, employers, and government in the 1980s.

In Italy, the period of "tripartite agreement" (1980–1983) could be considered as a phase of corporatism, even if rather irregular in that it was characterized by union weakness and considerable spreading of wage drift which led to a period of expanding wage differentials.[12] The agreement has helped to improve the industrial relations climate and to reduce conflict, at least in the private sector, allowing a reduction in the rate of inflation less costly in terms of growth.[13]

[12] Characteristics of the industrial relations system in this period could also be interpreted as a tendency toward a more pluralist and decentralized system (Dell'Aringa and Lucifora 1989).

[13] A different interpretation of the causes for the better improvement in Italy's performance than in Britain's is provided by Giavazzi and Spaventa (1989), who underline the

Table 11: Unionization Rates and Conflict.

	STRIKES Average index 1981–1986 (1965–1980 = 1)		UNION MEMBERSHIP (percentage of wage and salary employees)		
	Workers involved	days lost	1970	1979	1985
Concordance	0.18	0.14	33	33	30.50
High Corporatism	2.30	1.40	67	69	72
Medium Corporatism	1.23*	0.86*	53	53	52*
Weak Corporatism	0.60	0.49	38	46	48**
Pluralism	0.39	0.45	31.50	30.50	26.50
Japan	0.11	0.10	35	32	28
Switzerland	0.25	0.17	31	34	33
Austria	0.33	0.26	64	59	61
Norway	5.70	3.38	59	60	61
Sweden	0.87	0.57	79	89	95
Germany	1.35	1.14	37	42	43
Denmark	1.88	1.21	66	86	95
Finland	1.32	0.91	56	84	85
Netherlands	1.07	0.49	39	43	35
Belgium	nd	nd	66	77	nd
Australia	0.52	0.56	52	58	56
United Kingdom	0.85	0.61	51	58	51
Italy	0.82	0.48	41	51	45
France	0.12	0.37	22	28	nd
USA	0.22	0.27	31	25	17
Canada	0.56	0.63	32	36	36

Notes: * excluding Belgium.
** excluding France.
Sources: ILO, Yearbook of Labour Statistics (various years), and OECD, Labour Force Statistics (various years) for the strike data.
Bamber–Lansbury, 1987 and National Sources for the union membership data.

In 1983, Australia initiated a period of three-sided agreement which included political exchange and a neocorporatist type of centralized bargaining. The basic mechanism lies in the Price and Income Accord that was formulated in 1983 between the Labor government and the Associated Confederation of Trade Unions (ACTU), with the outside support of employer federations. The political trade-off consists of accepting a *de facto* wage freeze for two years, in exchange for a national health insurance system and a full indexation of wages to the cost of living. The wage determination system was modified in 1986, through a central government/union accord, in favor

importance of timing in the restrictive monetary policies carried out by the Bank of Italy.

of a two-tiered mechanism more closely linked to the economic conditions of individual firms.

In Finland, since the beginning of the 1980s, the level of cooperation and coordination among different union federations has grown. The biennial contracts signed in 1986 would indicate that the readiness, even by the white-collar workforce, to accept income policies has also increased.

The British case, however, shows the opposite tendency: That of a country with an already low level of corporatism and centralization which is moving toward the pluralistic model of the United States.

2.4 Which Model for the European Countries?

The EEC countries experienced the largest surge in unemployment in the years following the oil crises. Their industrial relations systems are also the most conflictive and difficult since they include union organizations powerful enough to somehow impose their interests, but too numerous and not encompassing enough to internalize the results. In the countries with systems closest to the neocorporatist model (Denmark, Germany), the prevailing tendency in the 1980s leans toward more decentralized and conflictive industrial relations, with work councils playing a larger role in bargaining.

Cross-country estimates of the impact of industrial relations on variations in the OKUN index during the 1970s and 1980s are shown in Table 12, and concern only the European countries (excluding Switzerland, whose socio-political system is too different from the other European countries to be used as a model). For these countries there are no substantial differences between rankings according to the degree of corporatism and those based on the level of centralization (the correlation coefficient between them is 0.97).

The results do not differ greatly from those corresponding to the set of sixteen countries considered earlier. The change in the OKUN index for the whole 1974–1987 period, compared to the period preceding the oil shocks (1960–1973), is explained rather well by the degree of corporatism and the level of conflict. The same is true for variations in the index during the stagnation period (1974–1982) compared to the previous period; however, the explanatory capacity of the degree of corporatism is cancelled out and the coefficient changes signs when considering changes in the OKUN index during 1983–1987 compared to 1974–1987. And neither is the "U"-specification of the corporatism ranking statistically significant. During these years, the differing performances of the European countries do not appear to be linked to the industrial relations systems prevailing in each country.[14] On the

[14] The variable indicating the level of conflict (days lost to strikes) is the only one to show a coefficient significantly different from zero, but the coefficient's sign is different than expected. Even if considering the variation in the degree of conflict rather than the average level, the same results are obtained.

Table 12: Corporatism and Performance in the European Countries.
Regression Analysis. European Countries Excluding Switzerland. Cross Countries OLS (t statistics in parentheses). Dependent Variable: Change in Okun Index between period averages.

	(1974–87)–(1960–73)			(1974–82)–(1960–73)			(1983–87)–(1974–82)		
	A	B	C	A	B	C	A	B	C
COSTANT	1.81 (1.87)	−1.70 (1.84)	4.55 (2.27)	2.39 (1.86)	−2.71 (−1.74)	5.46 (2.39)	−1.61 (1.16)	2.17 (1.27)	−3.38 (−2.42)
CORP	0.89 (6.23)			0.94 (4.98)			−0.14 (−0.70)		
L(GPS)		1.87 (4.58)			2.27 (7.20)			−0.98 (−2.83)	
CORPU			0.43 (1.46)			.43 (1.27)			0.15 (0.72)
R2 corr.	0.79	0.66	0.10	0.70	0.83	0.06	−0.05	0.41	−0.05
F	38.87	21.04	2.15	24.82	51.93	1.62	0.50	7.97	0.53

Variables: CORP, CENTR = corporatism and centralization rankings (see Table 3).
L(GPS) = logarithm of the average days lost to strikes in the 1965–1986 period. For the group of regressions relative to the (1974–1982)–(1960–1973) period, the strike variable relates to the logarithm of days lost during the period 1965–1982.
CORPU = corporatism ranking "u"-shaped: Austria, Norway, Sweden, Italy, France, United Kingdom, Germany, Denmark, Finland, The Netherlands, Belgium.
For the group of regressions relative to the latest period, CORPU is constructed placing at the top of the ranking the low corporatists countries: United Kingdom, Italy, France, Austria, Norway, Sweden, Germany, Denmark, Finland, Belgium, The Netherlands.

one hand, explanations for this trend can be found in the greater difficulty that highly corporatist countries had in reducing inflation since they began with moderate levels in the first place; explanations can also be found in modifications in the structure of the workforce and the representation system discussed in the preceding section.

European economic integration will surely have an impact on the industrial relations systems of the various member countries, if for no other reason than its repercussions on the economic performance of different sectors and its pressures on the regulation of labor/management relations and the cost of labor.

The questions arising at this point are the following: What type of modifications in the industrial relations system may be necessary (and feasible) to improve employment performance in the EEC countries? And what effects will European integration have on the industrial relations systems of the various countries? Although we are unable to answer these questions at this stage, several elements have surfaced in the analysis carried out here.

This analysis suggests that two types of institutional labor market structures exist that facilitate wage moderation and employment growth. One option is that of the fragmented and pluralist systems, such as that of the United States, where wage moderation and real wage flexibility are permitted by union weakness, fragmented bargaining, very low levels of wage indexation, and rather long contract periods. For many observers, this bargaining system and the extreme freedom and flexibility of firms in using the labor force are an important explanation for the strong employment growth in the United States between 1973 and 1986. However, the quality of these jobs is debatable: They were primarily low-paying, fixed-term jobs that only partially resolved the unemployment problem and increased the inequality of income distribution in the American system.

Certain elements of the model are spreading to the European countries (greater flexibility in the use of the workforce, growing importance of bargaining at the firm level instead of the central level, introduction of wage schemes tied to firm productivity); nevertheless, the American model does not seem feasible since it would require radical changes in wage bargaining practices, in the industrial relations system and in the social culture of the European countries.

The alternative offered by the example of the neocorporatist countries would permit a more direct method of confronting the unemployment problem, but this model appears difficult to implement as well. The prerequisites necessary for the system to work are rather binding. First, labor and employers' associations must be convinced of the need to give priority to the national macroeconomic problems over their own particular interests, and to give central organizations the required negotiating authority. Second, similar interests regarding economic and social goals are needed, both within the interest groups, between themselves, and with the government. These common objectives are necessary for a political exchange between wage moderation and for fiscal or social policies to be accpeted. Finally, central organizations must be representative enough to control their members and maintain consensus concerning the need for agreed upon policies and political exchange. As we have seen, the neocorporatist systems' greatest problems are tied to maintaining consensus for long enough periods, and, thus, controlling the deviating tendencies which are strongest in systems characterized by ideological or political divisions.

Perhaps the appropriate solution for the European countries is along the lines of what Tarantelli proposed: Encourage, on the one hand, systems and institutions which facilitate a certain degree of social agreement at a central level, so that mass unemployment becomes the central problem and is internalized by bargaining. On the other hand, in order to curb the deviating tendencies that undermine the agreement system, it is necessary to leave enough space to company bargaining within a system of clearly predefined rules concerning representation mechanisms and conflict regulation.

These elements have to go side by side with expansive employment policies, fiscal and social measures, support for professional training programs, and price controls, all of which give credibility to the political exchange.

The introduction of neocorporatist policies in the European countries, especially in the most fragmented (such as Italy, France, and the UK), is more necessary as the creation of a single market and monetary union draws near. An essential condition for creating an effective European monetary union is that wages and labor policies in the member countries converge. Economic integration and internationalization of firms should lead to a gradual convergence in the performance levels of different sectors, regardless of which countries they belong to. So as not to accentuate disequilibria between regions and countries, this process of integration should be accompanied by a renewal of the European social dialogue and the search for transnational systems of industrial relations.

References

Bamber, G. and J. Lansbury (1987): *International and Comparative Industrial Relations.* London: Allen & Unwin.

Bean, C., R. Layard, and S. Nickell (1986): The Rise in Unemployment: A Multi-Country Study. In: *Economia*, Vol. 53, Supplement.

Blyth, C. A. (1979): The Interaction Between Collective Bargaining and Government Policies in Selected Member Countries. In: *Collective Bargaining and Government Policies.* Washington Conference, OCSE.

Bruno, M. and J. Sachs (1985): *The Economics of Worldwide Stagflation.* Oxford: Basil Blackwell.

Calmfors, L. and J. Driffill (1988): Bargaining Structure, Corporatism and Macroeconomic Performance. In: *Economic Policy. A European Forum*, Vol. 6.

Cameron, D. R. (1984): Social Democracy, Corporatism, Labour Quiescence and the Representation of Economic Interest in Advanced Capitalist Society. In: Goldthorpe, J. H., *Order and Conflict in Contemporary Capitalism.* Oxford: Clarendon Press.

Crouch, C. (1985): Conditions for Trade Union Wage Restraint. In: Lindberg, L. N. and C. S. Maie, *The Politics of Inflation and Economic Stagnation.* Washington DC: The Brooking Institution.

Crouch, C. (1988): Trade Unions in the Exposed Sector: Their Influence on Neo-Corporatist Behaviour. In: *Markets, Institutions and Cooperation: Labour Relations and Economic Performances.* AIEL-IEA Conference: Venice, October.

Dell'Aringa, C. and L. Lucifora (1989): Trade Unions and Wages in Italian Industry. In: *Markets, Institutions and Cooperation: Labour Relations and Economic Performances.* AIEL-IEA Conference: Venice, October.

Freeman, R. B. (1988): Labour Market Institutions and Economic Performance. In: *Economic Policy. A European Forum*, Vol. 6.

Giavazzi, F. and L. Spaventa (1989): Italy: The Real Effect of Inflation and Disinflation. In: *Economic Policy. A European Forum*, Vol. 8.

Heitger, B. (1987): Corporatism, Technological Gaps and Growth in OECD Countries. In: *Weltwirtschaftliches Archiv*, nRd. CXXIII.

Jackman, R. (1989): Unemployment and Public Expenditure: Some International Comparisons. In: *Centre for Labour Economics*, LSE *WP*, 1152.

Klau, F. and A. Mittelstadt (1986): Labour Market Flexibility. In: *OECD Economic Studies*, Vol. 6.

Kyloh, R. (1988): The Wage–Inflation–Unemployment Nexus. In: *Occasional Paper I10.*

Lehner, F. (1987): Interest Intermediation, Institutional Structures and Public Policy. In: *Coping with the Economic Crisis*, Keman, H., H. Paloheimo, and P. Whitely (eds.). London: Sage Publications.

Lehner, F. (1988): The Political Economy of Distributive Conflict. In: *Managing Mixed Economies*, Castles, F., F. Lehner, and M. Schmidt (eds.). Berlin, New York: Walter de Gruyter.

McCallum, J. (1983): Inflation and Social Concensus in the Seventies. In: *The Economic Journal*, Vol. 93.

McCallum, J. (1986): Unemployment in OECD Countries in the 1980s. In: *The Economic Journal*, Vol. 96.

Newell, A. and Symons, J. (1987): Corporatism, Laissez-Faire and the Rise of Unemployment. In: *European Economic Review*, Vol. 31.

OECD (1986): *OECD Economic Surveys – Finland*, 1985–1986.

OECD (1987): *Structural Adjustment and Economic Performance.* Paris.

OECD (1988): *OECD Economic Surveys – Australia*, 1987–1988.

OECD (1988): *OECD Economic Surveys – Austria*, 1987–1988.

OECD (1988): *OECD Economic Surveys – Switzerland*, 1987–1988.

OECD (1989): *OECD Economic Surveys – Sweden*, 1988–1989.

Olson, M. (1982): *The Rise and Decline of Nations.* New Haven: Yale University Press.

Paloheimo, H. (1988): The Effect of Trade Unions and Governments on Economic Performance in 18 OECD Countries. In: *Markets, Institutions and Cooperation: Labour Relations and Economic Performance.* AIEL-IEA Conference: Venice, October.

Schmidt, M. (1982): Does Corporatism Matter? Economic Crisis, Politics and Rates of Unemployment in Capitalist Democracies in the 1970's. In: *Patterns of Corporatist Policy-Making*, Lehmbruch, G. and P. C. Schmitter (eds.). London: Sage Publications.

Schmidt, M. (1987): The Politics of Labour Market Policy: Structural and Political Determinants of Rates of Unemployment in Industrial Nations. In: *Managing Mixed Economies*, Castles, F., F. Lehner, and M. Schmidt (eds.). Berlin, New York: Walter de Gruyter.

Schmitter, P. (1981): Interest Intermediation and Regime Governability in Contemporary Western Europe and North America. In: *Organizing Interest in Western Europe*, Berger, S. D. (ed.). Cambridge: Cambridge University Press.

Soskice, D. (1983): Collective Bargaining and Economic Policies, Manpower and Social Affairs Committee. In: *OECD MAS*, Vol. 23.

Streeck, W. (1988): Industrial Relations in West Germany: 1980–87. In: *Labour*, Vol. 2 (3). Rome: Winter, p. 3.

Tarantelli, E. (1986): *Economia Politica del Lavoro.* UTET: Torino.

3 International Pressures on Industrial Relations: Macroeconomics and Social Concertation

Daniel J. B. Mitchell and Mahmood A. Zaidi

The industrial relations systems of the world's market economies are under common pressure, although the reaction to that pressure has varied considerably from country to country.[1] These pressures are moving world labor markets in an atomistic direction and thus are likely to have special significance for national systems which involve coordination and tripartite social concertation. Because the main forces acting on the various industrial relations systems are economic, countries which value the concertation approach will have a hard time over the long run maintaining their current systems.[2] As Ezio Tarantelli pointed out, successful social concertation for macro-economic purposes depends on the presence of a centralized IR system. Any move toward decentralized wage setting undermines such concertation.[3]

In making this argument, we do not downgrade the importance of other institutional arrangements – political, social, and legal. Rather, we view such arrangements as explanations of the divergent responses of various industrial relations systems that national observers have identified so far. Nonetheless,

[1] References to world developments are based in part on various papers presented at the September 1989 meetings of the International Industrial Relations Association, Brussels, Belgium. These papers are: *A Comparative View of U.S. and Canadian Industrial Relations: A Strategic Choice Perspective*, Kochan, Thomas, A. and Anil Verma; *Structural Change and Industrial Relations: The U.K. Case*, Beaumont, P. B.; *Structural Change and Industrial Relations: Australia*, Niland, John and Keri Spooner; *Structural Change and Industrial Relations in Japan*, Shimada, Haru; *The Coming Divergence in Dutch Industrial Relations*, Visser, Jelle; and *Structural Change and Industrial Relations in the Federal Republic of Germany*, Weiss, Manfred. A summary report based on these papers by Jacques Rojot was also helpful.

[2] The interrelationship between economic forces and the practice of industrial relations and human resource management is emphasized in: *The Economics of Human Resource Management*, Mitchell, Daniel J. B. and Mahmood A. Zaidi (eds.). Oxford, England: Basil Blackwell (1990).

[3] Tarantelli, Ezio (1983), *The Regulation of Inflation in Western Countries and the Degree of Neocorporatism*. Paper 60-83/sec. II(a)/4. Proceedings of the Sixth World Congress, Kyoto, Japan. Geneva, Switzerland: International Industrial Relations Association, pp. 45–77. See also his: (1986), The Regulation of Inflation and Unemployment. In: *Industrial Relations*, Vol. 25, pp. 1–15.

in all countries the element of industrial relations most at risk is collective bargaining and union representation. We believe that tendencies toward non-union workforces which have been most keenly felt in the United States will develop elsewhere, even if current trends are ambiguous. And faced with that situation, countries will have to choose between political representation of employee interests, *laissez faire*, or legal structures which maintain collective bargaining in the face of adversity. Countries which still have established methods of concertation have a mechanism for making that choice consciously. Those that do not – and the United States is a prime example – are likely to have the choice made for them by a collision of market and political forces.

3.1 Three Sets of Economic Influences

Three sets of economic influences are important to an understanding of the pressures on worldwide industrial relations: macroeconomic, financial, and technological. By *macroeconomic*, we mean primarily the forces that determine domestic wage and price changes and link these changes to the level of economic activity, that is, to unemployment. We also refer to external price determination and its linkage to domestic wage and price setting under the macroeconomic heading. By *financial*, we mean the so-called "market for corporate control" and the access to capital which is crucial to that market. We also refer to the financial approach to enterprise which depicts the firm as a malleable portfolio of assets. Finally, when we speak of *technological* change, we mean primarily production function influences which change the optimum scale of production.

If the response of industrial relations systems is placed on a spectrum ranging from little change resulting from these forces to substantial adverse impact, it is clear that the United States falls at the latter end of the spectrum. Managerial strategies of union avoidance are not new to the United States; they are certainly not creations of the 1980s. However, the American style of union/management relations and collective bargaining was especially vulnerable to the three economic influences as they developed in the 1970s and 1980s. As the economic influences supported the management strategies, unionization declined. Moreover, the United States industrial relations system lacked the institutional insulation provided to it in other countries. The degree to which such insulation was provided elsewhere has determined the relative pace of change which has occurred so far.

3.2 A Simple Macro Approach to Wage and Price Setting

To understand the macroeconomic influence, it is helpful to start with a simple model of wage and price setting in the context of a closed economy. In the labor market, the ultimate objective (or "target") is to set W/P, that is, the ratio of wages to prices, which is both the real wage as seen by workers and the product wage as seen by employers.[4] And in the product market, the object is to set P/W, that is, the markup of prices over costs, keeping in mind that in a closed economy costs of production other than labor net out in aggregate. For equilibrium to exist, target W/P in the labor market must equal the inverse of target P/W in the product market. Otherwise, adjustments must occur until equilibrium is reached.

Note that this is a bare bones, agnostic model. It does not specify exactly *how* the price and wage-setting process occurs. The process could be a classical supply/demand market story or a bargaining story. It could involve maximizing behavior or it could involve satisficing. Whatever the mechanism, whenever target W/P in the labor market exceeds the inverse of target P/W in the product market, inflation will tend to accelerate as a wage/price spiral sets in. When labor-target W/P falls short of the inverse of product-target P/W, there will be decelerating inflation.

How fast these adjustments occur will vary with institutional arrangements. For example, a centralized industrial relations system with a social concertation mechanism might bring about an initial reconciliation of the product- and labor-market targets, thus obviating the need for prolonged and painful periods of inflation or disinflation. Such an outcome is in keeping with the previously cited Tarantelli model.

The state of economic activity, as proxied by the unemployment rate (U) is the control rod in this model, absent a successful system of concertation. A higher U will tend to lower labor-target W/P and raise the inverse of product-target P/W, as sellers in both the product and labor markets are placed in a weaker position. That is, *other things being equal*, a slack labor market will make it difficult to sustain a high real wage. And other things being equal, a slack product market will make it difficult to sustain big price markups.

Consider, for example, a bargaining model of wage setting in which pay is negotiated by a union. With unemployment high, workers will not have an easy time finding alternative work. Strikes in support of pay demands will be hindered by worker insecurity. Management's hand will be strengthened by the ready availability of unemployed labor. Thus, in Figure 1, which shows W/P on the vertical axis and the unemployment rate U on the horizontal, the labor-market target function for W/P is represented as LL which slopes down, reflecting the weakening of labor's bargaining power in the face of increases in unemployment.

The product-market target for P/W is represented by pp in Figure 2. High

[4] We don't deny the possibility that there is an important element of "money illusion" (focus on the nominal wage W) in the short run. Indeed, there is considerable evidence of such a tendency. However, the text refers to the longer run in which inflation is "recognized", even if the recognition occurs with an adaptive lag.

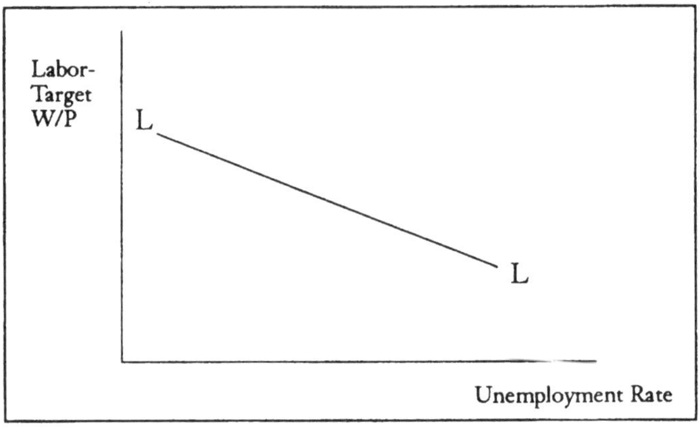

Figure 1: Labor-Market Target Function

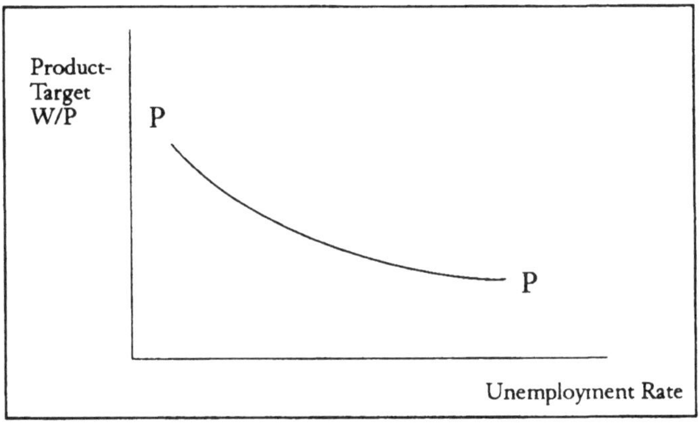

Figure 2: Product-Market Target Function

unemployment – slack in the labor market – will be associated with slack in the product market. Hence, markups will tend to be low. With substantial excess capacity, competition will tend to force firms to operate on lower margins. So pp – the product-target function – slopes down in Figure 2 which shows P/W on the vertical axis and unemployment on the horizontal.

To identify the equilibrium unemployment rate which is consistent with labor-target W/P=inverse of product-target P/W, it is necessary to transform pp to place it on a common diagram with LL. Since pp slopes down with P/W on the vertical axis, it must slope up on a diagram with W/P on that axis. The transformed pp thus appears in Figure 3 as an upward-sloping line.

With both LL and pp on the same diagram, the unemployment rate U*

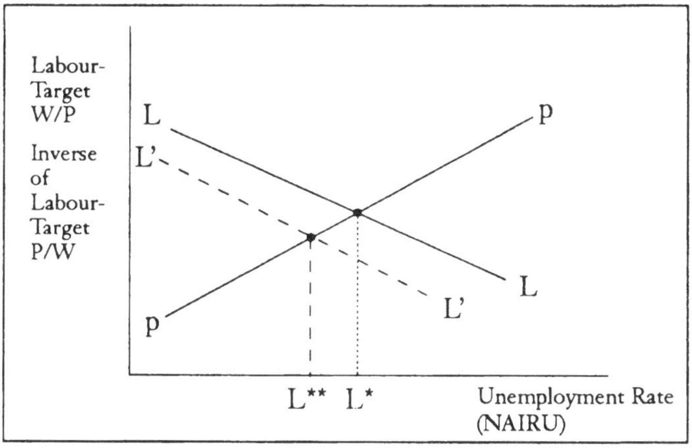

Figure 3: Effect of Weakened Bargaining Power on the NAIRU

which is consistent with labor-target W/P=inverse of product-target P/W can be determined. At that intersection point, there will be no tendency for inflation to accelerate or decelerate. Thus, U* in Figure 3 is what economists have sometimes called the "natural rate" and sometimes – and more accurately – the non-accelerating inflation rate of unemployment (NAIRU).

Institutional features can influence the relative push behind target W/P in the labor market. It is in that sense, countries will exhibit a real wage vs. unemployment trade-off. The United States was able to lower its NAIRU in the 1980s, compared with the 1970s, by following policies which reduced the push behind wages. Essentially, the union sector – where the push behind wages was centered in the 1970s – was shrunk in absolute size. This decline both lowered the union weight in total compensation as a matter of arithmetic and decreased the threat effect of unions. Thus, non-union propensities to follow union patterns were diminished. Furthermore, the rise of non-union competition weakened union bargaining power. This union shrinkage and weakening occurred under a barrage of unfavorable economic circumstances in heavily unionized sectors, deregulation in certain unionized industries, increasing importance of the financial approach to the firm (discussed below), and an adverse political/legal climate.[5] LL in Figure 3 dropped to L'L' (and U* dropped to U**) as the American wage-setting system became overwhelmingly non-union.

In certain other countries, while analogous forces developed, a reconciliation of product- and labor-market targets could not be made at low unemployment rates. Such countries had difficulty expanding employment in the

[5] Mitchell, Daniel J. B. (1989: 2), Wage Pressures and Labor Shortages: The 1960s and the 1980s, *Brookings Papers on Economic Activity*, pp. 191–231.

1980s without re-igniting inflation. That is, their LL and pp curves continued to intersect at high NAIRUs which had developed in the 1970s.

3.2.1 Policy Problems for a Closed Economy

In the closed economy model developed so far, the main short-term macro problem is that there may be a too high NAIRU from the viewpoint of policy-makers. Moreover, there may be shifts in the degree of upward pressure on wages – shifts in wage norms – which will increase the NAIRU.[6] Use of escalation (indexation of wages to prices) may create a problem if it establishes a high real wage incompatible with a low NAIRU. It may also affect the timing of the process by which labor-target W/P and product-target P/W are reconciled. But escalation does not create confusion between the real wage as seen by workers and the product wage as seen by domestic employers since the two are one and the same.[7] As already noted, if wage setting is centralized, the NAIRU can – in principle – be shifted down using an incomes policy based on social concertation or mandatory controls to lower the labor-target function (LL).

Although the United States economy has never been fully closed, until the 1970s external prices were not a source of substantial disturbance or divergence, that is, they tended to move along with domestic prices. This feature of pricing was partly due to the worldwide fixed exchange rate system then prevailing, partly due to a system of import controls on oil, and partly due to domestic farm price supports which sought to maintain "parity" between farm and non-farm prices. (Farm prices are effectively external for most of the domestic economy.) Wage setting could be undertaken *as if* the economy were closed.

In the union sector in particular, the rules of the collective bargaining process were learned and solidified within this quasi-closed economy. The macro problem of a too high NAIRU was addressed by the use of wage/price guideposts and controls in the Kennedy/Johnson, Nixon, and Carter administrations, although decentralized bargaining limited the success of this approach. Each of these episodes was based on the assumption that there was someone important to talk to on the labor side, that is, to the union leaders. By the end of the 1980s, however, the shift to a non-union workforce in the private sector would have precluded such attempts, even if there had been a political interest in trying them. And even in the 1970s, the shift to floating exchange rates and an open economy in 1973 led to severe pressures on

[6] The idea of wage norm shifts is associated with George L. Perry (1980: 1). See his Inflation in Theory and Practice, *Brookings Papers on Economic Activity*, pp. 587–602.

[7] The real wage is the nominal wage divided by a measure of the cost of living. The product wage in a given industry is the nominal wage divided by the price of the particular product being produced. At the aggregate level, the product wage is the nominal wage divided by a measure of the price of domestic output.

traditional bargaining in the United States which an incomes policy could not alleviate.[8]

3.2.2 Policy Problems for an Open Economy

Within an open economy, macro problems and their interactions with the industrial relations system become more complex. There are now two kinds of prices, domestic (P_D) and external (P_E). The real wage is now the ratio of wages to a weighted average of the two prices while the product wage is W/P_D. Thus, an exogenous upward shift in the external price will tend to raise target W/P_D. It will also raise target P_D/W, as firms seek to recover increased external costs as part of their markups. Since W/P_D and P_D/W cannot both shift up, a higher NAIRU rate is required to restore equilibrium.

Figure 4 illustrates this process. The labor-market target is now W/P_D as shown by LL while the product-market target P_D/W is represented by pp. An upward shift in external prices raises the labor-market curve to L''L'' (as wages must be raised relative to domestic prices to account for external prices). And it lowers the product-market target curve to p''p'' (as domestic prices must be raised to cover external cost increases). The combination of both adjustments moves the NAIRU to U***.[9]

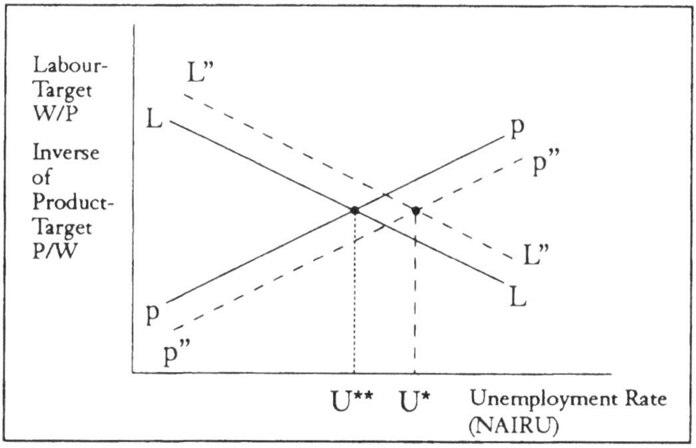

Figure 4: Effect of an External Price Increase on the NAIRU

[8] Results of the use of incomes policy varied from country to country. See, for example, Zaidi, Mahmood A. (1986): Do Incomes Policies Restrain Wage Inflation? Some Evidence from Australia, Canada, and the United States. *Economic Record*, 62, pp. 468–484.

[9] Note that moves from one unemployment rate to another as the result of shifts in the LL and pp curves could be consistent with a rise, a fall, or no change in the real wage. The model makes no prediction. Thus, it is consistent with the American experience in the early to mid-1980s which featured some erosion of the real wage (compared with

Various influences opened up a potential gap between domestic and external price movements in the 1970s, that is, between the real and product wage change. These include the previously mentioned shift to flexible exchange rates in the early 1970s, the development of OPEC as an independent force in setting oil prices, and a lesser willingness and ability (in the US at least) to maintain farm price parity with other prices. The new environment made formal wage indexation to prices a particular problem whenever external prices rose relative to domestic.

Put another way, guarantees of real wage protection became more difficult to offer from the employer perspective, and from the viewpoint of maintaining a low NAIRU, especially since worldwide productivity growth tended to deteriorate.[10] Where institutional arrangements insisted on maintenance of the real wage – or even improvements in the real wage based on the now obsolete productivity trend – the NAIRU was increased. In various countries, discussions concerning "real wage overhangs" and Keynesian vs. classical unemployment began to take place in the late 1970s and early 1980s. Social concertation became difficult under these circumstances since lowering the NAIRU often meant that one or both parties would have to take less in real terms to accommodate such factors as higher energy prices.

The gap between domestic and external prices also created a differential between union and non-union wages, where institutional arrangements permitted such divergence to occur. Union wages were more likely to be protected from inflation by formal or informal escalation. When external prices rose relative to domestic, union wages would rise relative to non-union, creating pressure on (and incentives for) management to choose the non-union route. In the United States, short-run success by unions in the 1970s in defending the wages of their members against inflation meant a rise in union/non-union differentials which set the stage for concession bargaining and shrinkage in the 1980s.

3.3 Financial Influences

Sometimes academic ideas have considerable influence on economic events. Financial theory, as it developed in the 1950s and later, suggested that traditional caution concerning corporate debt-to-equity ratios was unwarranted. Through portfolio adjustments, stockholders could adjust for the risks associated with high debt-to-equity ratios of particular firms.[11] This idea opened up

productivity trends) in the face of an increase in unemployment relative to the late 1970s. And it is consistent with the increase in the real wage that characterized some European countries in the face of chronically high unemployment.

10 Productivity improvements can be represented by parallel upward movements of LL and pp in Figures 3 or 4, leaving U* unchanged, but at a higher real wage.

11 The original idea appeared in Modigliani, Franco, and Merton Miller (1958), The Cost

the possibility of debt financing – the famous (or infamous!) "junk bonds" of the 1970s and 1980s – as a source of capital. Changes in bankruptcy laws – making it easier for firms to continue operating even if they could not meet their interest commitments, blurred the distinction between debt and equity in any case. At the same time, the related view of corporate organizations as simply financial assets within a portfolio suggested that ownership of such assets could be more fluid than had previously been the case.

The financial view of the enterprise raises an immediate problem for stable industrial relations, if such relations are conducted at the employer/union level. Collective bargaining relationships presuppose *continuity* of the parties, especially – as in the case of the United States – if long-term contracts are negotiated. Apart from the formal contract, there are numerous informal understandings which form part of the employer/union relationship. If the identity of one party to the bargain is constantly changing (or in danger of changing), there may be no real bargain at all. Revolving employers undermine employer-level bargaining.

Operating in a world dominated by the financial view makes corporate investment in human resources and in improving the employer/union relationship more difficult.[12] Such investments, unlike investments in physical assets, do not appear on the balance sheet. Rather, they appear as current costs on the income statement, and thus cut into profits. Failure to maintain past accumulated assets of goodwill in the employer/union relationship may raise measured short-term profits, since no "depreciation" of that type of goodwill is subtracted from such profits.

In theory, corporate shareholders might see through the veil of false accounting; in practice it is difficult for them to do so. Current management is therefore under pressure to obtain short-term labor cost savings. If it does not, an ownership change may lead to installation of a new management team which will do the job. In any case, the same uncertainty which affects the relation between the firm and its union(s) also affects the relationship between the firm and its managers. Managers are not necessarily continued in their posts when firms are restructured. Hence, managerial welfare is more likely to be linked to short-term profits than to long-term considerations (since the managers know they may not be around in the long term.

Undoubtedly, some observers may view such behavior as an American aberration, or – at any rate – an Anglo-Saxon phenomenon. But the financial

of Capital, Corporation Finance and the Theory of Investment. *American Economic Review*, 48, pp. 261–297. After publication, it took some time for the idea to be recognized as an important contribution to the theory of finance. See Miller, Merton H. (1988), The Modigliani–Miller Propositions After Thirty Years. *Journal of Economic Perspectives*, 2, pp. 99–120.

12 See Belous, Richard S. (1989), *The Contingent Economy: The Growth of the Temporary, Part-Time and Subcontracted Workforce*. Washington: National Planning Association, pp. 97–99.

model is clearly spreading to all market economies. Indeed, foreigners have been active players in the American market for corporate control; why should they not follow the same instincts at home? And when they do, their national employer/union bargaining systems will tend to erode just as the American system has. As union sectors shrink in importance, social concertation becomes more difficult. The question inevitably arises as to whether union officials can represent employee interests if the union sector is a (declining) minority sector.

3.4 Technological Change

It has been argued that new technology, especially that identified with computer applications, is making possible more customized production and is undermining older mass assembly line production. With such applications come pressure for "flexible specialization", the finding of changing market niches, and an emphasis on change rather than stability in workplace relations, job content, etc.[13] Again, a collective bargaining relationship dependent on continuity tends to be undermined by such developments.

It is difficult to say how widespread the kinds of changes just described will become. Plainly, there are examples in particular industries supportive of flexible specialization, and not all of these are in manufacturing.[14] However, the variation in the gap between domestic and external prices, especially through exchange rate gyrations, would have much the same effect as technically based flexible specialization. Shifts in relative prices create uncertainty and reduce the incentive to commit to large-scale, inflexible production runs.

Pressures from flexible specialization and the application of the financial approach to the firm both reduce the scale of operations. Peak production can be spun off to suppliers and subcontractors. Functions within the firm, such as maintenance or payroll accounting, can be outsourced to outside service vendors. Even within the firm, the core organization can be shrunk by using temporary employees to whom few commitments are made. Some of these employees may even work at home using computer terminals and related equipment. Temporary workers, "telecommuters", and workers at small supplier firms are more difficult to unionize than permanent workers at large enterprises.

[13] Piore, Michael J. and Charles F. Sabel (1984), *The Second Industrial Divide: Possibilities for Prosperity*. New York: Basic Books.

[14] For example, the Hollywood film industry has tended to disintegrate into collections of deal-makers and freelancers who come together for particular projects and then go their separate ways. Many employees in the industry do not have regular, ongoing employers. See Christopherson, Susan and Michael Storper (1989), The Effect of Flexible Specialization on Industrial Politics and the Labor Market: The Motion Picture Industry. *Industrial and Labor Relations Review*, 42, pp. 331–347.

From the viewpoint of industrial relations, the impact is much the same regardless of the source of change. Smaller firms and employing units grow relative to larger firms and units; big firm/big union relationships are undercut. Employer/employee relations become less stable. It becomes less and less plausible to argue that by influencing developments in big unionized firms, the rest of the economy will follow. Macro-oriented social concertation based on discussions with a few key players loses its rationale.

3.5 Interpreting Diverse International Reactions

Market forces of the type described will inexorably chip away at the kind of collective bargaining traditionally practiced in the United States; there is little in current American institutional arrangements which has been aimed at offsetting these forces. But in other countries, the institutions surrounding the workplace are different and have either slowed or, in some cases, prevented an American-style erosion of collective bargaining.

First, it is possible to erect *legal* barriers which either prevent management from following market-based incentives toward a non-union strategy or reduce the incentive to do so. Australia's arbitration system, under which the issue of union representation is a court decision, not an employer matter, is an example of such a legal barrier. (Nonetheless, Australian unions have had difficulty penetrating some of the newer sectors in terms of actual membership as opposed to legal representation.) Canada's slower rate of union erosion in the 1980s compared with the United States also seems to reflect tight legal controls and encouragement of public sector unionization. But note that legal structures can be changed, particularly when political winds change, as the British case clearly illustrates. The switch in Britain from a labor government to a conservative government with "new right" ideology reversed earlier unions gains dramatically.

Second, there may be *social* barriers to overt attempts to eliminate or marginalize unions. The German and Dutch cases seem to illustrate such social influences. But again, changes can occur. It might be argued, for example, that American management, too, was once inhibited by social pressures from following explicit non-union strategies. Thus, although American labor law has been little changed since the late 1940s, employer discretion under that law widened as the social barriers diminished. Foreign companies operating in the United States have adopted American-style union-avoidance strategies and may import these eventually to their home countries.

Third, *initial conditions* matter. Some countries started off with relatively high rates of unionization at the time that market forces tilted against collective bargaining. They could experience a substantial decline in union membership and yet still be left with significant unionization by the 1990s. The British case is illustrative; despite adversities similar to those felt by American unions, British unions remain more important players in aggregate wage determination than their American counterparts.

Fourth, market forces can be *accommodated* through enterprise-sensitive bargaining. Japan is a prime example of enterprise unionism. Particularly noteworthy is the bonus system which provides a variable element of pay reflecting company economic conditions. If union pay reflects enterprise conditions, managers have reduced incentives to follow a non-union strategy.[15] Of course, if – as some observers think possible – Japanese employees grow tired of high internal consumer prices, their willingness to accommodate may erode. In any case, even accommodative Japanese enterprise unionism has not forestalled a significant decline in union density.[16]

Finally, a fifth institutional arrangement which can reduce the adverse impact of market forces on unionization is coordinated "recognition" of the gap between real and product wages through *government guidance in wage setting*. In Australia, for example, the central arbitration authorities moved away from mechanical indexation of wages. Various social accords have sought to bring about adjustments to external price changes without resort to chronically high unemployment. Similar developments have occurred in Holland and other countries. Where real wages remain inflexible, however, high NAIRUs can result, producing chronic unemployment, especially among the youth who are the new potential entrants to employment.

3.6 Implications for Macro Performance

Atomistic labor markets of the type economic pressures are creating are likely to have different macroeconomic characteristics from those based on bargaining among major players. Although some European authors emphasize the power that even non-union "insider" workers can exert to influence employer policy,[17] it is easy to overstate such influence. It has long been known that non-union workers can withhold effort within small work groups. But by definition, non-union workers lack the organization needed to impose coordinated, organization-wide costs of their employers. Moreover, one element of the economic changes described above has been declining

[15] A partial alternative to enterprise-sensitive pay determination is the use of wage extension, that is, taking wages out of competition by extending union-set wages to all firms in an industry. Extension has been used in some European countries and is built into the Australian wage arbitration mechanism. American-style pattern bargaining – the extent it influenced non-union pay – played that role at one time. But with current low rates of unionization it no longer does so.

[16] Freeman, Richard B. and Marcus E. Rebick (1989), Crumbling Pillar? Declining Union Density in Japan, *National Bureau of Economic Research, Cambridge: Massachusetts*, working paper no. 2963.

[17] Lindbeck, Assar and Dennis J. Snower (1976), Wage Setting, Unemployment, and Insider–Outsider Relations. *American Economic Review*, 76, pp. 235–239.

employment tenure. At least in the case of the United States, there is evidence that the duration of spells of employment has been reduced.[18] Thus, insider power is becoming less of a factor in both union and non-union environments.

Non-union employers adjust wages with an eye toward recruitment and retention. As labor-market conditions change, they are likely to respond more quickly than employers who bargain their wages, especially under long-duration contracts. Non-union employers are unlikely to be committed to goals such as maintaining real wages in the face of external price increases.

On balance, the tendencies described in this paper suggest that wage setting is moving toward a greater responsiveness to labor-market conditions. Depending on assumptions, such responsiveness could produce a more or less stable macro economy. Sometimes, for example, lags and sluggishness can have a stabilizing influence in economic modelling. But real-world modern economies also feature monetary authorities who try to stabilize and avoid inflation. If the authorities find their task of inflation control easier, long and painful periods of stagflation can be avoided. A shift to a lower LL, with a steeper slope, suggests that episodes of inflation can be more quickly cut off without lengthy recessions. Given reasonable monetary policies, the net effect of a shift toward atomism is likely to be a more stable macroeconomic picture. Thus, one reason for countries to pursue social concertation – the pursuit of improved macro performance – is eliminated.

3.7 Social Concertation for Micro Goals

The key question in an atomistic labor market is whether employees will like inhabiting such a market and, if they are dissatisfied, what actions they will undertake. In the past, the answer was unionization. But there are alternatives to union representation available in the political arena. Thus, if social concertation has a role in the future, it will be in responding to micro-level employee concerns or establishing mechanisms to do so.

Even the atomistic labor market we have described should not be confused with a textbook auction market in which no employer/employee relationships – other than daily contracts – exist. In atomistic labor markets employees will still have ongoing jobs, will still have expectations about what obligations those jobs impose on the employer, and will still bear costs if they suffer job loss. Such costs tend to increase with the age of the employee and in most industrialized countries the median age of the workforce is rising. Thus, job security is an inevitable issue, and not one to which atomistic labor markets are prone to respond affirmatively. Economic uncertainty is pushing

[18] Jacoby, Sanford M. and Daniel J. B. Mitchell (1990), Sticky Stories: Economic Explanations of Employment and Wage Rigidity. *American Economic Review*, 80, pp. 33–37.

employers to cut back on commitments to workers, even as the age profile of the workforce pulls in the opposite direction.

In the United States, the clash between worker desires and employer offers has led to the phenomenon of mandated benefits and legalistic adjudication of employee complaints.[19] Some American states have required – or are considering requiring – that all but the smallest employers provide their employees with health insurance. Similar proposals are being made at the federal level, along with proposals for mandated family leaves in the event of childbirth or the need to care for an elderly parent. A federal law enacted during the 1988 presidential campaign now requires employers to provide 60-days' notice of plant closings and mass layoffs. State courts have become more receptive to individual "wrongful discharge" suits by terminated employees. As the union option for voicing complaints, filing grievances, and dealing with matters such as health insurance declines in the United States, the political/legal process is becoming the new employee representation plan. In an era when product markets were being deregulated, new regulations appeared in the labor market.

The difficulty with the political/legal process is that it tends to be piecemeal. Each issue – layoffs, health insurance, family leaves, wrongful discharge – is considered as an isolated matter. No mechanism exists for asking about the implications of each for the nature of the employment relationship or how the various proposals might affect economic performance.

Social concertation can be re-conceived as a process for dealing with the overall issue of what should be included within the employment relationship. Understood in that way, it could become an alternative to the older macroeconomic view of concertation as a way of avoiding inflation in a bargaining context. The older view is being undermined by shrinkage of the collective bargaining sector in many countries. But the question of who represents the employee interest in a forum of social concertation remains. As collective bargaining shrinks in coverage, other representational structures will be needed.

[19] Mitchell, Daniel J. B. (1990), Mandated Benefits, Voluntary Benefits, and the Changing American Workplace, *UCLA Institute of Industrial Relations*, working paper.

4 Economic Flexibility and Social Solidarity

Serafino Negrelli

4.1 "Disorganized Capitalism" and Micro Corporatism

In a recent paper, P. Schmitter (1989) acknowledges that changes in the international markets and technological advances have led to a turnaround in the tendencies of the corporatist trend in the Western capitalist societies. The signs which indicate the decline of the institutionalized and centralized systems of the representation of social and economic interests are clearly evident. Two of the nations which since World War II have developed, more than others, strong Keynesian policies, are Sweden and the Federal Republic of Germany. In these countries the governing social democratic parties, which in the past had ensured the regulations of relations between politics and economy on the lines of a class compromise (Bordogna and Provasi 1984), lost their majority positions, either temporarily or definitively, in the latter half of the 1970s or thereafter. On the other hand, in Great Britain and the United States, two neoconservative administrations won and maintained their control for the whole of the 1980s. Even in Italy, where there have been governments which were not anti-labor and where there has been a socialist executive, social concertation at a macro level has sharply declined since 1984.

It is hard to forecast the social settings which will evolve as a result of the crisis of the traditional macro-corporatist systems. We can identify at least two: First, a situation which could result from increasing tendencies toward what has been defined as "disorganized capitalism" (Offe 1985; Lash and Urry 1987). This would be the result of the rebirth of the competitive market, and therefore of the dispersion of capital at an international level, of a weakening of traditional working-class solidarity (weaker in terms of trade union power and in decline following the widespread diffusion of new occupations and of the service industry), and of the decreasingly interventionist and increasing deregulating role of governments, be they conservative or progressive.

Paradoxically, this rather left-wing view of economic and social change, concerned with the presumed decline of collective class action, corresponds to the neoconservative viewpoint which sees a return to the original form of capitalism, free private enterprise, and individualism as the only effective means of boosting the economy.

The English case represents an important example. Whether Labor or Conservative, post-World War II governments in England have always managed industrial relations by creating an organized system of collective bargaining within a pluralist context of concerted wage policies. Mrs. Thatcher's new legislation, however, tends to sidestep this approach, which in the past was considered mandatory, as is evidenced in the conclusions of the Donovan Commission Report (1968). The new aim of the governing Conservative body, rather than being that of defining the role of the trade unions, or of institutionalizing industrial relations, seems to be that of separating the trade union organizations from the workers. In doing so, much of the power previously held by the former in the area of collective class action has been taken away, and at the same time the workers have been given more flexibility with regard to the individual control and veto of trade union decisions (Crouch 1989). For this reason, Mrs. Thatcher could even be remembered as a neocapitalist revolutionary, because of her dedication to the task of reinstating the individualistic tradition of Common Law and of reconsidering in a negative light the rights of the trade union movement. This is exactly what was defined two centuries ago by the Jacobin law of Le Chapelier, which outlawed the right to form coalitions and to strike, countering the positive individual liberty to work with the negative collective liberty of association (Soboul 1962).

To complete, albeit briefly, the picture represented by those, who both from the left and from the right envisage the rebirth of individual capitalism, it is necessary to mention the rather more moderate position of Ralf Dahrendorf (1977, 1988) who, in his observation of the end of the social democratic century, proposes a new liberal agenda. The old class affiliations are disappearing, giving way to a new majority class of citizens which embraces many different levels of status and income, but which also has a fundamental equality of access. In this case, the new social conflicts would be concerned with the increase of personal freedom (chances), that is, the possibility for individual growth. The new liberal policy of entitlements, the legitimate right of access (Sen 1981), should therefore be oriented toward such problems as persisting unemployment, difficult living conditions in the inner city areas, regional disparity, and the lower-income bracket which all play a part in keeping people out of the majority group of citizens and which neither the old social democrats nor the new conservatives have been able to resolve (Dahrendorf 1988).

The second type of scenario in the future regulation of relations between politics and economy could be the prevalence of *social micro corporatism*, or rather of models of social and economic interest composition more decentralized with respect to the centralized composition typical of the Keynesian state which dominated the capitalist societies of the post-World War II era. It is widely agreed that the concept of decentralized corporatism, together with an increase in the development of technological innovations and substantial transformations in work attitudes and composition, constitutes a more suitable and successful answer to the problems of slow growth economies and of economies with unstable markets.

Almost a century ago, Durkheim had already defined the idea of a society consisting of a multitude of disorganized individuals as a sociological monstrosity. Durkheim thought, therefore, that the chances of a society remaining cohesive depended on the existence, between the state and the citizens, of "a series of secondary groups, close enough to the individual to be able to strongly attract him into their field of action, and to involve him in the general flow of life in the society" (Durkheim 1902: p. 33). In the industrial society which was forming at that time, Durkheim indicated exactly that intermediate level as being the one with the capacity of codecision on rules, to establish fairly and universally its own authority, and to exercise moral influence, thereby respecting rights and developing social solidarity. According to the French sociologist, one social group in a position to achieve these aims could be that formed by "all the agents of a particular industry, joined together and organized in the same body", which is therefore called a "corporation" or "professional group" (Durkheim 1902: p. 13).

As the basis of this form of decentralized common organization, Durkheim envisaged the establishment of distinct groups (possibly having antagonistic interests) such as employees and employers. These groups would be free to elect their own representatives to common administrative bodies. According to Durkheim, one of the vital functions of these corporative organizations was primarily that of differentiating and articulating the composition of social and economic interests, from a phase of mechanical solidarity into a phase of organic solidarity.

In the present day, the forms taken by this differentiation and articulation of the corporative organization may be multiple. There are at least four areas in which we can observe the practical functioning of this decentralized form regulating interests: economic sectors, territorial districts, groups of companies, and individual companies.

Economic Sectors. The importance of this level in the regulation of social and economic interests grew with the dominance of mass production and Fordism. Industrial trade unions replaced the old craft unions and developed collective bargaining for a whole category or industrial sector. Even today, in many European countries, including the Federal Republic of Germany, France, and partly also in Italy, this remains the dominant level of the national system of industrial relations. In this situation, the entrepreneurial trade associations and the trade union organizations of the principal industries (metalworking, chemical, textiles, etc.) have acquired a certain status and can now be considered a part of the "private government", that is, the public use of organized private interests (Streeck and Schmitter 1985).

This process has advanced to such an extent (and in a similar way, not only in the countries previously mentioned but also in others) that some researchers now have the tendency to consider these sectors as real social subsystems (Schmitter 1989: p. 178). This is true to such a degree that anyone who wishes to make a comparative study of capitalism is forced to abandon the typical global approach and adopt the sector as a central unit of analysis, differentiating and articulating national societies and economies.

Schmitter (1989: p. 179) maintains that it is in the economic sectors that "socially constructed" exchanges take place between producers and that many public policies are implemented at this level.[1] This is also true due to the existence of a "specialized organization" with a permanent administrative body like the entrepreneurial association (of which individual business companies are members), which is in a position to maintain continuous and direct contact with state organisms, trade unions, and other organizations. Schmitter does not believe that the inter-sectorial conflicts will substitute the old class struggle. However, in expressing his adverse position with supporters of "disorganized capitalism", he implicitly admits something of the sort by stating that capitalism is being reorganized according to new lines of solidarity and new divisions. Because the coalition of the interests of all the people involved in a particular economic sector, from owners and managers to blue- and white-collar workers (one could also add subcontractors, customers, and political lobbyists to this list), could be destined to increasingly oppose similar alliances in other economic sectors.

Territorial Districts. The corporative organization within the local community is today being re-examined as a result of the crisis of the Fordist production model and of the re-emergence of that which has been defined as the model of "flexible specialization" (Sabel and Zeitlin 1982; Piore and Sabel 1984).

This is a type of industrial organized based on decentralized production in small businesses with multi-purpose machinery and skilled workers, typical of the early industrial age.

[1] Schmitter defines the sector as a meso level, since it is situated in an intermediary position between the macro level of the entire economy and the micro level of the business company. This tends to reinforce his theory that macro corporatism is being replaced by a form of meso corporatism which is in a position to prevent society from disintegrating into the simple micro-corporative loyalties of a business company (Cawson 1985). The aim of this paper is not, however, that of expressing a preference for either type, but rather to identify the possible alternative or complementary set-ups. Therefore, the term "micro corporatism" is intended to refer to *all* the forms of decentralization of the old macro-corporative policies, assuming a Durkheimian point of view which tends to group together all those forms of corporative organization which lay between the state, central figure in macro-corporatist exchange, and the private citizen, principal figure in the return to individual capitalism.

This kind of organization is being revalued, above all, in certain areas characterized by the following factors: business activities conducted within the same vertically integrated industrial sector; the economic development of companies which are small but technologically up to date and have highly skilled workers; the diffusion of tighter links between businesses, suppliers, and customers; the existence of common attitudes and values, at least as far as work is concerned; and of rules and institutions which are in a position to transmit and ensure the respect of those values (Becattini 1989).

Some areas of the "Terza Italia" (Prato, Modena, Marche, Veneto, etc.) were among the first to be studied given their multi-factor evolution: the role and evolution of the peasant family; previous types of agricultural work; and the artisan specializations and the mediatorship which the local society and political forces are able to carry out in order to protect this type of industrial community (Bagnasco 1988). Other districts similarly homogeneous in terms of economy and society have been identified in the well-known studies carried out by Sabel: Baden-Wuerttemberg in Germany, Jutland in Denmark, Salzburg in Austria, etc.

The success of these forms of territorial corporatist organization is due to the fact that public bodies, regional administration, entrepreneurial associations, trade unions, political parties, and the church have established fiduciary relations (some of a formal and some of an informal nature), the effects of which, by mutual consent, are a dynamic regulation of the local labor market which constitutes the public wealth of the district. This is what Marshall defined with the term "industrial atmosphere"

Groups of Companies. Real corporatist pacts are being formed at this level even though, at least in Europe, until now they have primarily covered large public groups of companies or groups with a stable tradition of industrial relations (Treu 1988). Often the aim of these agreements is the mobility of labor within the group or the non-traumatic reduction of excessive workforces during the phase of industrial reorganization. However, it is not difficult to find examples of collaboration between management and trade unions also in the successive phase of development of the groups, with interesting examples of the increase of disclosure of information and consultative rights.

In Italy the example of the IRI (Institute for Industrial Reconstruction) protocol is an important demonstration of this innovative active involvement of trade unions in both the phases and not only instrumentally in the first. The IRI protocol is subscribed to by companies from various economic sectors, from the steel and food industries to computer sciences, aeronautical construction, telephone services, air transport, etc. Therefore, the agreement is drawn up by the IRI group directly with the Confederal unions CGIL, CISL, and UIL. We can but agree with those who maintain that these multi-company corporatist agreements constitute an interesting meeting point between the centralization and decentralization of industrial relations (Teubner 1987).

This kind of agreement can also form a basis for the introduction of new levels of conflict/mediation in the regulation of social and economic interests. The innovative character of the institution of trade union "group committees" has rightly been made known. These committees are formed by representatives of the workers of the various member companies and are now recognized in many European countries by law or by collective agreement. The status acquired by these representatives at the multi-company level has become more significant, at least with regard to recognition, than that of the shareholders of those individual companies which have not yet had the possibility to be represented in a similar coordinating body.

Individual Companies. The micro corporatism of the single company has been accepted as the symbol of the Japanese example of economic and social development. The lifelong employment for those who belong to the primary labor market of the large companies, the personalized wage system, and the company trade unionism are all factors which tend to reinforce the identification of the workers with one particular company. This contrasts with the experience of the Western, European, and Anglo-Saxon countries where the sense of belonging to a particular company has always been secondary to an identity related to craft if not to class.

The most recent studies, however, tend to belie this stereotyped image and to underline the presence, in Europe and the United States as well, of a trend toward stable employment of the central workforce, the reinforcement of company bargaining, the consolidation of trade union policies of an associative type, and the new role of company industrial relations systems (Brown 1986; OECD 1986; Negrelli 1988).

It is also known that in the European context, Italy, the Federal Republic of Germany, and Sweden have developed regimes of industrial relations which are very rigid with regard to external numerical flexibility and with trade union regulations designed to discourage dismissal policies. In the United States, however, external mobility has been more widely practiced and rigidity concerns, above all, the management of the internal labor.

Without deciding on which is the better system in a phase of rapid industrial change (Piore 1986), the most important issue is to understand, in the case of the European countries, if this reinforcement of the role of the trade unions has encouraged micro-corporatist policies within the company (Dore 1988).

In the latter case, the difference between this and the old universal criteria of solidarity of class or craft trade unions becomes important. In a corporatist-type business, collaboration at a company level between trade unions and management tends to grow on the one hand in order to maintain the privileges acquired, and on the other to share part of the profits resulting from this "micro-class compromise", by means of productivity agreements and profit-related wage increases. In his study, *British Factory – Japanese Factory*, Dore (1973) in defining a modern company as a "corporative collectivity", distinguishes between hierarchical micro corporatism, typical of the Japanese experience, and democratic micro corporatism which is the result of the negotiating process which takes place in those Western companies between representatives of all the main interest groups.

According to some researchers, it is a mistake to speak of sectorial or company corporatism, above all when looking at the internal labor market in the context of a "dualistic" system, because of the lack of public quality, an essential element of relational contracting (Streeck 1988).

It is probably true to say that the internal labor markets, which are born from a system of industrial relations of a predominantly contractual nature, are weaker and less efficient in the management of labor flexibility with respect to internal labor markets which are found within systems of industrial relations which contemplate their institutional protection. However, there can be no doubt that also in the former case regulatory and support action from public bodies has been increasing in recent times.

Sectorial, territorial, multi-company, and individual business company micro corporatism seem to be strengthening due to the role of state participation, at least with regard to three aspects. First, in establishing new rules of industrial relations with respect to representation, dispute, and collective bargaining, with a more definite trend toward legislative support. Second, by means of substantial financial resources. Consider, in the Italian context, the role of the "Cassa Integrazione Guadagni" (unemployment benefit fund) which has acted as a guarantee for the corporative pacts stipulated at multi-company and individual business company levels. Third, with the new deregulating form of employment contracts introduced in the 1980s by legislation in France, Italy, the Federal Republic of Germany, and Spain, which tend to facilitate employment security within the primary labor market, as has been seen to happen in the Japanese situation.

4.2 Can Economic Flexibility be a Source of Solidarity?

The sociological analysis of the relationship between economy and society has for too long been prisoner of the dichotomy between macro corporatism on the one hand and individual capitalism on the other. It is extremely difficult to interpret the Italian situation, which does not correspond to either model.

Like the majority of Western capitalist societies, during the post-World War II period the Italian economy witnessed the growth of a competitive sector, open to international competition, and a more protected one. This sectorial duality overlaps pre-existing territorial dualities and another based on company size. As a result of this, inter-sectorial and inter-company growth is highly differentiated. The effects of this economic development on industrial relations in a period of almost full employment have, up until now, been examined in the light of the traditional dichotomic model. The varying economic possibilities of different companies has led to wage drift; by means of centralized agreements and the coordination of national wages policies, the class-based trade unions would have tried to realize a "policy of wage equality". On the other hand, the associative unions would have preferred to decentralize the representative and bargaining structures, and to pursue local wage claims and forms of corporatism within the company (Pizzorno 1966). The fight against inflation which began in the latter half of the 1970s and lasted up to the "Craxi Decree" of 14 February 1984, seemed to reinforce, also in Italy, the Swedish-style macro-corporatist policies. However, the demand for economic flexibility, which had been expressed in the meantime by the national enterprises in the competitive sector, contributed to the inversion of these trends in Italian industrial relations. This came about due to the fact that the new goal, which was difficult to manage at a centralized level, was concerned essentially with sectors, districts, and company groups.

The fear that this move could be the prelude to a rapid transition from class-based trade unionism to company or associative trade unionism (if these old terms still have some meaning today), can be found in many publications, some of them recent (Dore 1987; Salvati 1988). However, to date, this does not seem to have been the destiny of industrial relations in Italy. On the contrary, the Italian case shows that between the two traditional corporatist systems of joint action (the Swedish-style macro-national corporatism and the Japanese micro-company corporatism), there is a whole range of intermediate possibilities. The latter have been, on the one hand, in a position to deal with the new managerial demands and initiatives in a more dynamic way, and on the other hand they have prevented the necessary decentralization of the industrial relations system from being transformed into a system of hierarchical micro corporatism.

How has this specifically Italian situation come about? Why is it that the evolution of the relationship between economy and society in Italy has not followed the same pattern as that of countries like the United States or Great Britain, where the acquisition of economic flexibility (read: extensive privatization) has been obtained with the result of widespread negative social effects? How can it be explained that the Italian micro-corporatist bodies, despite being unanimously recognized as weaker than those of countries with strong neocorporative traditions (e.g. Sweden and Germany), have been able to interact positively even with the rapid economic changes of the 1980s?

The following comparative table (Table 1) is concerned with the institutional aspects of the labor market and of the systems of industrial relations.

Table 1: Institutional Flexibility of Labour Market and Industrial Relations Systems.

Institutional Areas	Italy	USA	GDR	Japan
Labour Market	Numeric rigidity (large companies)	Numeric flexibility	Numeric rigidity	Numeric rigidity (life-long employment)
	Numeric flexibility (small companies, temporary employment contracts)	Functional rigidity	Functional flexibility	Numeric flexibility (temporary workers)
				Functional flexibility
	Functional rigidity (1970s)			
	negotiated functional flexibility (1980s)			
Industrial Relations Systems	Dualistic systems	National dualism	Single system	Company dualism
	private/public property	union system	codetermination	large corporations
	industry/services sector	non-union system		small companies
	company size small/large			

Looking at how Italy fits into this table, it can be seen that it emerges as a model of mixed rigidity and flexibility which combines the merits and defects of the prevailing models of the other countries. Some would say that it is this model of mixed rigidity/flexibility which has been able to guarantee a certain level of economic and social success in the Italian case, albeit with some flaws such as inefficiency in public administration and high unemployment in the south.

In comparison with the characteristics of the American labor market, Italy seems to have the benefit of the advantages of the German model in which functional flexibility is combined with numerical rigidity. According to some researchers this is the ideal solution for the achievement of aims regarding economic flexibility (Piore 1986). However, in Italy there is no shortage of economic sectors and employment contracts where American-style numeric flexibility prevails. Within Italian companies it is not difficult to find a fragmentation of the internal labor market, similar to that which is found in

Japan. This fragmentation gives a degree of employment stability to the central workforce, while those workers with temporary contracts are left to absorb the effects of market fluctuations. Finally, functional flexibility has become one of the principal subjects of trade union collective bargaining in the 1980s. This is in complete contrast with the concept of protecting functional rigidity, a common idea of the 1970s which still persists in some minority and "antagonistic" sectors of Italian trade unionism. With regard to this question, it has been noted how trade union action has transformed the flexibility of labor from a restriction to a resource (Regini (ed.) 1988). This transformation has given the trade unions the possibility to adopt, once again, an important role in collective bargaining on a theme which, by its very nature, demands a wide field of confrontation, from information sharing and consultation to the actual bargaining and finally to the application and verification of new agreements.

With regard to systems of industrial relations, the existence of pluralistic and dualistic situations, related to sector (industrial/service industries), property (private/public), and size (small/large companies), has resulted in a high level of differentiation in the management of economic flexibility. This differentiation, if not equal to that which can be found in America or Japan, is definitely higher than that found in Germany.

This institutional model, which provides both social guarantees and flexibility, may have contributed to facilitate economic and social change. However, this alone is not enough to explain the Italian case or to give exhaustive answers to the questions previously posed. Two other factors have been found to be even more important. The first of these refers to the existence in Italy of a *widespread institutional structure of industrial relations*, at least in comparison with other capitalist countries. The Italian bargaining system, as emphasized in the industrial relations handbooks as well (Cella and Treu 1989), has always been bipolar. Examples of this are the industry and company negotiations which took place in the national contract renewal period in the mid-1970s and the successive confederal and company negotiations. In fact, it is worth noting the extent of the institutional network, which has been able to involve, either one at a time or in combination, the four levels of bargaining previously identified; from confederal to industry and from district to company. Within this network, the questions raised by the problem of economic flexibility have been tackled in a rational and dynamic way, thus avoiding both the bureaucratic limitations of centralized agreements and excessive peripheral dispersion.

The second factor refers to the *supremacy of the industrial actors* within this widespread institutional network. It comes as no surprise that this leadership (both cultural and active) has evolved from those organizations belonging to the more internationally competitive sectors, and not from the more protected sectors of public and private service industries, which also happen to be the most conflictual sectors at the present time. Until just a few years ago, however, many of the sociological studies of post-industrial society seemed to predict the end of this kind of leadership and adaptation to economic change, which was claimed to be more typical of the period of industrialization. Few would have been able to foresee such an extension, both in terms of time and area, of the phenomenon which lasted until the end of the 1980s and maybe beyond.

Some indicators tend to confirm that this leadership in the transformation of economic systems is firmly in the hands of the "industrial" social actors, albeit with the appropriate updates and changes typical of a phase of transition and diversification in the sphere of industrial relations. The first of these signs can be inferred from the fact that the managerial initiatives in the field of industrial relations have come about chiefly within the large industries. The diffusion of these initiatives has in part been facilitated by those same entrepreneurial associations which, also in Italy, continue to maintain a higher level of organizational validity in the industrial sector than in the service industries sector. The latter sector is still undecided in its choice of associations both with regard to advanced services and within the small industries (Negrelli and Treu 1989).

In addition, the deregulation process which was predicted by many at the start of the decade has not come about. The "new" businesses and the "new" workers, both in the industrial and service industries sectors, continue to manifest a need for reliable rules. Economic flexibility therefore seems to require not so much the absence of rules as the introduction of new standards in the areas of management, workers' representatives, collective bargaining, and dispute.

Precisely these two factors, the widespread institutional network and the hegemony of the industrial social actors, have made it possible to manage economic flexibility in Italy within the sphere of collective action to obtain a common good. It is therefore possible to maintain that without this widespread corporative coordination between the social parties, the effects of economic flexibility on Italian society would have been considerably more traumatic. In this way, bargaining for economic flexibility in Italy has been a source of social solidarity, on condition that the latter is taken to mean any action carried out to reach a common good and an equilibrium between individual and collective interests (Pizzorno 1966; Cella 1989).

The *places* in which social solidarity has been practiced have already been noted; from sectors to areas, from company groups to individual companies. Now it is necessary to better define the *subject*, that is, the results. Subsequently it will also be necessary to specify the *type* of solidarity which is emerging within this context.

As far as the subject is concerned, we can observe the tendencies and the economic signs of the labor market and of industrial relations in Italian industry in two periods: the latter half of the 1970s and the 1980s (Baglioni and Crouch (eds.) 1990; Barca and Magnani 1989; Dell'Aringa 1989). During the first of these two periods, workforce mobility and turnover was notoriously low due to the rigid defensive strategies of the trade unions. At that time there was a combination of numerical and functional rigidity, which resulted in overemployment. At the same time in other countries, including West Germany, the number of workers employed by industry was dropping. Employment stability and revised working hours produced an increase in productivity of labor of approximately 3% per annum, which is the result of a corresponding increase in production.

The situation changed substantially in the course of the 1980s; businesses increased their demand for flexibility and this demand was of a *derivative* nature, that is, linked to the state of the product market (Salvati 1988). There was actually a reduction in production from 1981 to 1983 in Italian industry, but the corresponding drop of 3.5% per annum in the employment rate (after adjustment for redundancies), means that the annual 3% increase in labor productivity was maintained (Barca and Magnani 1989; Dell'Aringa 1989).

Given the changes which have taken place in the ratio of strength between trade unions and owners since the end of the 1970s (Salvati 1988), the explanation that trade unions and workers offered flexibility "because they had to", would seem tautological, as well as hurried. The English example seems to show the opposite; the increase in productivity of labor in industry was even higher (from 100 in 1980 to 137.8 in 1986 compared with 100 to 124.8 in Italy from 1980 to 1987), but this took place *in opposition to* the trade unions by means of special laws which re-evaluated the power previously held by the unions. In Great Britain, the alliance between entrepreneurs and government to achieve economic flexibility was a fatal blow to the trade unions. In Italy, however, governments which objectively were weaker were not in a position to oppose the trade unions so strongly. There can be no doubt that in both cases, English and Italian, there was some correlation between labor flexibility and changes in the industrial relations systems. However, the two phenomena took place following two diverging types of social solidarity.

Industrial reorganization in Italy was also facilitated by the possibility which companies had to free themselves of excess labor by recourse to unemployment benefits.[2] The combination of all these factors has led to an increase in production of 3.4% per annum in the period from 1984 to 1987, as well as a reduction in employment of 1.9%. The overall increase in labor productivity is therefore 5.3% per annum (Dell'Aringa 1989).

This maneuver to increase the competitiveness of manufacturing com-

[2] From 1981 to 1985 the net reduction in employment was 3.4% per annum, which becomes 2.5% after the adjustment for unemployment benefits (Barca and Magnani 1989).

panies was achieved thanks to the increased collaboration of the trade unions and workers, above all in the industrial sectors, which accepted self-limitation of their power. If the tendency toward increased efficiency in the national industrial system continues into the near future, there will be new opportunities for the trade unions to renew their initiative and to regain their bargaining power.

4.3 Interest-Based Solidarity

With reference to the concept of social solidarity, Gallino (1978) observed how eighteenth-century sociologists used the term to describe the capacity of the members of a community to behave as a single person toward others. This concept originates from Durkheim's idea of social cohesion and of solidarity as a source of consensus. Our attention is drawn to the classic problem of social order, or rather how stability and cooperation for the whole social system can be achieved. Solidarity, whether it be the "mechanical", community type, or the "organic" kind typical of modern society, is understood to be a "moral order" which permits the coordination (with a lesser degree of conflict and anomie), of individual and collective action. In this way, "all that which is a source of solidarity, which forces man to consider others and to control his actions according to something other than his own egoism, is moral" (Durkheim 1902: p. 389).

Some signs indicate the presence of this kind of *solidarity of moral order* in the modern capitalist societies. From the opinion poll carried out by R. Inglehart (1977) it can be seen, for example, that in the mid-1970s the dominant value in Europe and the United States was that of bringing down inflation. In Italy, the results of the 1985 referendum, which appealed against the government legislation of the previous year on the sliding scale, also seem to confirm a less materialistic collective viewpoint. As has been observed, the population was asked to "vote for more money in your pocket now against uncertain future benefits" (Provasi 1985). The victory of the "Nos" was evident above all in the modernized areas of the country and in the large cities. Those who voted "No" were mainly from the middle class and to some degree from the working class. It can be seen, therefore, that this solidarity of moral order has developed regardless of traditional class barriers in an atmosphere of "interclassness". It has been particularly strong with regard to the achievement of the common aim of increasing productivity of labor in industry, and has also been concerned partly with strategic sectorial and company flexibility. At this level capital and labor have now a similar viewpoint on the subject of the acquisition of economic flexibility, and it was exactly this type of solidarity (which is over and above the specific agreements between single-interest parties) that aided peaceful negotiation between collective actors.

Long after Durkheim's classic definition, the concept of social solidarity has been taken to mean, above all, a system of action which is opposed to the system of interest parties in that its aim is that of "equality of participation". An action which is directed toward the achievement of individual or group interests is based on distinction and on the improvement of relative social position. Solidarity, on the other hand, is orientated toward egalitarian aims within a particular community (Pizzorno 1966: pp. 252–254). In contrast with solidarity of a moral order, this type of solidarity is therefore a value which takes seed within a group or class. *Solidarity of egalitarian participation* can also lead to the temporary waivering of the bargaining power of a group or of individuals. This in turn produces a relative deterioration of the wealth and social standing of those involved, to the advantage of other weaker groups or individuals (Cella 1981).

The two different types of solidarity on which sociologists have theorized in the past can be defined in very strict terms. When Pizzorno counters "an action which considers the interests of the party" with "an action which considers solidarity between the parties", he states explicitly that these are two "pure systems" (Pizzorno 1966: p. 254).

It is becoming increasingly difficult to apply these definitions to daily life. There is always the risk of reintroducing the old divisions between optimists and pessimists who still clash over the different systems, when in reality the two types of solidarity – that of moral order and that of egalitarian participation – support each other; one cannot exist without the other. More specifically, the diffusion of the former is facilitated by the existence of the latter. The costs to society of economic flexibility are in fact more acceptable if based on their egalitarian division, at least within the classes.

Economic flexibility seems even more to accent the tendency toward mixed, rather than pure, systems of solidarity. Is it not true that what has been described as micro corporatism within economic sectors, districts, company groups, and individual companies, is perhaps the manifestation of systems of economic interest which also seem to develop a sense of belonging that contrasts with other group memberships? It is not difficult in these cases to see an increasing level of overlapping, almost a mixing, of the systems of interest and the systems of solidarity. In the systems of industrial relations at sectorial, territorial, and company level, it is possible to talk about true associative systems or systems of *solidarity of economic interest* since in this context mutual action facilitates exchange and the establishment of authority. This phenomenon has been observed within sectors, where alliances between interest parties which cross over the old class barriers are being formed, both at national and international levels. This fusion of interests and solidarity is even more marked in certain territorial communities involved in the "combined game of market and reciprocal action as a means of control" (Bagnasco 1988: p. 53) and in the recurring "institutionalization of solidarity between economically active groups" (Sabel 1986: p. 237). At company level, the "micro-democratic corporatism" described by Dore and by many other empirical researchers is also going in that same direction.

If it is true that economic flexibility seems to favor systems of solidarity which are increasingly linked to interest groups, then it is equally true to say that the macro-level neocorporative tendencies favored systems of "national" solidarity, in some way added to or combined with the systems of national economic interest. Micro-corporative tendencies serve only to bring about the decline of this fusion of interests and solidarity, preventing the outlet of neoindividualistic action. However, there is no doubt that that flexibility now constitutes "a means of contending international market shares" through national avenues, and therefore its implementation is effected through a virtual micro policy of wages (Boyer and Wolleb 1986). It is therefore difficult to insist that economic flexibility is only a phenomenon which the company owners have imposed on the trade unions. With regard to the Italian situation, it has even suggested that with the existence of a social buffer (i.e. the unemployment benefits), the trade unions have not insisted on the large-scale reduction of working hours or on forms of job sharing in exchange for flexibility because this move would not have been appreciated by the employees of the large concerns (Barca and Magnani 1989). These theories need careful examination, but they do, however, indicate the diverse nature of the problems to be faced within that associative order which is distinct from the community, the state, and the market, but which combines the three classical principles of solidarity, competition, and hierarchy (Streeck and Schmitter 1985; Lange and Regini 1987). Solidarity and the formation of a collective identity are becoming increasingly numerous within associations whose rational aim is the satisfaction of sectorial and/or professional interests, and which can be defined as "private governments" in that they benefit from a certain level of corporative/associative proxy of public tasks within the management of sectorial interests and therefore in the maintenance of corporatist order (Streeck and Schmitter 1985).

The solidarity formed within this type of association is obviously of a very different nature to that which is found in the traditional community or within social classes. Most of the researchers into neocorporatism have identified the fundamental characteristic of the social policy as being that of the combination of exchange, authority, and solidarity. First, Polanyi (1957) put forward the idea that as a means of social integration, reciprocity is rendered more efficient when it has the possibility to use redistribution and exchange for its own purposes. It is not enough, however, to identify the phenomenon of reciprocity in the facilitation of exchange and the establishment of authority. In fact it has already been noted that economic interests can become a source of identity, which brings us into contact with a different kind of solidarity, a real *associative solidarity* which becomes the main factor in the guarantee of corporative order even in the micro-corporative organization. In fact, with the advent of corporatism at macro or more decentralized levels, the traditional distinction between solidarity-based systems and interest-based systems has been surpassed, primarily because of the different nature of the criteria by which solidarity is regulated. This difference also applies to the combination of these criteria with those of exchange and authority.

This tendency is quite different from that identified by Pizzorno (1966), when he proposed that "State and class are systems of solidarity which are mobilized in an action aimed at the values of the system of interests. On the other hand, to the extent to which they express themselves in terms of actions based on solidarity, they do not give voice to individual interests." With the micro-corporative tendencies of economic flexibility (and also to some extent with the macro-corporative tendency of the fight against inflation), the opposite situation can often be found. In the latter case, it is the individual interests which influence the traditional systems of solidarity; it is almost as if the systems of interests can in turn modify in some way those very systems of solidarity. In the past, in a society characterized by continual economic growth, a link from solidarity (of class and values) to economic interests was the norm; in fact Pizzorno maintained that "the relationship between power, values, and interests is direct and necessary" (p. 255). However, with the advent of economic flexibility, the opposite relationship is becoming increasingly important. Economic variations are no longer certain and predictable and no longer seem to guarantee a univocal relationship between solidarity and interests.

We should not underestimate a further characteristic of the systems of solidarity of interest which have developed with the aims of reducing inflation and acquiring economic flexibility. These systems are also formed on the basis of the *perception of a common danger*, which may have encouraged some to believe that in this difficult present phase, society can remain intact only thanks to reciprocal and temporary pragmatic changes. If this was true, solidarity of interest would constitute only a tactical move by the large and small social actors, made in anticipation of a return to the distinction between interests and solidarity, in order to renew those long-term values which are able to give direction to the interests involved. The debate has only just begun and it promises to be very interesting, even though for the moment, curiosity predominates over the heavy contradiction which was predicted. There is a positive and stimulating aspect of the current attitude toward solidarity which should be mentioned. The fact that solidarity is *also* based on the awareness of a common danger could simply be another symptom of the disappearance of the sense of security derived from common possession or from the presence of a universal power, as was the case in the previous types. As maintained by the philosophical quest for truth, solidarity is increasingly becoming a progressive construction rather than a definitive discovery (Rorty

1989). For the moment, the system of action constructed from the combination of solidarity and the pursuit of interest may create discomfort for those who are used to dealing within the two categories separately. This combination must, however, be recognized as typical of the present phase.

4.4 Non Class-Based Solidarity: New Divisions and Old Social Identities

Until now the management of economic flexibility has definitely been directed toward favoring production needs while being reluctant to consider the needs of the individual subjects. An important example of this can be seen in the way in which many of the problems regarding micro flexibility of labor (e.g. flexible working hours, part-time contracts, incentive-based wages, and other new institutions) have been tackled. An increase in productivity of labor should have been combined with the equal division between the workers of cost and profit. In reality, the introduction of part-time contracts and new working hours has only in a few cases respected the individual preferences of the employees. In addition, employment contracts rarely reflect the characteristics of the job supply (Gallino 1985; Accornero and Carmignani 1986; Reyneri 1987; Cavalli and De Lillo 1988).

These tendencies seem to contradict the changes in work content, which, according to many researchers, should lead to the abandonment of the traditional Taylorist division between execution and conception, and toward professional recomposition. The latter would, in turn, lead to the redefinition of the traditional hierarchical functions, with new participative working regulations which would counter the old Fordist regulatory model (Piore and Sabel 1984; Kern and Schumann 1987; Boyer 1988).

This imbalance makes it very difficult to formulate any predictions on the stability of social order which accompanies the present management of economic flexibility, as also occurred in Italy. In the former half of the 1980s, gross profits in the industrial concerns with more than 200 employees increased from just over 25% to nearly 35% (Barca and Magnani 1989). In the same period, the increase in wages and hourly rates in the industrial sector, however, was less than 2% per annum. These facts have done nothing to improve Italy's position in the international league of inequalities in wages distribution. According to any of the indexes used to measure this phenomenon, in the period from 1978 to 1982 Italy was in sixteenth place among the first eighteen capitalist democracies, just ahead of New Zealand and Australia (Cameron 1988). In some countries, including Belgium and Holland, the presence of multi-class parties in the government has made it possible to keep these indexes of social inequality very low. The figures are even lower than those for some other countries like Sweden, Germany, and Norway where the participation of progressive parties in government decisions is positively correlated to medium-low indexes of inequality. In Italy, neither the lengthy reign of an inter-classist party, nor the sporadic experiences of governments with the participation of left-wing parties (like the centre-left coalition of the 1960s and thereafter, or that of national solidarity of the latter half of the 1970s, or again the socialist-led government of the early 1980s), have been able to alter the image of a country where the indexes of social inequality continue to be among the highest of all the capitalist democracies. For this reason, forecasts are risky, although it is probably fair to say that a complete return to the conditions of the post-1963 period (which fired the social explosion of the successive years) seems very unlikely (Barca and Magnani 1989: p. 72). This is due to the fact that today, unlike the past situation, economic productivity is no longer something which concerns only the owner, but it is also based on the wide consensus of workers within a company.

The development of social solidarity depends to a large extent on the attention paid to the individual needs of the workers, the changes in working conditions and the extension of individual and collective rights of status which tend to go some of the way toward correcting the "inevitable contractual asymmetry" which exists between the two actors, employees and employers (Streeck 1988: p. 674). If this does not happen, then there is reason to fear that even the consensus which has accompanied the management of economic flexibility in Italy until now could find less support in the future. The result would be the lack of equality of participation which is one of the essential elements of that same economic flexibility.

It is also necessary to consider the problem which arises from the fact that, unlike lower inflation which is a benefit to all and at the start of the 1980s constituted a source of macro-level corporatist solidarity, economic flexibility has become a source of solidarity, above all, at a decentralized level, thus giving rise to various forms of micro corporatism.

We must agree with some of the studies carried out by Salvati (1988) in which he points out that there is no hope of achieving social and economic success for societies, other than those of Japan and Sweden, unless some way is found of reconciliating economic efficiency with networks of solidarity extending beyond those concerning individual companies. It would, of course, be naïve to think that Italy, like Japan, is destined to produce a society which remains united only due to the micro-corporative loyalty of its members toward single companies.

Unfortunately, however, I do not believe that the answer lies in the equally naïve conviction that it is necessary to renew the important centers of class, national, or religious identity, or that it is necessary to seek new and improbable sources of widespread social solidarity. The problems created by these factors in the past and today in the recent evolution of state-sponsored collectivism are well known, and extend even as far as the transformation of modern democracies into authoritarian regimes. This has not necessarily only happened in societies which are characterized by individualistic fragmentation. The studies carried out by W. S. Allen (1965) gave plenty of examples of how, in Weimar Germany, despite the diffusion of intermediate associations, there was (even within the associations) a dominating and excessive class polarization.

It is necessary to accept the idea that in a modern capitalist society, the most important requisite is that of knowing how to live with numerous centers of social solidarity. These centers may at times be complementary and at others antagonistic, but it is from this balance that the capacity of a society to remain cohesive is derived. Society has become more complex in that it is necessary to know how to govern these multiple sources of social solidarity, not only in the horizontal direction, between the various forms of social regulation (community, state, market, and associations) (Streeck and Schmitter 1985), but also in the vertical direction, between different levels.

On the other hand, extensive economic and sociological analysis tends to counter economic flexibility (the subject of micro-level industrial relations), with social solidarity, which should be possible only as the result of macro-level agreement between the important social actors. The evolution of industrial relations in Italy tends to demonstrate the opposite – that economic flexibility and social solidarity can act together, even at decentralized levels.

The articulation of new centers of social solidarity within the nations, from sectors to districts and companies, does not, however, seem to be a threat to traditional class identity. This is due to the fact that the latter still crosses all those sections which could be defined as the new and not so new "socio-economic formations" of the country (Gallino 1978, 1987). This is true to such an extent that in using a "sectorial" model for the comparative analysis of capitalism, Schmitter (1978: p. 178) observes that the economic sector constitutes a method of differentiated structuring within the various national economies, but at the same time it also maintains similar characteristics between those same national economies. Similar considerations could be made about districts, company groups, and individual businesses.

As is already known, there are other structural factors which can be linked to the decline of the social classes. However, as is equally well known, there are other indications of persistence which counter these factors (Schizzerotto 1988).

It is significant that among the five aims noted by Dahl (1985) for the achievement of economic democracy, economic and political equity are considered with the same importance as efficiency, training, and economic freedom. Even without entering into a discussion on the merits of self-governing businesses, it is difficult not to subscribe to Dahl's general conviction that democracy at work will favor human development, increase the sense of political efficiency, create a community solidarity based on work, reinforce commitment to the ideal of general community good, weaken the attraction of personal interest, produce citizens who are actively involved and have a civic awareness with regard to the activities of the company, and finally will stimulate a higher level of participation and an increased citizenship spirit toward the government of the state. The most symbolic difficulties faced by the development of this same economic democracy are the obstacles which stand in the way of the realization of a common model of worker participation in the European companies of the future.

With regard to macro-corporatist policies, the realization of equality between classes and within the two class groups on the labor market has represented one of the principal aims of collective action (Streeck 1988). The situations experienced in Sweden and West Germany are often quoted, in contrast with those in Great Britain, because of their principal aim of reducing social inequality by means of innovative institutional measures. It is worth noting the position of those who have explained the decline of macro-level concertation in Italy in terms of the growing contradiction between, on the one hand, the widespread corporative consensus on the importance of the reduction of labor costs, and on the other hand, the scarce benefits to the workers of the new economic policies (Regini 1983). This explanation should, however, be enriched with a further concept, which is the "intrinsic asymmetry" between the trade union identity and political identity of the Italian workers (Baglioni 1986).

The present situation regarding the different forms of micro corporatism is significantly more complex, not so much because of the effects on the vertical inequalities between the classes (which, as has already been stated, do not seem to be of any great importance), but because of the horizontal inequalities of status which lead to increased segmentation between and within sectors, territorial areas, and companies. If the differences within and between the various socio-economic formations become abnormal, uncontrollable, and unjustifiable, then it will become increasingly difficult to avoid abnormal situations.

It is perfectly true that economic sectors, territorial areas, company groups, and individual businesses are focal points of social multi-identity, and that they therefore have more difficulty in generating those states of collective enthusiasm which were activated in the past by class struggle. The principles of solidarity of sectorial, territorial, and company interests are unlikely to prevail over the traditional principles of class, political, or national solidarity. In some cases, however, tension and conflict must not be considered out of the question even in the industrial sectors. There are the inevitable wage claims of the workers of companies with different productivity levels, or the territorial disparity with regard to economic conditions and working standards.

During the present phase, the emphasis remains on the associative solidarity at micro-corporative level which has led to the restructuring, and definitely not to the disappearance, of class action. It has also led to the restructuring, or to be more exact, to the articulation, of the macro-level systems of solidarity which were brought about by the neocorporative tendencies. This is, without doubt, a new and unexpected phenomenon; unexpected because the neocorporative tendencies are not countered by the well-publicized neoindividualism, but by an intermediate type of solidarity which is characterized by its false identity of economic interest. It is the instability of a model which is stuck between unacceptable macro-corporatist rigidity on the one hand, and individualistic relaxation (which until now has shown itself to be improbable) on the other hand, which seems to provoke that widespread sense of uneasiness among those who have taken it upon themselves to explain the functioning of social order. If, however, we consider that, from Durkheim to Keynes, the ideal dimension of the unit of organization and control between the individual and the modern state has always been of prime importance, the uneasiness may seem more tolerable.

References

Accornero, Aris and Fabrizio Carmignani (1986): *I paradossi della disoccupazione.* Bologna: Il Mulino.

Allen, W. S. (1965): *The Nazi Seizure of Power*, Chicago: Quadrangle Books.

Axelrod, Robert (1984): *The Evolution of Cooperation.* New York: Basic Books.

Baglioni, Guido (1986): Il destino delle pratiche concertative. *Prospettiva Sindacale*, 60, 5–22.

Baglioni, Guido and Colin Crouch (eds.) (1990): *European Industrial Relations: The Challenge of Flexibility.* London: Sage.

Bagnasco, Arnaldo (1988): *La costruzione sociale del mercato.* Bologna: Il Mulino.

Bagnasco, Arnaldo and Carlo Trigilia (eds.) (1985): *Società e politica nelle aree di piccola impresa. Il caso della Valdelsa.* Milano: Angeli.

Baldissera, Alberto (1984): Alle origini della politica della disuguaglianza nell'Italia degli anni '80: la marcia dei quarantamila. *Quaderni di Sociologia*, XXXI (1), 1–78.

Barca, Fabrizio and Marco Magnani (1989): *L'industria fra capitale e lavoro. Piccole e grandi imprese dall'autunno caldo alla ristrutturazione.* Bologna: Il Mulino.

Becattini, Giacomo (1989): Riflessioni sul distretto industriale marshalliano come concetto socio-economico. *Stato e Mercato*, 25, 111–128.

Bordogna, Lorenzo and Giancarlo Provasi (1984): *Politica, economia e rappresentanza degli interessi.* Bologna: Il Mulino.

Boyer, Robert (1988): Alla ricerca di alternative al fordismo. *Stato e Mercato*, 24, 387–423.

Boyer, Robert and Enrico Wolleb (eds.) (1986): *La flexibilité du travail en Europe.* Paris: La Découverte.

Brown, William (1986): The Changing Role of Trade Unions in the Management of Labour. *British Journal of Industrial Relations*, 24.

Cameron, David R. (1988): *Politics, Public Policy, and Distributional Inequality: A Comparative Analysis.* In: *Power, Inequality, and Democratic Politics*, Shapiro, Ian and Grant Reeher (eds.). Boulder: Westview Press.

Cavalli, Alessandro and Antonio De Lillo (1988): *Giovani anni 80.* Bologna: Il Mulino.

Cawson, A. (ed.) (1985): *Organized Interests and the State: Studies in Meso-Corporatism.* Beverly Hills/London: Sage.

Cella, Gian Primo (1981): Tra interessi e solidarietà l'azione sindacale nella crisi del pluralismo. Statoenercato, 2, 223–255.
Cella, Gian Primo (1989): *La solidarité possible*. Roma: Editioni lavoroz.
Cella, Gian Primo and Tiziano Treu (eds.) (1989): *Relazioni industriali. Manuale per l'analisi dell'esperienza italiana*. Bologna: Il Mulino.
CER/IRS (1986): *Quale strategia per l'industria?* Bologna: Il Mulino.
Crouch, Colin (1989): Le relazioni industriali in Gran Bretagna e in Italia oggi: convergenze e divergenze. *Sociologia del Lavoro*, 35–36, 357–376.
Dahl, Robert (1985): *A Preface to Economic Democracy*. Berkeley: University of California Press.
Dahrendorf, Ralf (1979): *Lebenschancen. Anläufe zur sozialen und politischen Theorie*. Frankfurt am Main: Suhrkamp Verlag.
Dahrendorf, Ralf (1988): *The Modern Social Conflict. An Essay on the Politics of Liberty*. New York: Weidenfeld & Nicolson.
Dell'Aringa, Carlo (1989): Produttività e retribuzioni: esperienze di relazioni industriali. *Rassegna di Statistiche del lavoro*, 1, 18–25.
Donovan Commission Report on Trade Unions and Employers' Association, 1958–1968. London: HMSO.
Dore, Ronald (1973): *British Factory – Japanese Factory*. Berkeley: University of California Press.
Dore, Ronald (1987): *Taking Japan Seriously*. London: Athlone Press.
Dore, Ronald (1988): La rigidità nel mercato del lavoro, *Stato e Mercato*, 22, 37–62.
Durkheim, Emile (1902): *De la Division du Travail Social*. Paris: F. Alcan. (Italian publisher: Milano 1962: Ed. di Communità.)
Gallino, Luciano (1978): *Dizionario di sociologia*. Torino: UTET.
Gallino, Luciano (ed.) (1985): *Il lavoro e il suo doppio*. Bologna: Il Mulino.
Gallino, Luciano (1987): *Della ingovernabilità*. Milano: Comunità.
Inglehart, Ronald (1977): *The Silent Revolution: Changing Values and Political Styles Among Western Publics*. Princeton: University Press.
Kern, Horst and Michel Schumann (1987): L'operaio duttile sostituirà l'automazione rigida. *Politica ed Economia*, 3.
Lange, Peter and Marino Regini (1987): Gli interessi e l'istituzioni: forme di regolazione sociale e politiche pubbliche. In: *Stato e regolazione sociale*, Lange, Peter and Marino Regini (eds.). Bologna: Il Mulino.
Lash, Scott and John Urry (1987): *The End of Organized Capitalism*. Oxford: Polity Press.
Milani, Rinaldo (1989): Contrattazione aziendale. In: *Cesos, Le relazioni sindacali in Italia. Rapporto 1987–88*. Roma: Edizioni Lavoro.
Mortillaro, Felice (1984): *Sindacati e no. Primo rapporto della Federmeccanica sulle relazioni industriali*. Milano: Edizioni del Sole 24 Ore.
Mortallaro, Felice (1986): *Aspettando il robot. Secondo rapporto della Federmeccanica sulle relazioni industriali*. Milano: Edizioni del Sole 24 Ore.
Negrelli, Serafino (1982): La Pirelli dopo l'autunno caldo. *Giornale di diritto del lavoro e di relazioni industriali*, 15.
Negrelli, Serafino (1987): La contrattazione della flessibilità in azienda. *Prospettiva Sindacale*, 66, 7–20.
Negrelli, Serafino (1988): Diversificazione e nuovi paradigmi dei sistemi di relazioni industriali. *Giornale di diritto del lavoro de di relazioni industriali*, 38.
Negrelli, Serafino (1989): Il caso Italtel. In Regini, M. and C. Sabel (eds.), Strategie di riaggiustamento industriale. Bologna: Il Mulino.
Negrelli, Serafino and Tiziano Treu (1989): *Scelte associative e scelte contrattuali di un gruppo imprenditoriale del settore televisivo privato: il caso Fininvest*. Rapporto di ricerca. Milano: Fondazione Seveso.
OECD (1986): *Flexibilité et marché du travail. Le débat aujourd'hui*. Rapport technique. Paris: OECD.

Offe, Claus (1985): *Disorganized Capitalism*. Oxford: Polity Press.
Olson, Mancur (1965): *The Logic of Collective Action. Public Goods and the Theory of Group*. Cambridge, Mass.: Harvard University Press.
Piore, Michael J. (1986): Una tesi contro la tesi sulla flessibilità nel mercato del lavoro. *Transizione*, 5–6.
Piore, Michael J. and Charles F. Sabel (1984): *The Second Industrial Divide*. New York: Basic Books.
Pizzorno, Alessandro (1966): Introduzione allo studio della partecipazione politica. *Quaderni di Sociologia*, XV (3–4).
Pizzorno, Alessandro (1980): *I soggetti del pluralismo*. Bologna: Il Mulino.
Polanyi, Karl (ed.) (1957): *Trade and Market in the Early Empires, Economies in History and Theory*. New York: The Free Press.
Provasi, Giancarlo (1985): Il referendum e la profonda crisi strategica del Pci. *Prospettiva Sindacale*, 56.
Provasi, Giancarlo (1987): La negoziazione sindacale: strategie e procedure. *Prospettiva Sindacale*, 66.
Regini, Marino (1983): Le condizioni dello scambio politico. Nascita e declino della concertazione in Italia e Gran Bretagna. *Stato e Mercato*, 9.
Regini, Marino (1988): Le prospettive delle relazioni industriali in azienda. *Giornale di diritto del lavoro e di relazioni industriali*, 37.
Regini, Marino (ed.) (1988): *La sfida della flessibilità*. Milano: Angeli.
Regini, Marino and Charles F. Sabel (eds.) (1989): *Strategie di riaggiustamento industriale*. Bologna: Il Mulino.
Reyneri, Emilio (1987): Il mercato del lavoro italiamo tra controllo statale e regolazione sociale. In Lange, P. and M. Regini (eds.), *Stato e regolazione sociale*. Bologna: Il Mulino.
Ricci, Maurizio and Bruno Veneziani (eds.) (1988): *Tra conflitto e partecipazione*. Bari: Cacucci.
Rorty, Richard (1989): *Contingency, Irony and Solidarity*. Cambridge: Cambridge University Press.
Sabel, Charles F. (1986): *Industrializzazione del terzo mondo e nuovi modelli produttivi. Stato e Mercato*, 17.
Sabel, Charles F. and Jonathan Zeitlin (1982): Alternative storiche alla produzione di massa. *Stato e Mercato*, 5.
Salvati, Michele (1988): Rapporto salariale e flessibilità. Ovvero: Teoria della Regolazione e "Political Economy". *Stato e Mercato*, 24.
Schizzerotto, Antonio (ed.) (1988): *Classi sociali e società contemporanea*. Milano: Angeli.
Schmitter, Philippe (1989): I settori nel capitalismo moderno: modi di regolazione e variazioni nel rendimento. *Stato e Mercato*, 26.
Sen, Amartya (1981): *Poverty and Famine*. Oxford: Clarendon Press.
Soboul, Albert (1962): *Précis d'histoire de la Révolution française*. Paris: Editions sociales.
Streeck, Wolfgang (1988): Status e contratto nella teoria della relazioni industriali. *Giornale di diritto del lavoro e di relazioni industriali*, 40.
Streeck, Wolfgang and Philippe Schmitter (1985): Comunità, mercato, stato e associazioni? Il possibile contributo dei governi privati all'ordine sociale, *Stato e Mercato*, 13.
Teubner, ?. ?. (1987): *Unitas Multiplex: Problems of Governance in Group Enterprises from a Systems Theory Viewpoint*. EUI paper.
Trentin, B., G. Amato, and M. Magno (1980): *Il piano d'impresa e il ruolo del sindacato in Italia*. Bari: De Donato.
Treu, Tiziano (1987): Rapporti tra sindacati e industria italiano negli anni '80: un caso di adeguamento positivo? *Prospettiva Sindacale*, 66.
Treu, Tiziano (1988): Gruppi di imprese e relazioni industriali: tendenze europee. *Giornale di diritto del lavoro e di relazioni industriali*, 40.

Trigilia, Carlo (1981): Le subculture politiche territoriali. *Quaderni Fondazione Feltrinelli*, 16.
Trigilia, Carlo (1986): *Grandi partiti e piccole imprese*. Bologna: Il Mulino.
Trigilia, Carlo (1989): Il distretto industriale di Prato. In: *Strategie di riaggiustamento industriale*, Regini M. and C. F. Sabel (eds.). Bologna: Il Mulino.
Williamson, Oliver E. (1986): *The Economic Institutions of Capitalism. Firms, Markets, Relational Contracting*. New York: The Free Press.

5 From National Corporatism to Transnational Pluralism: European Interest Politics and the Single Market

Wolfgang Streeck

5.1 Organized Interests and Regional Integration

Whatever the differences between the various versions of the theory, or "pre-theory" (Haas 1970), of European regional integration, organized interest groups were always assigned a prominent place.[1] Especially in the "neofunctionalist" image of "Europe's would-be polity" and of the way toward it, supranational interest group formation was expected to serve, in an important and indispensable sense, as a substitute for popular identification with the emerging new political community above and beyond the nation-state.[2] Most observers and, in fact, participants in the integration process fully expected that the citizens of Europe would for a long time continue to adhere to traditional, national passions and identities. They knew that if the united Europe had to wait until its citizens began to feel as "Europeans" – rather than Frenchmen, Germans, Italians, etc. – it would not in any foreseeable future come about, and Europe as a political entity would in their lifetime never be more than a small bureaucracy in Brussels with very fragile support in national politics.

One reason, nevertheless, why there appeared to be hope was that things were believed to be different with the professional leaders of organized interest groups. Unlike the voters, they were seen as likely to orientate themselves, rationally and calculatedly, to where the action was – that is, under the presumed logic of the neofuntionalist spillover process, to "Brussels". Indeed, in attitude and outlook, interest group officials and European civil servants could easily appear as birds of the same feather: both appointed rather than elected, both experts and technocrats, both susceptible to a cosmopolitan orientation and lifestyle, both professionally interested in the smooth

[1] In large parts, the present manuscript draws on ideas and material developed for a joint paper with Philippe Schmitter for a conference on "The United States and Europe in the 1990s: Trade, Finance, Defense, Politics, Demographics and Social Policy", American Enterprise Institute, Washington DC, 6–8 March 1990 (Schmitter and Streeck 1990).

[2] On the following see, in particular, Haas (1958: pp. 318–389).

management of complex interdependencies, and likely to be distinctly disinterested in the traditional rituals and symbolisms of nationhood. Just as civil servants like Jean Monnet had been persuading, cajoling, manipulating the elected politicians and the administrative machineries of national states into emergent supranationalism, so the *Geschäftsführer* of business associations and trade unions were expected to enlighten their elected leaders that their interests had migrated to a new place and that the offices and decisions of their representatives had to follow suit.

In fact, the relationship between European bureaucrats and the full-time managers of collective interests that was envisaged by integration theory was even more intimate. As pointed out, interest groups were believed to have a much better, much sharper, much more intense perception of the effects of spillover on the *situs* and *locus* of decisions than the average voter, and as a result were expected to make their appearance at the supranational level earlier than their less insightful fellow-citizens. But, more importantly perhaps, the move of organized interests on to the European scene was expected to be further accelerated by European bureaucrats who, in their search for a constituency, would be more than willing to promote interest organization on a scale coterminous with their supranational jurisdiction. Indeed, in the perception of early integration theory, especially its neofuntionalist version, there was hardly anything in which "Brussels" could be more interested than in cultivating an environment, around the Commission in particular, of powerful interest organizations negotiating with Community officials and each other – as an *Ersatz* for the elusive pan-European citizen humming a pan-European supranational anthem when facing the Barleymont office building.

Attracting a growing number of supranational lobbyists into the Community's decision-making process was seen as offering important pay-offs, especially for the Commission. Cooperation with organized interests not only provided civil servants with an indispensable input of detailed factual information in complex decisions. It also, and above all, was to bring about the socialization of powerful forces in European civil society into a world view compatible with that of European bureaucrats and with the requirements of continued "spillover".[3] Having been drawn into the ambit of the Commission, a multitude of political players would learn from experience that management from the top, from the center, from Brussels, was more efficient and effective than national policy-making. When returning to their natonal capitals, they – it was hoped and in fact predicted – would again become a lobby: This time not of their interest group *vis-à-vis* Brussels, but of Brussels *vis-à-vis* their national leaders, including their national governments. By fostering a transnational system of organized interest representation, the

[3] Which was, of course, the core concept of Haas's (1958) seminal, "neofunctionalist" theory of European and regional integration.

Community, and the Commission in particular, would thus contribute to its own growth as a policy arena and executive body, and lift itself out of the parochial entanglements of national politics and inter-governmental non-decision-making into a safely anchored new world of supranational political management.

In many ways, the status provided for organized interests in the future European polity bore strong resemblance with a model of interest politics that some time later came to be known to students of politics as "neo-corporatism". As in the latter, the integrated European polity was to be one that was primarily concerned with governing a "mixed economy", according to rules of technical and professional expertise whose prudent application was to help avoid social conflict and disruption. There also was to be a shift away from the territorial/electoral/parliamentary realm of politics, toward powerful mechanisms of functional representation of producer groups, and there was an emphasis on close linkage between state and society through privileged participation of organized interests in policy, and through mutually supportive organizational arrangements between the machineries of government on the one hand and of large, centralized interest organizations on the other. Above all, there was the idea of the future European political economy being kept together by a combination of technocratic professionalism, shared between all major players regardless of divergent, specific interests, and a web of dense and durable bi-, tri-, and multilateral bargaining relationships, involving public and private bodies alike that was seen as contributing to order, if not through common values and shared interests, then through strategic imperatives of self-restraint and compromise reflecting and respecting the complexity of a modern society and economy.

But while motivated speculation about the politics of a unified Europe prepared the ground for the (re-) discovery of (neo-) corporatism as a concept,[4] it was not at the European level that modern corporatism as a reality was finally found. When in the early 1970s students of European integration, in despair over their subject searching for new themes (Haas 1976), turned their energies to comparative politics, they recognized at the level of European nation-states something that looked conspicuously like what integration theory had long had in mind for Europe as a whole. At the time, European nation-states were almost universally turning to centralized bargaining between firmly institutionalized class and sectorial interest groups – facilitated, moderated, and supplemented by the government – as a reaction, first, to the turmoil of 1968 and 1969, and as a recourse, second, against the dislocations of the economic crises after 1973, and especially against the threat of inflation in societies with a strong labor movement whose governments were afraid of reneging on the post-war Keynesian welfare state com-

[4] This connection is particularly visible in the work of Philippe Schmitter. See Schmitter (1979, 1988a, 1989).

mitment to politically guaranteed full employment. In turning to "neocorporatist concertation", as it came to be called, national governments appeared to be doing precisely what integration theorists had been counselling the European Community and the European Commission: In order to integrate their political systems, they were relying more and more on deals with interest groups, as distinct from electoral and parliamentary participation; they were sometimes bypassing, and generally downgrading, their parliaments as places of political decision-making; they attempted to govern through compromises with and between organized interests; and they were generating obligations of special interests to the collective good, not through legislation passed by parliamentary majority, but through collective bargaining in all possible forms and manners (Lehmbruch 1979).

5.2 The Failure of Euro-Corporatism

Not that there was nothing like that at all at the European level. But compared to the prototypical national political systems of the time, interest representation around and within the Community always looked much more "pluralist" than corporatist: more organizationally fragmented; less hierarchically integrated; more internally competitive; and with a lot less control vested in peak associations over their affiliates, or in associations over their members. Tellingly enough, union and business association officials that were transferred to Brussels in the 1970s more often than not perceived this as a falling from grace at home and as a usually well-paid elimination from the excitement of domestic power games and succession struggles – rather than as accession to a new center of political power. By the mid-1970s at the latest it had become clear that, belying the predictions of integration theory, the Brussels system of functional representation had failed to develop into a corporatist engine of supranationalism.

Why was it that a centralized pattern of interest politics did not emerge at the European level when it was so common in national polities? On the surface at least, this was not for lack of trying. It is true that – compared to its predecessor, the European Community for Coal and Steel – the European Economic Community was from the beginning less *dirigiste*, more free trade, and less labor inclusive. Still, the Treaty of Rome paid tribute to the idea of an institutionalized tripartite "social dialogue", most visibly in the form of the Economic and Social Committee (ESC). While the Committee included representatives of national governments and the Community bureaucracy, its principal purpose was to give the "social partners", capital and labor, some form of privileged access to Community decision-making, as well as an opportunity to meet and, hopefully, deal with one another on, as it were, Community territory. However, given the overwhelming influence of conservative parties in the governments of the six Member countries, the ESC never assumed much substantive importance (Lodge and Herman 1980; Nugent 1989), and in spite of labor's ritual demands for a "social Europe" the "common market" remained essentially that: A customs union committed to liberalism and free trade.[5]

To an extent, this changed after 1968. With the accession to power of social democratic parties in major member countries, and with national political elites still suffering from the shocks of their respective "*autunni caldi*", the first Paris summit of the heads of states and governments inaugurated an ambitious program to extend the domain of the newly merged European Communities to a wide range of social policies. Subsequently, for a short, intensive period between 1970 and roughly 1974, it seemed that labor was about to capture the same or similar substantive concessions and institutional privileges at the European level as it was picking up simultaneously in individual countries. If at all, it was during this time that labor leaders, in the way predicted by early integration theorists like Ernst Haas, began to take "Europe" seriously as a political arena in which to launch strategic initiatives.[6] It seems, however, that the hopes of the early 1970s for a meaningful "social dimension" of the European Community dissipated as fast as they had grown – and clearly much faster than in national systems – and that the initial enthusiasm about a new "Europe of the worker" rapidly gave way to the sober realization that in a supranational polity, labor participation in tripartite governance is even more difficult to win and sustain than in traditional nation-states.

Rather than in neofunctionalist terms, the answer to the puzzle of the stagnant record of European interest politics will have to be given in a language that recognizes the importance of conflict and power and does not submerge politics in the technicalities of managing sectorial "spillovers". In a nutshell, there was and is no corporatism in Brussels because *labor* lacks the resources to impose it; because *capital* not only has no interest in it but has unique opportunities to prevent it; and because the European quasi-*state*, the Community, does not have the capacity to induce, facilitate, and underwrite it. Since the same factors are still at work and continue to shape the structure of interest representation in Europe, we will address them in some more detail.

(1) *Labor Weakness*. There is reason to believe that a high organizational

5 Where, in addition, the principal lines of cleavage were not between capital and labor but between "Gaullists" and "Atlanticists", and between the proponents of supranationalism and national sovereignty. As these conflicts began to dominate and eventually block the Community's agenda in the 1960s, introducing social questions in addition would probably have appeared hopeless from the beginning.

6 Not that Haas would have predicted, or approved, the substance of those initiatives which, to a large part, was clearly outside the spectrum of the "pluralist industrialism" of the 1950s and, in the eyes of many observers, signalled a return to "class conflict" and "ideology". See Haas (1976).

and political capacity of labor in the formative period of a polity is of particular importance for the growth prospects of centralized, publicly institutionalized interest politics. This is because more than anything else, it is the strength of labor as a collective actor that promotes the emergence of an active, interventionist, non-liberal state – a state which, in turn, may then institutionalize both labor and capital as principal participants in a centralized, corporatist bargaining structure. Since European labor was always as disorganized supranationally as it was organized nationally, there never was a chance for the kind of political power balance to develop that would have allowed the Community, as a state-in-waiting, to achieve enough "relative autonomy" to intervene in the organizational structures, not just of labor, but also of capital.

The low development of labor's organizational strength at the European level is above all related to the wide regional disparities in the European Community and the resulting divisions of interest between national labor movements (Alexander 1989; Campbell 1989; Visser 1989). This condition has existed for a long time, but it was exacerbated in the mid-1980s by the accession to membership of three Mediterranean countries: Spain, Portugal, and Greece. Average wages in Portugal are equivalent to less than 20% of the average West German wage.[7] The vast differences in trade union concerns and strategies to which this gives rise are reflected, among other things, in the traditionally low significance for their affiliates of European sectorial and inter-sectorial union confederations. While for trade unions from advanced economies a joint European strategy is unlikely to offer improvements over what they have already gained on their own, to unions from weaker countries common demands typically appear unrealistically ambitious and far remote from their everyday practical concerns. Moreover, to unions in rich countries, common labor standards, even if they are just to set a floor, may appear to threaten their own, higher standards. Still, and at the same time, they may *exceed* the marginal productivity of the workforces of less wealthy countries, thereby undermining their ability to take advantage of increased capital mobility and attract foreign investment (Padoa-Schioppa 1988). While it is *also* true that common standards may help unions in weaker economies to make more progress than they otherwise would, and while they may make it easier for more affluent working classes to defend their employment against capital migration, bringing the different interests together and finding a compromise acceptable for both sides is far from simple. Indeed, uniting national union movements behind European programs and policies – for

[7] According to *Eurostat Review 1977–1986*, hourly labor costs for manual and non-manual workers in 1984, expressed in ECU, were highest in West Germany. Portuguese labor costs amounted to 16% of the German level, and the respective figure for Greece was 28% (UK: 63; France: 86). Later data or more exact measures are not at present available.

example in the European Social Dialogue (Cressey 1989; European Foundation for the Improvement of Living and Working Conditions 1989) – always required great political effort and skill. Even where these were successfully applied, the joint policy platforms that were adopted often had to be left deliberately vague and rarely were more than symbolic in character.

In addition and exacerbating their difficulties, European union officials always had to face tendencies among their constituents either to seek national solutions and ignore the supranational level altogether, or to pursue their "European" interests through inter-governmental channels, using their access to home governments to work through the national embassy in Brussels in lobbying the Commission or, more likely, through the Council of Ministers (for a case study, see Teague 1989). Frequently such initiatives were coordinated with the respective national peak associations of employers, resulting in trilateral national coalitions pursuing joint objectives in competition with other countries and thereby effectively cutting out, or starving off, the European system of functional representation. This contributed importantly to the failure of attempts, especially by the Commission, to establish a trilateral European system of neocorporatist political bargaining and exchange in which the Commission could have played the part of a nascent central government (Wallyn 1988).

There is no reason to believe that a broadly institutionalized Social Dimension of the Internal Market, assuming for the moment that it will come to pass, will make consensus-building in European labor organizations less difficult. If outcomes matter more, interest differences assume more weight. Organizational, political, and ideological differences, important as they may still be, are likely to be less crippling in this respect than differences in national labor market structures, training systems, or living standards. Trade unions from rich countries traditionally offer their poorer counterparts assistance in the pursuit of aggressive demands for wages, holidays, social security benefits, etc. But what to them may appear to be internationalist concern for their fellow-workers' rights and well-being, these may be perceived as designed to protect their richer brothers from capital outflow and subsequent job loss (Streeck 1990b). As long as calls for Community-wide labor standards have no practical consequences, they are likely not to be opposed by unions in weaker economies. When confederal policies may have a real impact, however, their formulaton could become more contested.[8]

(2) *Business Resistance.* An important further reason for the organizational weakness of European labor is the absence, on a wide range of critical subjects, of an active interlocutor on the part of capital. European capital is strongly represented in Brussels by lobbyists for individual firms, as well as through sectorial and subsectorial trade associations (see Butt Philips 1985;

[8] I owe this point to a recent, unpublished paper by Peter Lange.

Sargent 1985; Platzer 1989). The interests that these defend are primarily those of enterprises and industries demanding protection and/or (de-) regulation of their product markets. While sometimes the same channels are also used to address social policy concerns – for example, in the 1970s, to defeat European Community directives on workforce participation and consultation – this is not their principal purpose. In fact, many of the *producer interests* firms and trade associations pursue in Brussels are, by and large, and more or less tacitly, shared by their workforces, with business interests often functioning in effect as vertical associations of "particularistic", "syndicalist" firm-specific or sectorial interests of workers.[9]

By comparison, the interests of firms *as employers* are typically not directed at extracting favorable policies from Community bodies. European business has consistently refused to contribute to a transfer of social policy matters from the national arenas to tripartite political bargaining in Brussels. While firms and their associations are always available for formal and informal consultations, binding decisions are typically opposed, usually with reference to widely different conditions and the need for "flexibility". In this respect, it is important to note that getting its will and keeping tripartite social policies at a minimum did not require any major organizational effort from business. Quite to the contrary, to protect the Brussels body politic from contagion by the neocorporatist disease that befell European nation-states in the 1970s, all business had to do was refuse its European peak associations the authority to enter into binding obligations on behalf of their national constituents. A trilateral polity can exist and grow only if all three sides are sufficiently centralized to take part in it. By not organizing strongly at the European level, employers were, and still are, able to confine institutions like the ESC and the Social Dialogue to a strictly non-binding, consultative status. The growing frustration of European trade unions, especially in the 1970s, with the minuscule results of long and complicated discussions in Brussels, and increasingly with the European Community as such, was in large part due to the political strength business was able to draw from its organizational weakness.[10]

Nowhere else is the contrast as stark between the neofunctionalist image of interest groups centralizing their organizations and activities at the European

[9] On the difference between class and producer interests, and its reflection in the organizational structures and strategies of business, see Streeck (1990a).

[10] In addition, of course, there was the fact that whatever consensus may have been reached between the "social partners" in, for example, the Economic and Social Committee, had to find the support of more powerful bodies such as the Council. Typically, in the past as today, employers objecting to centralization of social policy had reliable allies in national governments concerned about their sovereignty. To the extent that social policy is, formally or informally, subject to unanimity requirements, interest groups that prefer decentralized decisions need to find just one government to hold up any "corporatist" bargain that is not to their taste.

level and thereby pushing regional integration forward, and the realities of European business associations. The implicit assumption in much of the neofunctionalist writing is that in a set of interdependent economies, a centralized pursuit of group interests is always and unproblematically the rationally superior alternative to traditional, national, or subnational strategies. The example shows, however, that there may be indeed policy arenas, such as social policy and industrial relations, where *different levels of regulation favor different social interests,* and where groups that are favored by decentralized regulation or by the unfettered operation of "market forces" find it easy to *prevent centralization of regulatory capacity at the supranational level by refusing to "play" and build up the necessary organizations.* The result, clearly not foreseen in neofunctionalist thinking, is the *emergence of interdependencies in the process of economic integration without "spillover" into simultaneous growth of regulatory institutions* capable of controlling them, so that in such cases *integration and deregulation fall into one category.*

(3) *Lack of State Capacity.* Even and perhaps particularly in a democracy, large, encompassing organizations – if they are to grow, remain viable over time, and take part in sustained corporatist bargaining – need to be cultivated, supported, privileged, and monopolized by a sympathetic institutional environment, and preferably by an active state capable of more or less purposive and autonomous intervention in organizational structures. Much of the corporatist debate of the 1970s was on the question of whether a strong state is a precondition for strong associations or, conversely, whether strong associations can develop without, and may even substitute for, a strong state. Based on national observations and cross-national comparison, what seemed to emerge as a tentative consensus assigned a prominent place to the indispensable contribution of public power even in cases of "societal corporatism" (Cawson 1985; Grant 1985). From this perspective, the neofunctionalist expectation that a weak, fledgling non-state like the European Community should be able to launch a system of interest associations that would in return be capable of increasing the Community's power and its stateness, especially in relation to the established nation-states, appears vastly exaggerated.

The European Community does not command the legal and organizational design capacities necessary to reshape powerful interest organizations rooted in civil society. Whatever capacity it may have in this respect is vastly inferior to that of the Community's nation-states, from which it is derived in the first place. Moreover, the policy-making process in the Community is by far too fragmented and dispersed to place a sufficiently high premium on interest organizational centralization at the European level. In the history of the Community up to the present time, inter-governmentalism and the veto powers of individual nations were typically strong enough to pre-empt or modify centrally made decisions. In a situation like this, organized interests have no other choice, even if they were otherwise inclined, than to maintain a strong national base and to cultivate established channels of influence. This, as has been pointed out, holds in particular for groups and in policy areas *where the interest is more in non-decisions than in decisions.* As long as the Community – that is, its genuinely supranational institutions such as the Parliament and the Commission – cannot on its own appropriate policy issues, its ability to influence the structure of organized group interests will remain dismally low.

5.3 Corporatism, the Nation-State, and the Deregulation of European Economies

There are, however, more, and equally important and vexing, relationships between corporatism, nationalism, supranationalism, and the power structure of the political economy. The heyday of corporatism in the 1970s was a period of distinctly *national* responses to the catastrophic de-institutionalization of the capitalist world economy that started in the late 1960s, and the ensuing, rapidly rising domestic and international disorder. Apart from the United States where the absence of a European-style resurgence of labor militancy (see the book by Crouch and Pizzorno 1978) in 1968 had set the stage for a strategy of economic recovery through de-unionization and deregulation, governments almost everywhere experimented with centrally negotiated "social contracts" of all sorts, as a home-made replacement, or functional equivalent, for the now defunct set of international institutions that had in the past provided at least some form of stability for and among competing capitalist nations – by, for example, imposing and enforcing external "balance of payments constraints" that helped national governments keep domestic "discipline". To an important degree, corporatist concertation in the 1970s must be understood as a sometimes desperate turn to domestic political and institutional resources in a search for solutions to what really were international problems – a turn that reflected the almost complete absence on the eve of the crisis, in spite of three decades of international institution-building, of technically viable and politically legitimate mechanisms of international cooperation (McCracken *et al.* 1977). There is no doubt that the frequently made association of corporatism and economic nationalism has a strong basis, in fact, not only for the 1930s but also for the 1970s.

Recourse to corporatism, or attempted corporatism, in the early 1970s was also tried in particular by member states of the European Community. Indeed, if the Community was mentioned in Europe at all during that period, it was to point out how useless it had proven as an instrument for tasks like the restoration of a stable monetary environment; for working out a common energy policy with the United States and, perhaps, OPEC; or for fighting inflation and unemployment. The "dark age" of the European Community was, above all, a time when European national elites seemed to believe as a matter of course that the supranational European institutions they had set up in the 1950s and 1960s, embedded in a relatively stable world order, could not serve as a suitable tool for the restoration of that order, and that therefore everybody had to find their own, national solutions.[11]

Corporatism, we have maintained, was adopted as an alternative to international responses, including European ones. At the same time, the use of domestic concertation on a large scale was bound to make international concertation even more difficult, and thus contributed further to bringing the process of European integration, including the building of a European-level of interest politics, to a halt. This was not only because emerging national corporatisms diverted the attention of policy-makers and association officials away from "Brussels" and back to national capitals, or because attempts at international cooperation would have added further complexity to the domestic bargaining process, thus reducing elites' degrees of freedom and making compromise more difficult. It was also, and more importantly, because different countries turned out to be differently well equipped institutionally for corporatist concertation. While corporatism worked in some places, it dismally failed in others, and in yet others it worked for a while but created accumulated problems that later came home to roost. The economic performance of different capitalist economies thus became more divergent than ever in the 1970s, and as the history of European integration testifies, divergent performance is all but conducive to countries giving up a share of their sovereignty – the weak ones being afraid of becoming subservient to the strong ones, and the strong ones seeing no need and being afraid of diluting their national success.

Second, it almost follows from the above that the resurgence of European integration, as signified by the Single European Act and the Internal Market project, was more than just incidentally related to the demise of national corporatisms in the early 1980s. If anything, it had been the shared experience of a rapid decline in their "effective sovereignty" (Hoffmann 1989) that had undermined the capacity of national states in the developed capitalist

[11] Of course, the period in question – we are talking about the years from about 1970 to, roughly, 1975 – was also notable for vigorous attempts by unions and social democratic governments to move the European Community to the left. With hindsight, this may be seen as another manifestation of the general confusion and indecision of the period, when the Left was still benefitting from the momentum of 1968 while the Right was slowly beginning to mobilize its counterattack with the support of, as it were, 1973. Moves toward a "Social Europe" may, in this situation, well have been deemed as aggressive advances of Social Democracy at Community level, adding another reason for business and its political allies to hold back on European integration. Having not been able to escape national corporatism after 1968, there was no reason for them to accept supranational corporatism in addition at a time when the tide was already beginning to turn in their favor.

world to sustain the kind of social contracts that they had entered into in response to the crisis. The neocorporatist exercises of the 1970s had in large part been attempts to shore up the systems of economic and social policy-making that had been put in place under the post-war settlement (Gourevitch 1986), and prolong their life beyond that of the international environment in which they had originally been embedded. Ultimately, it turned out, this was not possible. The changes in the international position of the United States that had exhausted its capacity to act as a benevolent hegemon, had gradually given rise in the 1970s to a domestic move away from the New Deal compromise, to a political economy that sought competitiveness through deregulation and de-unionization and abandoned the social democratic principle that wages and social conditions were to be taken out of competition. After the final defeat of the Labor Law Reform Act in 1978, the Federal Reserve could feel free to respond to the second oil crisis with a dramatic increase in interest rates, ending inflation at the price of de-industrialization and causing a further, probably irreversible decline in union organization. In the early 1980s, with effectively deregulated, worldwide integrated capital markets, the destruction of American trade unions paid off handsomely in that it gave the United States the "flexible" markets and the "confidence" of financial investors required to underwrite an expansionist fiscal policy that has been ironically characterized as "Keynesianism in one country".

From the perspective of other capitalist countries, the term would appear to have carried a particularly ominous connotation. As the French socialist government after 1981 was soon to find out under the watchful eyes of other political elites, the dynamics of the international political economy after the second oil shock were governed by the old Roman imperial maxim, *quod licet Jovi non licet bovi.* Keynesianism had ceased to be universally available; it had become limited not just to one, but to *only* one country. Being so much larger than everybody else and, as a consequence, so much less internationalized; having broken its unions; being still in control of the *de facto* world currency while no longer accepting the responsibilities of world banker; and for all these and other reasons being able to attract and maintain the confidence of what is euphemistically called "the financial markets", in spite of gigantic and growing deficits in its budget and foreign trade – the United States could effectively and successfully apply fiscal stimulus, whereas the others could not without their capital running away and holders of financial assets dropping their currencies at their doorsteps. In fact, arguably one reason why they could not was that the United States could, and did, siphon off resources that, in earlier, better times, would have gone into industrial investment in other countries.

The important point here is that some sort of effective Keynesian/expansionist capacity would appear to be indispensable for the kind of corporatist concertation and social contract bargaining that was to stabilize non-American capitalisms in the 1970s. As much as these systems may otherwise have differed, under the rules of corporatist bargaining a state that cannot with any reasonable prospect of success promise to apply its fiscal and monetary policy tools to alleviate unemployment, cannot possibly hope to gain concessions from unions or to influence settlements between unions and employers by, for example, offering to improve the terms of the bargain through a corresponding economic policy (Regini 1986). To put the use of its sovereignty up for negotiation, a state needs to have sovereignty in the first place. As the effective sovereignty and, subsequently, the Keynesian capacity of European nation-states faded, so did corporatism – and with it the social democratic project of polically guaranteed full employment.

Of course, not all of the causes for the demise of sovereignty and, therefore, national corporatism originated in the de-institutionalization of the international economy or in the internal politics of the United States and the "deflationary bias" it introduced in the world capitalist system. A more general explanation should be found in the growing interdependence between capitalist economies – or better: Inside the capitalist world economy – which in the typical West European country has now increased the external contribution to its national accounts to a level where it can no longer be treated as a mere addition to a primarily domestic economy. As the French have learned, and everybody else from the French, interdependence does not make it impossible to create jobs by Keynesian stimulus; but unless a country has the size, the currency, and the social system of the United States, chances are that many of those jobs will emerge outside the territory whose government has increased the national debt to create them. Given the absence of international institutions to manage such interdependence, governments in the early 1980s felt hard pressed, or saw a golden opportunity depending on their political complexion, to withdraw the political full employment promise of the post-war period and yield control over the restoration of prosperity and employment in their internationalized national economies to "the market", including a deregulated labor market – in effect accepting the increasingly demanding conditions placed by capital holders on industrial investment and conceding what Burnham once called "domestic sovereignty" to what is euphemistically referred to as "market forces".

Deregulation thus spread – from the United States to Britain, the country with the most open capital markets, and from there to the European continent. What it involved was a more or less forceful, and more or less successful, attack on the accumulated "rigidities" that more than three decades of "mixed economy" had left. In many cases, this included the dismantling, or at least the disregard, of structures of collective bargaining and domestic compromise that already under the late Keynesian regime had more and more been perceived as obstructing industrial adjustment. Where dismantling got stuck, the proven inability of governments to deliver on employment, and their growing unwillingness to try, together with the insistence of unions on concessions and institutional monopolies that capital and governments felt they did no longer need to provide, created the atmosphere of "Euro-pessimism" and "Euro-malaise", not to mention "Euro-sclerosis", which was so pervasive in Europe during the first half of the 1980s.

The Internal Market project emerged at this time and in this context.[12] If one wants a shorthand explanation for the renewed momentum of European integration in the mid-1980s, one would probably account for it as the result of an alignment between two broad interests: (1) large European firms struggling to overcome perceived competitive disadvantages in relation to Japanese and American capital; and (2) state elites seeking to restore at least part of the political sovereignty they had gradually lost at the national level as a result of growing international interdependence. Unlike in the crisis years of the 1970s, European large firms seem to have resolved at some point in the early 1980s that using their clout in national political arenas to get protection from foreign competition through subsidies, technical standards serving as non-tariff trade barriers, or privileged access to public procurement contracts – had become counterproductive given the increased size of production runs and investments required for world market competitiveness. Instead of trying to benefit from the economic nationalism that had made European integration grind to a halt in the 1970s, business throughout Europe seems to have become willing in the 1980s to join forces with political elites which, under the impact of their economies' poor performance, and with worldwide policy coordination with the United States and Japan out of reach, found themselves under pressure to seek a *supranational pooling of eroded national sovereignties over economic policy*, to recapture collective autonomy in relation to the United States and to begin to organize a competitive response to the Japanese challenge.

The main concession governments seem to have made in return for business giving up previous claims for national protection was that the future European political economy was to be significantly *less subject to institutional regulation – national or supranational – than it would have been in the "harmonization"-minded* and *social democratic 1970s when employers found themselves forced to obstruct the "Social Dialogue" and struggle against a Community Directive that would have made German-style codetermination obligatory for all large European firms. In the 1992 compromise*, unlike in the European Community's more mixed economy-minded past, *the project of European integration became bound up with a deregulation project.* As has been pointed out elsewhere, the principal assurance for business that supranational sovereignty would be used just for the *external reassertion of*, and not for *internal intervention in*, the European economy

[12] For more detail, see Sandholtz and Zysman (1989), and Streeck (1989).

was the adoption of a novel method of defining and governing the Internal Market known under the label of "mutual recognition" – which for all practical purposes is a subtle form of *de facto* deregulation (Hoffmann 1989; Streeck 1989).

Deregulation is almost by definition inimical to corporatism. The "negative" mode of integration implied in mutual recognition both undermines national corporatisms even where the national political resources of labor are still comparatively strong, as well as stands in the way of an eventual replacement of national by supranational structures of corporatist concertation. To the extent that corporatism requires a sovereign state, a supranational pooling of national sovereignties is not likely to produce a renaissance of corporatist arrangements at national level. And, as we shall see in more detail below, at the supranational level the bargain that underlies 1992 will very likely prevent the European Community as a supranational government from asserting domestic sovereignty over the market in a way comparable to the traditional nation-state.

5.4 The European Community: A New Type of Non-State

The character of the emerging European polity has puzzled the literature on European integration since the 1950s. As it became clear that "regional integration" was an exclusively European phenomenon – the number of cases being no higher than one – the question became irrepressible of what the "dependent variable" was that integration theory expected to explain (Haas 1975); toward what "final state", if at all, the integration process was moving; and what "the nature of the beast" was that students of European integration, like in the parable of the blind men and the elephant, were trying to grasp (Puchala 1972).

Unlike in the early, "motivated" theorizing (until de Gaulle rehabilitated realism, both with and without a capital R), today hardly anybody[13] expects that the supranational European polity of the future will be a replication of the European nation-state of the past. Wherever else students of European politics may disagree, and they like to disagree a lot, as a minimum it now seems to be accepted that the political system of the post-1992 European Community will be fundamentally, and by a quantum leap, *more complex* than anything that has preceded it. For example, while Europe as a whole will undoubtedly exist as a unified political entity of some as yet undetermined sort, the *nation-states* that now constitute the European Community will not disappear in that entity but will co-exist with it (Puchala 1972). Nor will

[13] The exception being the "federalist" tradition of thinking about the European Community, with its strongholds in Italy (the tradition of Spinelli) and, remarkably, in the United Kingdom (cf. Burgess 1989).

Europe be simply an institutionalized system of *international, or intergovernmental relations*; yet at the same time such relations will continue to play an important part in Europe, alongside and in interaction with other relations (Keohane and Hoffmann 1989). And, similarly, Europe will have *supranational institutions* contributing to the governance of what will be a domestic Western European polity; but these will have to share authority with national, as well as with a dense web of international and transnational institutions which, too, will be constitutive elements of the emerging political system of Western Europe (Schmitter 1989).

Europe's future polity, that is to say, will be composed of traditional domestic relations *within countries*, traditional international relations *between countries*, less traditional transnational relations between both individuals and organizations, and entirely non-traditional supranational relations *between European-level public institutions* on the one hand and, on the other, a *European civil society* consisting of domestic, international, and transnational forces and relations, and including both nation-states and, in manifold national and cross-national combinations, their constituents. The possible dynamics of this unique, and uniquely complex, system of governance are as yet only poorly understood, and there is very little theory, if at all, to guide such understanding. This applies not least to the literature on *state formation* and the role of *class conflict* in it. While there always were more and other actors involved in the shaping of state structures than socio-economic classes – for example, regional, ethnic, and cultural communities and interest groups – in the case of European integration classes, as well as other forces in civil society, have to compete for control over the newly emerging central level of governance with a qualitatively different set of players: A number of already existing, sovereign (or better and increasingly, "semi-sovereign") nation-states. One reason why the latter's continued presence inside the European polity makes a difference is that the international boundaries between them constitute powerful, additional lines of cross-cutting cleavage inside classes and interest groups that stand in the way of their fast and effective polity-wide organization. Moreover, unlike in the nineteenth century when the system of European nation-states was formed, social structures today appear too differentiated, and political problems too variegated, to be easily organizable along bipolar class lines – a condition that, while it is gradually yet fundamentally transforming the political make-up of established nation-states, can be expected to exert a much more powerful, formative influence on the only now emerging polity of the integrated European Community.

There is, furthermore, a growing suspicion that conventional models of the growth of the *modern European welfare state* may not be applicable to the European Community. For some time to come, whatever will occupy the place of the supranational Single European State governing the Single

European Market will likely resemble a *pre-New Deal liberal state* with, in Marshall's terms:

1. A high level of *civil rights* enabling citizens freely to engage in contractual relationships inside and across national borders, accompanied by well-protected *human rights* to equal treatment before the law, freedom of movement, etc. Here the European Court of Justice is of crucial importance, and also the Council of Europe although it is not, of course, a European Community institution.
2. A low level of *political rights*, with the European Parliament continuing to play only a minor role in the system of European institutions. This holds in spite of the fact that the Parliament's direct election and its new powers under the Single European Act have vastly improved its status over what it was in the mid-1970s.
3. An even lower level of *social rights*, these being essentially limited to a set of European-wide health and safety standards. Historically, intervention on health and safety matters represents the earliest stage in the history of the modern welfare state. Present efforts to attach a "Social Dimension" to the Internal Market by starting with a set of generally binding health and safety standards are aimed at replicating the familiar national trajectory of welfare state development. But in the face of the retarded advancement of European-level political rights, there is little reason to expect such efforts to be particularly successful, given in addition:
4. The almost complete absence of a European system of *industrial citizenship* that would give workers and unions rights to representation in industry as a functional domain at the European level, separate from the territorial domain of electoral politics. The closest the European Community will come to being a source of industrial citizenship – that is, to creating and safeguarding European-wide institutions of industrial relations and collective bargaining – is in providing for some form of labor participation under the European company statute. But whatever this will in the end entail – and we comment on this in more detail below – it is likely to pale into insignificance when compared to some of the national systems of union rights that were part of the post-World War national settlements.

State structures matter for interest politics and interest representation, and they certainly do for corporatism. The emerging shape of the European "non-state" – or even "post-Hobbesian" state (Schmitter 1989) – does not bode well for a reconstitution of corporatism at supranational level. In the final part of this paper, we will try to trace the implications of what we think we know about the future shape of the European polity for the structure and function of organized interest groups. In this, we will follow Puchala's (1972) advice and organize our account by distinguishing three levels of policy-making and interest articulation: (1) a subnational, regional level, (2) the nation-state, and (3) the supranational institutions of the European Community. Given the diffuse and fragmented nature of sovereignty in the Community's polity, levels are conceived as interdependent – forming an incompletely unified, loosely coupled, highly diverse institutional complex which confronts an at least equally diverse civil society acting in what after 1992 will be an integrated market.

5.5 The Future of European Interest Politics

5.5.1 At Subnational Level

At the core of the 1992 process is the abolition of national boundaries between the markets of the twelve Member states of the European Community (Bieber *et al.* 1988; Calingaert 1988). As a result, the twelve formerly "national" economies will become *regional subunits* of a larger economic and political entity – a *region* being a *territorial society without sovereignty over its borders*. At the same time, the existing regional subunits of European nations, being no longer fenced in by common, national economic boundaries, are themselves becoming subunits in their own right of the larger, integrated European economy. This tranformation of national into regional economies, and of subnational regions into subunits of a supranational economy, society, or polity, amounts to a *regionalization of Europe* as well as, at the same time, a *Europeanization of its regions.*

The potential importance of the regional level for the developing political economy of Europe is underlined by the rich literature on *industrial districts* (e.g. Brusco 1982; Sabel 1989). Its underlying theme is that of a strong, positive contribution of a dense, social/institutional infrastructure to the vitality of regional economies – like Baden-Wuerttemberg in West Germany or parts of the "Third Italy" – that engage in "high valued-added", "flexible specialization" (Piore and Sabel 1984), or "diversified quality" (Sorge and Streeck 1988) modes of production. In many of these prosperous and world market-competitive areas, unions in particular seem to play an indispensable part in the negotiation of distributional compromises, the building of growth and productivity coalitions, the formation of public/private interfaces, the provision of a protective institutional exoskeleton for small, innovative firms, the generation of collective factor inputs, and the creation of institutions that allow for non-zero-sum cooperation among firms, as well as between capital and labor at the workplace and beyond.

Recent developments seem to indicate that the former regional subunits of European national economies may be about to become independent actors on the European Community stage.[14] A number of Eurpean regions, most prominent among them Catalunia, Lombardia, and Baden-Wuerttemberg, have set up permanent offices in Brussels that bear conspicuous resemblance with embassies. Moreover, their heads of government are reported to have met several times to discuss strategy and form coalitions concerning their interests *vis-à-vis* the European Community. If this trend was to continue, regions would join nations, classes, sectors, and firms as participants in European interest politics, adding another category of players and further complexities to a scene that is already highly complex and pluralistic.

Europeanization of regional interests, and especially inter-regional political competition for Community resources, is far from being universally welcomed.[15] For one thing, while it would improve the position of the Commission, it would also and *ipso facto* tend to weaken further what is left of sovereignty at the national level – which is why national governments have been found to actively resent the formation of direct connections between Brussels and "their" subnational governments. Also, if regions are admitted to European politics, regional subunits of *federal* states, having independent powers of legislation, taxation, budgeting, etc., will likely have an advantage over regions of more centralized countries, namely the absence from the above list of, say, the Midlands.

The impact of the possible emergence of a regional level of interest politics on the form and role of functional representation in Europe, and on the prospects of corporatism in particular, depends to an important extent on the likely composition of ruling regional coalitions. The main question here seems to be for the sources and conditions of labor-inclusiveness of regional regimes – especially whether regional power resources of labor can be generated *endogenously* inside the region, or need to be mobilized *exogenously* using national power resources under the protection of a sovereign border. Regions, it may be remembered, are societies that have no control over their boundaries. As European nation-states turn into regions of an integrated market economy, nationally legislated labor market regimes are likely to lose much of their force, and the same holds for protective barriers against cross-border competition; this, after all, is what the expected deregulatory effect of 1992 is all about. The survival and growth of regional labor-inclusive institutions inside the integrated Internal Market, and with it perhaps that of regionally based non-price-competitive production, would then have to depend on non-national, regionally indigenous forces – or would require that functional equivalents for national-level supports be found to balance the decline in national political capacities that is associated with 1992.

[14] For a strong statement to this effect, see Majone (1989).
[15] The following discussion owes must to a set of unpublished papers by Gary Marks.

Much of the literature on regional political economies seems to take the position that the composition and survival of their regimes is indeed, and always was, largely independent from national institutions. Typically, the institutional infrastructure of economically successful European regions is described as based in *local* cultures, traditions, and politics that, by implication, would be unlikely to be destabilized by an attenuation of national sovereignty. However, apart from the fact that culture and tradition may rapidly lose vitality in the modernizing, internationalizing post-1992 European economy, a case could be made that, certainly as far as the presence of unions and of a tripartite power balance in regional economies is concerned, this severely underestimates the role played in the past by *national* power resources (Korpi 1978), like labor law creating or supporting various overt or covert mechanisms of union security, or protective monetary and trade policies.

Regions, not being states, are by definition unable to insert coercive power in the voluntary contractual and communitarian relations between their citizens. Their social organization is that of a civil society undistorted, as it were, by public intervention. In particular, regions lack the capacity to provide the kind of public support that has generally been found to be required to transform unstable, voluntaristic, pluralistic unions into institutionally "mature" ones that are capable of looking, in corporatist fashion, beyond the individual enterprise or occupational group to the sector, the country as a whole, or, for that matter, the region. Regionally based unionism in the European Community would have to do without external sources of associational monopoly, without authoritative stabilization of bargaining arenas, and without recourse to a public sphere balancing the manifold advantages employers enjoy in the marketplace. It is not easy to see how the disabling effects on union movements of the erosion of institutional supports at national level should be counterbalanced by unions turning to the regional level where such supports have never existed.

In any case, even if it was somehow possible to create stable tripartite systems of regional governance, one would want to resist the temptation to refer to this as (regional) "corporatism". Corporatism requires encompassing organizations that internalize a significant part of the externalities of a group's collective action and interests, and allow for hierarchical coordination between different levels of interest aggregation and group activity. Neither condition would be met in a "Europe of regional tripartisms". If national-level corporatisms have been undermined by growing international interdependence beyond the control of the parties at the bargaining table, regional arrangements are even more affected by the shrinking "effective size" of modern polities. The "tyranny of external effects", as it has been called, may be and clearly is on the advance at the national level; but it certainly is incomparably more severe in the much smaller action space of a subnational region – especially after the demise of national regulations that in the past have taken a core set of social and constitutional conditions out of inter-regional competition.

Moreover, in moving their organizational center of gravity toward the region, as most of the industrial district literature more or less explicitly advises them to do, unions would write off any aspiration they may have had for playing a role in the political management of inter-regional externalities. Regionalized unions would inevitably be partners, junior or not, of regional capital trying to survive in inter-regional free-market competition. For example, they would have to cease seeing themselves as agents of inter-regional redistribution. While the *mezzogiorno* policy of Italian unions in the 1970s, which relied on the movement's centralized, national power to demand regional development programs for the impoverished South of the country, may not have been particularly successful, a regionally decentralized union movement would have been unable to agree on any such policy in the first place. Today, regionalized unionism would for the same reasons be incapable of a political response to the involvement of regional economies in the larger European and global economic context – an involvement that has become deeper than ever and that, incidentally, fundamentally distinguishes today's regional economies from those of the past.

It is conceivable that political control over economic interdependence is presently beyond recapture, and that union organizational domains may for a long time or forever be bound to be significantly narrower than whatever the relevant "market" may be. But decentralization of unions and industrial relations toward regional arenas will clearly not remedy this condition, and to the extent that it ratifies the, possibly inevitable, effective fragmentation of organized interests, it actually amounts to the very opposite of corporatism. The emergence of regional arenas of interest politics seems to advance, not the organization of labor or, for that matter, of capital, but rather its *dis-organization*. In the 1992 environment in particular, new opportunities for interest articulation at the regional level would appear to increase actors' range of *choice* between political channels widely beyond what would be compatible with the orderly world of corporatism. In addition to the enterprise, the sector, the nation, and perhaps Europe as a whole, struggling factions inside interest associations, and especially inside unions, would have yet another option for pursuing sectional interests separately and on their own, in coalition with other categories of interests, and with ambitious local governments. By undermining associational monopoly and inter-associational hierarchy, the fragmentation of interests and the pluralist proliferation of political opportunities that is entailed in the "regionalization of Europe" thus adds to the decomposition of national-level corporatisms.

5.5.2 At National Level

Initial analyses of the decay of national corporatisms in the late 1970s and in the 1980s tended to locate its causes in the economic problems of the period, and especially in slack labor markets and high unemployment (on the following, see also Schmitter 1988b). The implication was that a recovery of corporatist macro-economic management and bargaining was possible together with and as a consequence of economic recovery. It only later transpired that this overlooked the qualitative changes in social structures, in domestic political systems, in the economy, and in the international environment that had been occurring since the early 1970s and that had, imperceptibly at first, eaten away at corporatism's structural foundations. While this is not the place to review the literature on these trends in any detail, three such trends will be briefly described:

1. *Increasing differentiation of social structures and collective interests in advanced capitalist societies.* Neocorporatism "assumed" an underlying social structure that could be plausibly conceived as polarized in two large producer classes, "capital" and "labor". There are strong reasons to believe that this assumption was already highly counterfactual when Western European countries in the late 1960s increasingly moved toward neocorporatist forms of governance. However, for a while, the *corporatist working hypothesis of a bipolar organization of societal cleavages and identitites*, while from the beginning no more than a *heroic simplification* of a much more complex reality, could be kept alive with the help of the powerful institutional reinforcements that both business and labor as organized actors had received from their beleaguered governments. Underneath the organizational structures, however, social change continued and perhaps even accelerated; 1968 wrought not just a strengthening of the institutional position of labor movements, but was also the birthdate of a new, highly educated and politically outspoken *middle class* that increasingly found its specific concerns insufficiently represented in the post-1968, class-political institutional set-up. Subsequently, during the 1970s and 1980s the substantive content of interest conflicts and the focus of policy attention shifted away from class-based lines of cleavage toward a panoply of discrete issues focusing on consumer protection, quality of life, gender, environmental, ethical, and other problems, each with their respective movements. As is well known, in most countries this weakened the capacity of social democratic parties to govern or, alternatively, strained the alliance between social democracy and the union movement. Both were far from conducive to corporatist governance.
2. *Market instability and volatility, and pressures on firms to increase the "flexibility" of their product ranges, technologies, and social organization.* New production technologies based on microelectronics and cutting

across traditional job classification systems and professional categories have created possibilities for flexible production in relatively small units. In one sense, these processes increased the need for active assent on the part of workers – and, therefore, the need for capitalists to bargain with them over the quality as well as the quantity of their contribution. But, in another sense, this is occurring in highly differentiated settings not easy to cover by a standard contract and difficult for intermediaries to control. Indeed, both trade unions and employer associations are today finding themselves increasingly shut out of workplace-specific deliberations and bargaining between their respective local constituents.

3. *Changing roles and structures of interest associations.* In the new social and market environment, negotiations aimed at establishing standard national solutions for the regulation of the employment relationship appear of decreasing relevance, and at times may even be counterproductive, when what is demanded are policies tailored to improving the productivity and international competitiveness of specific sectors and even individual enterprises. As a result, the role of intermediary institutions, especially trade unions and employer associations, changed from the point of view of members and interloculors, both of whom are searching for more differentiated mechanisms of representation. While decentralization may have taken very different courses in different countries, what it had inevitably in common was a weakening of the center – and it is there that corporatist bargains are traditionally struck.

Moreover, the shift of employment from traditional manufacturing to the services and, in some cases, to public employment in a number of countries changed the "character" of unions in that unions from the public and private service sector became the largest units in national confederations, weakening the organizational discipline maintained by traditionally unionized manual workers, especially in the metalworking sector (Crouch 1988). These unions, whose industries were exposed to world market competition, have in the past typically been willing to maintain wage restraint in exchange for political concessions. Their sectors have often been hard hit by de-industrialization, and such workers as remained after successful restructuring – if they joined unions at all – are employed in more scattered sites with much more individuated tasks. The very categories upon which macro-corporatist compromises were built have thus become disaggregated and dispersed, and as a result centralized negotiations on wages, benefits, and working conditions came under severe pressures. In some cases (e.g. Sweden), the system only survived by shifting to a sectorial level.

At least as important as the domestic causes of the decline of national-level corporatisms were the profound changes in the status and performance of the *nation-state* that occurred during the past two decades. Since a corporatist policy regime requires a government able to protect the expectations and reward the concessions of its partners in collective bargaining, the decline of the nation-state undermined neocorporatist arrangements even where they had been comparatively well established. As has been pointed out, the 1992 project must be seen as a response to the apparently irreversible loss of effective national sovereignty that was so painfully experienced by the political elites of European nation-states in the early 1980s (Streeck 1989). Its thrust, however, is toward Europe's external environment rather than its domesitc economy, and this is another important factor that in all likelihood *precludes* a return to corporatism. Indeed, part and parcel of the pooling of sovereignties (Keohane and Hoffmann 1989) under the Single European Act, and of the political deals that made it possible, is a redefinition of the relationship between the Community's "domestic" institutions and "the market", under which the latter stands to gain unprecedented freedom from intervention by the former. The mechanism, to recapitulate, is "negative" integration through pre-emption of national regulatory regimes, without a simultaneous supranational restoration of regulatory capacity. In addition to obstructing a rebuilding of corporatism at the level of European nation-states, this also is likely to prevent the emergence of corporatist governance at the supranational level.

Seen from a national perspective, 1992 amounts to a formal devaluation of vast political resources that have come to be organized in and around the nation-state. Declining effective sovereignty had long been chopping away at the value of the investments in national political power that had been accumulated and cultived for more than a century; this, after all, was why corporatism was eventually becoming untenable. The 1992 principle of mutual recognition may well be understood in analogy to the cut of a collapsed currency – an inevitable but nevertheless painful adjustment to reality, with significant distributional side-effects in that currency holders are more severely affected than owners of real estate or productive capital. In present-day European nation-states, with the successive layers of political, industrial, and social rights that have been built into them in the domestic struggles of the nineteenth and twentieth centuries, it is clearly labor that is in the former, and capital that is the latter position. While mutual recognition and the resulting inter-regime competition devalue nationally institutionalized power resources, they leave property rights untouched, or even increase their value. As neocorporatism has always been conditional on a measure of political strength of organized labor, the prospects for its restoration in the post-1992 European nation-states are therefore dim.

Not everything that has in the analyses of the 1970s and 1980s come to be associated with corporatist modes of governance will disappear in Europe. Pragmatic sectorial partnerships between state agencies and groups of business firms, oscillating, as it were, between agency capture and *Selbst-*

verwaltung, are likely to continue, to the extent that they are comfortably embedded in national policy styles and as long as they do not run afoul of European Community competition law – which they well may. Especially if they have from the beginning been labor-exclusive "private interest governments", as we have called them elsewhere, they may remain viable for some time, due to the savings on transaction costs they entail and regardless of the weakening of their sponsors in national state and legal systems. Multi-employer collective bargaining arrangements between trade unions and employers' associations may not disappear either – at least, again, for the time being. But corporatism as a national-level accord between encompassingly organized socio-economic classes and the state, by which an entire national economy is comprehensively governed, is a matter of the past.

5.5.3 At Supranational Level

Tripartism never really worked in Brussels (Sargent 1985), and where it was tried it was always too encapsulated and marginal to come in any way close to a neocorporatist model of governance. There is no reason to believe that this will change. The negative integration mode of the 1992 process – the move away from harmonization to mutual recognition – ensures that the eroded domestic sovereignty of nation-states will not be recreated at the supranational level. Unlike in older, more naïve images of regional integration, national political arenas, themes, and regulatory instruments that are rendered obsolete by integration do not always and necessarily have to be reconstructed at the level of the emerging supranational polity. Rather than being moved upward, they may as well dissipate in the newly emerging, more complex, and less orderly institutional system, or they may, more or less intentionally, be turned over to the voluntarism of market and civil society. Where this happens, it obviously deprives what might aspire to become a European federal government of a range of subject-matter and decisional discretion that it otherwise could use, and indeed would need, to build the mutual give-and-take in and between interest groups and public bodies that is the indispensable basis for stable neocorporatist exchange.

A case of limited state capacity at the European level reducing the incentives for comprehensive organization of economic interests is the absence of a European Central Bank (Holm, forthcoming). Historically, tripartite corporatist bargaining has typically involved the government's use not only of its fiscal but also of its monetary policy instruments. The need to be represented in bargaining over monetary policy was an important reason for socio-economic interests, in particular for employers, to get organized. However, the European System of Central Banks, if it will at all come into being, will be carefully shielded from political pressures, not least by its diffuse and decentralized internal structure. Moreover, a European Central Bank is likely for a long time to continue to be subject to strongly institutionalized deflationary, "monetarist" preferences (Delors Committee 1989) – if only beause the European Community as an imperfectly unified actor in the world economy will need time to get used to the reflationary possibilities offered by a large economy with a currency that could compete for the role of world money.

Another important ingredient of 1970s-style neocorporatism – centralized collective bargaining between capital and labor – is entirely missing at the European level, and nothing is in sight that would indicate its impending appearance. In the past, centralized collective bargaining was often advanced by encompassing employers' associations forcing unions to unify their policies and organizational structures (Swenson 1989). No such support will be forthcoming at the European level in the foreseeable future, not least because the inter-regional mobility of capital will, perhaps indefinitely now, exceed that of labor, and because centralization would deprive capital of the strategic advantages of competition-driven collective bargaining at regional or enterprise level. The same applies to the other historical source of external facilitation, government intervention. European institutions are unlikely to develop an efficient capacity to serve as carry-over mechanisms from the unionized to the non-unionized sector, thereby protecting employers in the former from competition by employers in the latter.

A further factor that would appear to stand in the way of European-level collective bargaining is the mutual incompatibility of existing national industrial relations systems. While in some countries collective agreements are negotiated at the *enterprise* level, in others they are concluded for all firms that belong to a specific *sector* on a given national or subnational *territory*. The latter, as a rule, requires the presence of a strong employers' association and is in addition greatly facilitated by state-sponsored extension mechanisms making agreements binding on non-affiliated firms. Moreover, the success of sectorial/territorial collective bargaining depends crucially on the large and more prosperous firms being included in the bargaining unit; otherwise unions would be unable to increase their bargaining power in small firms by enlisting the willingness to settle and the ability to pay of large firms as their ally. In the absence of supranational employer associations and facilitating state intervention, it is hard to see how European-level collective bargaining could ever become sectorial/territorial in scope; all unions can hope to accomplish in building what the Commission has euphemistically called a "European industrial relations system" (Commission of the European Communities 1988), are consultations and, perhaps, negotiations with the headquarters of large multinational firms (Campbell 1989). However, while this would tend to be compatible with national industrial relations systems based on enterprise bargaining, a European enterprise agreement might *de jure* or *de facto* exempt that enterprise's subsidiaries from the purview of sectorial/territorial bargaining. The result would be a weakening of national multi-employer bargaining regimes. Since sectorial/territorial bargaining is used by unions to reduce regional and inter-firm wage differentials, there would be not just organizational but also political reasons for unions to object to European enterprise-level bargaining – even though this would appear to be the only possible form of supranational collective bargaining on offer.

Even if, then, the Commission and its allies were much more successful than can be realistically expected in moving the European political economy toward a broad Social Dimension, Europe is not likely ever to become a neocorporatist, tripartite, bargained economy. Collective bargaining in Europe – this is one of the few predictions one can feel safe to make – will always remain nationally and regionally fragmented. European-level relations between capital and labor, instead of forming the institutional core of the European political economy, will largely remain compartmentalized in the private sphere of large multinational enterprises; they will essentially be non-political and voluntaristic in character. Where labor/capital relations enter the political arena, they will mainly take the form of a set of discrete "labor" and "social policy" issues, outside any "ideological" context. As such, they will lend themselves to being dealt with by bureaucrats, experts, and inter-governmental committees in the same way as, for example, labelling rules regarding the cholesterol content of palm oil, or proposals for the recycling of mineral water containers. That is, rather than driving the constitutional bargain underlying the political system, the traditional class issues of industrial society will have to compete on an equal plane with "post-industrial" themes like environmental protection, consumer rights, equality between men and women, etc. – issues that by their nature defy integration in an encompassing framework of "class" politics.[16]

The evolutionary alternative to Thatcherism as a model for the European political economy is clearly not (German or Scandinavian) neocorporatism. More likely appears an American trajectory: A political system of "disjointed pluralism" or "competitive federalism", organized over no less than three

[16] In part, this reflects a process, or "style", of decision-making that is specifically "European". In brief, its integrity and continuity is achieved by decontextualization and depoliticization of the issues at stake – "pragmatically" isolating them from "ideological" meanings and as much as possible avoiding their incorporation in any coherent political symbolism. Didactically helpful in this respect is the recurrent discovery in European Community bodies that apparently identical political arrangements and outcomes can sometimes be of completely contrary significance in different national, political, and ideological environments – for example, legally based co-determination rights in Britain and West Germany. After policy "issues" have been divested of their emotional and ideological aura, and fragmented and individualized, their treatment can be assigned to "experts" – specialists, that is, in comparative inventories of decontextualized and depoliticized problems, positions, and compromises, and in the extraction of the smallest common denominator from such inventories.

levels – regions, nation-states, and "Brussels". As in the United States, and perhaps even more so, this system would be characterized by a profound *absence of hierarchy and monopoly* among a *wide variety of players of different but uncertain status.* Interest associations, and many of them, will certainly be among those. But they will have to compete for attention with national states, subnational regions, large firms, and specialized lobbyists, leaving their constituents with a wide range of choices among different paths of access to the political center and enabling them to use threats of exit to coerce their representatives into pluralist responsiveness. Just as fundamental constitutional questions of sovereignty and hierarchy inside the Community's quasi-state – in the relative status of regions, nations, and supranational bodies – will remain unsettled and uncertain, so will the hierarchical relations between firms, sectorial associations, and peak associations in its system of functional representation.

Given the constitutional bargain that underlies the relaunching of the European Community in the 1980s, no mechanism is in sight that could rationalize its political system, help crystallize its *mélange* of actors and processes, and establish corporatist monoplies of representation, inter-associational hierarchies or, for that matter, a predominant position for the Commission's bureaucracy and technocracy. Whatever turn the European Community may take after 1992: It is not likely to reverse the tide and reorganize European capitalism in the neocorporatist cast.

References

Alexander, J. (1989): Divergent European Community Unionism: A Threat to Single Market Unification? Unpublished manuscript.

Bieber, R., R. Dehousse, J. Pinder, and J. H. H. Weiler (1988): Introduction. Back to the Future: Policy, Strategy and Tactics of the White Paper on the Creation of a Single European Market. In *1992: One European Market?*, Bieber, R. R. *et al.* (eds.), pp. 13–31. Baden-Baden: Nomos Verlagsgesellschaft.

Brusco, S. (1982): The Emilian Model: Production Decentralization and Social Integration. *Cambridge Journal of Economics*, 6, 167–184.

Burgess, Michael (1989): Federalism and European Union: Past, Present and Future in the European Community. Unpublished manuscript.

Butt Philips, A. (1985): Pressure Groups in the European Community. *UACES Occasional Essay*, 2. London: University Association for Contemporary European Studies.

Calingaert, M. (1988): *The 1992 Challenge from Europe: Development of the European Community's Internal Market.* Washington DC: National Planning Association.

Campbell, D. C. (1989): Multinational Labor Relations in the European Community. *ILR Report*, 27, 7–14.

Cawson, A. (ed). (1985): *Organized Interests and the State: Studies in Meso-Corporatism.* London: Sage.

Commission of the European Communities (1988): *The Social Dimension of the Internal Market: Interim Report of the Intergovernmental Working Party.* Special edition of *Social Europe.*

Cressey, P. (1989): Trade Unions and the Social Dialogue. Paper presented at the IRRU

conference on *Industrial Relations and the European Community*, University of Warwick, 17–19 March.
Crouch, C. (1988): Trade Unions in an Exposed Sector: Their Influence on Neo-Corporatist Behavior. Paper prepared for a conference on *Markets, Institutions and Co-Operation: Labour Relations and Economic Performance*, Venice, October.
Crouch, C. and A. Pizzorno (eds.) (1978): *The Resurgence of Class Conflict in Western Europe Since 1968*, 2 vols. London: Macmillan
Delors-Committee (Committee for the Study of Economic and Monetary Union) (1989): Report on Economic and Monetary Union in the European Community.
Grant, W. (ed.) (1985): *The Political Economy of Corporatism*. London: Macmillan.
Gourevitch, P. (1986): *Politics in Hard Times*. Ithaca/London: Cornell University Press.
Haas, E.B. (1958): *The Uniting of Europe: Political, Social and Economic Forces 1950–1957*. London: Stevens & Son.
Haas, E.B. (1970): The Study of Regional Integration: Reflections on the Joy and Anguish of Pretheorizing. In: *Regional Integration: Theory and Research*, Lindberg, L.N. and S. Scheingold (eds.), pp. 3–42.
Haas, E.B. (1975): *The Obsolescence of Regional Integration Theory*. University of California–Berkeley: Institute of International Studies.
Haas, E.B. (1976): Turbulent Fields and the Theory of Regional Integration. *International Organization*, 30, 173–212.
Hoffmann, S. (1989): The European Community and 1992. *Foreign Affairs*, p. 27–47.
Holm, E. (forthcoming): The Politics of Europe's Money. In: *European Self-Assertion: A New Role for Europe in International Affairs*, Crawford, B. and P. Schulze (eds.).
Keohane, R.O. and S. Hoffmann (1989): *European Integration and Neo-Functional Theory: Community Politics and Institutional Change*. Unpublished manuscript.
Korpi, W. (1978): *The Working Class Under Welfare Capitalism: Work, Unions and Politics in Sweden*. London: Routledge & Kegan Paul.
Lehmbruch, G. (1979): Liberal Corporatism and Party Government. In: *Trends Towards Corporatist Intermediation*, Schmitter, Ph.C. and G. Lehmbruch (eds.). London/Beverly Hills: Sage.
Lodge, J. and V. Herman (1980): *The Economic and Social Committee in EEC Decision-Making. International Organization*, 34, 265–284.
Majone, G. (1989): *Preservation of Cultural Diversity in a Federal System: The Role of the Regions*. Unpublished manuscript.
McCracken P. *et al.* (1977): *Towards Full Employment and Price Stability: A Report to the OECD by a Group of Independent Experts*. Paris: Organization for Economic Cooperation and Development.
Nugent, N. (1989): *The Government and Politics of the European Community*. Durham: Duke University Press.
Padoa-Schioppa, T. (1988): Questions About Creating a European Capital Market. In: *1992: One European Market?*, Bieber, R., R. Dehousse, J. Pinder, and J.H.H. Weiler (eds.), pp. 283–292. Baden-Baden: Nomos Verlagsgesellschaft.
Piore, M.J. and C.F. Sabel (1984): *The Second Industrial Divide: Possibilities for Prosperity*. New York: Basic Books.
Platzer, H.-W. (1988): *Transnational Politics of Interest Groups in Western Europe*. Unpublished manuscript.
Puchala, D. (1972): Of Blind Men, Elephants and International Integration. *Journal of Common Market Studies*, 95–128, 267–284.
Regini, M. (1986): Political Bargaining in Western Europe During the Economic Crisis of the 1980s. In: *Economic Crisis, Trade Unions and the State*, Jacobi, O. *et al.* (eds.), pp. 61–76. London: Croom Helm.
Sabel, C.F. (1989): Flexible Specialization and the Re-emergence of Regional Economies. In: *Reversing Industrial Decline? Industrial Structure and Policy in Britain and Her Competitors*, Hirst, P. and J. Zeitlin (eds.), pp. 17–70. New York: St. Martin's Press.

Sandholtz, J. and J. Zysman (1989): Recasting the European Bargain. In: *World Politics*, pp 95–128.

Sargent, J. (1985): Corporatism and the European Community. In: *The Political Economy of Corporatism*, Grant, Wyn (ed.), pp. 229–253. London: Macmillan.

Schmitter, Ph. C. (1979): Still the Century of Corporatism? In: Trends Towards Corporatist Intermediation, Schmitter, Ph. C. and G. Lehmbruch (eds.), pp. 7–52. London/Beverly Hills: Sage.

Schmitter, Ph. C. (1988a): Corporatism (Corporativism). In: *The Encyclopedia of the Social Sciences.*

Schmitter, Ph. C. (1988b). Corporatism is Dead! Long Live Corporatism? Reflections on Andrew Shonfield's "Modern Capitalism". In: *Government and Opposition*, p. 54–73.

Schmitter, Ph. C. (1989): *A Sketch of an Eventual Article on The European Community as an Extreme Example of a Newly Emergent Form of Political Domination.* Unpublished manuscript.

Schmitter, Ph. C. and W. Streeck (1990): *Organized Interests and the Europe of 1992.* Paper prepared for a conference on "The United States and Europe in the 1990s: Trade, Finance, Defense, Politics, Demographics and Social Policy", American Enterprise Institute, Washington DC, 6–8 March.

Sorge, A. and W. Streeck (1988): Industrial Relations and Technical Change: The Case for an Extended Perspective. In *New Technology and Industrial Relations*, Hyman, R. and W. Streeck (eds.). Oxford: Basil Blackwell.

Streeck, W. (1989): *The Social Dimension of the European Economy: A Dicsussion.* Paper prepared for the 1989 Meeting of the Andrew Shonfield Association. London: Andrew Shonfield Association.

Streeck, W. (1990a): Interest Heterogeneity and Organizing Capacity: Two Class Logics of Collective Action? In: *Rational Actors in Institutional Settings*, Czada, R. and A. Windhoff-Heretier (eds.). New York: Westview Press.

Streeck, W. (1990b): *More Uncertainties: West German Unions Facing 1992.* Paper presented at the Seventh International Conference of Europeanists, Washington DC, 23–25 March.

Swenson, P. (1989): Fair Shares: Unions, Pay and Politics in Sweden and West Germany. In: *Cornell Studies in Political Economy.* Ithaca, New York: Cornell University Press.

Teague, P. (1989): Trade Unions and Extra-National Industrial Policies: A Case Study of the Response of the British NUM and ISTC to Membership in the European Coal and Steel Community. *Economic and Industrial Democracy*, 10, 211–237.

Visser, J. (1989): Trade Union Diversity in Western Europe: Dimensions, Origins, and Consequences. Paper presented at the IRRU conference on *Industrial Relations and the European Community*, University of Warwick, 17–19 March.

Wallyn, L. (1988): The Social Policy of the Community and Participation of the Social Partners in Decision-Making at European Level. Social Europe, 1, 13–20.

6 Weakness of Pluralism in Latin America – What Are the Prospects for Social Concertation?

Gian Primo Cella

6.1 The "Story" of Pluralism

I will try to give a brief account of a phenomenon which has played an important role in the history of this century – that of pluralism as a form of interests control, as a procedure for competition between groups and the composition of conflicts, and also, as far as possible, as a political theory. Latin America does not hold a very important position in this story, and this has not been without significance for its past, nor will it be for its future, especially in these years of delicate and decisive transitions from authoritarian regimes to democracies. We will look at the reason for this absence. But before we begin the tale, let us look at what we mean by Latin America as a whole. Several important and authoritative works warn us to proceed with caution. The first of these is the recent publication by Hirschman, who is convinced that "the most important factor characterizing recent events in this region is diversity and the most interesting facts are linked to the specific experiences, often contrasting, of the individual countries" (1987: p. 305). O'Donnel's work (1988: p. 18) is also interesting. Looking at the comparison between Latin America and Southern Europe with regard to the transition from authoritarian regimes, he writes that the former is less homogeneous. Does this heterogeneity prevent global discourse regarding a single subject (and perhaps a single historical subject) or not?

The considerations and research which, for example, revealed the lack of consistency in the long-accepted well-known theory of authoritarianism as a "natural" state of affairs in Latin America helped, if not to prevent, certainly to make these arguments more cautious (see Malloy 1987: p. 246; Seligson 1987: p. 10). However, in political and social sciences, the theme of "regionalism" is a long way from being satisfactorily resolved. The balanced and wise ways of tackling it, like those proposed in J. Sheahan's useful contribution of political economy (1987: pp. 17–18), are convincing in their invitation to use cautious methods, but they do not obstruct the constant flow of questions, impressions, and images in connection with Latin America as a whole. These questions, we have to admit, are raised, almost imposed, also by an extraordinary and enduring literary culture made up of writers like Carpentier, Asturias, García Marquez, Vargas Llosa, and Roa Bastos (who have dealt specifically with aspects and implications of authoritarianism). I will therefore leave the theme in the background, and for the time being I will content myself with putting forward only one negative specific regional aspect, which is far less exacting, that is to say that in this century Latin America has *not* been the area of pluralism. I do not intend to suggest mandatory historical/political interpretative methods, but just to discuss the current lack of capacities to manage some of the macro problems in Latin American society which can be partly blamed on this absence. But let us go back to our brief outline of the well-known "story" of pluralism.

In European experience, the end of the society of liberal individualism, based on the competitive market and on limited suffrage; the spread of large organizations representing group interests (industrial trade unions, entrepreneurial associations, farmers' organizations), of collective bargaining, and of bargaining relations in general; the advent of broadly based parties (Socialist/Labor or Christian/Social), and of universal suffrage, mark the advent of pluralism. It is a form of regulation, and a theory, which is perhaps the greatest political "invention" of the century, or rather, to quote Pizzorno, I believe, "the pride of Western political inventiveness".

This "invention", in its opposition to individualism, and also to monism, continues to have contrasting links with democratic theory and practice. Pluralism is like a precondition necessary for the appearance and consolidation of liberal democratic situations, and yet it can erode the foundations of political equality, weaken democratic leadership, and prejudice the pursuit of collective interests and long-term goals (S. Veca's analysis (1990) is excellent). Dahl's arguments with regard to these aspects, that is, the tension existing between democracy and pluralism but also the need the former has of the latter, are very enlightening. The areas of tension in the path of democratic pluralism are: the specter of the emergence of political inequality; the distortion of the civic conscience; the distortion of the hierarchy of aims; and the loss of ultimate "control" (taken to mean the reciprocity of actions or preferences between different groups) (R. Dahl 1982: p. 40). But pluralism is necessary: "The change in the democracy scale from the city-state to the nation-state has led inexorably from monist democracy to pluralist democracy" (R. Dahl 1988: p. 26). Dahl goes on to mention Stein Rokkan's effective allusion, and to say that of course in pluralism "votes are important, although often organizational resources are the decisive factor" (ibid., p. 25). However, polyarchy and pluralism are closely and fundamentally linked. On the other hand, the forms and directions of pluralist organization are not the same everywhere, and some have been more successful at partially solving the tensions with democratic situations than others. Furthermore, "polyarchic" paths not based on a pluralist culture may be dangerous for these situations (this can be seen in the current situations in Eastern Europe, which has been "plunged" into democracy). In fact, pluralism provides a fundamental intermediary, operating alongside the political system, between civil society and state, for greater correspondence between *demos* and *polis*.

In the more specific field of regulating interests, and the corresponding conflicts, pluralism has provided, and still provides, above all, a set of procedures (such as collective bargaining, as a structure and a process). Its advantages and disadvantages all derive from this characteristic, and its main disadvantage (it does not provide values for creating a hierarchy of aims or demands) stems precisely from its fundamental advantage (the creation of a type of procedure within which to control the competition of organized groups between themselves or with the state).

Its procedures are the main legitimization of pluralism and its logic of controlling interests. This legitimization comes from the feedom to organize oneself, from participation in negotiation exchange, and from the possibility of voicing (even as a voice of conflict) one's own interests on the sole condition of maintaining the mutual survival of the parties (e.g. employers and trade unions) and the complete framework of the procedures (Cella 1989: p. 14). This purely procedural nature should be respected also on the level of theoretical planning. As such, pluralism, at least in its European form, is badly suited, on closer examination, to becoming a *theory*, or the distortion of theory, an *ideology*. The critics of pluralism, and especially Fox (1973), were the ones who dragged pluralism down to these levels, for the sake of controversy. But the deeper significance of pluralism, as the great Otto Kahn-Freund (M. Grandi 1982) noted with regard to the position occupied in it by labor law doctrine formulation, remains on the one hand of an organizational/procedural type, and on the other of an analytical/explanatory type.

The uninterrupted process of negotiations, concessions, and compromises is the mechanism that prevents the disintegration of the pluralist system by the competing groups (Clegg 1975), and the onset of generalized conflicts (devastating conflicts which in pluralism are not impossible, but improbable). The market, although not that of individualist competition, but an "organized", almost oligopolistic one, provides the basic criteria for controlling the system. In this framework the participation and incorporation of the masses is not necessarily a danger to democracy.

But procedures, or analytical systems, do not result in the creation of ethics or values. The fact that it is impossible (or absurd?) to put pluralism forward as an ethical theory, or at least as a framework of ethical reference, is the reason for most of its difficulties. These difficulties, especially in moments of economic/social crises, derive from its inability to foster the pursuit of common goals (if not of the "common good"). Goals not only like the reduction of inflation or of unemployment, but also of economic development as such (as Olson (1984) mentioned, in the macro-social application of his famous collective action model). And objectives regarding social groups (among these, for example, large sectors of marginal laborers) employed outside pluralistic relations. Or those of harmonization of the demands of the various groups represented, or of the pursuit of goals which truly regard collective goods. This certainly happens in pure pluralist systems, still quite far off "organized" pluralism, but we have to refer to it in order to grasp the basic dynamics.

The other major forms of regulation and representation of interests which have characterized the twentieth century are divided into the events, the successes and failures, and the strengths and weaknesses of pluralism: From the corporatism tending to state control of countries with weak pluralism, practiced by the authoritarian or right-wing totalitarian regimes in the Mediterranean or Eastern Europe between the two World Wars, to the collaboration, association, and participation situations (called "Neocorporative" in the vast and important political science literature of the 1970s) of the European social democratic-type experience after World War II, up to the attempts to return to market individualism made by advocates of neoconservatism (the 1980s in the US and the UK).

The break between pluralism and corporatism tending to state control is clean but, from many points of view, so is that between pluralism and the new returns to conservatism. Meanwhile, the continuity between pluralism and association/collaboration or "neocorporative" systems is evident. The latter could be defined as more or less "organized" pluralism. In fact, the large organizations operating within it continue to find their strength in their capacities of representation, even if they are aided by the delegation of public functions. The organized and controlled market does not stop providing criteria of regulation and reference. Collective bargaining does not disappear, replaced by laws; in fact in many cases it becomes stronger, albeit with more centralized structures. In the mechanisms regulating the relationship between state and society, the role of the "private governments" of associations, the participation into policy-making institutions, and the delegation of powers and responsibilities by the state is consolidated.

6.2 A Gap in the "Story"

If pluralism is the great political "invention" of the twentieth century, it has unfortunately found no wide or effective room for "application" in Latin America. The "story" has no characters, important events, or significant images in this part of the world. This is a point on which all the experts agree. O'Donnel (1976: p. 208) speaks for all and in a clear manner when he says that "Latin American society has never been (at least in the sense understood by the English-speaking parts of the world) pluralistic". The role of the political parties and the government has been very different from that of the constitutional democratic system: Furthermore, the "vertical" relations between the various social spheres have considerably complicated the structure of the "horizontal" class divisions. We can say (if a little simplistically) that clientelism and patrimonialism have represented the initial forms of articulation of civil society and of links with the state.

O'Donnel is echoed by those who analyze the various political cultures, starting from that in Argentina (Vacs 1987), which possesses to a greatest extent some of the conditions for helping the consolidation of pluralist relations, the first of these being the presence of a labor movement with organizational resources and industrial-type structures (the type of trade union which in other experiences was the main protagonist in the spreading of bargaining relations). "From the corporatist-ultrareactionary, through the economically liberal-politically dictatorial, to the leftist-authoritarian positions", A. C. Vacs wrote in a recent paper on the transition to democracy in Argentina (1987: p. 39) "a wide spectrum of anti-democratic groups have attacked the basis of pluralistic coexistence with different degrees of success."

The reasons for this gap, or latency, in the Argentine republic, as in other Latin American societies, are to be found on various planes: economic, social, and political. The market is fragmented and has never reached a sufficient level of "organization". Also, the exceptional dependence (political and economic) on foreign countries has prevented autonomous bargaining relations from establishing themselves within it. This factor can also be held responsible for the lack of "pure social protagonists" (Touraine 1987: p. 13), which can be defined as such independently of their political status, who are the fundamental creators of pluralist relations. Large-scale industry was slow to establish itself and, if it managed to, it did so as a result of state initiatives (similar in this case to the experience of European countries with weak pluralism like Italy).

In the early decades of the century the class structure did not reach the "simplifications" (such as the establishment of a large working class) that favor the development of large collective organizations. Income distribution in this area is still extremely unequal (J. D. Sachs 1988); in fact it is the most unequal in the world. Such distribution can herald explosive conflicts and strong pressure on the political system: It certainly does not encourage aggregation into large groups with negotiable aims. The trade union organization was, and still is, very fragmented: Industrial trade unions are not the typical form of organization (except in Argentina). The most widespread form of organization for labor remains that of the enterprise union (many of them multinational companies); confederate bodies have little organization resources or powers of negotiation (again Touraine 1987: pp. 44–45). The industrial system is too unequal and divided to give rise to effective representative organizations.

The claims, aspirations, and initiatives of state regulation of collective relations are considerable. The entire area is characterized by a glut of legislation governing labor relations, determining the limits of trade union freedoms and the right to strike, and limiting collective autonomy, with the sole exception of Uruguay. The latter is perhaps the only country with a voluntaristic tradition in industrial relations (H. Lucena 1989: pp. 15–16).

In this situation we cannot be amazed that the political system is still a long way, in general, from a liberal democratic situation; that the mobilization of civil society may appear a threat to the survival of these situations; and that the *polis* has few instruments for responding to changes in the *demos*. The dominant political culture seems more well disposed toward zero-sum conflicts than toward competition and cohabitation of groups. But the culture of civil society has also had difficulties considering democracy as a permanent value and not purely as a tactic (for these points of view, see also A. Stepan 1988: p. 129). On this level, significant changes are taking place (e.g. the transition in Chile). It will be necessary to see to what extent a new and perhaps fragile political culture will be handicapped by the weakness of pluralist relations.

6.3 Pluralism or Populism?

The 1930s were decisive years for changes in the forms of regulation of interests in Europe and North and South America. In Europe and North America the ways of reacting to the great crisis sparked off by governments and large organized groups resulted in either consolidation of the pluralistic situations (characterized by forms of association or collaboration) or, with the abandonment of pluralism, the abandonment also of democracy for right-wing totalitarian regimes. In the first case (North European countries and the US under Roosevelt) the result was the compromise between classes and groups which in the post-war period was known as Keynesian. The large groups which expressed pluralistic interests were in some way associated in the development and application of economic and social policies, on a permanent basis in Scandinavian countries, much less so in the United Kingdom and the United States. In the second case (symbolized by the end of Weimar Germany), it proved to be impossible to overcome the crisis and preserve democracy without making deep changes in the pluralistic situation. One of the most characteristic facets (or destinies) of pluralism was confirmed: That of a form of regulation required for liberal democratic regimes to be successful, which in a condition of tension or socio-economic crisis may, if not corrected, turn into a factor which aggravates the crisis. Corrections may, for example, prevent union action being totally dependent on the trends of the economic cycle, with the resultant collapse during phases of great depression. These forms of pluralism, based on organization and collaboration, had already been experienced by some countries during World War I (e.g. in the UK, with the *Whitley Model*). In some ways these are precursors of "political exchange". It is precisely that process of collaboration, and of "exchange", that it was not possible to spark off in the last years of the Weimar Republic, despite significant attempts to do so (for this subject, cf. Fauvel-Rouif 1966; Rusconi 1977; Cella 1979).

These were also decisive years for changes in the form of regulation of interests and political and trade union representative organization in Latin America. In these societies *populism* was a form of mass incorporation, of regulation of demands and protests, and of participation in development, which offered an alternative to pluralism. If one wants to find phrases to fit the purpose, one could say that from a practical and theoretical point of view populism constitutes the "corrected" pluralism typical of Latin American societies. This is a unique way of changing the previous forms of regulation, bringing about a process of incorporation of large sectors of the population and integration of the organized groups (especially the labor representative bodies, the groups which almost always become the fundamental instrument of support of populist experiences). Touraine (1987: pp. 139–170) pointed out the reasons for the peculiarities of these paths in countries in which the process of modernization, and of industrialization, is largely imported, or managed from outside. The theme of autonomous characterization of the economic development was an element missing from contemporary and successive European experiences. Touraine's words are quite effective "To overcome the external nature of economic and sometimes political power, the idea emerges that the purpose of development is not that of increasing the capacity to invest, but the level of participation and integration of a national society broken up or divided in two by the effects of heteronomous modernization. This is the definition of populism" (ibid., p. 139).

In this case, too, experts agree on the definition of the basic issues populism in the 1930s and the years after World War II was responding to. In the first place, to discover models of economic growth capable of reacting to the difficulties, aggravated by the crisis of the traditional model based on primary exports (this leads to the well-known strategy of import "substitution"). In the second place, to set up institutions capable of "incorporating" the new sectors and social groups on which the political mobilization is based (the trade union movement first of all). Finally, the formation of efficient coalition governments to guarantee the first two aims (Malloy 1987: p. 238. For a comparison between Cardenism, Peronism, and Varguism, cf. Ianni, 1989; on the Brazilian experience, also Weffort 1978). Generally speaking, populist policies lead to the balance of power (and the distribution of resources) being in favor of the urban classes. With the adoption of the "import substitution strategy" it becomes possible (in particular in Argentina) to increase salaries and the rate of unionization (Sheahan 1987: p. 84).

Populism, however, tends to link up with traditional processes of clientelism, and to refer to "patrimonial" relations. The model remains that of vertical integration. The social groups, or group coalitions, do not compete "pluralistically" with each other, or with other coalitions or the state. The systems of pluralistic competition are not able to develop. The groups instead belong to the apparatus of a political coalition, in the retinue of a strong political leadership. This is a consequence of the absence, or lack, of mediation between the state and the civil society by the political system. In a dual process of mass mobilization, and state control of civil society, it comes as no surprise that populistic situations are almost always accompanied by institutional transformations of a corporatist type, albeit of the type that Stepan (1978) defines as "inclusive", making a distinction between the two poles of state corporatism (the other being the "exclusive" pole toward popular sectors). The experiences of Brazil and Argentina are examples of this, although there are large differences between the two, for example that of the strength of the "incorporated" trade union movement. In the original structures and residues of the Vargasian *Estado Novo* the Brazilian trade union movement is weak (cf. B. Fausto 1986, and in particular L. Martins Rodrigues 1986). The Argentinian movement, on the other hand, was strong under the different Peronist governments (cf. J. E. Miguens and F. C. Turner 1988). From this point of view the Brazilian corporative system is the closest to the European corporatist tradition, even if it is characterized by a comprehensiveness and an "inter-sector" and "inter-category" extension rarely reached in Europe (see the neopatrimonialist practices that led to the so-called "cartorial" capitalism, i.e. capitalism based on concessions and protection; cf. Camargo 1989: pp. 28–33). The real exception is the Peronist system, the only historical case of corporatism based on strong, centralized trade unions with great capacities of mass mobilization and incorporation (J. C. Torre 1988).

The deterioration and failures of populism (in the 1950s in Argentina, the 1960s in Brazil, and again in the 1970s in Argentina, to mention the most sensational examples) led in some cases corporatist institutions developing toward "exclusive" (and more explicitly state-controlled) institutions, to use Stepan's image. Rather surprisingly, the populist experiences have substantially the same economic and political dynamics. They have several factors in common: the urban-based government, policies of redistribution, and the collapse of monetary reserves (Sachs 1988).

Somehow, and in some ways (e.g. the political result), the experience of the European countries with weak pluralist systems between the two World Wars (Italy, Spain, the Eastern European countries, but also Germany in that it was characterized by a weak pluralistic system within a strong industrial structure) is repeated.

In the authoritarian regimes that followed one another in Latin American societies during these years, this "exclusive" corporatist/statist-type of transformation was not, however, the rule. In some cases it was attempted with little success. The failure of General Ongan's attempt to create a coalition of the conservative/corporatist type during the period of the so-called Revolución Argentina (1966–1970) demonstrated the (residual) strength of the populist coalition. In this crisis, the Peronist trade union movement headed by the wing of the powerful leader Augusto Vandor backed the attempt to create an authoritarian corporatist system (Cavarozzi 1988: pp. 54–55). In this it revealed attractions to corporatist solutions (also of the state-controlled type) not lacking in other Latin American systems (cf. Valenzuela 1988), but also not unknown in the history of trade unions in Europe during the early decades of the century.

In other occasions and situations military governments did not even attempt to develop new corporatist structures or relations. The exclusion brought about by authoritarian regimes did not necessarily pass through the adoption of reinforcement of corporatist institutions. For example, after 1976 under the military governments, again in Argentina, there was a tendency to break off all links between economics and politics, reinforcing the alliances with the economic liberals sectors, lifting protectionist barriers, and putting the trade unions under military control (Vacs 1987: pp. 21–22). As has been clearly stated, the attempt to free the state from all corporative influences brought it under the aggregating influence of the military corporation or led to the construction of a "military regime dictatorship", free from any kind of links with civil society in its decision-making (Delgado and Stiletano 1988: pp. 59–69).

Pinochet's regime in Chile also tended to sever all the links between state and society, with the atomization of the society and moving away from the past, especially with the past of populist policy "incorporation" (Borzutzky 1987: p. 86). Unlike the Argentinian military regimes, however, it took on the distinct characteristics of a personal dictatorship. C Huneeus (1988: p. 93) noted accurately that "the personalization of power by General Pinochet as an element of the structure of the authority of the political system constitutes an exception among the *new authoritarian states*". This personalization did not require a very high level of "institutionalization" (Huneeus 1989: p. 158). As a consequence of this, there was perhaps less institutional innovation during the Chilean dictatorship than during the Argentinian one (cf. Cuevas (1989) on Chilean authoritarian institutions). The roads leading to corporatism were not, having been abandoned by the Brazilian military regimes, although with different emphasis before and during the period of *abertura*. The liquidation of populism, which turned out to be "incapable of reproducing a competitive social order or of spreading a capitalist ethos" (Martins 1988: p. 136), was carried out by the Brazilian army without rejecting all of the *issues* which populism was an answer to. The most important of these was that regarding industrial development guided and "administered" by the state.

From this point of view it is possible to redimension the significance of O'Donnel's famous definition (1987, although his first work on this theme was published in 1972) of bureaucratic/authoritian-type regimes. These have the following characteristics: (a) higher government positions are occupied by people coming from bureaucratic organizations; (b) political exclusion of working-class sectors is carried out not only by using repression, but also through corporatist controls of trade unions; (c) economic exclusion in the sense of deferment of all aspirations of participation; (d) cancellation of political involvement carried out through agreements between organization managements; and (e) deepening of the aspects of "dependent capitalism", although not completely separately from intensive industrialization (ibid., 1987: p. 21).

O'Donnel's definition would appear to be applicable only to authoritarian regimes which have followed corporatist paths (exclusive and tending toward state control): Brazil and Argentina in the second half of the 1960s. For the other areas of the Southern cone (Chile, Uruguay, and Argentina in the 1970s) a definition like "market/authoritarianism" (Sheahan 1987: p. 9) is more suitable. This means a forced return, using the main instrument of monetary policies, to regulation through typical criteria of market individualism, with drastic destructive effects on the already weak pluralistic fabric in these societies. We can imagine what a writer like Karl Polanyi, who died before their appearance, would have written about these regimes. He would have found dramatic confirmation of the "destructive" effects of the individualistic market on solidarity within societies.

It is not only out of a pure love of symmetry that we wish to mention how a process of this type, albeit with the formal protection of the rules of democracy, but with a noticeable reduction of the prerogatives and the autonomy of pluralistic relations, also took place during the same period in some of the major industrialized countries: the United States and the United Kingdom. These were the typical "birthplaces" (or "places of discovery") of pluralism, and also the situations which had made the least progress along the path of transformation of pluralism. It is as if pluralism and populism were watching each other from a distance, the former more solidly rooted than the latter, but not alien to some of the events of the latter, albeit always experienced in a less dramatic and devastating manner.

This is how the weakness of pluralism accompanies, and to a considerable extent explains, the weakness of democracy in Latin American societies. The Latin American alternative, populism, has certainly not been a solid base for polyarchies. This weakness is also present in the political culture of the left, where it has long been a minority idea.

However, if in the experience of this century, pluralistic organization and political democracy have mutually supported each other, it is also true that the crises, excesses, and difficulties of the former are a serious threat to the latter. Tensions in the field of pluralistic relations or economic/social problems (e.g. inflation) not manageable within or according to the logic of pluralism may lead to the collapse of democracies. This is what happened to the European experiences of weak pluralism which collapsed during the thirties under right-wing totalitarian regimes. Something of the sort happened also to the Latin American experiences through the ups and downs of populism, the form of regulation which had great opportunities of "incorporation", but little capacities of mediation between state and civil society, or of approach between *polis* and *demos*.

The path of collaboration/association in "organized" pluralism is the one that has guaranteed to the major industrialized countries more solid democratic situations. Our "story" (what radical critics of pluralism like Fox would call a "fairy-tale") should conclude that something of the kind could take place in Latin America, even if the conditions do not seem to be of the most favorable. In fact, populism has been accompanied by corporatist channels of the type tending toward state control, first of "inclusive" type but then, in the face of the crisis of populism itself, of exclusive type. From this point of view, the links between populism and liberal democratic situations appear to be very problematic, both in the rise of the former, and in its moments of crisis. Furthermore, the fragmentation of society, following the failures of populism, soon turned into phenomena of "pretorianization", that is, the sort of exasperated pluralism, without rules or methods, that comes about when different sectors of society come face to face over questions of power and the distribution of resources in the absence of institutions or organizations of mediation. Phenomena of this type preceded, or accompanied, the progressive militarization of society in Brazil, Uruguay, Chile, and Argentina (O'Donnel 1976; Moneta 1987).

The gap between populism and pluralism, in both their rise and their fall, widened as the century progressed. The hope remains that the logic of "pacts" will be able to help Latin American societies in their transition from authoritarian regimes. This logic ironically "brings a political community to democracy using non-democratic means" (O'Donnel and Schmitter 1988: p. 68). Pluralism had not supported the Latin American democracies, but "organized" versions of the same pluralism could bring these back on the scene after the drama of military dictatorships. It is well known that not everything which serves democracy is necessarily a part of democracy.

6.4 Possibilities of Associative Regulation

The weakness of the pluralistic organization of society and the related relations makes the transition to situations of collaboration/participation in Latin

America (or of "neocorporatism", if one wishes to use a concept which was invented for the leading industrial countries) difficult and problematic. These situations could turn out to be precious both to aid the change-over to democratic political regimes (from the preceding bureaucratic/authoritarian or market/authoritarian experiences), and to save these regimes traumas and tensions which could result from the pressure of excessive demand, particularly in the early stages of the transition to democracy and in rough economic situations (caused by inflation, unemployment, external or internal debt).

On the other hand, if pure pluralist organization and logic are not present in Latin America, then perhaps they are not desirable by those who pursue the polyarchic consolidation of these societies. Pluralism within a social structure which still has strong inequalities, within a segmented and weakly organized market, with poorly centralized representative organizations, and without great capacities of mediation in the political system, could have rapidly destructive effects on democracies in the transition stage, or in any case in the early stages of their life.

To further the success of associations as forms of social regulation, it may be useful to retain some of the institutional structures from the corporatist tradition (naturally of inclusive type), combined with the success of essential traits of pluralism, in particular those linked with the freedom to organize trade unions and of collective bargaining. Observers such as Diniz and Boschi (1988) agree on this fact. After noting that "a pluralist model, like a corporatist model, in its pure state can by no means be said to exist in modern-day reality", they recognize the "possibility of developments of the Latin-American systems toward more complicated structures, combining their strong tradition of corporatism with emergent pluralist arrangements" (p. 62).

The main features of pluralism are, however, necessary to make the system of industrial relations and representation of interests dynamic and flexible (by means of its partial transfer from the legal regulation, to partially subordinate it to the criteria of market regulation, to prevent degeneration into clientelism and to promote, as in Argentina, or to consolidate, as in Brazil, the spread of autonomous associations in civil society. The importance of these associations must be stressed. It is this presence which makes the Brazilian situation on the path of pluralism look positive in the Latin American panorama, despite the far from brilliant performance of the political system. In fact, as has been noted, "civil society became the political celebrity of the abertura"; in its role of opposition to the regime, it encouraged the establishment of links between groups which from other points of view were antagonists (like the entrepreneurs and metalworkers of the state of São Paulo) (Stepan 1988: p. 5). This collection of organized groups comprised a wide range of elements from the economic and industrial world, wide segments of the Catholic

Church, the lawyers' association, and even a new model of industrial trade unions (Duncan Baretta and Markoff 1987: pp. 46–48).

The crucial problem on the path toward polyarchic consolidation appears today to be that of regaining capacities of "incorporation" of wide sectors of society (from some aspects the same as the best moments of populism), not just to create distributive coalitions, but rather to reach common goals (some of which are real collective goods of wide-ranging significance: reduced inflation, debt management, more efficient public structures, the fight against social emargination, reduced unemployment, etc. The path of "social concertation" (whether or not this term is accepted) seems to have been laid, and to follow it requires social pact logic, political exchange relations, and the creation (or preservation/transformation) of institutional structures of the "neocorporatist" type (e.g. for industrial policy management). These are the structures which could lead to the creation of a source of consultancy and of decisions outside the political one, perhaps a "gradual" way of applying democracy, alongside legislation limiting inter-party competition and electoral choices. But as O'Donnel and Schmitter remind us (1988: pp. 26–28), the democratic process can allow such "gradual steps".

From a theoretical point of view, the advantages of this type of associative control are clearly outlined in an important essay of a few years ago by Streeck and Schmitter (1985). The essay arrived at the close of the debate and the research into neocorporatist situations, and perhaps was not fully appreciated. Again, the remarks refer mainly to the principal industrial countries, the pluralism of the strong, we could say. But the pluralism of the weak, in its excesses, can have similar problems of regulation from several points of view. "Associative control", based on government by private associations, may become an important source of social order, confounding a consolidated belief: "In the field of modern political and social thought, associations have always been considered more than anything else a cause of disorder" (p. 50). The functional advantages of private governments seem in some cases to be considerably important in comparison to other forms of regulation (the well-known trilogy of Polanyan origin): voluntary community action, state intervention, and market competition. There are advantages, for example, in the field of policy implementation (the associations which draw up agreements are the same ones ensuring that they are respected by their own members). And in the field of policy legitimation (a delicate and important matter in the context of a policy-making culture as strife-marked and characterized by ideological overloading as that of Latin America). It is the leaderships of the associations (e.g. entrepreneurs and trade-union) who sustain (appealing to widely divergent values, images, and traditions) the validity or value of a policy decided in an agreement between their members. There are also advantages on the level of the authority control of individual action which is necessary to furnish the collective good, but which may also be impossible in the voluntary logic, is destined to fail in market logic, and is unacceptable in a democratic state. Streeck and Schmitter affirm that "corporative/associative order emerges in mixed political contexts" (p. 78). These are contexts in which state intervention acts as direct regulation, but in which large areas are also left to the pluralist market. However, the authors continue, "public use of organized private interests requires a strong state rather than a weak one. It is true that association-based social order involves the delegation of state functions to intermediaries of interests, but this must be accompanied by the simultaneous acquisition by the state of the capacity to design, lead, and control the new systems of self-regulation" (p. 79).

This is an important statement, not just because of the conceptual status of associative control (in fact, some could doubt the theoretical autonomy of this form, and label it as a variation of state regulation), but also because of its practical implications in experiences like that of Latin America, where the fear that groups could attack the state apparatus through the channels of patronage and clientelism is always rife. This fear could be an element of legitimization of regressions to authoritarianism.

If it is certain that democracies can have comparative advantages over authoritarian regimes in their capacity for commanding respect of agreements or policies by exploiting, for example, fair cost allocation (Sheahan 1987: p. 120), it is equally true that all of this is only possible within structures of concertation and social regulation. Democracies should have the strength and the capacity (i.e. suitable institutions) to delegate duties of regulation to private associations. It is only through this type of institution that "unorthodox"-type anti-inflationary programs which combine income policies and tax consolidation policies, for example, have some chance of success (E. A. Cardoso 1989: pp. 40–41).

What conditions could make these situations of regulation possible in Latin American societies, and in particular those with a certain level of pluralist organization (cf. Cuevas 1986: pp. 59–83)? It is important not to exaggerate when establishing the conditions, and to bear in mind Hirschman's (1987) invitation to think not only and not so much in terms of probability, but in terms of possibility, in an attempt to overcome the *fracasomania* or the structuralist catastrophism typical among Latin American intellectuals. It would seem, above all, necessary for there to be sufficiently centralized and concentrated organizations representing interests, backed by adequate pluralist experience. From this point of view, if we continue in our comparison between Argentina and Brazil, the former would seem to be in a better position as far as organizational structures are concerned, and the latter as far as experience of pluralism goes. More centralized specialized structures would also be useful in the field of collective bargaining: for large sectors of industry on a national level in Argentina, and perhaps for industry on a state level in Brazil; in any case, bargaining structures which break the mold of exclusive bargaining by companies or in any case on a decentralized level, characteristic of bargaining experiences in Latin America (with the exception of Argentina), as in other areas with "weak" economies. This type of bargaining model leads to an adequate level of pluralistic organization within societies, although it does not prevent explosions of demands, and makes it difficult to pursue wage fairness policies. If a comparison is made between these two important experiences, as Sheahan has done very convincingly (1987: pp. 179–203), apart from the differences, we see the common necessities as far as cooperation and control of group "aggression" is concerned. However, a simple and crucial question comes to mind: "Can such systems perform well enough in economic terms to maintain their acceptance?"

Other necessary conditions regard the presence (or creation) of institutional bodies to implement concertation and also vertical participation/collaboration, and to avoid degeneration into clientelism and patrimonialism (cf. Malloy 1987). These institutional bodies will have to be linked to the existence of a political system which does not tend to superimpose itself onto civil society and its dynamics but, on the contrary, acts as intermediary between the political/institutional sphere and that of pluralistic relations (cf. Diniz and Boschi 1988: p. 89).

I will make a comparison between attempts at concertation and "pacts" in Brazil and Argentina elsewhere, as these two experiences make it possible to evaluate the possibilities of success of association-based regulation situations emerging from situations of weak pluralism within contexts of former (or still partial) corporatism. However, significant differences immediately emerge from the two contexts of regulation. In Brazil, some of the necessary conditions are missing, but policies (e.g. industrial policies) ever since the period of *abertura*, have featured some very interesting moments (we could mention the case of market reserve for the computer industry, which resulted in an alliance between the political left and the army; Stepan 1988: p. 126), and a few signs of willingness from the entrepreneurial sectors (Tavares de Almeida 1986). Even after the end of the military regime the possibilities of this kind of corporative arrangements still exist, although the influence of the organized groups does not appear to be exercised through explicit negotiations, but instead is limited to veto power. This confirms characteristics which have been a constant in the "transition modernization" in Brazil since the period of Vargas. Over the last few years the entrepreneurial associations have been excluded both from talks on the debt and from anti-inflationary policy-making talks. The employers will tend to react to these measures with their power of veto (Camargo 1989: p. 23). The regulating influence of the Brazilian state in the economic (and social) sphere is impressive from many points of view, and it has increased during the period of authoritarian rule, as can be seen by the disproportionate number of regulation councils and commissions set up in all fields by the military presidents, in particular the last one, J. Figueiredo, 1979–1984 (W. Guilherme dos Santos 1989: pp. 511–522). The institutional step necessary to guarantee the success of situations of concertation is the transformation of regulating corporatist bodies of this type into places for collaboration and negotiation capable of strengthening and "organizing" the pluralistic structure of the society.

In Argentina, the situation of competition and conflict of interests has been called one of "anarchic corporatism". This means it is a situation in which the protagonists, which are real corporations (trade unions, industrial and agricultural entrepreneurial associations, "privatized" segments of the state organization, the armed forces, etc.), act in the great public arenas uniquely in their own interests, without political mediation capable of imposing any general interest (O'Donnel 1984; Acuña *et al.* 1988: p. 27). This is a weak, but also "wild" and aggressive pluralism, which turns into "anarchic corporatism" because of the political system's incapacity to act as mediator. The traditional culture of much of Peronist trade unionism completes the picture: A unique mix of business unionism, conservative culture (with traces of authoritarianism and patrimonialism), attachment to the strong institutional power, and the memory of great movement in the past. This culture has led to systematic opposition of the economic policies of president Alfonsin, which resulted in an incredible thirteen general strikes under the first democratic government after the fall of the military dictatorship (Palomino 1989).

The situation of group aggressiveness and the traditional trade union culture have considerably undermined the favorable conditions for concertation in Argentina which are in some way present in the union representative structures (the Argentinian trade union movement is, after all, the only great unitary labor movement in Latin America). Another important feature is the shallowness of the military government policies (especially those of the "market authoritarian" type which followed the fall of the Peronist return governments), whose only skill was that of hard repression. However, the policies of the subsequent democratic governments have not been much better, and large areas of entrepreneurial sectors are still unwilling to collaborate (cf. de Riz *et al.* 1986).

6.5 The "Story" and Its Future

We have come to the end of our short "story" of pluralism. It has been short, but it corresponds to the history of the principal industrial countries during this whole century. The "story" relates the events, conjures up pictures, and evokes practices which have little in common with Latin American societies. It has been noted that the weakness of the structure of pluralism in society can certainly act as an obstacle to democracy (this has been the case in the past, and could still be so in the future for the democracies which follow a long period of military dictatorship).

However, it is not as certain that we should wish for the widespread application of pluralist logic and dynamics. The risk of a slow or rapid return to the path of populism (the logic and form of representation still more deeply rooted in these societies, where it has been an alternative to pluralism) could be more than just a theoretical possibility. And in this case the danger of the resurrection, as Malloy astutely notes (1987: p. 239), of the populism/anti-populism cycle which is the driving force of the authoritarianism/democracy cycle would emerge. With regard to this, nobody is sure that it will ever be finally replaced, perhaps because of the favorable international political situation, with a trend of development from the first to the second.

The path of regulation of the type based on association/collaboration would seem to be the best one to consolidate the polyarchies. It could perhaps make use of some features of the populist tradition (and also of inclusive-type corporatism heritage), made more dynamic and "controllable" by the spread of pluralist practice and criteria. It could happen this way, but this is only a hope for the future, which as in the European countries where pluralism has a strong framework, practice based on association/collaboration (or "neo-corporatism") has controlled (or blocked) the political business cycle (cf. Bordogna and Provasi 1984), in Latin American societies it could prevent the democracy/authoritarianism cycle or significantly reduce its political/social significance and relevance. The hope is that this path, too, will strengthen the implementation of democracy in the future, and not frustrate a pluralist political culture which, it must not be forgotten, is still a novelty among Latin American intellectuals and politicians. This is in order not to make the risks of "banal democracy" embodied in these sceptical words by a Brazilian political writer (Renato Lessa 1989: p. 182) come true: "Beyond the theme of institutional decadence there is also that of banal democracy, a political system characterized by freedom of association, great electoral incorporation, a multi-party system, elections at all levels, freedom of the press, of worship, of belief, etc., but in which nothing happens."

References

Acuña, C., M. Cavarozzi, L. de Riz., E. Jelin, and O. Oszlak (1988): Estado, politica y actores sociales en la Argentina contemporanea. In AA. VV. (1988): *Hacia un nuevo orden estatal en America Latina?*, Vol. 1. Buenos Aires: Clacso.

Bordogna, L. and G. Provasi (1984): *Politica, economia e rappresentanza degli interessi.* Bologna: Il Mulino.

Borzutzsky, S. T. (1987): The Pinochet Regime: Crisis and Consolidation. In: *Authoritarians and Democrats*, Malloy, J. M. and M. A. Seligson (eds.). Pittsburgh, Penn.: University of Pittsburgh Press.

Camargo, A. (1989): As dimensões da crise. In: *Continuidade e mudança no Brasil da Nova República*, Camargo, A. and E. Diniz (eds.). São Paulo: Vertice-IUPERJ.

Cardoso, E. A. (1989): Hiperinflação na América Latina. *Revista de Economia Politica*, 9 (3), 21–42.

Cavarozzi, M. (1988): Ciclos politicos na Argentina a partir de 1955. In: *Transições do regime autoritario. America Latina*, O'Donnel, G., P. C. Schmitter, and L. Whitehead (eds.). São Paulo: Vertice.
Cella, G. P. (ed.) (1979): *Il movimento degli scioperi nel XX secolo*. Bologna: Il Mulino.
Cella, G. P. (1989): *La solidarietà possibile*. Roma: Edizioni Lavoro.
Clegg, H. A. (1975): Pluralism in Industrial Relations. *British Journal of Industrial Relations*, XIII (3).
Cuevas, A. (1986): *Democrazia e sviluppo*. Roma: Edizioni Lavoro.
Cuevas, A. (ed.) (1989): *Le istituzioni autoritarie*. Roma: Edizioni Lavoro.
Dahl, R. (1982): *Dilemmas of Pluralist Democracy*. New Haven, Conn.: Yale University Press.
Dahl R. (1988): Poliarquía, pluralismo y magnitud. *Opciones*, 14, 9–28.
Delgado, D. G. and M. Stiletano (1988): La participación de los militares en *los nuevos autoritarismos*: la Argentina del «proceso» (1976–1983). *Opciones*, 14, 55–88.
Diniz, E. and R. R. Boschi (1988): La consolidación democratica en Brasil: procesos sociales, intermediación de intereses y modernización del Estado. In: AA. VV. (1988), op. cit.
Duncan Baretta, S. R. and J. Markoff (1987): Brazil's *Abertura*: A Transition from What to What? In: Malloy, J. M. and M. A. Seligson (eds.), op. cit.
Fausto, B. (ed.) (1986): *O Brasil Republicano. 3. Sociedade e Politica (1930–1964)*. São Paulo: Difel.
Fauvel-Rouif, D. (ed.) (1966): *Mouvements ouvriers et dépression économiques de 1929 à 1939*. Assen: Van Gorcum.
Fox, A. (1973: Industrial Relations: A Social Critique of Pluralist Ideology. In: *Man and Organization*, Child, J. (ed.). London: Allen & Unwin.
Grandi, M. (1982): Otto Kahn-Freund: un «pluralista» atipico? In: *Il pluralismo e il diritto del lavoro*, Balandi, G. G. and Sciarra, S. (eds.). Roma: Edizioni Lavoro.
Guilherme dos Santos, W. (1989): El siglo de Michels: Competencia oligopolica, logica autoritaria y transición en America Latina. In: *Muerte y resurrección. Los partidos politicos en el autoritarismo y las transiciones en el cono Sur*, Cavarozzi, M. and M. A. Garreton (eds.). Santiago: FLACSO.
Hirschman, A. (1987): Economia e politica nello sviluppo dell'America Latina: un'analisi comparata. *Stato e Mercato*, 21, 305–343.
Huneeus, C. (1988): El Ejército y la politica en el Chile de Pinochet. Su magnitud y alcances. *Opciones*, 14, 89–136.
Huneeus, C. (1989): La derrota del general Pinochet. *Opciones*, 15, 155–179.
Ianni, O. (1989): *A formação do estado populista na América Latina*. São Paulo: Editoria Atica.
Lessa, R. (1989): Reflexões sobre a gènese de uma democracia banal. In: *Modernização e consolidação democrática no Brasil: Dilemas da Nova República*, Diniz, E., R. Boschi, and R. Lessa (eds.). São Paulo: Vertice-IUPERJ.
Lucena, H. (1989): Il ruolo dello stato nelle relazioni industriali in America Latina. *Industria e Sindacato*, 46.
Malloy, J. M. (1987): The Politics of Transition in Latin America. In: Malloy, J. M. and M. A. Seligson (eds.), op. cit.
Martins, L. (1988): A «liberalização» do regime autoritário no Brasil. In: O'Donnel, G., P. C. Schmitter and L. Whitehead (eds.), op. cit.
Martins Rodrigues, L. (1986): Sindicalismo e classe opéraria (1930–1964). In: Fausto, B. (ed.), op. cit.
Miguens, J. E., and F. C. Turner (eds.) (1988): *Racionalidad del peronismo*. Buenos Aires: Planeta.
Moneta, C. (1987): Fuerzas armadas y gobierno constitucional después de la Malvinas: Hacia una nueva relación civil-militar. In *Sintesis*, 2, 300–324.
O'Donnel, G. A. (1972): *Modernización y Autoritarismo*. Buenos Aires: Editorial Paidós.

O'Donnel, G. A. (1976): *Sobre el «corporatismo» y la cuestión del Estado*. Documento Cedes/Clacso, 2, Buenos Aires. (In: *Sviluppo capitalistico dipendente e regimi burocratico-autoritari*, Cerase F. P. (ed.). Roma: Carucci, 1984.)
O'Donnel, G. A. (1984): *Y a míque me importa?* Buenos Aires: Estudios Cedes.
O'Donnel, G. A. (1987): *Reflexões sobre os estados burocráticos-autoritários*. São Paulo: Vertice.
O'Donnel, G. A. (1988): Introdução aos casos latino-americanos. In: *Transições do regime autoritario. America Latina*, O'Donnel, G. A., P. C. Schmitter, and L. Whitehead (eds.). São Paulo: Vertice.
O'Donnel, G. A. and P. C. Schmitter (1988): *Transições do regime autoritario. Primeiras conclusões*. São Paulo: Vertice.
Olson, M. (1984): *Ascesa e declino delle nazioni*. Bologna: Il Mulino.
Palomino, H. (1989): *Democratización y crisis: los dilemmas del sindicalismo argentino*. Paper presented to the CLACSO Symposium on «Sindicalismo y transición democrática», Santiago, 1989.
de Riz, L., M. Cavarozzi, and J. Feldman (1986): El movimiento sindical y la concertación en la Argentina actual. In: *El sindicalismo latino-americano en los ochenta*. Santiago: Clacso.
Rusconi, G. E. (1977): *La crisi di Weimar*. Torino: Einaudi.
Sachs, J. D. (1988): Social Conflict and Populist Policies in Latin America. Paper presented to the Seminar on «Markets, Institutions and Cooperation: Labour Relations and Economic Performances», Venezia, Ottobre, 1988.
Seligson, M. A. (1987): Democratization in Latin America: The Current Cycle. In: Malloy, J. M. and M. A. Seligson (eds.), op. cit.
Sheahan, J. (1987): *Patterns of Development in Latin America*. Princeton, NJ: Princeton University Press.
Stepan, A. (1978): *The State and Society: Peru in Comparative Perspective*. Princeton, NJ: Princeton University Press.
Stepan, A. (1988): *Rethinking Military Politics*. Princeton, NJ: Princeton University Press.
Streeck, W. and P. C. Schmitter (1985): Comunità, mercato, stato e associazioni? Il possibile contributo dei governi privati all'ordine sociale. *Stato e Mercato*, 13, 47–86.
Tavares de Almeida, M. H. (1986): Sindicalismo brasileiro e pacto social. *El sindicalismo...*, cit.
Torre, J. C. (ed.) (1988): *La formación del sindicalismo peronista*. Buenos Aires: Legasa.
Touraine, A. (1987): *Actores sociales y sistemas politicos en America Latina*. Santiago: Prealc-OIT.
Vacs, A. A. (1987): Authoritarian Breakdown and Redemocratization in Argentina. In: Malloy, J. M. and M. A. Seligson (eds.), op. cit.
Valenzuela, S. (1988): *Labor Movements in Transitions to Democracy: A Framework for Analysis*. «Working Paper» n. 104, Kellog Institute, Notre Dame (In.).
Veca, S. (1989): *Una filosofia politica della cittadinanza*. Paper presented to the seminar of Cortona, Fondazione G. Feltrinelli, on «Libertà e cittadinanza sociale, I due '89: dalla rivoluzione francese alla seconda internazionale».
Weffort, F. (1978): *O populismo na politica brasileira*. Rio de Janeiro: Paz e Terra.

7 Social Concertation in Mexico

Francisco Zapata

The Mexican political system, closely related to Schmitter's definition of corporatism (1979),[1] is a prototype of social concertation, conceived in terms of a system where economic activity, investment, and in general terms, political, economic, and social development does not result from the operation of a free market (where private entrepreneurs play the central role) or from dictatorial, State initiative but from concerted action among unions, entrepreneurs, and the government. The identification of Mexican corporatism with social concertation results from the permanence of this system. Indeed, for the last fifty years, Mexico has been managed by arrangements institutionalized in the Institutional Revolutionary Party (Partido Revolucionario Institucional, PRI) which is composed of three "sectors": the worker, peasant, and popular organizations. Concertation between the leadership of these "sectors" and of each of them with their respective rank and file members has been the dominant characteristic of political life in Mexico since the 1930s when it was implanted during the government of president Lázaro Cárdenas (1934–1940). The entire decision-making process rests upon a structure centered on the PRI which is directly accountable to the president of the country who thus controls both the State and the party. As we shall see, most of the decisions concerning the role of labor and business in the process of economic development have been the result of concertation imposed by the government on both of these actors, in the various scenes where they are represented (National Commission of Minimum Salaries, the Mexican Institute for Social Security, National Institute for Public Housing, etc.). Even collective bargaining can be subject to this procedure because the Ministry of Labor tends to fix maximum salaries or acceptable fringe benefits. Historically speaking, the structure we have described forces all political and social

[1] Schmitter's definition (see Schmitter, Philippe (1979): Still the Century of Corporatism. In: *Trends Toward Corporatist Intermediation*, p. 13, Schmitter, Philippe and Gerhard Lehmbruch (eds.). Sage Publications) reads as follows: "Corporatism is a system where constituent units are organized into a limited number of singular, compulsory, non-competitive, hierarchically ordered and functionally differentiated categories, recognized or licensed (if not created) by the State and granted a deliberate representational monopoly within their respective categories in exchange for observing certain controls on their selection of leaders and articulation of demands and supports".

actors to act in relation to one another in the context of a *primus-inter-pares* identified with the government.

In recent years, the impact of economic and political crisis (closely related to the debt problem) has strained Mexican corporatism. But, and this will be the point of view we will argue in this paper, the system has been able to face those strains and pressures and is trying to renovate leaderships and institutions, and has committed itself to reform everything, from the Labor Law to the Electoral Law passing by less significative matters, such as the access to public television, para-estatal enterprise, and the primary school curricula. The promotion of these reforms is tied to the objective of re-establishing legitimacy toward the political system, which has been questioned recently by the appearance of higher levels of opposition to the governing party and which reflected clearly in the 1988 presidential elections. At the same time, the implementation of reform has reflected in the magnification of social concertation as "the" mechanism to make them work. Present-day Mexico is witnessing systematic efforts to place concertation at the center of a strategy of economic and political relegitimation. Therefore, the content it takes, while specific to the national context, can also have some interest for other situations. This will be the stance taken here: Simultaneously describe the Mexican situation and consider its wider implications.

7.1 The Historical Legacy

When the House of World Labor (Casa del Obrero Mundial) was created in 1912, Mexican labor acquired representation within the revolutionary process that had started in 1910, achieving an identity it did not previously possess. This participation led to the agreement signed in 1915 whereby the Casa committed its support to the so-called "constitutionalist" fraction of the revolutionary movement, in exchange for economic and social benefits (Carr 1974).[2] At this time, what would later become a basic commitment on the part of the State to respond to workers' support, became established. The principal labor confederations, the Mexican Regional Workers' Confederation (Confederación Regional de Trabajadores de México—CROM) created in 1918 and the Mexican Workers' Confederation (Confederación de Trabajadores de México—CTM), created in 1936 would encarnate the political project that consolidated in the 1920s and 1930s as a result of the institutionalization of the revolution. Specifically, the promulgation of the Mexican Constitution of 1917 and the passage of the Federal Labor Law in 1931 (regulating article 123 of the Constitution) were the institutional mechanisms through which labor adhered to the State and subordinated its strategy to it. Both the CROM and the CTM represented explicit commit-

[2] See Carr, Barry (1974): *El movimiento obrero y la politica en México: 1910–1929*, Secretaría de Educación Pública (SEP), Colección SRP-60, México.

ments of labor to the pursuit of the objectives of the Mexican revolutionary State. Their leaders, Morones, Lombardo Toledano, and, later, Fidel Velazquez, became ministers, headed political organizations and parties, wrote about the coincidence between the aspirations of the workers, and the ends pursued by the State.

This process entailed benefits for the expansion of the labor movement. Unionization increased, collective bargaining expanded in the oil, mining, and textile economic branches. During the 1930s and 1940s control was not extensive on leftist presence but, ideologically, the left responded favorably to the populist project pursued by the regime. This permitted across the board alliances and support of the large industrial unions to the political project of the State. It was only at the end of the 1940s that these agreements began to break up and that the CTM acquired total control of labor's manifestations. In any case, "class confrontation" was never central to Mexican politics. Conflict was centered more on foreign domination of the economy, especially in the oil industry, but also in railroads, electricity production, and mining. This is very clear if we remember the decision to nationalize the oil companies, taken by president Lázaro Cárdenas in 1938. In this instance, which began as a simple labor relations problem between the foreign oil companies and the various unions representing the workers, it is clear that confrontation was not the result of the disagreements between capital and labor but between the State and the foreign companies. Cárdenas gave his support to the unions and ratified an alliance that had been in the making since 1912. The corporatist structure was becoming gradually established.

The description of this process would not be complete without mentioning the capacity of the State to incorporate the business group into the political structure.

Indeed, the promulgation of the Law of Business Chambers (Ley de Cámaras) in 1936 was the basis for the consolidation of ties between the Mexican State and entrepreneurs. In a similar way as relations were established with the workers' organizations, those established with business interests tended to be related vertically to the State. Not only for corporate objectives such as prices, credits, or guarantees for foreign loans but also for political reasons, linked to the space that business groups wanted to occupy to put forward their views on the future of Mexico, was this scheme built. In the next decades, this arrangement was to prove its efficiency for the management of Mexico's economy and political system. As Roger Hansen argues (1970),[3] each actor in the corporate structure fulfilled a part of the total responsibility of organizing the development of the country. Labor assured wage control through different pacts, the most significant of which was signed during World War II and permitted intense use of productive facilities.

[3] See Hansen, Roger (1970): *The politics of Mexican development*. The Johns Hopkins Press: Baltimore.

Business assured investment through different schemes, the most important of which was perhaps the one established with Nacional Financiera, Mexico's development bank. The State, the third partner in the arrangement, not only acted to guarantee agreements between capital and labor but also actively intervened to invest on its own parastatal sector (steel, oil, sugar). It is important, then, to keep in mind this situation to understand adequately the way in which the Mexican corporatist system has been operating for the last fifty years.

The results of the control upon capital and labor paid off in terms of the resulting high rates of economic growth. The Gross Domestic Product grew at a rate of 6.1% in the 1941–1946 period, at 5.7% in that of 1947–1952, and at 6.4% in the period 1953–1958, all average rates for the periods involved. Real salaries actually decreased and did so up to 1958–1959 when they began an upward trend that did not last very long, given that in 1974 inflation began to be felt in the economy. In addition, the average salary in thirty-five industries declined some 26% over the period 1939–1950, showing the decade of the 1940s to be the one with the most intense accumulation. Where the process was acutely felt was in agriculture where the rural minimum salary fell 46% in the same period mentioned before. Such income data demonstrate the existence of a very efficient system of allocation of responsibilities for Mexico's development. Capital accumulation enjoyed optimum conditions and did not imply political instability, as it did in other countries. On the contrary, for most of the period, labor peace was the rule rather than the exception, especially in comparison with the Cárdenas period, when labor mobilization was rampant. However, one ought to mention that despite the decline in real salaries, worker benefits in housing, education, health, and social security experienced substantial improvements in the same period. The creation of the Mexican Institute for Social Security (Instituto Mexicano del Seguro Social—IMSS) in 1940 and twenty years later of the Institute for Social Security for the Workers in the Service of the State (Instituto de Seguridad y Servicios Sociales de los Trabajadores al Servicio del Estado—ISSSTE) as well as other institutions in the housing field (Instituto para el Fomento de la Vivienda de los Trabajadores—INFONAVIT), without mentioning the fact that education from kindergarten to the university is free, point toward the existence of a type of trade-off between real salary deterioration in the period 1940–1960 and the promotion of the welfare state. What labor did not obtain in salaries it obtained collectively through benefits provided directly by the State rather than by entrepreneurs. Such improvements help to explain why the alliance has persisted even if the economy has undergone serious pressures from foreign debt, decline of growth rates, unemployment, and lack of productive investment.

Mexican labor maintained a relationship with the State that relied not only on the satisfaction of employment and salary demands but also and especially on the satisfaction of the collective needs of the country's workers, such as housing, social security, health benefits, and education. This trade-off resulted from the mediating character of the labor movement which gave the Mexican State its support in exchange for those benefits. At the same time, it assured labor's quiescence: In fact, strike activity was very weak all through the period of industrialization through import substitution, especially if one compares it to the high proportion of workers that were unionized.[4] This means that the labor movement was and is an essential agent of control of workers' demands. This benefitted the State in political terms and the business class in economic terms. Business' needs for a stable workforce, for limits on salary increases, for labor peace, and for adequate facilities for the reproduction of the working class were amply satisfied by the social concertation that was practiced in the long period 1940–1976. Trade-offs of economic and political demands between labor and the State reinforced the process of capital accumulation and maintained the legitimacy of the political system.

But, obviously, since 1976, things have began to look a little different. Starting with the devaluation of August 1976 and the crisis of the years 1977–1979, which were interrupted by the oil boom of the period 1980–1982 for a short while, and continuing with the never-ending crisis derived from the debt, the Mexican political and economic system has been undergoing radical pressures that have questioned the "business as usual" attitudes of some politicians. Several processes are taking place in parallel: On the one hand, the liquidity (or cash flow problem) question puts the State in a difficult position with respect to its capacity to honor its side of the trade-off with the labor movement. It is harder and harder to finance subsidies to health, education, housing, and basic food (milk, "tortillas", and transportation). On the other hand, an apparent effort to curb corruption by the De La Madrid government did not prosper but the Mexican people got a glimpse of what was going on in the oil industry, for example (through the incarceration of the director general of the national oil company, Petroleos Mexicanos). But, clearly, the most recent and most serious challenge to the system came at the 1988 presidential elections when the official candidate almost lost. It is clear that the present president, Salinas De Gortari, who is in charge for the period 1988–1994, will have to face increasing challenges on all three fronts: economic, social, and political. It is here that the theme of this paper becomes central; indeed, social concertation has began to be the principal mechanism through which challenges to the Mexican political system have began to be faced. This process has been centered on the control of inflation but, through it, many other aspects of the crisis have been countered. Let us try to see in more detail the type of social concertation that is presently going on in

[4] See Zapata, Francisco (1986): *El conflicto sindical en America Latina*, El Colegio de Mexico; also Zapata, Francisco (1983): Les conflits du travail au Mexique depuis 1934. *Problèmes d'Amérique Latine*, p. 69. Paris.

Mexico and focus on some of the implications this concrete experience may have for other national situations.

7.2 Social Concertation in the 1980s

Increases in inflation, serious drops in real salaries, prices of public services falling behind costs, instability in the foreign currency market, erratic fluctuations in the Mexican exchange, and, last but not least, high degrees of uncertainty in the perspectives of the international markets, to which Mexican products are exported, forced a decision that took the form of a *Pact of Economic Solidarity* signed by business, labor, and the government on 15 December 1987.[5] In this pact, specific policies on public income, public expenses, salary policy, price control, trade policy, currency policy, and monetary policy were determined and coincided with the objective of stabilizing an economic situation that was going out of hand. It was explicitly stated that "today, to the governmental leadership has been added the solidary attitude of all the productive sectors of the nation and thereby, in a common front, give solutions to the issues that affect us". In addition, in the conclusion to the text of the pact it is said: "protected by the law and with the support of the *institutions* that the people have created and through the National System of Democratic Planning, solution has been given to participation and the contribution of everyone. The common objective is to eradicate inflation, make the economy grow under sane bases and suppress social hatred; in sum, to advance with greater speed in the construction of the *great national project*". These sentences are evidences that confirm the importance of the pact, conceived as a social concertation mechanism, to face the difficulties of the country. If the pact is to be treated as a specific economic strategy, the way to put it into practice has involved political measures of profound significance. A comparative evaluation of these pacts for Argentina, Brazil, and Mexico has shown that it has worked in this country essentially because the political dimension has played such an important role. In the other countries, all through 1986–1987 and 1988, some types of pact have been put into place but all have failed because of the absence of the political coincidence between the three actors: labor, business, and government (Roxborough 1989).[6]

[5] The text of the *Pact of Economic Solidarity* appears in Banco Nacional de Mexico (BANAMEX), *Examen de la situación económica de México*, January 1988. Analytical comments appear in: [No anthon], Ni pacto, ni solidaridad, *El Cotidiano*, 21, January–February 1988, and Rangel, José, La inflación como recuperación de la ganancia, *El Cotidiano*, 23, May–June 1988. Its implications for the relation between labor and corporatism, see De la Garza, Enrique, Para-estatales y corporativismo, *El Cotidiano*, 28, March–April 1989.

[6] See Roxborough, Ian (1989): Organized Labor: A Major Victim of the Debt Crisis. In: *Debt and Democracy in Latin America*, Stallings, Barbara and Robert Kaufman (eds.). Boulder, Colorado: Westview Press.

Nevertheless, not all rests upon the mere signing of a document in the presence of the representatives of all actors involved. In recent months, the State and the labor movement have consistently tried to maintain social cohesion among workers and unions by showing the centrality of the labor movement in the political system and their responsibility in putting the country out of the mess it is in. A good indicator of the relative success of this strategy has been the incapacity of the political opposition to recruit support among the members of the "official labor movement". Blue-collar workers have not changed political allegiance massively. The PRI seems to retain a virtual monopoly over worker ideological views. No animosity against the State seems to originate in the labor sector. The few demands that the pact has granted are presented as if they resulted from the strength of the labor movement in the political sphere and not as a direct concession of the State. Thus, labor's confederations appear as efficient representatives of labor demands and the State accepts this as the price to pay for the relegitimation of the system. How has concertation operated in the recent period? What are the attitudes of the actors concerned and what has been the form that concertation has taken? Finally, what are the levels at which concertation has operated and what have been the principal outcomes observed? These questions are at the core of the analysis of the Mexican's situation but, at the same time, the answers we can give to them can contribute to a general conclusion about the significance of contemporary social concertation.

7.2.1 Attitudes of the Actors in Social Concertation

Trade unions, employers, and the State continue to interact within the corporatist structure that was established in the 1930s. The change of name, with the introduction of social concertation has not modified the essential character of the way these actors behave in relation to one another and especially in relation to the State. Unions and business chambers recognize their subordination to the State while contributing to the implementation of the objectives promoted by it. Thus, one cannot identify important changes in the strategies of these actors as a result of present-day social concertation. Perhaps the institutions where they come together work more intensively and the rhetoric associated to the implementation of the Pact of Economic Solidarity has become overwhelming. One good example of this situation is the present negotiation about reforms to the Federal Labor Law where the three actors are discussing accommodations to the needs of the new economic strategy in the labor field. The State has confirmed the maintenance of the social security apparatus while recommending the introduction of measures geared toward the flexibilization of procedures concerning hiring and firing of personnel, the operation of promotion through merit schemes instead of seniority, the elimination of clauses in collective contracts that limit management's prerogatives in the workplace, and, last but not least, liberalization of salary conditions with the elimination of minimum salaries. While not yet approved, it is clear that a new trade-off is in the offing. It takes away from unions and workers certain benefits but maintains others, such as those associated to social security, that give them some guarantee that the modernization of the social relations of production will not end all their historical achievements. In this way, State intervention in labor relations is not receding. Trade unions and employers have accepted to renovate their traditional ways of interacting and have been able to process change and modernization without "rocking the boat" in dangerous ways. One can conclude that actors have been able to maintain corporatist institutions within its structural limits.

7.2.2 Form of Concertation

It is clear, from what has been said up to now, that Mexican corporatism is operating today under the guise of social concertation. In our opinion, there are no fundamental changes in the structure of the system. It is perhaps operating under pressure and within time constraints derived from the difficulties in honoring trade-offs between the State and trade unions and from the external demands for the payment of the foreign debt. In addition, one must mention the problems derived from the electoral results of July 1988 and the appearance of a stronger opposition in front of the PRI. But, by no means is the game played out. The system is experiencing serious challenges from within and from without but it is using, to the full, the mechanisms that were established in the 1930s to confront them.

Therefore, the form that social concertation had taken in the implementation of the solidarity pacts does not mean that the corporatist structure has changed its contents. On the contrary, the labor movement, business organizations, and governmental representatives are interacting with one another more efficiently than ever before because now the challenges are there, pressuring them to really solve what is in front of them. Inflation, salary control, interest rate control, price control are all subject to negotiation and the implementation of the strategy signed in December 1987 and renewed in December 1988 reflects basic agreements among these actors. Traditional forms have shown their validity and their operational capabilities in present-day Mexico.

In general terms, one can say that the Mexican arrangement shows that when a structure is present where actors are able to interact on the basis of non-ideologically motivated consensus, and where this consensus results from a long history where all three central actors have played a central role, the feasibility of present-day social concertation is much higher than when these elements are not present. In addition, social concertation taking place within this context is not something new: Actors have played other "plays" in different circumstances, perhaps in more positive circumstances and are therefore able to confront present challenges with much more maturity than if they didn't have that history behind them. Their capacity to concur within solutions that are acceptable to each of them taken separately is enhanced by the existence of this corporatist structure. It is evident, then, that social concertation is not more than another name for corporatism in a situation, such as the Mexican one, where this system has been in operation for such a long time. But, it is also evident that it is much harder to operate when such a corporatist structure is not in existence and where it is necessary to build from scratch. The feasibility of social concertation in this second scenario is harder to imagine than in the first one.

7.2.3 Levels of Concertation

Concertation and corporatism are located, by definition, at the macro level. State supervision is ever present and, frequently, the operation of the system results from direct intervention of the State in the promotion of specific objectives. Nonetheless, some degree of concertation has been taking place at the sectorial level, in the telephone, steel, and railroad sectors. Discussions about technological modernization, lay-offs, revision of collective contracts to eliminate clauses that block innovation, or promotion through merit, have resulted in new agreements. Clearly, they have not been easy to implement. Tensions have arisen, especially in the question of collective lay-offs in the steel sector. Here, the official labor leadership, fully incorporated into the corporatist structures, has succeeded in forcing workers to accept lay-offs in exchange for emergency employment programs. Nevertheless, the importance of some of these measures (in the case of one steel plant, more than 25,000 workers were laid off, in another more than 8,000) has resulted in dissatisfaction derived from the incapacity to implement the trade-offs in an efficient way. Animosity has appeared against the labor leadership that is more and more identified with management. Loss of labor's legitimacy is rampant in steel, mining, air transportation, the oil industry, and urban transportation. It may also erupt in the automobile industry where foreign competition may force the transnational corporations in charge to pressure workers to accept less salaries and less fringe benefits to assure the competitive position of the industry in the future.

Finally, no micro or meso concertation has taken place in this country. It would be contradictory for the corporatist structure and would endanger the central role occupied by the State in the promotion of the strategy. Social concertation, located at the highest level, has not been decentralized nor sectorialized. Perhaps this is so because the strategy is too young for it to have engendered a more localized impact, for example, in the level of the enterprise. But, it is evident that, sooner or later, it will have to do so. Indeed, macro-level strategies for the control of the overall economy, or reform to the labor law will have to become much more specific to take into account the needs of sectors, regions, markets, etc. Something has happened in this respect in the off-shore industry located in the northern border of Mexico where management and labor have succeeded in signing contracts where worker participation has been almost non-existent and thereby have been able to grant most of what the foreign managers of the companies could want. Nevertheless, it is not likely that this will be easily generalized to the rest of the economic sectors and particularly to the principal enterprises of the public sector such as steel, oil, electricity, railroads, telephones, and air transportation. The labor leadership will have to take into account a more militant rank and file that will not agree easily to the kind of things that are being applied in the north.

7.2.4 Outcomes of Social Concertation

If measured in terms of the *Pact for Economic Solidarity*, weekly evaluations made by a commission made up of government ministers, labor leaders, and business representatives show that the process has been very successful. Indeed, inflation has decreased to 19.2% in the period April 1988–April 1989 from 161.4% in the period April 1987–April 1988. The peso/dollar parity was fixed for the whole year 1988. Only interest rates have shown resistance to decreasing their high levels, superior to 50% on average during the period 1988–1989, thus giving an important premium to savers who keep their money in Mexico. Also, the control of wages has succeeded, given that they have not increased more than half of what inflation has increased in the same period.

Thus, social concertation has been able to stabilize the economy and at the same time it has been successful in promoting the new development project geared toward non-traditional exports. Business sectors have been cooperating by penetrating foreign markets and modifying their internal strategies to face stiff competition from imports that have been arriving as a result of decreases in customs rights. The entrance of Mexico into GATT was not as traumatic as some businessmen thought and, apparently, Mexican industry has been successful in facing foreign competition.

However, it is difficult to predict what will happen if some of the prerequisites of the pact are not operational. For example, if demands for salary increases exceed the capacity of the State or of business to grant them (that has began to appear in the teacher's union strike of April—May 1989) or if the peso/dollar parity has to be changed dramatically to permit interest payments of the foreign debt, it will be inevitable to see growing inflationary pressures in the economy. Thus, present concertation efforts could enter some turbulence if the actors in specific places of the political and economic structure begin fighting for particular benefits.

The same thing will happen if the political pressures that appeared after the presidential elections of July 1988 continue to exert their toll on the institutional system. As was made public at that time, electoral results did not coincide with the vote count[7] that was certified by the representatives of the different political parties, especially of the opposition. Thus, suspicions about manipulation of electoral results became generalized and questioned the legitimacy of those candidates that became elected. This event put pressure upon the corporatist structure given that even some candidates proposed by the official organizations in the labor and peasant sectors of the PRI did not get elected. It is possible to think that voter control, at the grass-roots level, has lost some of its efficiency and many people voted not as they were told to but as they wished to. Infighting within the organizations of the PRI has been rampant and conflicts at middle levels in different states have been much publicized. Renovators, supported by the president and by the apparatus of the party have had to confront so-called "dinosaurs", partisan of maintaining the old ways. Relations between the government and the opposition continue to be tense. Modernization of the political system does not appear to be as easy as the governing group, headed by the president, thought it would be. Perhaps, through electoral reform, which is in the making, elections will acquire a transparency they have not had up to the present. This, by itself, could give some breath to the renovators and assure the modernization of the corporatist structure and assure at the same time the correct operation of social concertation. Nevertheless, it is still too early to evaluate what will come out of this initiative, but it is possible to recognize its importance for the future of social concertation in Mexico.

The electoral system, within a corporatist structure, seems to be more important than one could think in abstract terms. Indeed, in spite of the controls that corporatism exerts on labor, business organizations, and government officials, there remains the fact that people are at the bottom of this structure. And contradictions may appear between the control that corporatist structures may have on individual citizens and the concrete behavior that they may have on events such as elections. This will be the principal

[7] This apparent contradiction rests on the fact that the vote count has to be confirmed by Electoral Commissions that meet one week after the election to revise it and produce the so-called electoral results that are the only official results. Many negotiations take place between voting day and revision day and that explains the differences. Surprisingly, even opposition parties agree to this procedure because, in the past, due to the total domination of the electoral process by the PRI, it was the only way to obtain some type of representation. For the forms of *fraud*, see Gómez Tagle, Silvia, Nos ganó la democracia, *El Cotidiano*, 25, September–October 1988, and by the same author: Conflictos y contradicciones en el sistema electoral mexicano, *Estudios Sociológicos*, VI, 16, January–April 1988.

challenge that social concertation will face in the future because it is limited to agreements among actors located at the macro level of the corporatist structure and their links with the rank and file workers, peasants, businessmen, bureaucrats, middle classes, students, and intellectuals are not as solid and institutionalized as the leadership of these organizations may think.

7.3 Conclusion

The relatively short experience that Mexico has had in the implementation of social concertation does not allow for very general conclusions. On the contrary, one has to be very careful in not projecting the apparent success that present formulas for concertation are having to the future. However, at the same time that caution must be exercised, one cannot sufficiently underline that the Mexican experience of the period 1987–1990 has been by far the most successful in comparative terms, within the Latin American context.

The labor movement has been able to enjoy the diverse trade-offs we have mentioned in this paper and business interests have also been flexible enough not to pressure for price increases that would have imperilled the solidarity pacts signed with the government. At the same time, we need to keep in mind that social concertation in Mexico has been restricted to the control of economic aspects. While some initiative has been oriented toward the electoral question, given the relative loss of legitimacy of the political system, by large the most effort has been put into the design of methods to control inflation, eliminate pressures on the national currency, maintain salaries, and prices restrained. Only time will allow for a fully fledged analysis of the Mexican type of social concertation. For the time being, we can only say that it has inherited the capacity that the old "corporatist system" had for making all sectors of society participate in relatively legitimate goals without having to deal with radical class conflict as happened in other countries of Latin America in the last fifty years.

In general, the Mexican experience shows that when a structure of concertation has been in operation for a long time and has shown its usefulness for the actors that make it up, it is possible to use it in time of crisis for the pursuit of different objectives than the ones it was built for. Thus, one precondition for the successful operation of social concertation in the contemporary situation is the existence of a corporatist framework where a learning process has facilitated the mutual knowledge among social and political actors. On the other hand, it is important to underline the fact that present-day social concertation is strictly focused on economic problems and most of the success it has enjoyed in Mexico derives from the fact that it was put into place before political pressures began to question the legitimacy of the corporatist structure. Now that profound interrogation arises about the degree to which the system is really representative of the opinions of the citizens of the country, doubts may appear that ultimately will impact the social concertation process. Therefore, close observation of the way in which social concertation will operate in the future, given the legitimacy crisis, may provide additional insights on the conditions of the successful operation of this mechanism.

8 European Labor Relations and the Prospects of Tripartism

Hans Slomp

8.1 The Nature of European Labor Relations

Most of the comparative literature on labor relations points to the differences between the European nations, and to the existence of national traditions of conflict and conflict resolution, bargaining, consultation, and cooperation. The prevailing approach of nation-to-nation comparisons tends to hide the fact that (Western) European labor relations have much in common, when viewed in a wider perspective. Common characteristics are:

Collective bargaining at the industrial branch of sector level, probably the most outstanding common feature of European labor relations. Although the extent and scope of this kind of contact between unions and employers' organizations differs widely among the European nations, the branch or sector level represents an important forum of decision-making with respect to labor conditions or procedures of conflict resolution.

Worker participation, in one form or another, at the enterprise level. This feature shows even more national variations than branch or sector bargaining. National differences on this point concern the extent and the degree of formalization of worker participation, the position of the enterprise union representation *vis-à-vis* works councils, and the existence of codetermination at management or Board-level.

A relatively high level of *government involvement* in the regulation of labor relations, and of government interference in employer/union bargaining and conflict. Treating European labor relations as a two-party affair would seriously miss the mark: Three, not two parties are involved, including the national government, though the status of this third party may be different from that of the other parties.

In combination, these three distinct features determine the nature of European labor relations as one consisting of *three parties* interacting at *three levels*. National organizations and the national government meet at the central or national level; branch organizations at the industrial branch or sector level; unions, management, and the company workforce at the enterprise (and workshop) level. At the branch and enterprise levels the government is often involved indirectly at most, making the rules, but it may also be active as a mediator or arbitrator. Moreover, activities at the three levels are related to each other.

The definition of European labor relations as a three-party and a three-level affair gives only some indications about the nature of the relations between the parties. Collective bargaining may be a recurrent phenomenon without much conflict or it may be studded with conflicts. Worker participation may involve a number of controversial issues, and it may be a highly contentious issue in itself. The national government's role may range from a bargaining partner or a mediator to one of a frequent target in political strikes and other political action.

Despite the many variations, the features listed are not without significance. They do allow a distinction of labor relations in (Western) Europe from those in other industrialized countries and regions in the world. Outside Europe one has to go a long way to find such an interplay between three parties and three levels. In other industrialized countries either the central level or the branch level is less developed as a forum, or an arena, of unions, employers' organizations, and national government.

8.2 Three Parties and Three Levels at Work

European labor relations are a three-party and a three-level affair. This does not imply that European labor relations are uniform. Within this general framework there exist as many variations as there are nations.

Only some countries have known periods in which the levels functioned as three stages in the process of wage bargaining. As examples might be cited Italy's "articulated bargaining" and the Irish "wage rounds" of the 1960s. More often the three levels were related less closely and different subjects were discussed and decided at each level. For instance, social security at the national level, payment and working hours among the branch organizations, and the introduction of new technology at the enterprise level. Even more important, in a number of countries labor relations seem a two-level rather than a three level affair. In France, union/employer contacts at the national level have almost been absent. In that country, the central or national level derives its importance mainly from frequent union/government conflicts. In a few other countries the enterprise level seems underdeveloped, though in Germany and the Netherlands union absence at this level is compensated for by strong works councils.

With respect to the relative importance of each of the levels and the nature of the contacts between the three parties at each level, a distinction can be made in three models of labor relations. The nations within each group share a number of elements which have been rather consistent over a long period of time.[1]

[1] The distinction in three models is worked out more in detail in: Slomp, Hans (1990):

The *British model*, partly applying also to Ireland, represents the oldest type of labor relations. It consists of a combination of craft or sector bargaining, between craft unions or general workers' unions and employer organizations, and enterprise and shopfloor-level talks between management and shop stewards. Craft and sector agreements mainly concern conflict procedures; most substantive bargaining is done at the enterprise or plant level. The highly decentralized and informal system of enterprise bargaining, coordinated only to some extent by the craft and branch agreements, has shaped the British model as one of fragmentation and of great variations between sectors and even between enterprises and plants. Indeed, one could hardly speak of one model (as a matter of fact most British are very reluctant to regard their labor relations as a system), except by making this degree of variation and lack of coordination the core of the model. The model has proven to be state-resistant. Neither statutory wage control nor incidental union efforts of voluntary union restraint have met with success. This failure and the fragmentation of bargaining were among the backgrounds to the recent conservative policies to change the system of labor relations in Great Britain. These efforts had hardly any precedent: Labor relations and politics have always been separate fields of activity, with different actors. Political strikes were almost unknown in Britain. Even the foundation by the unions of the Labor Party in the beginning of the century served this separation, rather than being the start of political union activities.

On the European continent national politics has acted as an agent of national and international uniformity in labor relations. At the end of the nineteenth century the system of dispersed craft unions gave way to a labor movement combining industrial and political action, or became part of such a movement. The political aims reinforced the importance of the central, or national, organizations. One of their functions was to mobilize workers for political action. Hence, there was a (slow) transition from craft unions to industrial unions, organizing both craft and general workers. These developments shaped continental labor relations. Again, there exists a wide range of national variations, but two more general models emerged at the turn of the century.

In the *northern European model* (Germany, Scandinavia, the Low Countries, and Austria, and to some extent also Switzerland) there were intimate links between the socialist party and the socialist union movement. The efforts to organize workers in industrial unions allowed the rise of collective agreements between unions and employer organizations. In turn, the implicit or explicit peace clauses in such agreements reduced the frequency of political strikes by the unions. After the great political strikes in the first decade of the twentieth century a neat distinction was made between

Labor Relations in Europe, A History of Issues and Developments. Westport, CT: Greenwood Press.

the political arena, or forum, in which the political party was active, and the industrial forum, reserved to the unions. The formalization of collective bargaining and the relative absence of political strikes allowed national government to occupy the position of a neutral party in talks with employers and unions, and as a neutral arbitor or mediator in labor conflicts. This neutrality did not develop overnight. It was established in the early 1920s, as the outcome of a process in which the *Massenstreiks* at the beginning of the century, union/government relations during World War I, and the wave of militancy and turmoil during the aftermath of that war played a role. In the 1930s and even more after World War II it became something of a sacred principle in northern European labor relations. Although outsiders might question the degree of neutrality, especially in view of postwar wage policies, what counts is not strict neutrality but the fact that employers and unions regard the national government as a neutral force, more or less irrespective of the government's composition.

In the *southern European model* (France and the Mediterranean countries) the dominant union movement (syndicalist, revolutionary Marxist, anarchist) at first was not linked to a political party, or at least the link was much weaker. One of the backgrounds to this separation was the labor movement's view that parliamentary politics was a less promising field of action than the industrial arena. This attitude opened the road to frequent political strikes, in various forms, as an alternative to parliamentary pressure. Such strikes could range from industrial conflict developing into political strikes to local and national general strikes, and to industrial action as a form of political action. This overlap or even unity of the industrial and the political arenas made the national government a target in many labor conflicts, and a possible target in any action, which was not a favorable condition for a role as a neutral arbiter or mediator. The communist domination of a large part of the labor movement after World War II reinforced this process. In the northern European model a government may be "unsympathetic" to labor or to the employers, due to its composition, but both parties will accept or at least comply with the measures taken by that particular government. In the southern European model such a government is a hostile force, to be combated and defeated by all means, including labor conflicts. Of course, this politicization of labor relations has been a more outspoken trend in France and the Iberian Peninsula, dominated by rightist governments for most of the twentieth century, than in Italy with its coalition cabinets.

8.3 Tripartism in the Three Models of Labor Relations

The differences between the three models of labor relations apply also to tripartism, that is, to negotiations or consultation between the central, or national, employers' associations, union confederations, and the national government. The literature on neocorporatism has pointed to two conditions which have to be met if such central-level contacts are to develop. First, it must be possible to confine such contacts to a small number of umbrella organizations, which are thus given an oligopoly or even a monopoly of representation. A second precondition, of even greater importance, is the need of membership discipline within the organizations involved. The two conditions require hardly any explanation. Any form of bargaining requires a limited number of participants and some guarantees that the bargaining partners speak on behalf of their members and are able to enforce the bargaining results. A third precondition is state neutrality, at least in the view of the other two parties involved, employer associations and union confederations. The state must be independent from any of the other parties and it must have something to offer to both employers and unions. A lasting state bias in favor of one of these parties reduces the willingness of the other party to participate.

Given these preconditions, it is not difficult to explain the lack of success of tripartism in the British and the southern European models of labor relations. In the highly decentralized British model the organizations lack the means to impose any bargaining results. Moreover, neither of the parties involved has viewed the national government as a neutral party. Rather, it was an outside force, to be kept at arm's length from the sphere of labor relations. Neither employers nor the unions were willing to accept any form of state involvement in labor relations, let alone their own involvement in state legislation with respect to labor relations or labor conditions. The incidental examples of tripartism in the British Isles served the goal of a statutory or informal wage policy, and they failed. The national government took the initiative, and even if the organizations were willing to participate, they were unable to enforce the outcome of the talks. In Britain this applied to both the TUC and the CBI; the two-party Irish Employer/Labor conference had a better performance.

In the southern European model the preconditions are not met either. In particular the position of the state is too much a source of friction. In the unions' view the (mostly rightist) national governments are an enemical force, a target of political action rather than a neutral bargaining partner. Employers consider any (incidental) leftist government as a possible successor to the *front populaire* of the 1930s and they cherish their own informal contacts with the national governments. In accordance with this politicization of labor relations, membership discipline within the unions is an instrument of member mobilization for political protest, rather than a tool to enforce the outcome of central-level negotiations. Moreover, political mobilization does not involve a high degree of membership discipline. The unions are often under pressure of their own membership to call political strikes or engage in other forms of political action. In France, CGT leaders prefer to refrain from signing agreements (even if they participated in the talks), in order to keep their hands free in case they find themselves confronted with member protests against the agreement. The history of Italian national talks is even more a fascinating succession of political mobilization by the unions, union involvement in central-level talks, the rise of autonomous membership initiatives against the agreements, and new political mobilization in order to ensure the life of the union organizations.

In contrast, northern Europe, from Austria to Norway, is covered by tripartite councils, committees, and informal union/employer/government meetings. Tripartism became a conspicuous feature of northern European labor relations (and politics) especially in the course of the postwar reconstruction policy. Its rise was related to state intervention, in the economy, and in some countries also to statutory or voluntary wage policies. Since most of the countries in this part of Europe have a long tradition of substantive collective bargaining and of institutionalized labor peace, membership discipline is a normal ingredient of labor relations. This does not only apply to membership discipline within the sectorial or branch organizations, but also the latter's compliance with decisions made by the national organizations. In a number of countries the strong position of these national organizations was established in the labor truces of the 1930s, like the Norwegian basic agreement (1935), the Belgian National Labor Conference (1936), and the Swedish Saltsjöbaden agreement (1938). Wartime agreements, for instance in Finland (1941) and Belgium (1944), reinforced this position. Even countries with relatively high strike rates, like Finland and Belgium, have their share of tripartism. The existence of a number of competing union (and employer) organizations, for instance in the Low Countries, has given rise to disputes on the division of seats in tripartite bodies, but such problems have been solved rather easily. The same applies to the recent admission of *cadre* organizations in both countries. State neutrality is visible in the continuity of tripartism after changes in cabinet composition. The literature on neocorporatism stressed the link between socialist, or better social/democratic, union and the social democratic party, and the latter's participation in government as favorable conditions or even as preconditions of corporatism, including tripartite contacts. These conditions may have played a role in the postwar start of neocorporatism; in later years tripartism has been continued under governments in which social democrats did not participate.

With respect to tripartism there is one major exception in the northern European model: West Germany. This country shares all the characteristics of northern European labor relations, including the predominance of highly formalized sector bargaining by strong organizations. Tripartism is absent, however. The position of Germany has some very specific backgrounds in the postwar period in which the nation was (re)established. As a guarantee against a few fascist *Gleichschaltung* of the unions, and against a possible

Table 1: Three Models of Labor Relations[2]

Models	National level	Branch level	Enterprise level
British	mainly serving wage policy	collective bargaining	informal bargaining
French	union–government conflict government–employer consultation	collective bargaining	worker militancy worker participation
German	consultation, and coordination of bargaining (tripartism)	collective bargaining	worker participation

communist take-over, the central level was played down, and the position of the state became that of an outsider in labor relations, like in the British model (the TUC was helpful in the formation of postwar labor relations in Germany). State abstinence was laid down in the famous *Tarifautonomie*. It also implied the absence of tripartism, since the latter would invariably involve state activities in the field of labor relations. Both unions and employers have stubbornly defended this state abstinence, rather than state neutrality. The German position confined tripartism to the smaller nations of the northern European model, which gave rise to the notion of smallness as a precondition of tripartism.[3] The German position is also the reason to use the terms "northern European" and "southern European" models, rather than "German" and "French" models, beside the British model. Since tripartism is the main subject of this contribution, one would be forced to speak of the "German model with the exception of Germany". Diagram 1 summarizes the main elements of the three models of labor relations, including tripartism.

Since tripartism is mainly confined to the northern European model of labor relations, the question of its future is a twofold one. The first is, will tripartism be continued in that model? The second is, will the southern European and the British models also adopt forms of tripartism?

8.4 Tripartism in the Northern European Model

Tripartism, as practiced in the smaller northern European model nations, serves two functions:

First, union and employer *consultation* by the national government, a function well covered by the extensive literature on neocorporatism. The process prevails in social and economic policy, and it has been extended to a

[2] Compiled from: Slomp, Hans (1990): *Labor Relations in Europe, A History of Issues and Developments*, chs. 3–4. Westport, CT: Greenwood Press.

[3] As argued in: Katzenstein, Peter J. (1985): *Small States in World Markets, Industrial Policy in Europe*. Ithaca, NY: Cornell University Press.

wide range of policy fields, including housing, health care, and education. In recent years environmental policy has become the latest topic of tripartite talks. In contrast to the formal councils of the Low Countries (the Belgian NAR/CNT and the Dutch SER), Scandinavia (and Belgium in some periods) have preferred more informal consultation, like the Swedish "Thursday club".

Second, the *coordination of collective bargaining* which takes place at the branch and enterprise levels. During most of the postwar period the national union and employer organizations took care of this task in a form of bipartism. In some countries the national confederations supervised or monitored the process of sector bargaining very strictly, in other countries the sector organizations enjoyed more autonomy.[4] Especially in the 1960s central-level bargaining, or at least central-level coordination of wage bargaining, became a general trend. Its expansion was related to a number of economic and political changes, including changes in technology, the rise of indicative planning, and the start of the Common Market. The national government hardly participated, with the exception of the first years of postwar reconstruction (and the Dutch "guided wage policy"). In the course of the 1970s governments became increasingly involved in the coordination of wage bargaining, in formal or informal talks, bypassing the formal institutions of tripartism: The official separation between consultation and collective bargaining was still adhered to, though in practice the two were often interwoven (as they traditionally have been in Austria's Paritary Committee). In the course of the talks, governments committed themselves to legislation in the fields of social security benefits, taxation policy, or even worker participation, in exchange for wage restraint. These state concessions allowed the national organizations to advise or impose wage restraint upon the branch organizations. A more popular form of government involvement was the announcement of some form of statutory wage policy, followed by tripartite talks to find a compensation, or to substitute voluntary restraint for the government measures. Examples of this kind of tripartism were the Swedish Haga meetings, the Danish government involvement in central bargaining, and the Belgian informal meetings in the late 1970s and early 1980s.

Among the backgrounds to the transition from two-party to three-party activity in this field were the high wage demands during the period of increased worker militancy following May 1968, the oil crises of 1974 and 1980, and the rise of inflation and unemployment in the course of the 1970s and 1980s. Other motives for national governments to take part were related to the links between wages and social security benefits, which contributed to the rise of social security costs, and the position of the state as the nation's

[4] Slomp, l.c., chs. 10, 12. Michels, Ank and Hans Slomp (1990): The Role of Government in Collective Bargaining: Scandinavia and the Low Countries. *Scandinavian Political Studies*, 13 (1), 21–35.

largest employer. National governments allowed not only a growth in the number of state employees, but also granted them more bargaining rights. This affected the uniformity of labor relations, since public sector, or public employees' collective bargaining has not always followed the same trends as labor relations in the private sector.[5] In the 1980s the second function of tripartism was more frequent in Scandinavia than in the Low Countries, where the very high level of unemployment enforced wage restraint right away.

The first function of tripartism has survived dramatic changes in economic conditions, from high growth rates to recession, and from full employment to high unemployment. It was also rather immune to changes in political conditions, in particular in cabinet composition. The second function also survived under different political and economic conditions, so there is no need to fear for its future.

Of course, tripartism could be adversely affected by changes in membership discipline and in the position of the state. The tradition of membership discipline has lost some of its force, indeed, but there are no signs of a general erosion of union (and employers' associations) authority. A more serious threat seemed the decline of the rate of organization, in particular in the early 1980s, since it would confront the unions with the problem of the non-members' discipline. The decline has hardly been a general trend, however, and it has affected the other models of labor relations more than the northern European model.[6] Moreover, the least organized category of workers, clerical workers in the private sector, have also shown the least willingness to strike. This lack of strike propensity could affect the unions' power in the long run, but it does not affect their membership discipline. State neutrality was endangered in the 1980s, due to wage measures without tripartite consultation and by cuts in public spending which gave rise to public employees' strikes and protest actions. In most countries the unions have joined this protest, or they have been active in organizing it, even in the Netherlands, a country without any tradition of such protest. However, the actions have been limited in frequency and extent, and they seemed especially related to the recession of the early 1980s. As a consequence, the preconditions of tripartism have not changed substantially. Tripartism is still firmly established.

The future of both functions of tripartism looks even brighter in view of a phenomenon which is gradually changing this German model of labor rela-

[5] Cf. Treu, Tiziano *et al.* (1987): *Public Service Labor Relations, Recent Trends and Future Prospects*. Geneva: ILO.

[6] Armingeon, Klaus (1989): Arbeitsbeziehungen und Gewerkschaftsentwicklung in den achtziger Jahren, Ein Vergleich der OECD-Länder. *Politische Vierteljahresschrift*, 30 (4), 603–628. Cf. Visser, Jelle (1990): *European Trade Unions in Figures*. Deventer: Kluwer.

tions to some extent, the decentralization of collective bargaining. The partial shift from branch to enterprise level increases the need of coordination at the central level, and also of legislation to provide general rules for the many enterprise-level innovations in labor contracts and working hours. Such new developments strengthen each of the two functions separately, and their combination at tripartite meetings, at which both legislation and collective bargaining are important topics of debate and negotiations. The extension of tripartism offers a guarantee for the continued hold of the national organizations over collective bargaining. Indeed, the very backgrounds to the decentralization of bargaining provide (new) fields of legislation and tripartite coordination:

The powerful ideal of democracy and worker participation in enterprise decision-making has been at the root of agreements and legislation to extend the powers of works councils and the union representation in the enterprise. This trend has not been affected by adverse economic conditions. The extension has been the subject of national agreements or legislation (and consultation) in all smaller nations. A related topic has been codetermination, that is, the appointment of worker representatives in the management team and/or in the Supervisory Board. The European Community has also been active in the field of participation (the Vredeling Directives are an example), but its record is not impressive.

The ongoing shift from manual to clerical work also favored the position of the enterprise level and reduced the role of "outside" forces like the branch organizations of employers and unions. This trend to "exclusion", American style, will probably motivate the development of general rules, for instance about career patterns, paid educational leave, fringe benefits, and protection against dismissal.

The growth of female labor has been (or better, should have been) accompanied by enterprise child care provisions and enterprise activities to increase the number of women in higher echelon functions by way of positive action. Legislation and tripartite agreements on these subjects and on protection against sexual harassment have been called forward by the European Community's Directives. Despite the slow start in most countries, this is a growing field of state activity. Some of the more progressive governments try to catch up with Sweden's policy with respect to female workers. The rear is pushed by the European Court of Justice's judgements in cases of direct as well as indirect discrimination.

The extension of flexi-time has given rise to detailed provisions at enterprise level. In some countries, in particular Denmark and the Netherlands, its popularity is linked to the growth of female employment especially. But the trend toward a division of labor along sex lines between full-time working men and part-time working women is visible in other countries as well. The deviation from traditional working hours requires adaptation of existing social legislation and new general guidelines on working time as well as shop opening hours. In several countries legislation has been passed or at least the discussion has been reopened. A general example has been the lifting of the ban on nightwork by women. It served sexual equality, by removing specific protection of female workers, and allowed the extension of flexi-time to nightwork.[7]

The introduction of new technologies has prompted enterprise-based union or works council responses. The fast speed of technological change in production and office work continues to motivate such responses rather than branch-level solutions. This is another promising field of legal and tripartite frameworks.

Several other topics of enterprise bargaining are related to changes in economic conditions, like employment level, vocational training, and early retirement. They have also been subjects of central-level agreements and legislation.

To summarize, the trend of a partial decentralization from branch to enterprise level is due to lasting social and economic changes which in themselves offer new opportunities for tripartism. These opportunities constitute a response to the challenge which decentralization poses to the established position of unions and employer organizations. The result could well be an even more balanced "division of work" among the three levels of European labor relations.

8.5 Tripartism in the Southern European and British Models of Labor Relations

Tripartism has never been a constituent part of the southern European model of labor relations. In a few southern European countries there exist economic and social councils, but their functions are different from those of the tripartite councils in the northern European model. The latter comprise the major union and employer confederations. Their size, up to 50 members, allows effective consultation and coordination of bargaining. In contrast, the Italian CNEL numbers 111, the French CES even 230. Not only sheer size prevents any such activities, membership is also spread over a larger number of organizations. In the French CES various kinds of cooperatives, mutualities, and family associations participate.[8] This represents a kind of multipartism, which is ineffective almost by definition in France, at least as a device of decision-making.

In addition to the lack of formal tripartism, informal three-party talks have

[7] Cf. Delsen, Lei (1990): European Trade Unions and the Flexible Workforce. *Industrial Relations Journal*, 21 (4) 260–273.

[8] European Trade Union Institute (1990): *The Role of Economic and Social Councils in Western Europe*. Brussels: ETUI.

been rare, in contrast to the Scandinavian countries, in which they take the place of formal tripartism. Even two-party (union/employer) meetings have been rather uncommon in the southern European model. Only Italy has a (limited) tradition of central-level wage agreements, covering wage indexation, wage differentials between the northern and the southern parts of the country, and between clerical and manual workers.

The main factors which have prevented the rise of anything like tripartism have been immanent in the relationship between the three parties. In the relation between unions and employers' associations conflict rather than compromise has been the dominant tradition during most of the twentieth century. The nature of this relationship and the limited extent of collective bargaining have been conducive to membership militancy rather than membership discipline at both sides. Outbursts of member militancy have at times overpowered the unions' and employers' organizations, forcing them to revise their position on the relevant issues. In the northern European model such developments were mainly confined to the period of increased militancy between 1968 and the mid-1970s.

Probably the most outstanding single factor explaining the absence of tripartism in the southern European model is the position of the state. It has never been able to acquire the status of a neutral party. In contrast, it has been a partisan force favoring employers most of the time. Without exception, autonomous trade unions have been suppressed by indigenous forms of state corporatism or fascism in the course of the twentieth century – which is another contrast to most northern European nations. Although the period of suppression lasted only a few years in France, other countries did not enjoy union freedom until recently. The relation between the state and the unions has remained a highly explosive one ever since. Even at times of a state/union *rapprochement*, like the start of the French Fifth Republic in 1958 and the time of the unions' EUR line in Italy in the late 1970s, they were soon followed by growing friction or by a new wave of militancy.

Are there, then, no changes going on, or to be expected in the near future, which could stimulate a transition to tripartism? The conditions of trade unionism in the southern European model do not point in that direction. A conspicuous development has been the decline in membership numbers and in rate of organization. In the southern European model membership decline was larger than in any other European country in the 1980s.[9] In France, the rate of organization has sunk to United States proportions and one is tempted to speak of the remnants of what *used to be* the French labor movement. A more recent trend is the ideological drift of the major union organizations. They have long been dominated by communists and have been affected by the events in Eastern Europe. Though it is still difficult to assess the effects of the

[9] Armingeon, Klaus (1989): l.c., 625–626.

landslides in Eastern Europe, a process of ideological reorientation of the communist-dominated unions seems inevitable. The Italian union movement occupies the best position in this respect. The Italian communist-dominated union organization and the communist party have always been more open to ideological debate than in the other countries. The unions have built a tradition of cooperation, which has not always been easy, but which has certainly stood the test. Moreover, the Italian rate of organization is still on a level with that in some northern European countries, and even higher than in the Netherlands.

The decline of unionism in some of the other countries has made them a rather marginal movement. Union authority has been put to the test several times, and in this respect Italy shares the problems of the southern European model. The *cobass*, which have risen recently, are just another variation to a traditional Italian theme.[10]

However, more important for a future of tripartism than changes in union membership and union organization could be a shift in the position of the state. In particular, in France and Spain, socialist governments of the 1980s have done their best not to alienate employers, almost up to the point of alienating the unions. Measures like the Auroux reforms in France have reinforced this trend of depoliticization. National governments have still been the target of major national actions, but in general the unions' and employers' organizations attention has shifted somewhat from the state to collective bargaining. As a consequence, national government has moved a certain distance along the road to a less partisan and a more neutral position *vis-à-vis* the other parties. Similar reforms were implemented in Greece in the first half of the 1980s. The measures in these countries have contributed to an extension of collective bargaining, in particular at the enterprise level – in line with the traditions of the southern European model. The recent two-party national agreements in France on a number of hot issues like flexi-time and worker protection are probably also related to this process of depoliticization. They show that the conditions favoring tripartism in the northern European model are also a good base of central-level contacts in the southern European model. In the latter, two-party agreements rather than three-party tripartism cover the new issues of the late 1880s and the 1990s. If the trend toward depoliticization continues, national governments might well become involved in due time, as a neutral force this time. But in contrast to the stable northern European model, the southern European one is full of surprise. A shift to rightist governments could well lead to a new process of politicization, a new wave of mobilization and militancy, and to a concomitant increase in union membership numbers.

To sum up, the southern European model, though with national variations,

[10] *Cobas* re-emerge in difficult bargaining around. *European Industrial Relations Review*, 196 (May 1990), 18–20.

has changed in at least two respects: In the willingness of the parties to bargain and in the position of the national government. Both changes constitute preconditions of a move toward tripartism, like they are in the northern European model. The predominance of enterprise bargaining in the southern European model has always acted as a stimulus of central-level activities, be it conflict rather than bargaining. The change in conditions might transform this tradition of conflict into one of relative *concertation* and bargaining, that is, of tripartism. The political scene, union decline, and the recurrent rise of members' militancy represent imponderables for this development, however.

In the *British* model, and in *Germany*, the central level has been least developed. The recent legislation (to be) imposed by the national governments on British and Irish labor relations have not brought about any change in that respect. Moreover, the formalization of bargaining and the relative centralization from workshop talks to enterprise bargaining do not raise any need of tripartite coordination. In Germany, free bargaining without government intervention has been even more of a sacred principle. The integration of Eastern Germany will not change this situation, since in that country the state is regarded even more as an evil institution than it has been in the labor relations of the Federal Republic.

8.6 The European Community

The depoliticization of the southern European model and the decentralization in the northern European model point to a certain degree of convergence in *European labor relations*. In both models a number of conditions seem to offer chances for tripartism. New chances in the southern European model, and an expansion of tripartism in the small nations of the northern European model. Only in the British model, and in Germany, is the central level not sufficiently developed to allow for tripartism. The convergence reaffirms the nature of European labor relations as a three-party and a three-level affair. It is the nature of the relations between the parties involved that changes most.

What about the *European Community* and "1992"? The answer to that question is a simple one. One look at the economic and social conditions which contribute to the decentralization of collective bargaining in the northern European model will show that most of these processes constitute part of the preparations for "1992". Although other backgrounds should not be overlooked, for instance internationalization and responses to the labor market, several of the conditions mentioned have been consciously framed to anticipate the opening up of the internal market. Examples are the introduction of new technology, flexi-time, and the extension of all kinds of education and vocational training. The same applies to the political changes in the southern European model. The changes in this model have been part of frantic efforts to bring social legislation and collective bargaining in line with the situation in the northern European model. Portugal is the only country hardly affected by this trend. As a consequence, the changes which have been described form a part of "1992", and will continue afterward. Because of the high risen expectations their pace of development could well be faster until 1992 than after that fateful year!

Tripartism might even extend to the Community level, in particular with respect to issues dealt with by the Community, like female employment and worker participation. However, the extension of tripartism to that level is only in an infant stage. National governments still determine the Community's freedom of action in the social field.[11] Hence, the further development of tripartism depends on the experience of the national governments and on the expansion of tripartism in the southern European model, rather than on "autonomous" Community-level changes. Though the former British Prime Minister was often blamed for her negative attitude toward such tripartism (and toward the unions in general), one should not forget that British unions and employers' organizations have never favored national-level tripartism. Their rejection has been shared by their German colleagues, most of the time. Even if this stance becomes a minority position within the Community, it will certainly function as a brake for Community-level tripartism. Moreover, who is prepared to accept the second function of tripartism (the coordination of collective bargaining) at Community level, including Community calls for wage restraint?

[11] Corbey, Dorette (1990): *European Integration and the Survival of Trilateralism*. Paper, Conference on "The Future of Industrial Relations in Europe", Maastricht, June.

9 Macro-economic Policies and Collective Bargaining in Ireland

Kevin P. O'Kelly

9.1 Labor Costs and the Economy

The one area of continual controversy during the postwar era has been the degree of influence governments should have over the fixing of wage levels, and the relationship between the level of labor costs and the level of job creation. From the different methods of pay bargaining experienced in the Irish economy since 1946, no system has emerged with universal acceptance for any sustained period of time, or justified its retention on a permanent basis.

As social demands and economic indicators rise and fall, so also do the attitudes of employers and employees change. There has not been any long-term commitment to any particular method of pay bargaining, rather each party has decided its attitude to future negotiations during each National Wage Round. The attitudes of both sides depends on what is perceived to be the most suitable system to achieve their respective sectorial objectives in a given economic climate.

In the Irish context, the acceptance of centralized bargaining arrangements as a means of determining labor costs has been inevitable. This is a consequence of the economic situation within which Ireland operates on the periphery of larger, very competitive markets. It is a natural consequence also of the consistent commitment of the trade union movement to the achievement of full employment and of the ongoing concern of both employers and government to achieving efficiency and competitiveness in the industrial and services sectors. While these objectives may appear mutually exclusive, enough common ground has been found on which to base centralized agreements when all three parties have been committed to the consensus approach.

At times of transition from one system to another, governments have considered it essential to intervene to protect the economy from the effects of chaos in the determination of wage costs. Intervention ranged from persuasion to threats of statutory control. In more recent times, the involvement of government has gone from full participation with trade unions and employers in agreeing a total package of social and economic items, including pay, to the other extreme of allowing the levels of labor costs, including those of the public sector, to be fixed by market forces. With the change of government in 1987, there was a return to the tripartite approach.

Successive governments have considered the fixing of wage levels as an important tool in their control of the economy, based on the premise that increases in incomes are a matter for political as well as economic judgement.

After a period of ten years of centralized National Wage Agreements, a return in 1981 to the system of plant level and sectorial bargaining which prevailed during the 1950s and, to a large extent, during the 1960s, was a consequence of the prevailing economic philosophy in Western industrial countries which argued that government intervention is ineffective and not necessary in a market economy which is, in effect, self-regulating. This economic view, in its extreme version, reasons that unemployment would not exist with wage structures which are responsive and flexible to the prevailing market, and that governments should not take on the responsibility of providing full employment in the face of trade union attitudes which attempt to hold rates at an unnecessary high level. Consequently, centralized bargaining is an unacceptable way to fix labor costs in an open and free market economy.[1]

9.2 Employment and Inflation

So, in most Western economies, full employment has been replaced by high levels of unemployment because during the 1970s the policy priorities of governments changed from a concentration on maximum job creation to a reduction of inflation and to control of the money supply, regardless of the economic and social consequences. In line with other governments, Irish administrations have been following similar policies and much of the resulting impact has put social objectives in a position of dependency on the success of monetary policies.

While full employment was never achieved in Ireland, the pursuance of such policies has also resulted in higher than normal unemployment rates with the conequential problems of poverty and emigration.[2]

Therefore, in attempting to balance and compare the three basic wage bargaining systems which have operated within the Irish economy since 1970 – namely, centralized bipartite bargaining, tripartite bargaining, and local-

[1] Minford, P. (1983): *Unemployment: Cause and Cure*, Oxford. Also, Hawkins, K. (1984): *Unemployment*, pp. 96–102, Pelican; Outlines the arguments of Friedman, M. (1975) in: *Unemployment versus Inflation?* IEA Paper No. 44. Also, Cairncross, A. (1984): Is Employment Policy a Thing of the Past? *The Three Banks Review*, No. 139, as quoted by Conniffe and Kennedy.

[2] Conniffe, D. and K. A. Kennedy (eds.) (1984): Employment and Unemployment Policy in Ireland, chs. 1, 2, and pp. 324–325. Dublin:Economic and Social Research Institute. Also, Peillon, M. (1982): *Contemporary Irish Society* (London: Gill and Macmillan), p. 160, on the effects of economic development on employment.

level bargaining – it is essential to take into consideration the various factors dictating government action and government responsibility in the bargaining process and its effect on employment levels.

Since the foundation of the Irish State, successive governments have never hesitated to become involved in setting up State companies to exploit specific development opportunities not undertaken by private enterprise and, consequently, have promoted economic growth, thus providing a high level of employment in the commercial and non-commercial public sectors.[3] Likewise, in promoting development and expansion in the private sector, the State has invested heavily in the manufacturing, industrial, and services sectors through its development agencies, making almost all employment in these sectors dependent, at an early stage, on State support.

This commitment by successive Irish governments to a close involvement, through financial, training, and management support in the promotion of employment, has drawn them more closely into the mainstream of economic activity and job creation. Society has come to expect this level of involvement and, in turn, governments have taken on the role of coordinating the development of the national economic potential, both its manpower and physical resources, and in the redistribution of national wealth. In undertaking these responsibilities, it has also been expected that the State would protect living standards of, in particular, the dependent groups within the community and also provide essential social services such as education, health, housing, and welfare, in keeping with the mores of a Western European society.

This trend has made the modern State an all-powerful consumer of national production with the responsibility of balancing the economic and social consequences.

It has become the major consumer, the major investor, the major employer.[4]

In these circumstances, it was the position of the trade unions, both in 1979 and again in 1986, that it is not possible, with this degree of domestic interdependence, to separate economic actions from their social consequences. Conversely, to achieve soical objectives, it is essential to have regard for the resulting economic realities. The two are interwoven.

[3] Lemass, S. F., TD (196): The Role of the State-Sponsored Bodies. In: *Economic Development and Planning*, Chubb, B. and P. Lynch (eds.), Dublin: Institute of Public Administration (IPA). Also in: Conniffe and Kennedy: On analysis of employment in non-commercial semi-State bodies, op. cit., p. 258.

[4] Peillon, M. (1989): Strategies of State Mobilization in Irish Industrial Relations. *Ninth Countess Markievicz Memorial Lecture* (Dublin: Irish Association for Industrial Relations (IAIR)), p. 4; Peillon also covers this point in his book (op. cit.), pp. 158–159.

9.3 International Influences

Apart from the internal considerations of pursuing a policy of reducing government involvement in wage bargaining as part of an overall economic strategy, there is also the more complex international dimension. The rapid postwar movement toward interdependence of the economies of the free world, and the emergence of major trading blocks such as the European Community, make it more difficult for governments, who represent the nation at an international level, or, indeed, even exporting industries within a country, to act independently in economic decisions. This restraint is particularly relevant to the peripheral nature of the Irish economy and in attempting to influence the outcome of collective bargaining, successive governments have argued that pay increases must be kept in line with international trends so as to keep Irish exports competitive in these international markets.

The present level of international integration suggests that the only viable option to stimulate economic activity is to participate and cooperate in agreed policies with the other members of the trading block. The recent developments within the European Communities toward fully integrated internal markets by 1992 and the ratification of the Single European Act has made the Irish economy even more dependent on its partners in Europe. Heretofore, in the absence of agreed policies for international coordination, the room to maneuver for an Irish government in controlling State expenditure and expanding employment was substantially reduced.

As the Irish economy has a minuscule share of world trade and does not have a significanctly high share of European markets,[5] a slight upturn in trade with the rest of the world can be of immense benefit to the economy and to national prosperity. However, production costs remain a large factor in competitiveness within the European Community, as do extra inbuilt costs, such as the cost of transport and the cost of imported raw materials, neither of which are experienced by member states located nearer the major market centers. While considering these inherent economic disadvantages, and in order to take advantage of the new developments within the European Community, the importance of developing an integrated approach to industrial, manpower, and wage policies was accepted by the government and the national organizations of influence.

The objective of these policies was to strive for a maximum level of employment creation and for the achievement of other social objectives

[5] *Economic Review and Outlook* (Dublin: Government Stationery Office (GSO), 1980 to 1986). Also, European Community, *Eurostat publications*, e.g. Irish exports to the other nine EC member countries was 1.3% of total EC exports, and 0.4% of total world exports (1983 figures). Seventy-two per cent of Irish exports are to the other eleven EC countries, while 67.3% of imports come from the same countries (Central Bank of Ireland Report, Autumn 1987).

within the context of centralized bargaining. A key element of the strategy was to reconcile conflicting attitudes toward the determination of labor costs.

9.4 National Policy Approach 1977–1987

During the 1977 to 1979 period, the Department of Economic Planning and Development (EPD) provided the embryo institutional structures at government level which had the potential to provide a focus for the parties to identify agreed national objectives. The planning work of this department resulted in the first formal coordinated attempt at resolving the conflicting interests of employers, trade unions, other representative organizations, and the government.

The First National Understanding was a product of this planning process and the wide-ranging consultation undertaken by EPD. It laid the foundation for integrated policies which would balance the economic realities of the time with the social objectives, including employment targets and planned wage increases. It provided all parties involved in the negotiations with a model on which to build and improve further national planning.

The Second National Understanding developed and extended this approach, bringing into the discussions a wider range of national policy issues as a basis for an integrated agreement, even though the political priority was shifting from a social commitment to full employment to the restoration of stability in the national finances and the pre-eminence of monetary policies in line with the "new realism" approach in neighboring economies.

An interval of six years followed the two National Understandings during which the determination of pay levels reverted to local, plant, and sectorial levels. The negotiations on income increases both in the public and private sectors took place against the background of pay guidelines issued by the government in line with their stated economic and social objectives which reflected the new political/economic philosophy.

As the international economic climate improved and the Irish economy responded accordingly, the need for a more structured approach to the formulation of national economic and social policies began to be sought by the trade union movement. The employers were not anxious to return to a situation of centralized bargaining, although the experiences of local-level negotiations were not as successful as they had expected.

9.5 Programme for National Recovery 1987–1990

Following the 1987 General Election, the new government reverted to the central planning concept which was designed to integrate financial control into a programme of economic development and implement a comprehensive programme of economic recovery.[6]

The new centralized agreement, the Programme for National Recovery, outlines the commitment of all parties to work together to overcome the difficulties facing the economy and thus to bring about an expansion of growth and employment.

While the economic and financial situation within which this agreement was framed reflects the monetary concerns of recent years, much of the original concept still remains. It restores special consideration for the low paid, a feature which was absent at local- and plant-level bargaining and also restores the starting and termination dates for the National Wage Rounds which have operated since 1946. However, one major change in this Programme is that the agreement, including pay policy, will run for a duration of three years – more than twice as long as the National Understandings. Apart from a centralized pay agreement, non-pay items which are included in both the Understandings and the Programme for National Recovery are commitments to taxation reform, social welfare and health, education, housing, and labour and industrial relations issues. The development of employment creation opportunities by the private sector, rather than involvement by government or State underwriting of job targets, indicated that this aspect of national policy remains subject to monetary and national financial policies.

9.6 Conclusions

For the acceptance of the tripartite approach to national planning, it is essential that the limitations it imposes on the parties must be understood by the community. Policies resulting from consensus place a responsibility on the parties to deliver on their commitments within the agreements without undermining the complementary roles of the other parties.

While governments can consult the representative bodies and allow its policy formulation to be influenced in the interests of a successful conclusion to tripartite negotiations, it is dependent on changing attitudes through the power of the other parties to deliver on the issues agreed. The government can, however, play a vital role in generating a positive national environment within which the creation of national wealth and employment opportunities evolve, but this can only be achieved by recognizing the contributions and broad social/economic roles of the trade unions and employer organizations, outside the narrower confines of the industrial relations system.

[6] Programme for National Recovery. Fianna Fail document published for the general election, 7 February 1987, p. 3.

In the pursuit of tripartite agreement in recent decades, the government has been posed with a dilemma on how to balance its roles within the economy. In the final analysis, the government of the day is answerable to all sectors of the community, not just those with which it reaches agreement. It must, therefore, reserve its constitutional right to take the final decisions on the effects of centralized tripartite agreements as they relate to its social responsibilities on the wide range of policies not included in such agreements and in the "national interest".

It is the contention of this paper that to do this, governments have to intervene in the planning and working of the economy to a significant extent so that the industrial, agricultural, and services areas become more efficient and competitive and provide quality value-added products for the national and international markets. Thus economic development resulting from such a consensus approach will result in wealth creation, a growth in real incomes and in employment, and the Irish workforce taking full advantage of the potential of tripartite planning.

> One can accept that Irish business has faced very real and severe difficulties in the seventies and eighties, and that much of this derives from a vast collective imprudence, not of its making, in the generation of the inflationary wage–price spiral of the seventies, yet (...) it is simply not realistic to pretend that the private sector can generate enough employment to come anywhere near meeting our national needs. The conclusion is inescapable. The State has to be the main engine of economic development in Ireland. So it was in the beginning, and so it still is.[7]

[7] Brady, J., SJ (Summer 1985): Wealth, Work and Employment, p. 158. *Studies*, Dublin.

10 Social Concertation in Australian Industrial Relations

Alan Brown

10.1 Introduction

The term social concertation is not a familiar one in Australian industrial relations. It has been defined as "the whole set of procedures and bodies conceived to allow employers and workers or their representatives to settle their problems through a concerted approach" (Ministry of Labor and Employment). Treu (1989: p. 2) sees concertation as the "active interplay and consensus of the many social actors" to deal with the major problems of industrial societies such as innovation and economic adjustment, controlling inflation, and implementing effective management policies. It is not a process which relies on market forces or authoritarian state intervention. According to Treu, some of the features of concertation are: first, less adversarial and more convergence and interdependence of interests in industrial relations; second, a focus on long-term collaboration and broad social issues rather than narrow self-interest objectives; and third, concertation tends to be tripartite in nature.

10.2 Background to Social Concertation in Australia

Australia has always had a relatively highly centralized industrial relations system due largely to the existence of various State and Federal Conciliation and Arbitration Commissions. The Federal Commission has played a central role in wage movements through National Wage Cases and support for the principle of comparative wage justice whereby wage agreements and working conditions in key industry sectors (e.g. metal trades) have traditionally set the benchmark for movements in other industries.

Between 1973 and 1981 the Commissions adopted a quasi-incomes policy with a system of wage indexation for all Federal and State awards, covering some 90% of the Australian workforce. This was primarily directed at controlling high inflation rates. The Liberal Government, in office from 1975 to 1983, was not interested in any social concertation with the union movement. To complement a restrictive monetary policy, it supported a tight centralized incomes policy through the Commission to the extent that this was possible. On a number of occasions the Conciliation and Arbitration Act was changed by the government in an effort to gain greater control over the Commission's independence.

In July 1981, following the abandonment of wage indexation for various reasons, including increasing occurrences of industry wage agreements outside the guidelines, Australia experimented with a short period of wage deregulation leaving the parties to seek their own settlements on a case by case basis. This resulted in some substantial wage increases, such as in the metal industry, which had flow-on effects to other industries. This took place at a time of economic downturn, thus contributing to an increase in the unemployment rate, particularly in the manufacturing industry.

In order to try and moderate wage increases, the Federal Government introduced a wages pause (not freeze) for its employees in 1982. The Commission followed this example by suggesting a voluntary wages pause for private sector wage negotiations.

In March 1983 the ruling Liberal Government was replaced by a Labor Government led by an ex-Australian Council of Trade Unions (ACTU) President, Bob Hawke. Part of the electoral platform of this new government was an Accord struck between it and the ACTU (Accord 1983). This social contract covered many areas including education, taxation, social welfare, government expenditure, and wages. In the area of wages policy, the union movement gave a commitment to moderate wage demands and limit industrial disputation in return for a system of full inflation-indexed wages and other government programs, such as increased expenditure on training, the unemployed, education, social welfare, and taxation. Indexed wages was a big advantage for many of the weaker unions who had suffered reductions in real incomes during the period of the pause and deregulated wages policy. The Accord also provided for consultation between the ACTU and Federal Government on the range of issues which it covered, thus offering the ACTU a significant input into Government policy-making.

To ratify the principles of the Accord and seek employer commitment to it, an economic summit was held soon after the election. Despite the employers being reluctant participants, a joint communiqué was released at the conclusion of this summit which provided support for, amongst other things, a return to centralized wage fixation. Given this tripartite support, and following a series of conferences chaired by the Commission involving the ACTU, Confederation of Australian Industry, and State and Federal Governments, the Arbitration Commission handed down its National Wage Decision in September 1983 which provided a return to centralized full wage indexation. Consensus and corporatism became the important themes of industrial relations and macro-economic policy in the 1980s. This could be seen as Australia's entry into social concertation, although initially it was primarily bipartite than tripartite in nature due mainly to the lack of a united employer strategy.

10.3 New Challenges to Social Concertation

Economic. Whilst trends in economic growth and unemployment levels have been relatively favorable, a significant challenge for social concertation and the Accord has been the growing internationalization of world economies, and the need for Australian industry to become internationally competitive. Declining world prices for Australian agricultural and mineral products in the mid-1980s, a significant part of Australia's export income, brought a recognition of the need to diversify its export base, particularly manufactured goods.

Since 1986, the deterioration in Australia's balance of payments and growth of foreign debt has been the focal force for macro- and micro-economic policy. At the macro level, fiscal and monetary restraint have been adopted, whilst at the micro level, industry efficiency, productivity, and competitiveness have become important themes for policy. The Labor Government has been keen to pursue an industry restructuring policy which has involved reducing industry protection, and promoting concepts such as quality management, technological reform, and employee participation aimed at a world competitive manufacturing strategy (NIES 1988). Part of this strategy in the area of micro-economic reform includes plans for the Australian car, steel, footwear, clothing and textiles, heavy engineering, and waterfront industries.

In the area of labor market reform, recent government policy statements have indicated that "a greater degree of labor market flexibility" is high on its agenda (DEIR 1988). The term flexibility is used here in the broader meaning of "improving the ability and willingness of institutions and individuals in the labor market (...) to respond to the economic and social needs of the country" (DEIR 1988: p. 8).

Social. A social trend with important implications for the union movement has been the growth in the service and financial sectors of the economy and substantial decline in manufacturing. These growth sectors generally have a low level of unionization and often a large portion of female and part-time employees. As a consequence, despite a growing workforce, there has not been a growth in union membership levels, rather a decline from over 50% of the workforce to 42% (ABS). At its 1989 biennial congress, the president of the ACTU acknowledged the importance of this problem and indicated that whilst the ACTU had exerted a very successful influence at the macro level, this may have been at the expense of the rank and file at the micro level. This trend poses a future challenge for the union movement in terms of its representativeness and power and is significant given that a Labor Government has been in office.

Frenkel (1989) has also identified other demographic trends affecting the workforce. These include a growth in the female participation rate and a decline in the male levels, an increase in the immigrant workforce and a growth in part-time female employment. These also pose particular problems for union organization.

Political. Since 1983 the Australian union movement has not faced a hostile Federal Government. Furthermore, many Australian states also have Labor governments in office. Whilst the Accord has been modified and unions have suffered real wage reductions of around 10% since 1983, there remains an important cooperative relationship betweeen the government and ACTU. The government has also demonstrated a willingness to work closely with the business community. Social concertation has therefore not faced major political challenges.

10.4 Attitudes and Policies of the Actors

Unions. The leadership of the peak union body, the ACTU, specifically the president, Simon Crean and secretary, Bill Kelty, have had a substantial impact on the direction of the Australian trade union movement in the 1980s. Close links with the Labor Government have provided a favorable political context which has enabled the union movement to have an important input to policy at a time when its power could have been expected to decline. Niland and Spooner (1989) have also suggested that the institutional framework of conciliation and arbitration in Australia has given unions time to consider alternative strategies in the face of change and management militancy.

Two important documents released by the ACTU have helped establish strategic directions. In June 1987, Bill Kelty released a discussion paper concerning Future Strategies for the Trade Union Movement (ACTU 1987). Essentially, it proposed particular strategies which the union movement needed to seriously consider for its long-term viability and survival in the face of strong employer attacks through the media and legal system. Some proposals included the amalgamation of Australian unions into twenty large industry-based groupings, support for the Conciliation and Arbitration system, restructuring the ACTU, and increased emphasis by the ACTU through the political system.

Also released, in 1987, was a document titled "Australia Reconstructed", a report on an overseas study mission to Western Europe undertaken by the ACTU and Trade Development Council (ACTU/TDC 1987). The report endorsed a cooperative rather than confrontationist approach to industry restructuring in the face of competitive pressures and made a number of policy recommendations in areas such as industry unionism, wages and prices, industry policy, industry training, and industrial democracy. It also called for the development of a productivity consciousness and culture.

Both documents stressed the need for unions to be adaptive and to be proactive in promoting change. This has been forthcoming, particularly in the areas of industry restructuring and wages policy. Unions have given support for a new wages system based on efficiency, restructuring and productivity, and the ACTU leadership has sought strong commitment from the entire union movement for changes made by the Australian Conciliation and Arbitration Commission to wage-fixing principles in March 1987, August 1988, and August 1989. The union movement remains committed to centralized wage fixation and the Conciliation and Arbitration system which helps to explain why it has been prepared to accept restructuring and efficiency in the face of some employers who would prefer to dismantle the centralized system altogether. This also helps to ensure continuity in policy if the government should change.

The ACTU has also shown strong support for increased employee participation. An important development has been the issuing of a joint statement by the ACTU and Confederation of Australian Industry on employee participation (ACTU/CAI 1988).

Individual unions such as the Metal Workers (AMWU) and Footwear, Clothing, and Textile workers have also adopted a reformist approach. They represent large portions of the workforce in industries which have suffered considerably from past ineffecienies and foreign competition. These unions have a goal to help rejuvenate such industries in order to create more employment. The Industrial Democracy Officer for the Metal Workers Union, Max Ogden, sums up this view by suggesting, "If we simply go for direct confrontation on wages and conditions, then in the context of the global reorganization of manufacturing, it's likely to mean a further rapid fall in the number of jobs in manufacturing" (Ogden 1986: p. 39).

Union reform in terms of amalgamations away from craft-based toward industry-based unions is also on the agenda. Provisions in the new Industrial Relations Act of 1988 will facilitate this. Some amalgamations have taken and are currently taking place. Although not all are along industry lines as recommended in Kelty's ACTU paper, they are producing larger unions which will have greater economies of scale.

However, whilst the Australian union movement has been relatively successful in influencing the direction of industrial relations at the macro level and not suffering a substantial decline in power such as in Britain or the United States, a recent problem to emerge has been declining union density. As indicated above, this figure has fallen from over 50% to around 42%. The problem stems from in part an apparent alienation of the rank and file, declining real incomes, and the inability of unions to organize new groups of employees in the growth sectors of the economy such as leisure and tourism and financial and business services. This problem poses an important one for the union movement to address in the 1990s.

Overall, in the face of strong economic and social threats and also the push from employers for decentralized industrial relations, the union movement has been remarkably flexible (e.g. suffering real wage losses and changes in relativities) and coherent as a group since the early 1980s managing to maintain considerable influence over the direction in wages policy and industrial relations generally. Much of this can be attributed to the leadership of the ACTU and their ability to "sell" it to their affiliates. A crucial question is whether this can be maintained in the 1990s.

Employers. Faced with the economic challenges of the 1980s, two main approaches to industrial relations reform have been advocated by employers and employer associations. First, that of gradual reform within the conciliation and arbitration system and, second, a more militant approach involving the reassertion of managerial prerogatives with calls for legislative changes to reduce the power and influence of unions. Despite the differences in means, both share the same goal of decentralizing industrial relations with a greater emphasis on enterprise-level relations between management and workers. Two new influential groups to emerge have been the Business Council of Australia (BCA), and the "New Right".

The Business Council of Australia was formed in 1983 and consists of chief executives from Australia's large corporations. It has contributed significantly to the industrial relations debate in areas of enterprise-based industrial relations, work practice reform, and wage reform with many of its proposals being introduced within BCA member organizations (BCA Bulletins, various). Unlike the New Right, they have not pursued wholesale deregulation of the labor market, but rather focused on proactive reform, particularly in promoting enterprise level-industrial relations. This includes favoring the development of employee participation. They have also played a major role as business lobby group on the Labor Government.

The Confederation of Australian Industry (CAI), traditionally the main peak employer association, has tended to prefer to remain within the system of Conciliation and Arbitration and seek gradual reform. Because of this it has come under some criticism from other employer groups such as the Australian Federation of Employers. Nevertheless, it has been instrumental in the development of the two-tiered productivity wage system in 1987 and the joint statement on employee participation in 1988.

Whilst not strictly an employer association, a new group espousing a particular ideological approach in industrial relations emerged in 1986 and has received considerable media publicity from their involvement in several important industrial disputes. The H. R. Nicholls Society, consisting of political activists and business leaders, was established and became known as the New Right. Several employer organizations loosely involved with the New Right include the National Farmers Federation, the Australian Federation of Employers, and the Melbourne Chamber of Commerce.

The main objectives of the New Right are to reduce the power of the union movement, deregulate the labor market by removing the Conciliation and Arbitration Tribunals, and introduce labor contracts enforceable through common and business law (Dabscheck 1987). This is aimed at providing greater flexibility at the enterprise level.

Several well-publicized industrial disputes, namely Dollar Sweets, South East Queensland Electricity Board (SEQEB), Mudginberri, and Robe River, involved or had New Right support. The main elements of these important disputes were: The use of trade practices and common law against industrial action by unions resulting in financial penalties, attempts to reform work practices which inhibit efficient use of labor, the use of contract labor to perform work previously done by union labor, and union members circumventing their leadership in seeking agreements with their employers. All disputes, particularly because of their high profile in the media, helped to influence the industrial relations agenda throughout Australia quite apart from the specific workplaces involved. It could be argued that the threats from the New Right have forced the Labor Government and the ACTU to alter their strategies as originally specified in the Accord.

Whilst the initial developments amongst the business community were somewhat reactionary to the prospect of a Labor Government being in office for many years, more recently, there has been considerable support for the movements to productivity and efficiency as primary criteria for wage setting. However, a major limitation to social concertation is the inability of Australian employers to develop a united industrial relations strategy. Frenkel (1989; p. 22) has suggested that "employers have shown greater unity regarding wages policy recently but this has not led to organizational restructuring". The New Right are ideologically opposed to corporatism.

The State. The Australian Government has been a particularly important force in the social concertation which has taken place during the 1980s. Initially, the Accord set the direction for economic and social programs and offered substantial benefits for the workforce and wider community. However, faced with the growing trade deficit and wishing to substantially reduce public sector spending, it has adopted a tight fiscal and monetary policy since 1986.

In order to moderate wage growth to help promote the competitiveness of Australian industry, the government has supported the move to productivity and award restructuring as concepts of wage adjustment with the abandonment of full wage indexation. It has assisted in the form of income tax reductions to increase disposable income and also has various micro-economic reform packages in place.

Whilst the traditional association with the union movement has permitted their involvement, the Hawke Labor Government has also tried to involve the business community in its reform programs. A problem is that whilst there is one voice for the union movement, there are many for the employers.

Industrial Commissions. A fourth actor in the Australian context which has played a significant role in the process of social concertation is the Australian Industrial Relations Commission (formerly Conciliation and Arbitration Commission). To a large degree it provides the structure through which the various actors desired wages policies are processed in the concertation process. An important catalyst for widespread change was contained in two important National Wage Case decisions in March 1987 and August 1988. The principles which were outlined in these decisions marked a substantial departure from previous decisions, and also the Accord, which had been implemented in 1983.

Toward the end of 1986 there were signs of the need for changes to be made in wage-fixing principles, mainly as a result of the economic circumstances as outlined above. A review of the existing system resulted in a two-tiered wage system being introduced in March 1987. The first tier consisted of an immediate ten-dollar wage increase to all workers covered by Federal awards (this was also accepted by State Tribunals) and a further wage increase in October 1987 not to exceed 1.5%. The second tier offered a wage increase of up to 4% based on criteria of restructuring and efficiency. Unions and employers were free to negotiate wage increases, providing they met these criteria and could then have these agreements ratified by the Commission. This decision signalled the abandonment of full wage indexation with productivity and efficiency becoming the primary principles for wage adjustment. This landmark wage decision had several objectives, namely:

to reduce wage growth based on cost of living adjustments (i.e. abandon wage indexation);
to encourage productivity bargaining with an enterprise focus;
to reduce the reliance on wage relativities as a means of wage adjustment (ACAC, 1987).

The departure from previous wage fixing meant that unions and employers were now forced into direct negotiations rather than rely on the Commission to hand down decisions.

Further reinforcement of this new direction in wages policy was made by the Commission in its National Wage decision in August 1988. In handing down its structural efficiency principle, a wage increase of 3% was granted to all workers covered by awards on the understanding that unions give a commitment to engage in restructuring their awards. The principles included: establishing skill-related career paths, removing impediments to multiskilling, and allowing more flexible working patterns (ACAC 1988).

The August 1988 decision had several objectives, particularly to encourage industrial award restructuring with a view to:

> establishing skill-related career paths;
> eliminating impediments to multiskilling and broadening the range of tasks which a worker may be required to perform;
> ensuring that working patterns and arrangements enhance flexibility and meet the competitive requirements of the industry (ACAC 1988).

These two decisions have been further supported in National Wage cases of the Australian Industrial Relations Commission in April and August 1989. The decisions sought continuation of the rewriting and modernizing of all awards to provide career paths, training, and skills acquisition. Pay rises are based on award restructuring. The significant aspect of the decisions is that they seek to promote increased labor flexibility whilst at the same time, place a ceiling on wages growth.

10.5 The Form of Concertation

As indicated above, in Australia, an important vehicle for social concertation is the Australian Industrial Relations Commission. From the turn of this century it has become centrally important in establishing the terms and conditions of employment by means of industrial awards. Its National Wage Case decisions have national implications since some 90% of workers are covered by industrial awards. Various principles have been adopted by the Commission for these decisions including capacity to pay, productivity, needs, and cost of living indexes.

However, it is important to note that the Commission's decisions are largely influenced by the submissions which are presented to it in the wage hearings by governments, unions, and employers. In addition, a requirement under the Parliamentary Act which governs the Commission's operation is that it takes account of the state of the economy in handing down a decision. There has traditionally been much reliance on the Commission for setting the direction in industrial relations policy with very little direct interaction between the parties.

Prior to 1983 there had not been much direct social concertation in Australia at a national level; instead, the primary industrial relations actors made their submissions to the Commission. The election of the Labor Government in 1983 signalled the start of some concertation by means of the Accord although this was bipartite. The government has established various tripartite committees concerning industrial relations, industry policy, and training.

In the late 1980s there has been a considerable level of agreement amongst these actors on overall directions in industrial relations policy. This has included wages policy moving away from wage indexation and maintenance of relativities (comparative wage justice) toward productivity, efficiency, and skills. Most recently it has concerned the restructuring of industrial awards away from narrow job specializations and clear demarcation boundaries to provide for greater flexibility involving multiskilling, broadbanding, skill-based career paths, greater employee participation, job redesign, and work reorganization. This has enabled the Industrial Relations Commission to move wages policy in a different direction. There is not, however, a formal tripartism structure in operation apart from various committees. Nevertheless, there is now a strong inducement for greater labor management cooperation to take place, particularly at the enterprise and industry level in the context of award restructuring.

10.6 The Levels of Concertation

What commenced as a macro-level social contract between the Federal Labor Government and the ACTU has now been considerably modified, placing greater emphasis on industry and enterprise-level reform with the award restructuring process. The macro level still remains important in setting the parameters for the micro reform with the Industrial Relations Commission playing a central role. The significance of the guidelines is illustrated by the 1989 pilots dispute where the pilots sought to negotiate a wage increase in excess of the guidelines as determined by the Industrial Relations Commission. The lengthy dispute which resulted drew the wrath of the Federal Government and ACTU for their "selfish" claim.

The Australian Industrial Relations Commission and various State industrial relations tribunals have handed down decisions imposing less reliance on them to determine substantive employment conditions, particularly wages. The tribunals have established the broad parameters for wages policy and endeavored to place an emphasis on negotiated settlements at the industry or enterprise level. However, in order to limit the possibility of a wages blowout, it has set broad parameters within which it will ratify negotiated agreements. There have been several problems as a result, particularly an increasing number of groups who consider themselves to be special cases and therefore pursuing claims beyond the guidelines (e.g. schoolteachers and airline pilots).

Macro Concertation. Prompted by several National Wage decisions, this has been an area of substantial change in Australian industrial relations in the past three years. The decision by the Australian Conciliation and Arbitration Commission in the National Wage case of August 1988 helped promote further changes in this area with strong support from the Federal Government and ACTU, and also support from the CAI and BCA. The labor market reform policy released by the Federal Government in August 1988 sought to promote award restructuring (DEIR 1988). These actors play a major role in establishing the direction for industry and enterprise concertation.

The August 1988 wage decision offered all workers covered by Federal awards a pay increase of 3% on the basis that their respective unions give a commitment to engage in award restructuring. A further flat ten-dollar increase would be granted in March 1989 where such action had taken place. Essentially, the Commission was hoping to build on developments which had taken place since the earlier restructuring and efficiency decision of March 1987. A further national Wage Base of April 1989 provided a wage increase guideline of 6.3% for 1989. The August 1989 case also endorsed the earlier award restructuring principles. Thus, the structural efficiency principles set the criteria for all negotiations at the industry and enterprise levels ensuring integration between them.

Industry Concertation. In late 1986 and early 1987, the main employer and union federations in the metal industry produced draft proposals for reform aimed at preventing further job losses. Considerable common ground existed between the parties and included: the need for a completely new award with substantially fewer job classifications, scope for multiskilling, career structures and training, job security, and consultation. Negotiations are still taking place on this new award which seeks to reduce over 300 separate job classifications into 9 with three main streams. A major element of this restructuring is the emphasis on pay based on skills attained rather than work performed (Dufty 1989).

The growth in the Australian tourism industry and the need to provide for greater flexibility in employment conditions has resulted in several new industrial relations agreements. One, the Offshore Island Resorts Agreement 1988, was a negotiated agreement between the Australian Workers' Union and an employer group, Offshore Islands Resorts Association (Austalian Financial Review, 28 August 1988). It covers some 2,000 employees employed on 15 island resorts off Queensland and aims to increase labor flexibility in the geographically isolated resorts. Benefits for employees include an average pay rise of 18% and training schemes, while for employers, the removal of penalty pay rates for weekend work and demarcation barriers. It was strongly influenced by a special agreement which covered the World Expo '88 in Brisbane.

In the public sector, broadbanding has been introduced where once up to 100 different promotional positions have been placed into a few bands. This permits greater movement of employees in the public service within each band and reduces the number of promotional appeals. In the Australian Public service, an agreement was reached whereby a single office-based structure with 8 classifications replaced some 100 separate classifications for a large number of clerical, administrative, and keyboard staff (DEIR 1989). The agreement aims to provide more flexible working arrangements and improved career paths.

Enterprise Concertation. Examples of where restructuring has taken place at the enterprise level have mainly been at "greenfield" sites, particularly in the mining industry with new projects such as Argyle Diamonds and Worsley Alumina in Western Australia. During the planning phase of these ventures discussions between management and selected unions resulted in enterprise-based awards, usually involving only three to five unions, very few job classifications, and a considerable amount of multiskilling. This permits much greater management flexibility, increased job satisfaction, and fewer demarcation disputes. In most cases, pay levels are based on an employee's skill level rather than the actual work performed.

10.7 Objectives and Outcomes

The initial objectives of concertation were primarily a wages policy emphasizing the maintenance of real wage growth whereas the new objectives emphasize industry productivity and efficiency, the restructuring of industrial awards, and reform of work practices. The overriding theme is to make Australian industry more efficient in an effort to improve its international competitiveness.

At the macro or national level, the main objective is to control nominal wage growth in times of relatively healthy economic growth. This is why the Industrial Relations Commission sets maximum wage guidelines in its National Wage cases.

At the intermediate or industry level, the main participants in various industry groups are involved in industry restructuring and rationalizing industrial awards.

Within enterprises, there is also some degree of concertation taking place. This is mainly in medium to larger-sized organizations. Unions, management, and employees are involved in negotiations concerning job design, training, employee participation, and other matters of common interest.

This transformation has created several problems. First, at the operational level, rigidity of the Commission's wage guidelines, particularly maximum wage levels, has caused some difficulties. Severe skill shortages in a buoyant economy means that many employers need to offer wages in excess of award rates in order to attract and retain workers.

A second operational difficulty is that for many unions and employers, the new wage-fixing principles are a completely new *modus operandi* where negotiations are the primary means of handling issues rather than relying on conciliation and arbitration. This has led to problems such as cost offset deals rather than true productivity bargaining, leading to the development of some cynical attitudes concerning future award restructuring deals. Also, some restructuring packages have been hastily prepared, only to find considerable rank and file resistance when being implemented. A further problem concerns the interpretation of the meaning of restructuring by the parties. In effect, the new principles have meant a learning process for all parties.

A third major problem concerns those groups of employees who consider themselves to be "special cases". The wage-fixing principles provide little guidance for what constitutes a special case, simply stating that such considerations must be heard by a Full Bench of the Arbitration Commission. The lengthy pilots' dispute arose from their attempts to consider themselves as a special case.

In evaluating concertation in the 1980s, several criteria can be used. First, the level of nominal wage increases, in terms of which there has been some success in limited wages growth. In a relatively buoyant economy, wage growth has been largely contained within the parameters established in the National Wage cases. Combined with the devaluation effects of the Australian dollar, this has enhanced Australia's comparative labor costs. Second, the level of industrial disputation has been relatively low. Third, the adjustment of industries to new economic challenges will be a longer-term issue.

Compared with the incomes policy operating between 1975 and 1981, and the deregulated approach between 1981 and 1982, it has been relatively successful, not only in terms of outcomes but in achieving an attitudinal shift amongst many of the industrial relations actors about the merits of a cooperative approach to industrial relations. This is in marked contrast to the traditionally adversarial nature of Australian industrial relations.

10.8 Conclusions

Australia began experimenting with social concertation following the election of a Federal Labor Government in 1983. The close ties between the political party and the union movement produced the Accord which provided the blueprint for wages and other economic and social policies. It had a macro focus and was seen as a system which would provide non-inflationary growth for the Australian economy. Despite being a bipartite arrangement, its wages policy of full wage indexation was accepted by the Industrial Commission providing the background for industrial relations in the 1980s.

The last three years has seen significant changes to the Accord as most of the main industrial relations actors have shown a willingness to be flexible in responding to changing economic circumstances. The emphasis is now on economic adjustment at the industry and enterprise level in order to raise productivity rather than maintaining a centralized wage indexation policy. However, the National Wage Decisions of the Industrial Relations Commission still establish the parameters for these industry and enterprise negotiations. In effect, Australia is attempting to achieve greater industrial relations flexibility and structural adjustment within a centralized system with the Industrial Relations Commission acting as the medium for the actors to determine wages policies. The movement toward a more flexible and decentralized form of concertation has been the response to predominantly economic challenges of the mid-1980s.

An important medium for handling concertation in Australia has been the Industrial Relations Commission. In the 1980s it has shown itself to be capable of adjusting to new economic, social, and political challenges with wages policy moving away from cost of living indexation to productivity and award restructuring.

The reforms which are taking place in Australia show what can be achieved through negotiations between the important parties to industrial relations without substantial legislatively imposed changes or a completely deregulated approach. More reform than was imaginable at the start of the 1980s is taking place and at the same time, industrial disputation has been the lowest for many years. Greater flexibility in industrial relations has occurred as a response to changing circumstances. These changes signal greater emphasis on industrial negotiations at the enterprise level although social concertation at the national level still remains important to establish the framework and guidelines for these negotiations.

The major reasons for this have been a reformist-oriented Federal Government and national union body (the ACTU) and some key unions. Employers, particularly the BCA at the national level, have also been instrumental in promoting important changes. The industrial tribunals have also played a vital function in promoting changes from traditional industrial relations practices.

At the end of the decade, Australian industrial relations is in a state of considerable transition and structural adjustment with a number of significant developments taking place. Recently commenting on this, the Director of Labour Relations of the CAI indicated that he has seen more changes in the past 5 years than the previous 30 (Noakes 1989). Much of this reform is taking place through negotiation and concertation amongst the parties rather than being enforced through a legislative approach or by conflictual bargaining. The attitudinal shift amongst most of the industrial relations actors in Australia has produced a great deal of consensus regarding the direction for industrial relations for the next decade.

References

Australian Bureau of Statistics (ABS): Trade Union Members, Industrial Disputes. Canberra: Australia, 1988.

Australian Conciliation and Arbitration Commission (ACAC): National Wage Case Decision, March 1987, Print No. 86800. Melbourne.

Australian Conciliation and Arbitration Commission (ACAC): National Wage Decision, August 1988. Print H4000. Melbourne.

Australian Council of Trade Unions (ACTU): Future Strategies for the Trade Union Movement. Melbourne, 1987.

Australian Council of Trade Unions–Trade Development Council (ACTU/TCD): Australia Reconstructed: ACTU–TDC Mission to Western Europe. Canberra: Australian Government Publishing Service, 1987.

Australian Financial Review, 28 August 1988.

Business Council of Australia Bulletin, various issues.

Confederation of Australian Industry and Australian Council of Trade Unions, Jount Statement on Participative Practices. Melbourne: Bradley Printers, 1988.

Dabscheck, B. (1987): New Right or Old Wrong? Ideology and Industrial Relations. *Journal of Industrial Relations*, 29, 425–449.

Department of Industrial Relations (DEIR): *Labour Market Reform – The Industrial Relations Agenda*. Canberra: Australian Government Publishing Service, 1988.

Department of Industrial Relations (DEIR): *Award Restructuring – The Task Ahead*. Canberra: Australian Government Publishing Service, 1989.

Department of Employment and Industrial Relations (DEIR): *Industrial Democracy and Employee Participation: A Policy Discussion Paper*. Canberra: Australian Government Publishing Service, 1986.

Department of the Treasury: *Economic Round-up*, October 1989. Canberra: Australian Government Publishing Service, 1989.

Dufty, N. F. (1989): *Award Restructuring and Education in the Metal Trades*. Discussion Paper. Perth: Western Australian Labor Market Research Center.

Dufty, N. F. (1989): *Second Tier Wage Increases in Western Australia*. Report. Perth: CEDA.

Frenkel, S. (1989): *Restructuring Industrial Relations in Australia: A Battle Still to be Won?* Working Paper. Department of Industrial Relations, University of New South Wales.

Industrial Relations Act. Canberra, 1988.

Ministry of Labour and Employment (Belgium): Social Concertation in Belgium. Brussels, September 1989.

National Industry Extension Service (NIES): World Competitive Manufacturing. Canberra, July 1988.

H. R. Nicholls Society: *Arbitration in Contempt*. Hobart: Mercury-Walch, 1986.

Niland, J. R. (1989): *Transforming Industrial Relations in New South Wales: A Green Paper*. Sydney: Government Printer.

Niland, J. R. and K. Spooner (1989): *Structural Change and Industrial Relations in Australia*. Paper presented to the 8th World Congress of the International Industrial Relations Association. Brussels (September).

Noakes, B. (1989): *Address to National Convention of the Industrial Relations Society of Australia*. Alice Springs (April).

Ogden, M. (1986): Industrial Democracy and New Management Techniques in the Australian Metal Industry. *Journal of Australian Political Economy*, 20, 39.

Plowman, D. H. (1987): Economic Forces and the New Right: Employer Matters, in 1986: *Journal of Industrial Relations*, 29, 84–91.

Report of the Committee of Review: *Australian Industrial Relations Law and Systems*. Canberra: Australian Government Publishing Service, 1985.

Rimmer, J. and J. Zappata (1988): Labour Market Flexibility and the Second Tier. *Australian Bulletin of Labour*, 14, 564–591.

Statement of Accord by the Australian Labor Party and the Australian Council of Trade Unions Regarding Economic Policy (Accord), 1983.

Treu, T. (1989): *Industrial Relations, Tripartism and Concerted Actions: Where do we Stand?* Paper presented to the 8th World Congress of the International Industrial Relations Association. Brussels (September).

Walton, R.B. and A. McKersie (1965): *Behavioral Theory of Labor Negotations.* New York: McGraw-Hill.

11 For a New Income Policy. Growth, Prices and Wages in the Italian Model

Renato Brunetta and Leonello Tronti

The paper recounts the recent history of incomes policy in Italy, its nature, peculiarities, specifics, anomalies, and accomplishments, seen both in relation to the particular economic situation of the later 1980s and in the perspective of the single European market in 1992.

Premised on a theoretical framework on incomes policy as an evolutionary, cooperative game, and on a schematic "Italian model" of economic and social development, the paper examines the recent government/union agreement to eliminate fiscal drag (26 January 1989), and the working of revised *scala mobile*. It then offers guidelines for long-run incomes policy, capable not only of managing real gross and net wages but also, and above all, of guaranteeing the efficient allocation of the benefits of productivity gains.

11.1 Premise: Incomes Policy as a Cooperative Game

Starting from the lesson provided by the Italian incomes policy experience of the 1980s, this paper presents a new framework to interpret the performance of incomes policy agreements and institutions, and proposes new strategies for the 1990s.

In this analytical framework, incomes policy is viewed as the cooperative, evolutionary outcome of a non-cooperative long-term game among several players (workers, unions, firms, government, parliament, etc.), along the model sketched up by Brunetta and Carraro (1990) (Chart 1). In that model, being the cooperative outcome of such a game unstable (due to several reasons, one of which is workers' and unions' time-bounded rationality), a set of norms or rules (institutions) must emerge for the agreement to be sustainable in the long run. In such a situation, evolutionary game theory can be used to describe the emergence, in the long run, of stable incomes policy settlements.

Several conditions make the actual implementation of incomes policy possible. Among others, incomes policy agreements must be policed by appropriately designed norms and institutions (enforcement technology), and these

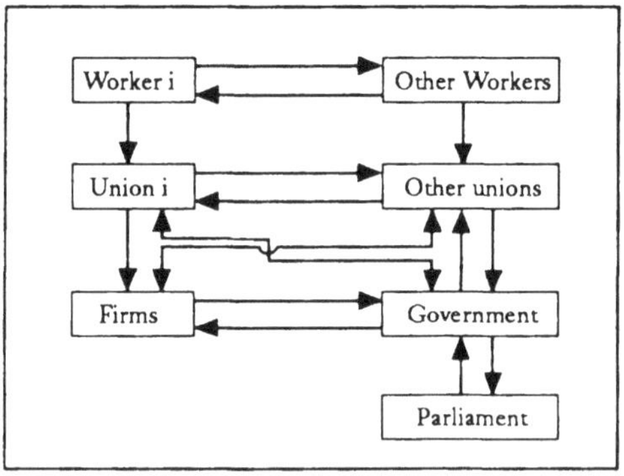

Source: Brunetta and Carraro 1988

Chart 1: The Structure of the Brunetta and Carraro Model

agreements are likely to be inequality-preserving. In a perspective different from Weitzman (1984), gainsharing (profit- and/or productivity-sharing) is then viewed as a major mechanism capable of sustaining and enforcing long-run cooperative agreements.

The basic assumption in the analysis is that incomes policy is a way of achieving cooperation among conflicting social groups. This implies recognition that economic agents interact, and that a group of agents' action can negatively affect other agents' welfare (or profit). The presence of externalities, thus, can lead the government to intervene, in order to redistribute welfare gains that can be achieved through harmonization of agents' behavior.

This approach is not totally new. Tarantelli (1986: chs. 2 and 3) proposed a similar approach to incomes policy by viewing wage and price stabilization as a public good. His analysis makes use of a static model that prevents the understanding that incomes policy can never be adopted by social parties (not even in a completely centralized setting) if the intertemporal dimension of the decision process is not taken into account.

In contrast, following Brunetta and Carraro (1990), this paper proposes to view incomes policy as a dynamic, long-term agreement – on growth targets no less than on distribution patterns – that can be sustained as an equilibrium growth-path by appropriately designed institutions (rules). In the short run, the agreement can be modified in order to react to transitory shocks affecting the economy, and the rules must properly allow for such temporary modifications.

In this context, agents' behavior is represented as an intertemporal non-cooperative game, in which both conflict and cooperation are possible outcomes that depend on the agents' strategies (and all agents have different objectives). Conflict and cooperation are possible strategies among others, but cooperation (incomes policy) has been shown to emerge as the best policy in the long run, after agents have learned and compared different strategies (evolutionary strategy, and the related equilibrium concept).

The plan of the paper is the following: In the next section is sketched out a schematic model of the Italian economy, and of the main anomalies in its labor market. Ironically, peculiar disequilibria have succeeded in assuring till now a relatively comfortable performance to the economic system, but this is not likely to last forever, and will not favor the completion of the single European market.

The need to envisage and implement new strategies is stressed, too, by the present period of profound wage reform (including industry-wide labor contracts, wage indexation mechanism, and severance pay), as is argued in Section 3. Furthermore, the abandonment of the cooperative game of a concerted incomes policy after 1984, and the poor results of more recent attempts in this direction (the agreement to eliminate fiscal drag of 26 January 1989 and the following two agreements on labor costs of 25 January and 6 July 1990) signal the urgent need for a new round in tripartite concertation.

Section 4 examines the working of the *scala mobile* agreement, a rule of the game enforced from 1986, and suggests its modification as to make it an efficient and flexible tool for incomes policy. The managing of real gross and net wages is viewed not only as a means for safeguarding workers' purchasing power, but to guarantee the efficient allocation of productivity gains, as well as a prerequisite for a long-term, cooperative incomes policy. A strong help to the successful performance of such a concerted strategy is seen in price control through public prices management.

The last section presents a few concluding remarks that stress the opportunity to establish the invoked new round in incomes policy game on two general principles (rules): First, that wage increases in any sector never exceed gains in productivity, unless through agreements reached by concertation; Second, that all automatic mechanisms in incomes formation be abandoned, in favor of more flexible and functional policies within a general concertation framework between business, unions, and government.

11.2 The Features of Today's Italian Model

An interpretation of the current trends of the Italian labor market, as well as of its potential future outcomes, cannot do without at least the implicit adoption of a model of the Italian development, as it has emerged over the past two decades. This is indispensable because the labor market is a faithful reflection (as well as a fundamental element) of the actual economic and social condition of the country. And it is also helpful in view of the strong performance of the Italian economy since 1984, in order to weight the likelihood of the current expansion's continuing in the future.

In simplified form, with a "stylized" portrayal of some features of recent economic evolution, the schema set forth here takes as its starting point a number of distinctive features and anomalies, observable within the Italian labor market and the structural development of the Italian economy (see also Tables 1 and 2). Those considered are:

(1) an employment rate significantly lower than the average for the industrial economies;
(2) female participation rates as much as 10 points lower than those of Northern Europe;
(3) self-employment accounting for a significantly larger share of total employment than elsewhere, and still rising;
(4) an underground economy that employs an estimated 2.4 million people;
(5) a part-time ratio more than 5 points lower than the European average;
(6) one of the highest propensities to save in the industrial world;
(7) inflation averaging about twice the rate as in its major competitors;
(8) fixed capital formation about one-third slower than the average for the industrial countries;
(9) public debt slightly over GDP, with an annual budget deficit of the order of 12% of GDP, and a primary deficit (net of interest payments) of 4%.

The functional interactions among these divergences and anomalies may

Table 1: The Italian Economy, 1970–1988.
(Annual Percentage Changes: 1980 Prices)

	GDP	Gross fixed capital formation	Private consumption	Public consumption	Consumer price deflator
1971	1.6	0.1	3.5	5.2	5.5
1972	2.7	1.3	3.7	5.1	6.4
1973	7.1	8.8	6.9	2.6	13.8
1974	5.4	2.0	3.7	2.5	21.3
1975	2.7	7.3	0.3	2.5	16.6
1976	6.6	0.5	5.2	2.3	17.7
1977	3.4	1.8	4.1	2.8	17.6
1978	3.7	0.6	3.4	3.5	13.2
1979	6.0	5.7	7.3	3.0	14.5
1980	4.2	8.7	5.6	2.1	20.5
1981	1.0	3.2	1.4	2.7	18.1
1982	0.3	5.2	1.3	2.9	16.9
1983	1.1	0.9	0.6	2.9	15.2
1984	3.0	4.5	2.1	2.5	11.8
1985	2.6	1.4	3.1	3.5	9.0
1986	2.5	1.6	3.8	2.9	5.8
1987	3.0	6.8	3.9	3.6	5.1
1988	3.9	4.9	3.8	3.0	4.9
1989	3.2	5.1	3.8	0.5	6.3

Source: Istat, National Accounts 1990.

Table 2: The Italian Economic System—Selected Indicators
(Annual Change in Percentage: 1980 Prices)

	GDP at market prices	Employment		Cost of labour	GDP per person employed	Cost of labour per unit output
		Total	Wage and salary earners			
1971	1.6	0.1	1.1	14.6	1.7	11.5
1972	2.7	0.6	0.9	11.6	3.3	7.1
1973	7.1	2.2	2.4	20.5	4.9	12.2
1974	5.4	2.0	1.8	24.7	3.4	18.6
1975	2.7	0.1	−0.1	20.7	−2.8	24.2
1976	6.6	1.5	1.5	22.7	5.0	15.2
1977	3.4	1.0	1.3	22.3	2.3	18.0
1978	3.7	0.5	−0.6	15.8	3.1	13.0
1979	6.0	1.5	1.3	21.5	4.4	14.8
1980	4.2	1.9	1.3	23.0	2.2	18.8
1981	1.0	—	−0.7	21.7	1.0	21.4
1982	0.3	0.6	0.2	16.4	−0.2	16.4
1983	1.1	0.6	−0.8	15.1	0.5	15.5
1984	3.0	0.4	−0.1	11.6	2.6	8.9
1985	2.6	0.9	1.4	11.7	1.7	8.2
1986	2.5	0.8	0.4	7.7	1.8	5.5
1987	3.0	0.6	0.4	9.8	2.4	6.8
1988	3.9	1.4	1.6	10.5	2.5	6.1
1989	3.2	0.2	0.5	9.2	3.0	6.0

Source: Based on Istat data 1990.

suggest the formulation of a causal framework, capable of explaining the resiliency and the efficiency of the Italian model (Chart 2).

In the last twenty years, Italian economic development has achieved a strong, dynamically responsive equilibrium with respect to the economic cycle, taking advantage of historical characteristics and the peculiar features of the organization of society. Above all, the underground economy, and to a lesser extent the comparative importance of self-employment, is crucial to an understanding of both Italy's lower female participation rate and its low part-time rate, and therefore of the low overall employment rate. Hence widespread tax and social security evasion, the high saving rates, and the private sector's great capacity to finance the public debt. Meanwhile, public expenditure is largely directed to defusing conflict and fostering consensus; in other words, it is directed to the dynamic maintenance of the model.

On the other hand, Italy's historically inflationary economy has entailed a relatively undersized productive apparatus, and a curtailment of the economy's ability to provide jobs, notwithstanding the high saving rate (Tronti 1987a). One of the most immediate harmful effects of sustained relatively high inflation is, in fact, the uncertainty it induces in estimating return on private investment, especially when the expected profits are

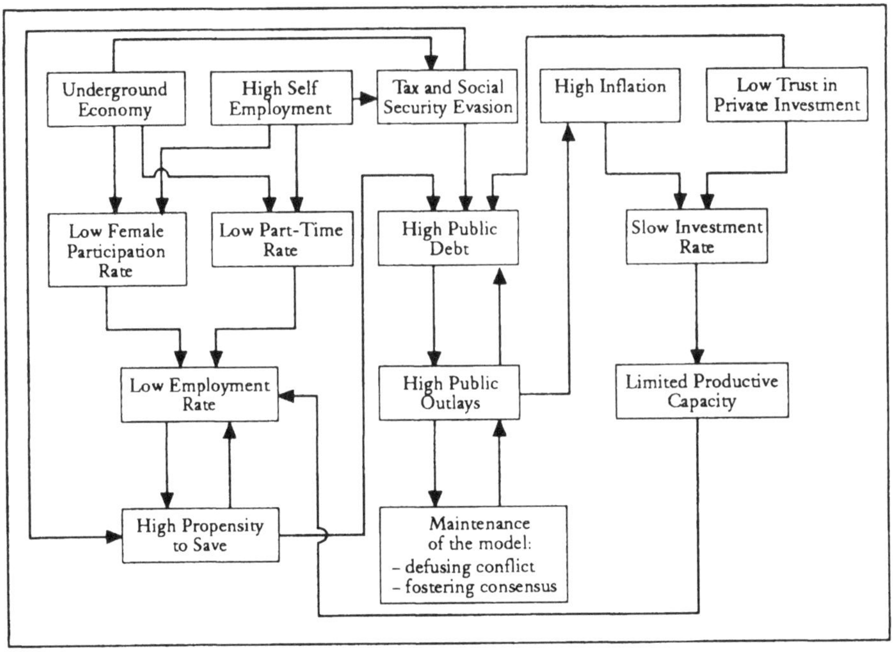

Chart 2: The Italian Model

weighted heavily toward the last years of investment's life. The still inadequate dimension of Italy's productive plant, thus, may well be related to the country's particular propensity to inflation. All the more so, when one considers the traditional mistrust of Italy's small savers in private equity markets, as reflected in the very modest development of the stock exchange (as compared to public debt), as well as the very large role of Government in the economy: This overall assessment fits best to the most undercapitalized sectors of the private economy (farming and livestock raising, some industries and service branches, and social investment), and above all to the regions of the South.

The model thus summarily sketched has managed, despite the persistence and recurrent exacerbation of glaring disequilibria, to weather both the social and economic shocks of the 1970s, as well as the massive restructuring of the 1980s, without any great social trauma and even at what remains, fundamentally, a relatively modest cost in terms of unemployment (Giavazzi and Spaventa 1989).

As the decade draws to a close, the question policy-makers and all economic agents have to face is whether this model can withstand the European integration of the 1990s without strong corrections, when Italian savings can flow directly into international markets, and the constraints of competition will be increasingly widespread, stringent, and hard to elude. In other words, 1992 will test whether real integration into Europe and the overthrow of pervasive and disingenuous domestic equilibria will once again arrive as a *deus ex machina* – certainly at higher cost to all agents – or whether this time the Italian economic system will manage by itself to follow the guidelines needed to accomplish to the European integration, without bitter surprises and in the best possible fashion.

On the answer to this question necessarily depends the formulation of consistent policy indications for the coming decade, for the entire economic and social body. In particular, for the purposes of this paper, on that answer depends the most appropriate model for playing the incomes policy game in the 1990s.

11.3 Wage Reform and the Agreement of 26 January 1989

In the present contractionary phase for the Italian economy, the revision of the *scala mobile*, and more generally the safeguarding of the purchasing power of wages, is closely connected with the possibility of reformulating incomes policy. In fact, today we are in the midst of a renovation of virtually the entire "pay packet". In 1989 and 1990, by a singular coincidence, the agreements covering all the major items have expired: Not only the indexed portion (*scala mobile*), but also the negotiated portion (industry-wide labor contracts), and the deferred portion (severance pay).

The present lack of clarity and ideas afflicting relations between Government and the two sides in industrial conflict springs, in our view, from the overhasty abandonment of the cooperative game of a concerted incomes policy resulting from tripartite negotiations. The last such measure was taken more than five years ago, with the so-called Valentine's Day agreement of 1984 and its legislative implementation (Chart 3).

The abandonment of the tripartite incomes policy game was largely due to the opposition of one player, a part of the trade unions – chiefly the communist stream of Cgil, whose majority was always opposed to it. But the corresponding indifference shown in recent years by the other players (Government and employers' organizations) can only be understood, ironically, in the light of the economic successes achieved with disinflation and the windfall from the world economy, especially with the oil "countershock" in 1986.

Today, however, the chickens have come to roost. The condition of international economy are no larger favorable, and the perspective of European integration sets stringent tasks on the Italian economic system. Labor dispute has also persisted, and in a few cases augmented, showing new types of conflict differing from the traditional dispute over wages and hours.

These new types of conflict are indeed over economic issues, but they take

Objective	Instruments 22 January Agreement	14 February Agreement
Cost of labour	Change in *scala mobile* agreement State assumption of social security contributions	Fixing of maximum number of *scala mobile* points for first 2 quarters
Employment, Labour market reform	More flexible first-job hiring procedures mobility hiring reform hours reform	Institution: observer, labour agency Solidarity contracts On-the-job-training contracts Revision of hiring procedures
Industrial relations	Removal of causes of micro-conflict	
Prices and charges	Ceiling (13%) on increases, but merely as a target	Ceiling (10%) with specific tools for implementation Modulation of increases Self-regulation of unregulated prices Postponement of increases in rent-controlled apartment rents
Taxes	Change in income tax Neutralization of fiscal drag	Modification of VAT, local real-estate income tax (ILOR), imputed capital gains tax on property (INVIM), etc. Target for tax revenue increase by elimination of evasion (10 trillion lire) Correction of tax brackets
Public spending	Control of enlarged public sector deficit	Control of enlarged public sector deficit Restructuring public expenditure
Health and social security	Reduction in prescription fee for low-income groups Modification in sick pay New disability pension rules	Reform of local health units New drugs regulations Reform of family allowances and social contributions Renewal of conventions with private clinics

Objective	Instruments 22 January Agreement	14 February Agreement
Industrial policy		Strengthening of CIPI (Interministerial Committee of Industrial Policy) "Horizontal" measures (depressed industries, formation of companies for new investment opportunities, active role for public demand
Southern development		Promotion of employment opportunity (cooperatives) Support and incentives

Chart 3: Two Tripartite Agreements Compared: 22 January 1983 and 14 February 1984.
Source: Brunetta and Pozzana 1984.

place directly in the sphere of economic, fiscal, and welfare policy, over and above the ordinary wage claims. This was the case in the dispute over the Government's budgetary decree-law, against which the unions did not hesitate to call a general strike over an economic policy issue (direct taxation and fiscal drag), far removed from the traditional bargaining platforms. And it was evident in the general strike against the Government's recent decision to increase presciption and diagnostic service charges for clients of the National Health System.

The offsetting of fiscal drag has been one of the union demands with the most far-reaching policy implications. The labor movement has asked that Government ensure a stable tax bite on incomes, despite the automatic shift to higher tax brackets due to inflation. In this, the unions have opposed the *de facto* tax raises imposed with no explicit decision (or bargaining), hence not being the fruit of reason and consensus, but of the blind operation of the economy (thus an unfair tax).

It is worth recalling that the combined effect of fiscal drag and social security tax relief for employers is to transfer a certain amount of resources from wages to profits (Giavazzi and Spaventa 1989). This circuit did yield the benefit of facilitating the recovery in investment and the economic adjustment after the shocks of the 1970s, but its introduction was nevertheless not decided consciously and came about without the explicit consent of worker organizations. It slowed down the rise in net wages and fuelled union demands for wage safeguards.

The neutralization of fiscal drag and the reform of the *scala mobile* must also be seen in relation to changes in indirect taxation. With a view to the completion of the single European market, the Government is proceeding to align Italian VAT rates with those in the European trading partners. The first step was raising items taxed at nil and 2% to the 4% rate. Further adjustments are foreseen that will produce additional revenue of 3,8 trillion lire in 1990, and 4,0 trillion in 1991.

The VAT adjustment meant, in turn, that the *scala mobile* had to be sterilized against its effects. Otherwise wages and salaries would have risen more than proportionally, triggering off a new wage/price spiral. The most authoritative econometric analysis projected an initial impact in the year (net of demand effects) of between 0.32 and 0.62 percentage points on the cost of living, depending on the reference index selected. This explains a part of the resurgence in inflation at the beginning of 1989. Because of this price effect, the Government announced the need to sterilize the wage indexation mechanism, and the trade unions, for their part, asserted their right to discuss and bargain over the measure. It is established practice that no modification of the *scala mobile* shall be made without the consent of the unions, or at least without an effort to obtain their assent (as in the agreements of 22 January 1983 and 14 February 1984). Thus the Government proposed to trade off the two measures – neutralization of fiscal drag against VAT increases sterilization – having previously enacted the reform of income tax brackets, and a controlled revision of the rules on conventional tax assessments (the so-called "condonation" of unpaid taxes by the self-employed).

This complicated political exchange, anyway, did not work. The unions upset the plan by proclaiming a general strike; and, in order to ward this off, the Government agreed to the questionable pact of 26 January. General strike, anyway, was not avoided but only delayed to the next dispute – the one on increases in National Health System charges, a few months later – and, once again in Italian postwar history, after a general strike the Cabinet had to resign.

The 26 January agreement was a partial and misleading understanding that resolved only the fiscal aspect of the problem (and far from optimally, at that), while neglecting the crucial issue. This, in our view, can only be the design of a new, effective economic development policy, appropriate to the current cyclical phase and the array of deadlines and commitments facing the economy over the next few years. Such a policy, as we have seen in Section 1, has to hinge on a long-run income policy in the perspective of European integration, based on regular, institutionalized consultation and shared responsibility between union, Government, and business in all sectors of the economy, and must be endowed with the appropriate enforcement technology as to avoid "free-riding" behaviors by single agents (Tarantelli 1988).

The perilous political and technical fragility of the 26 January pact may be viewed as the result of a failure to understand that all the issues mentioned – the upcoming expiration of the *scala mobile* agreement (in the background);

the reform of VAT; income tax reform; and the reduction of tax evasion and measures to make the underground economy surface – must be dealt with within a unified, consistent development strategy (cooperative game).

This long-term policy must usher in a new stage in incomes policy, going beyond the limits of emergency measures and form part of a broad project, truly European in outlook.

The bilateral (Government/unions) fiscal pact of 26 January 1989 could perhaps be viewed as the first step toward a new era in Italian incomes policy. Afterward, in fact, two further centrally concerted agreements were signed: (a) a bilateral (unions/firms) understanding on industrial labor cost, in view of nation-wide labor contracts renewal (25 January 1990); (b) a trilateral (unions/firms/Government) understanding on labor cost in the whole economy and on cost-of-living allowance (7 July 1990) (Chart 4).

Unfortunately, however, these are insufficient steps, and dangerously away from any policy reflecting the economic realities and the need of a strategy for development and European integration. Such inadequacy, both technical and political, demands further, broader reflections, such as could be made during the present negotiation on labor cost and wage structure, begun on 1 June 1991.

In the long run, apart from cyclical and countercyclical maneuvers, the equitable and efficient regulation of the growth in income from labor and from capital depends strictly on the ability to create and enforce an appropriate distribution of the economy's productivity gains (Tronti 1987b).

Recently, as the 1988 report of the ASAP (Association of State Petroleum Corporations) makes clear, the distribution of productivity gains across economic sectors, achieved thanks essentially to the performance of the industrial sector, has been questionable to say the least. A part of the gain went to profits, a part was taken by taxes (chiefly, from 1986 on, as a result of fiscal drag), and also a part to wages in the public sector (Figure 1, Table 3). It thus turns out that, except for the part going to profits, the real protagonists of the surge in productivity, those who bore the burden of industrial restructuring and rationalization, received only a tiny portion of the benefit.

The rise in tax revenues was unplanned and unexpected, not the result of any explicit program for broadening the tax base (such as might have been achieved, for instance, by taxing retained profits, taxing capital gains, and so on); rather it stemmed principally from fiscal drag and the characteristics of the economic expansion. Nor, certainly, have the wage gains of public employees been obtained by virtue of improvements in their productivity (as difficult and controversial as the measurement of this is), but rather by virtue of that sector's "monopoly" position.

Thus, the present Italian incomes policy problem appears to be how to regulate the long-run distribution of the added income due to productivity gains. To solve this problem, as we have seen above, means to build a major

	Fiscal equity	Anti-inflation
Income from labour		
– wage and salary earners	Total elimination of fiscal drag	Sterilization of scala mobile against VAT increases
	reduction of health service contributions to 0.64% as of 1 June 1990	
– self-employed	Prepayment of income tax in two instalments per year	
	Lowering ceiling for conventional tax regime from 36 to 19 million lire per year	
	Recalculation of past fiscal history (condonation)	
Income from capital	By May 1991, rationalization and harmonization with EEC rules on financial incomes	
National income tax	Reform of standards for deductible expenses (interest payments, medical expenses, funeral costs, educational costs, insurance and voluntary health and pension contributions)	
	Measures to combat tax avoidance, with definition of actions considered illicit tax avoidance	
	Limits to public relations expenses, *et al.*, for tax purposes, conferences; taxation of merger profits	
Local income tax	Pledge to combat evasion	
	Extension of taxing powers for local authorities in 1990	

Chart 4: Government Commitments Under The Pact Of 26 January.
Source: Brunetta and Trout, 1989.

mechanism capable of sustaining and enforcing long-run cooperative agreements. Naturally, from a technical standpoint, the efficient solution of the problem requires this to be done without neglecting the interconnections with wage indexation and the other areas of incomes policy.

The transformation of the economic picture since 1983, when disinflation got under way, the length and the strength of the current expansion, and the prospect of the single European market now allows us to tackle the problem in a new climate. The outlook today is for sustained, relatively non-inflationary growth, largely free of grave economic emergencies (despite such burdensome legacies as massive joblessness, the huge public debt, and the persistent

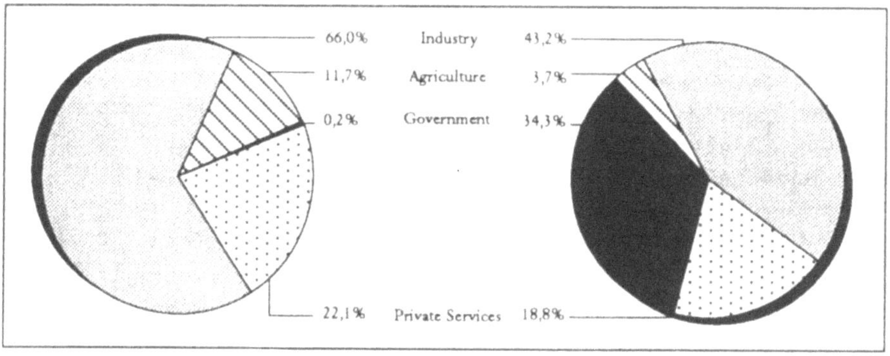

* Value added per unit labour at 1980 prices
* * Real earnings per unit labour
Source: Brunetta and Tronti 1989

Figure 1: Distribution of Productive Gains* ... and Wage Gains**
Weighted Contribution to Increase, 1983–1987

Table 3: Productivity Gains and Wage Increases, 1983–1989.
(Percentage Increases)

	Productivity*	Wages**
Agriculture	20.72	1.13
Industry	29.98	10.71
Private services	6.88	5.70
Government	−0.93	12.68

* Value added per unit labour, 1980 prices.
** Real gross earnings per unit labour.
Source: based on Istat, National Accounts data 1990.

inefficiency of the public sector), and marked above all by the calendar for European integration.

11.4 For a new Incomes Policy

In formulating a dynamic, long-term incomes policy, consistent with a Europe-oriented strategy for economic development, a useful starting point is Italy's budget legislation, which now requires that the Finance and Budget Acts supply a three-year economic and fiscal program (the medium-term financial plan), on the basis of a programmed inflation rate for each fiscal year, allowing for the effects of the projected deficit on macro-economic aggregates.

The programmed inflation rate was the linchpin of the income policy launched in 1983–1984, as of economic and financial policy in subsequent years. It has come to represent a fixed medium-term point of reference for all economic agents. The programmed inflation rate thus estimates the maximum rate of price increase compatible with the targets for balanced economic growth, limitation of the public debt, control of the balance of payments, and Italy's alignment with Europe.

The transition from an incomes policy aimed at disinflation and adjustment, under the impact of external shocks, to one of dynamic planning consistent with medium-term economic policy goals requires that the indexation of both gross wages (*scala mobile*) and net wages (control of fiscal drag and the tax wedge) will no longer be entrusted to automatic economic mechanisms. Rather, it must be determined in tripartite negotiations on the basis of the programmed inflation rate.

The extent and the technique of indexation can be reformed along the lines suggested by Ezio Tarantelli to combat the wage/price spiral (i.e. predetermination of *scala mobile* points for a year, with annexed guarantees and sanctions) (Tarantelli 1988). This would avert the protraction of automatic purchasing power safeguard mechanisms that, in acting upon unforeseen and unmanageable domestic or international shocks, may easily generate damaging multiplier effects on costs and prices. When this happens, economic policy is obliged to compensate with tardy and artificial sterilization and correction.

The forthcoming expiration of the three-segment wage indexation mechanism introduced in 1986 (Chart 5 and Figure 2) makes further reform possible. Any proposals for change, of course, should not be judged prior to a thorough examination of the results achieved by the new system's brief application. Let us recall that the new system brought in by law 38 of 26

Frequency	Semi-annual
Index	Trade union cost-of-living index. Reference is to the ratio of average level of the index in the six months covered to the average for the previous six months, rounded to two decimal places.
Form and size of adjustment	This system remains in effect through 31 December 1991. Salaries are indexed as follows: A fixed portion of 580,000 lire monthly is 100% indexed; the portion from 580,000 to the contract minimum for each grade, plus accrued cost-of-living allowance, is 25% indexed.
Application	All wage and salary earners in public and private sectors.
Disadvantages	This system was designed to correct the excessive wage levelling of its predecessors. As ex-post adjustment to inflation it is an automatic defense mechanism, not an instrument of incomes policy.

Chart 5: The Present Scala Mobile.

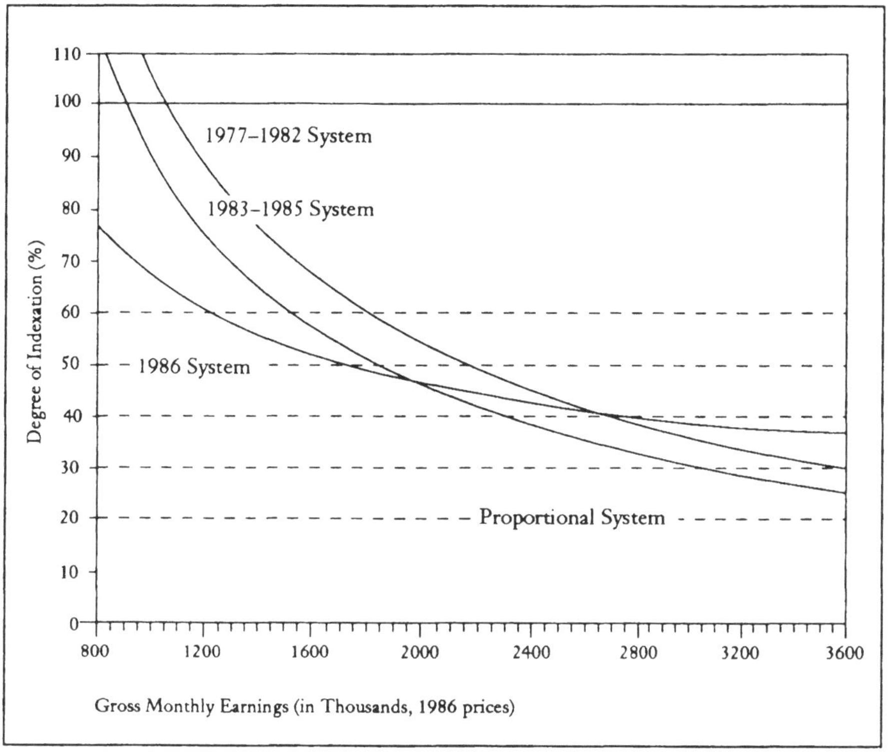

Source: G. Faustini 1987

Figure 2: Different Wage Indexations System (1986 Prices)
(This Figure shows how the new system provides less unequal degrees of coverage for different income levels, with less complete coverage of lower incomes and more complete coverage of higher ones.)

February 1986 had three distinct purposes, in addition to defending the purchasing power of wages. These were:

(a) Macroeconomically, curbing the automatic increase in the wage bill and ending the inflationary price/wage-price spiral by accompanying disinflation with a reduction in the degree of indexation coverage;
(b) In industrial relations, enlarging the negotiated portion of earnings and diminishing the automatically indexed portion, thus enabling the unions to retain their collective bargaining role on wages;
(c) Microeconomically, combating the excessive wage-levelling of years past, which had meant disincentives and lack of rewards for skill, a trend closely connected with the introduction in 1975 of the uniform cost-of-living allowance point, and the steady increase in the proportion of total wages accounted for by the allowance.

In its brief three-year existence, the system has answered well, though not perfectly, to the purpose of safeguarding gross wages, as well as to the first two of the three additional goals. Specifically, the macro objective has been virtually attained. In 1987, nominal GDP increased by 9.3%, and was only very slightly outpaced by total income from wages and salaries, which rose 9.8%. In 1988, however, gross wages (net of employer contributions) rose at the same 10.1% rate as nominal GDP. It is thus hard to argue that overall salaries, in the past two years, have produced any independent impetus to inflation.

The new *scala mobile* can thus be said to have worked quite well although, as some acute observers have pointed out, at a time of decelerating inflation the shift from quarterly to semiannual wage adjustment has ironically delayed rather than speeded disinflation.

The second industrial relations objective also appears to have been quite largely attained. In industry excluding construction the share of the rise in the average wage accounted for by the cost-of-living allowance has plunged from 59% in 1986 to 40% in 1987 and 32% in 1988. The degree of coverage of gross earnings has declined sharply, owing in part to the recent upturn in inflation (Table 4), but not to the detriment of real wages. The unions have vigorously resumed wage bargaining, without negative repercussions on the purchasing power of the average wage, which has risen by 2% per year.

Table 4: Scala Mobile: Degree of Coverage of Average Gross Yearly Earnings of Manufacturing Employees.

Year	Degree of coverage (%)[1] Using union index	Using Istat index
1982	78.9	76.9
1983	76.6	71.8
1984	51.5	53.8
1985	61.7	60.2
1986	56.9	54.8
1987	57.3	68.0
1988	47.0	50.0

[1] Ratio of percentage rise in salaries due to scala mobile and percentage rise in cost-of-living indices.
Source: Mariani 1989.

Much more questionable is the presumed role of the revised *scala mobile* in the renewed widening of wage differentials. The restoration of differentials between grades and between industries and sectors has been under way since 1982, and has now brought earnings variability back to the levels of the 1970s (ASAP 1986–1989). The causes of the widening of the range of variation between sectors are uncertain and complex, but the importance of wage drift in enhancing differentials by grade is clear (Dell'Aringa and Presutto 1986.

The present *scala mobile* mechanism provides 100% indexation of a salary band valued at 750,900 lire monthly as of 1 May 1990; this is the equivalent

Table 5: Incidence of 100% Indexed Portion on Average Gross Earnings.

Date	Size of indexed portion (monthly)	Percentage of average earnings*	Average incidence on yearly basis**	
As of 1.5.86	580,000	36.94		
As of 1.11.86	595,776	35.79	1986	37.11
As of 1.5.87	613,054	35.73		
As of 1.11.87	629,055	34.57	1987	35.55
As of 1.5.88	645,348	34.39		
As of 1.11.88	662,385	33.65	1988	34.25
As of 1.5.89	679,806	33.69		
As of 1.11.89	703,123	33.03	1989	33.60
As of 1.5.90	724,217	33.08		
As of 1.11.90	750,868	—	1990	32.96

* Gross earnings per unit labour (annual figure, Istat, National Accounts).
** Using monthly values.

of 33% of 1990 average gross earnings (Table 5). It also provides 25% indexation of a second salary band, which covers the difference between the first band and the minimum contract wage for each grade. A third portion, that is, salaries above the contract minimum, is not indexed at all. The putative differentiating impact of the mechanism, however, has no effect whatever on wage drift; it affects only the variability of the second wage band, which in turn is defined by collective bargaining.

Looking at the engineering and chemical industries, which renewed their labor contracts during the period, we find that between 30 April 1986 and 31 October 1988 (on the even, i.e. of the new *scala mobile* increases) there was a slight increase in the spread between the "overall wage" (defined as the sum of the first two contract salary bands) of the highest and lowest grades. The spread rose from 130.8 to 135.1 in engineering, and from 131.5 to 133.3 in chemicals (Table 6). This widening of contractual wage differentials is very modest indeed, however, in view of the fact that range of effective earnings was, in 1987, 230–100 in engineering and 198–100 in chemicals (data from Assolombarda, Lombardy industrial firms association). From this follows clearly that the new *scala mobile* has played only a very minor role in the restoration of wage differentials, which itself has not been especially pronounced.

Anyway, apart from the assessment of the working of the new mechanism over this short period, what is notable is its feebleness as an element in the launching of a new stage in incomes policy, oriented to the long run. This weakness stems from two main factors: (a) the indexing mechanism is based on a price index that itself is not a planning target; (b) it is automatic, essentially an *ex-post* corrective to economic events that have already taken place. It simply cannot be viewed as an effective, sensitive instrument for a

Table 6: Overall Contractual Monthly Wages, by Grade, in Engineering and Chemical Industries.

Grade	Engineering 30.4.86	31.10.88	Grade	Chemicals 30.4.86	31.10.88
A	—	1,592,308	7	1,315,193	1,540,465
8 B	1,351,981	1,547,664	6	1,252,700	1,462,252
7 C	1,283,186	1,468,736	5 S	1,195,876	1,394,526
6 D	1,210,856	1,385,774	5	1,157,685	1,346,341
5 E	1,164,659	1,335,484	4	1,104,762	1,283,721
4 F	1,132,813	1,296,282	3	1,076,067	1,247,458
3 G	1,096,408	1,252,174	2	1,045,045	1,208,759
H	—	1,233,520	1	1,000,000	1,156,021
2 I	1,068,140	1,217,647			
1 L	1,033,868	1,178,648			
Range, index	130.77	135.10		131.52	133.26

Source: Based on Mariani 1989.

cooperative, long-term incomes policy game between the economic agents.

Once the programmed inflation rate has been set (in the Government's Forecasting and Planning Report and the Finance Act), a new, cooperative *scala mobile* mechanism should fix in advance the size of the increase in pay packets needed to safeguard the buying power of gross wages consistent with that rate. The anticipated increase could exert a beneficial announcement effect on inflation expectations. The lump sum benefit could be based on the average amount payed by the *scala mobile* in the last semester, adjusted for inflation by the programmed inflation rate. In this way the degree of coverage equal to 100% only for minimum wages, would decrease at the wage-level increases. The semi-annual cost-of-living adjustment could be retained; at the end of the first six months the amount paid would correspond to half of the programmed inflation rate, while at the end of the year the remainder would be paid, adjusted up or down in line depending on the divergence of actual from programmed inflation.

An arrangement along these lines could easily not alter at all the volume of resources distributed as cost-of-living allowance nor the degree of coverage, but it would profoundly change its philosophy. The *scala mobile* would be transformed from a strictly defensive, rigid and automatic safeguard mechanism into a flexible, responsive economic policy instrument, the symbol of an ever evolving cooperation on the part of business, labor, and Government in playing the game of planning the future course of the economy.

The safeguarding of net wages might also be entrusted, at least in part, to a similar procedure for predetermining increases. Given the pattern of gross wages, the fate of net wages is determined by the "tax wedge", that is, the

Table 7: Gross Wages, Tax Wedge, and Total Labour Cost.
(Percentages).

	Economy		Industry		Industry excl. construction	
	1980	1987	1980	1987	1980	1987
Net wages	59	54	58	53	58	52
Tax wedge:	40	46	41	47	41	47
Income tax	9	12	8	12	8	11
Employee soc. contr.	4	6	5	6	5	6
Employer soc. contr.	21	23	21	23	21	24
Gross wages	79	77	79	77	79	76
Cost of labour	100	100	100	100	100	100

Source: Brunetta and Tronti 1989.

total income and social security taxes on salaries (Table 7). Institutionally, the size of the wedge is affected by all measures concerning income and social security taxes, charged both to firms (employers) and to employees, such as tax reductions, social security relief, and tax reform. In terms of the spontaneous evolution of the economy, it is influenced by fiscal drag and also by the composition of employment (by income, sex, age, skill, region, and employee or self-employment status), by virtue of the differing tax treatment of different types of income earners.

Once the indexation of gross wages has been determined, then, safeguarding the purchasing power of net wages depends on the course of the tax wedge and its components, which we feel should be made the object of specific, targeted policies of predetermination. In particular, in order to avoid the rigidity of the automatic adjustment of the tax bite to inflation, as stated in the bilateral agreement of 26 January 1989, the structure of income tax brackets and its modification over time could be programmed, for example, for a three-year period, consistently with the programmed inflation rate and other economic policy objectives (redistribution objectives, employment targets, and so on).

Similarly, the revision of social security contributions and their distribution among categories and between employers and employees should be planned, jointly, taking into account strategic objectives and projections of the future of the welfare system, to ensure that over time entitlements are compatible with contributions. It is worth repeating, in this regard, that safeguarding real net wages depends on a strategy for broadening the tax base, which can be done essentially by combating tax evasion and also by measures to bring underground activities to the surface, with legal and fiscal incentives for both unions and employers.

Among the ordinary economic policy instruments at the disposal of Government, one final bulwark of incomes policy is institutionalized control of prices. This is not a novelty in recent Italian economic policy. For the implementation of Valentine's Day accords, the Government did not adopt any price freeze, as was being done with scant success throughout Europe. Rather, it planned the course of monitored prices (those covered by the Central Statistical Institute's consumer price index), public tariffs, and administered prices, so as to keep their increase, on average, within the set disinflation target.

The results exceeded the most optimistic forecasts. In 1984 the rate of increase of monitored and other controlled prices slowed sharply, by 7.3 percentage points, while the overall CPI slowed by 3.9 points (Figure 3). Since controlled prices had a weight of about 24% of the overall basket, their deceleration accounts for about 45% of the overall slowdown that year, and a significant share of disinflation over the next couple of years as well. More recently, the room for maneuver of public price setters has reduced but, nonetheless, the 1989 new inflationary trend and the 1990 reduction of the allowed oscillation band for the Italian lira around its central EMS parity, require to renew the use of this economic policy tool.

As we have seen, the formulation of a new, dynamic, long-term incomes policy requires the use of different tools, aimed at different goals as safeguarding gross and net wages, programming product and wage growth, controlling the evolution of taxation, and curbing inflation. With disinflation having come to a halt, no room for exchange rate movements and the single European market impending, only a powerful, renewed tripartite pact can prevent the triggering off of another round of wage catch-up, such as those that afflicted the private and public sectors alike in the 1970s.

11.5 Conclusion: Two Principles of Reform

The objective of safeguarding real gross and net wages, while minimal, is a worthy one, because it underlies a socially acceptable prerequisite for all players to play incomes policy as a cooperative game. As always, anyway, this is not the real problem. What has to be done is not to squabble over how to cut up the income pie changing, with greater or less cunning, the rules of the game. Rather, for the game to be a long-run one, the conditions must be firmly established, under which the pie can grow for everybody, with equity and efficiency for the entire economic system, and with a view to its integration into the single European market in the best possible state.

What is involved is advance programming to distribute the benefits of productivity gains among those who helped achieve them, in such as way as to attain the desired social and economic goals. Today this problem, no

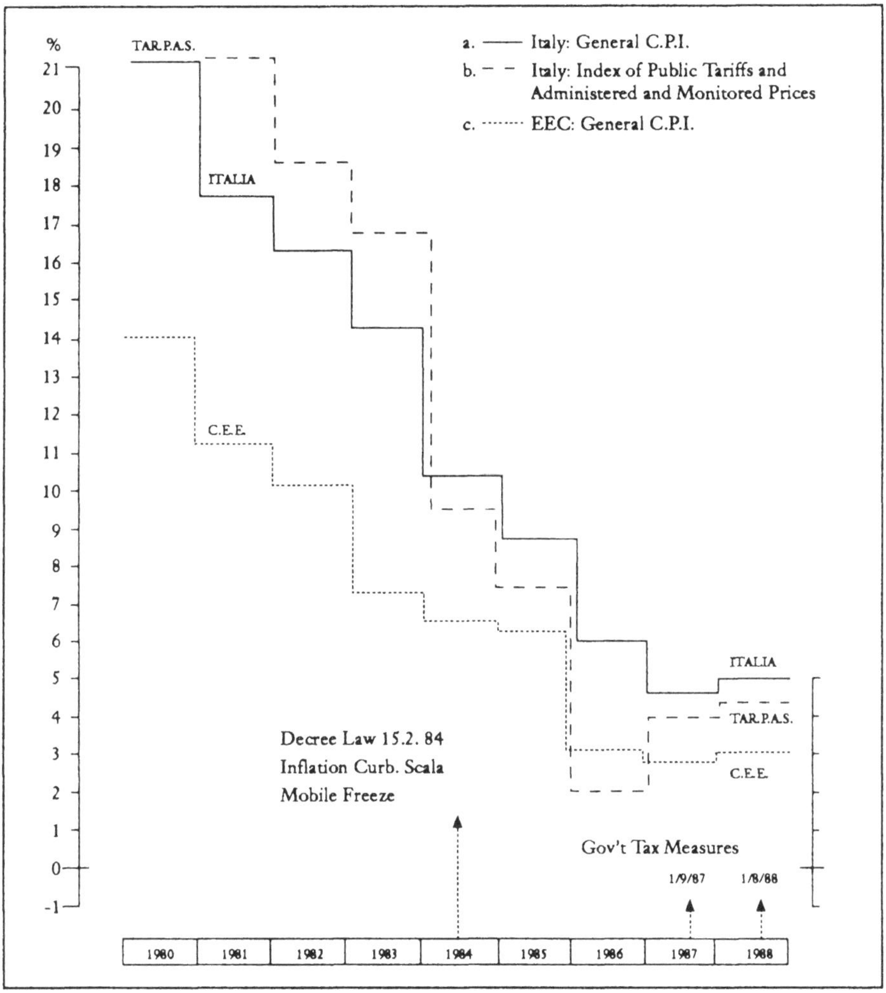

Source: Brunetta and Tronti 1989

Figure 3: Year-on-Year Variation in Consumer Price Index

newcomer to economics, can then be dealt with concretely, through a cooperative incomes policy.

As we have seen, in recent years the productivity gains in industry have largely gone to increase incomes in other sectors, especially in Government employment. This sort of unplanned transfer triggers off rising expectations, positions of privilege, inefficiency, and wage rivalry with its perverse price impact. The first step to avert such negative effects is, in our view, to lay down with absolute firmness a general principle that can serve as a norm (institution) in the new incomes policy game for the 1990s, namely that wage increases in any sector can never exceed gains in productivity.

Looking to the future, applying this principle means that, in collective bargaining, unions and firms must tie wage increases to expected gains in productivity, taking account of planned investment, its financing out of profits, and the need to curb price rises so as to improve competitiveness and gain new market shares, as well as of social preferences concerning employment and working hours.

Certainly, the rate of labor productivity growth in the various segments of the economy also depends on structural factors, relating to the type of organization of production, and quite independent of institutional matters. As a rule, for instance, in the services (private and public alike) productivity does not increase as fast, by the very nature of the process entailed and the lower returns to technical progress. Nevertheless, it would be a step forward toward the common goal of determining in advance the main macro-economic variables, to state for incomes policy the norm that for all working people wage gains must be conditioned by productivity gains. Exceptions to the general rule could be negotiated in special cases (in accordance with structural and/or "solidarity" motives), as long as they were consistent with overall economic requirements and with social consensus.

It is thus necessary for all the themes of incomes policy to be reconsidered one by one by the agents in the game, in the light of the changing state of the economy and the outlook. As they must be treated in a way consistent with the general rules of the game (mainly Government's economic policy), with a view to medium-term perspective (i.e. full European market integration after 1992).

Finally, it is worth stressing that this reconsideration need to be governed by a further norm, that can be spelled out as a second general principle: The elimination of all automatic mechanisms, wherever located and for whatever purpose instituted, in favor of more flexible, thorough, and functional policies of concertation and programming of all aspects of incomes policy. The purpose of this second principle is not so much to change the volume of the resources moved (as we saw in the case of *scala mobile*), as to attain two different goals. First, to make incomes policy adjustment prompter and more flexible; and, second, to improve, broaden, and enrich the cooperative policy game, by installing among business, labor, and Government the practice of joint, shared responsibility for economic management, in conformity with the rules of the market.

References

ASAP (1986–1989): *Rapporto sui salari.* Milan: F. Angeli.

Assolombarda, *Indagine sulle retribuzioni e costo del lavoro dell'industria manifatturiera nella provincia di Milano.* Milan, 1989.

Brunetta, R. and C. Carraro (1988): *Incomes Policies as Cooperative Strategies: Lessons from the Italian Experience of the 1980s.* Paper presented at the EALE Conference, Venice. Forthcoming in: *Labour Relations and Economic Performances*, Brunetta, R. and C. Dell'Aringa (eds.). London: Macmillan.

Brunetta, R. and R. Pozzana (1984): La politica dei redditi nei paesi industrializzati. *Economia & Lavoro*, 2.

Brunetta, R. and L. Tronti (1989): Riforma della scala mobile e politica dei redditi. *Rassegna di statistiche del lavoro*, 2.

Brunetta, R. and L. Tronti (1991): Nuove possibilità nuovi obiettivi della politica dei redditi in Italia. Forthcoming in: *ASAP, Rapporto sui salari 1990.* Milan: F. Angeli.

Brunetta, R. and A. Venturini (1987): *Microeconomia del lavoro.* Venice: Marsilio.

Dell'Aringa, C. and G. Presutto (1986): Lo slittamento salariale. *Economia & Lavoro*, 2.

Faustini, G. (1987): A New Method of Indexing Wages in Italy. *Labour*, 2.

Giavazzi, F. and L. Spaventa (1989): Italy. The Real Effects of Inflation and Disinflation. *Economic Policy*, 8.

Government Forecasting and Planning Report, Ministero del Bilancio: *Relazione previsionale e programmatica.* Rome, yearly.

ISTAT: *Annuario di contabilità nazionale.* Roma, 1990.

Mariani, I. F. (1989): Esperienze di tre anni di applicazione della legge sulla scale mobile. *Industria e Sindacato*, 8.

Tarantelli, E. (1986): *Economia politica del lavoro.* Turin: UTET.

Tarantelli, E. (1988): *L'utopia dei deboli è la paura dei forti.* Milan: F. Angeli.

Tronti, L. (1987a): Slowdown e aggiustamento: la produttività del sistema economico italiano, *Rivista di politica economica*, 3.

Tronti, L. (1987b): La produttività nell'industria. *Spazio Impresa*, 4.

Weitzman, M. L. (1984): *The Share Economy.* Cambridge, Mass.: Harvard University.

12 Social Concertation in Latin America

Emilio Morgado

Latin American experiences and perspectives on social concertation are presented in this paper. On the first subject, national cases reviews are preceded by some general comments on peculiarities of this social process in Latin America.

12.1 Latin American Experiences

12.1.1 General Comments

In Latin America concertation and social pacts are viewed with considerable interest. But, certainly, there are not frequent or many cases in which they have originated pacts of considerable duration.

Various reasons would help to explain such phenomena, mainly those associated with the presence of inadequate basic assumptions which make possible a concertation. One of them concerns broad democratic liberties in order to sustain and be supported within a regime of trade union freedom and also the genuine representation of participating social organizations and the existence of a sharing and balanced power to facilitate the dialogue. In addition are the harmonic, complementary, and correlative relations among concertation processes and those proper of constitutional powers of State, particularly the Parliament, and the technical support and necessary information to facilitate the dialogue and agreements.

To the insufficient presence of those factors, some other subjective ones used are to be added: the weak dialogue vocation, which is self-explained by emphasized opposing traditions, both authoritarian and paternalistic, as well as, in many cases, the lack of authenticity when pretending to use concertation as a strategy or as a trick to delay definitions. To the said factors, which conform to the *corpus* and *animus* of concertation, is added one no less important: the absence of a previous or parallel political agreement to facilitate and make it efficient, particularly in such unbalanced and dissenting societies.

Most relevant experiences have taken place in *Argentina*, *Colombia*, *Chile*, *Guatemala*, *Honduras*, *Mexico*, *Uruguay*, and *Venezuela*.

Among the characteristics of these experiences it is important to highlight the following, related to participant parties and their roles, subjects covered, levels, formalities, enforcement procedures, and some factors that surround this social process.

1. *Participant Parties.* Governmental participation in concertation processes is in line with the old and well-established Latin American tradition of public intervention in labor relations: With very few exceptions, the State is practically considered the principal part of them. In many cases the State interventions have been predominant and concertation agreements have resulted in social endorsements of governmental policies. The real degree of social participation in the elaboration of those policies can be discussed. On the contrary, it seems undeniable that social participation has proved to be determinant in the success of such policies.

Almost all the experiences have had a tripartite nature. The only exceptions have taken place in *Colombia* (Labor Relations Agreement 1982) and *Honduras* (Commitment Act 1985). But in fact, the Government played some role in the Colombian case. In the Honduran experience, the Army and Parliament had significant intervention.

2. *Concerted Matters.* Most concertation processes deal with economic matters, mainly anti-inflation policies, productivity improvements, economic adjustments, prices and tariffs, and international trade. A majority also deals with labor relation subjects, mainly trade union rights and freedom, collective bargaining, employment security, and vocational training; only one (the Colombian Agreement of 1982) constitutes a kind of declaration of conduct in labor relations. Another one (the Venezuelan Workers/Employers Agreement of 1958) established the web of rules for the settlement of industrial conflicts.

The preservation and consolidation of democratic systems have been a central issue in the agreements signed in *Chile* (1990), *Honduras* (1985), *Uruguay* (1984), and *Venezuela* (1958 and 1989).

3. *Levels.* All the agreements have been designed for having effects on the national level. Some of them (for instance, the Mexican Agreements signed from 1987 to 1991) have also dealt with matters concerning some branches of the economy, such as the agricultural sector.

4. *Formalities.* Most concertation experiences have taken place without formalities or procedures previously established. Relevant exceptions are Chile (1990) and Uruguay (1984).

Pacts resulting from concertation processes have been written and duly signed by the parties' representatives. In some cases they have set up some institutional bodies to facilitate negotiations (for instance, the Chilean Agreement of January 1990 and the Venezuelan Agreement of 1989), or for the follow-up and evaluation of the agreement (Mexican Pacts from 1987 to 1991).

No specific provisions have been adopted about technical support and access to information.

5. *Enforcement Procedures.* The contents of social pacts have been mainly enforced through the enactment of legislation, the issue of decrees, the approval of decisions by specialized bodies, or the incorporation of specific clauses in collective agreements.

6. *Some Factors Linked to Concertation Efforts.* Concertation and pacts assume that social parties have appropriate aptitudes, that is to say, knowledge, information, and proposals concerning macro-economic and social aspects. In Latin America, with few exceptions, workers' and employers' organizations have been able to develop some aptitudes, mainly referred to social and micro-economic aspects, due to strongly decentralized labor relation levels. Furthermore, in those countries in which such said relations are either centralized or given at various levels, they have hardly developed an integrating aptitude, since these labor relations have been mainly centered around interests of very definite economic or professional sectors. Generally, there has not been a tradition for inter-sectorial or inter-professional dialogue. Also, it must be stated that social concertation compels to use a macro-economic language to those who talk nothing but micro-economic language when referring either to specific company, sector, or professional problems.

12.1.2 Review of Cases

1. In 1973, the General Confederation of Labor (CGT), the Economic General Confederation (CGE), and the Government, headed by President Perón, subscribed in *Argentina* the National Commitment Act (Acta de Compromiso Nacional), in which the main emphasis was to settle and determine a wages and salaries policy. These wages and salaries would be determined in such a way as to watch over their acquisitive capacity and the productivity improvement, within a framework of general anti-inflation policies.
2. In 1981, *Colombia* started a Tripartite Intersector Commission, integrated by Government representatives, the Colombian Workers Union (UTC), the Workers Confederation of Colombia (CTC), the General Confederation of Labor (CGT), the National Industrial Association (ANDI), the Colombian Popular Association (ACOPI), the National Federation of Commerce (FENALCO), and the National Association of Financial Institutions (ANIF). As a result of their negotiations two important laws were issued about indirect forms for salaries: the new law for Family Subsidy and the Consumer Bylaws. Concerning the first law, the coverage of Family Compensation Funds was increased, the monetary subsidy was significantly raised for work-

ers earning less income, and the investment of resources was re-oriented in order to satisfy basic workers' needs in health, food, education, and housing matters. The Consumer Bylaws (Law 73, December 1981) issued protecting measures to prevent consumers against speculation and poor quality of products and to freeze housing rents. Within the Committee negotiations, they also undersigned a Labor Relations Agreement (25 November 1982) allowing, among its results, the strengthening of tripartite systems for minimum wages fixing.

3. In *Chile* the concertation and democratization processes are closely united. After various approaches, a significant political concertation of the democratic parties was produced when they decided to participate together in the plebiscite which was called by the Government, thus opposing the extension in office of the military ruler.

The broad victory won by the "concerted" parties strengthened their position and allowed them to issue a concertated Government program, which was presented by the democratic candidate, who was elected on 14 December 1989 and assumed the Government on 11 March 1990.

Social concertation was favored by the success achieved by the political concertation. In late 1989, the Unitary Workers Central (CUT) and the Confederation of Production and Commerce (CPC) published a joint communication showing their disposal to strengthen and extend the dialogue initiated among those workers' and employers' central organizations. On 31 January 1990 those organizations undersigned an agreement under the title of "Terms of Reference for the Dialogue Between the Unitary Workers Central and the Confederation of Production and Commerce". In this Agreement, the parties expressed their basic principles which would guide their negotiations, within joint committees which they agreed to create, in order to discuss certain aspects of labor relations, collective bargaining, trade union organization, and subjects of social economic nature of common interest.

As a result of the activities developed by those committees, on 27 April 1990, they adopted a Basic Agreement (Acuerdo Marco) with the signatures of Manuel Bustos and Arturo Martinez representing the CUT, Manuel Feliú representing the CPC, and by the President of the Republic Patriciø Aylwin and his Ministers of Finances (Alejandro Foxley), Economy (Carlos Ominami), and Labor and Social Security (René Cortázar). The Government participation had been announced by President Aylwin during his inaugural speech of 12 March 1990.

The Agreement is entitled "Chile, a Historic Opportunity". Its contents has one part with statements which emphasized the necessity to conciliate development with equity and democracy in a context of economic, political and social liberties, distributive justice and institutional stability, and modernizing the social economic structures.

Then the Agreement points toward essential requirements for development with equity and states and fixes the views of both parties about a future with stability and prosperity for every Chilean. Also, the Agreement sets which role corresponds to the workers' and employers' organizations; it appraises needs, objectives, and scopes of the social dialogue and the social agreement and clarifies that the Basic Agreement does not replace but facilitate the seeking of direct agreements among workers and employers, as well as among them and the Government.

The following matters are remarked upon as appropriate for independent or joint initiatives of the parties: (a) the quality of education and training, in particular those corresponding to young people; (b) the quality, efficiency, and extension of health programs, both preventive and curative; (c) housing for workers and their families; (d) salaries and minimum pensions policy, family allotments, and other basic coverage; (e) the labor legislation which assures equity in labor relations; strengthens autonomy of the workers' and employers' organizations; protects both parties' rights; permits a balanced collective bargaining, extended to the largest number of workers; rules and prevents conflicts and procures a satisfactory employments stability – these legislation changes must be adequate for the needs of productivity, competence, technological changes, and the increase of employment opportunties; (f) management of the public sector giving special attention to fiscal austerity; (g) the public labor inspection system; (h) the governmental economic activity, with a tendency to describe properly its competence, harmonizing its responsibility of promoting an institutional frame and development goals with the common welfare, directing it essentially to improve the situation of the poorest segments of the society, with a leading and growing paper of the private sector; (i) the economic growth and developing policies, emphasizing the purpose of full employment; (j) social participation policies, including permanent forms of information and consultation and facilitating the development and representativity of social partners.

Finally, the Agreement has two types of immediate actions. Ones which associate the three signing parties and other ones which compromise the Government and the CUT.

The tripartite commitments refer to: the support of the bill raising the minimum wage as of 1 January 1990, and which would be adjusted a year later to keep its acquisitive power, as well as the increasing purchasing power if it is consistent with the national economy situation and with employment levels; the support to direct negotiations at the company level for the transportation and food bonus payments to those workers earning a minimum income; the search for the best possible agreement in preparing bills reforming the labor legislation; the affirmation that fiscal expenses proceeding from the Agreement will not produce fiscal imbalance, and to the need of maintaining a permanent dialogue with respect to treated matters on the Basic Agreement. In turn, bilateral commitments are referred to the establishment, by means of the law, of increments of the family allowances for workers with lower income and the increase of the "family subsidy", as well as the raise of 10.6% of all minimum pensions and assistance payments, at the moment that inflation accrues 15% of inflation since the date of the last adjustment.

There are strong and various reasons to think that this Basic Agreement will have deep and significant impacts within the social and political development of the country. Everything seems to indicate that the agreement is a clear expression of a fundamental change in the Chilean labor relations system, and that it would have left its conflictive and opposing characteristics, becoming a participative model of mutual recognition among parties and of explicit acceptation of a model for development and society.

These assumptions have proved to be realistics. A new national trilateral agreement was signed on April 30, 1991. Together with Ministers of Labor, Economy and Finance and the representatives of the CUT and the Confederation of Production and Commerce (CPC) and some of its associated employers' organisations of the agriculture, commerce, mining industrial, banking and building sectors, two other social organisations signed the agreement. They were the National Association of Public Employees (ANEF) and the National Confederation of Small and Medium Size Enterprises, Articrafts and Services. So, the social and economic coverage of these national agreements has been expanded.

The new agreement is based on the previous one of 1990. It deals with many subjects, among them: (a) technical considerations for future minimum wages fixing, including those related to productivity; (b) minimum wage increases to 33.000 chilean pesos per month (about US$ 100), from 1st September 1991 (this raise was to be approved by the Parliament while the other remunerations are to be fixed by the parties); (c) promotion of joint initiatives for the development of employment information systems; (d) establishment of a consultation machinery and joint proposals to improve the access to new markets, the technological level and the ecological balance, in the framework of productive modernisation policies; (e) study of sound economic and technical proposals to improve the protection of the unemployed; (f) development of joint initiatives for the establishment of new vocational training policies and for the establishment of tripartite consultative bodies in two institutions of the Labor Ministry (the Program for the Development of Technical Education and the National Service for Training and Emloyment – SENCE); (g) promotion of joint activities to prevent work accidents, including improved functioning of bilateral committees at the enterprise level; (h) recognition of the importance to prevent inflationary trends and recognition of the importance of this National Agreement in the betterment of worker's consuming power. It was also recognised the need to develop policies to promote employment creation as a tool to improve the workers' living conditions.

Besides these tripartite compromises and declarations, the National Agreement includes a bilateral agreement (CUT and the governement) in the fields of family allowances and pensions.

4. In *Guatemala*, as a result of the First Regional Tripartite Economic Congress (May–June 1945) – sponsored by the Government of President Juan José Arévalo – a number of resolutions were passed, most of them in labor matters, under the name of Escuintla Triangle (Triángulo de Escuintla). Those resolutions played an important role in the enactment of new labor legislation.

5. In *Honduras* the Commitment Act (Acta de Compromiso) was signed in May 1985, mainly to solve certain political problems connected with the appointments for judges of the Supreme Court and the process for the election of a new President of the Republic. In paragraph 7 they establish commitments to assure "the active participation of the workers and peasant organizations to build a democratic, pluralized, and participating society". On this matter they agreed to complement systems which would allow their participation in the definition of objectives and in the preparation of national development strategies; also to establish ways of joint participation of workers, peasants, and additional social sectors in governmental bodies, as well as the promotion of workers' force enterprises. It was also agreed that the National Congress would adopt the correspondent legislation to comply with these agreements. By the Commitment Act, political parties recognized "the vital mediation of workers and peasants to accomplish agreements allowing it to overcome the present political and institutional crisis, and at the same time to consolidate the country's democratic process". In turn, such said social sectors stated that through their organizations, they would keep "the permanent watching for a true fulfillment of the contracted commitment". The Commitment Act was signed by the highest representatives of the National Party, the Liberal Party, the Christian Democratic Party, the Innovation and National Unity Party, the Honduras Workers Confederation, the Workers Central, the Country Workers National Central, and the Honduras Peasant Federation.

6. There have been various experiences of social concertation in *Mexico*, among them the 1945 Industrialist Workers Pact (Pacto Obrero Industrial) and the 1977 Alliance for Production which covered salary limitations. Then the Tripartite Pact of National Solidarity (Pacto Tripartito de Solidaridad Nacional), of December 1982, August 1983, directed to face the economic crisis and to express support, understanding, and solidarity with the National Development Plan. In December 1987 a Pact of Economic Solidarity (Pacto de Solidaridad Economica), was signed by the Government and the workers' and employers' sectors. The Pact included resolutions taken by the Federal Government, with the support of undersigning organizations, in taxation matters, prices and rates for the public services, public budget, exchange

rates, international trade, minimum wage, guaranteed prices for basic products, land capitalization, and improvement of peasant standards of living.

Also, the Pact covered commitments regarding productivity and efficiency matters; salary adjustments, decrease of labor absence rates; increase of land and cattle outputs; elimination of intermediate, redundant, and unnecessary processes; vocational training; reviewing of guaranteed prices; increase of the national offer of basic products; moderation of price changes; and of increases of contracted salaries. The Pact also provided the integration of a follow-up and evaluation committee.

The provisions of the Pact were renewed and amended, thus securing its positive impact over the economy. In December 1988 it was replaced by a new agreement: the Pact for Stabilization and Economic Growth (Pacto para la Estabilidad y Crecimiento Económico). The Pact contained provisions concerning the Government, employers' organizations, and trade unions. The Governmental compromises dealt with subjects related to balanced public finances; prices and tariffs for public commodities; exchange policy providing minimum and fixed daily devaluations; new custom rates schemes for imports; the establishment of a program to eliminate unnecessary economic regulations that results in the creation of unjustified costs or obstacles for pursuing legal economic activities; promotion of agricultural productivity to raise incomes and living standards of peasants; and promotional price policy for the agricultural sector of the economy.

The private enterprise sector assumed the responsibility to recommend its members not to raise prices unless circumstances defined in the Pact were met. It was ratified with recognition of the trade unions rights to review collective agreements. It also established a Commission for the follow-up and evaluation of the Pact.

The most recent renewal of this Pact took place in May 1990 (it will end on 31 January 1991). In the preliminary paragraphs of the Pact, it is stated that due to the concertation process, inflationary rates were reduced from 160% in 1988 to 20% in 1990, and that similar improvements were attained in other economic indicators such as the deficit in public finances (reduced from 16% in 1987 to 5.8% in 1989).

The Pact is named PECE (Initials of its Spanish title) and was signed by Fidel Velasquez (Secretary General of the Mexican Confederation of Workers – CTM), Maximillano Silerio Esparza (Secretary General of the Peasant National Confederation – CNC), Lorenzo Duarte Garcia (President of the Congress of Labor), Rolando Vega Iñiguez (President of the Private Enterprise Coordinating Council), and Arsenio Farell Cubillas (Secretary of Labor). The parties agreed on the following subjects: (a) workers' and employers' sectors will negotiate a National Agreement for Higher Productivity at the enterprise and economic sector of activity levels. That agreement must deal with the training program and equity in the distribution of fruits of productivity increases; (b) the parties ratify the need of peaceful social climate and labor relations, within the law and without violence; (c) the Government assumes obligations in regard to public finances, lower daily devaluations, promotional policies for the development of the agricultural sector, improved ecologic conditions, and moderated price raises of energetics; (d) prices revision process will include the appraisal of its impact on real wages; (e) private sector will not transfer to prices the additional costs resulting of the implementation of the Pact and (f) the representatives of workers, peasants and private enterprise sectors in the Follow-Up and Evaluation Commissions will insist in the appropriate fulfillment of the Pact provisions.

Until the end of 1990, the economic results of the Pact have been relevant despite the fact that no agreement has been reached on productivity, as stated in point 2 of PECE.

7. In *Uruguay*, once the democratic Government was elected, the National Program Concertation (Concertación Nacional Programática) took place, with participation of representatives from political parties together with representatives of the inter-syndical Plenary of Workers and National Confederation of Workers (PIT/CNT) and other organizations of workers, employers' representatives, such as the Chamber of Industries, the National Chamber of Commerce, the Constructions Chamber, the Employer Confederation of Uruguay, the Country Producers Association, and the Mercantile Chamber. In addition, other social organizations participated. The objective was to bring up proposals for solutions to be applied once the Government assumed its functions (March 1985). The mechanisms for concertation included an Executive Board and Working Groups dealing with the economic policy education and culture, health, housing, employment, salaries, social security and civil rights.

As a result of the concertation process, they stated policies for each one of the above-mentioned subjects. For example, about salaries and pension schemes they determined to stop their accelerated deterioration. To comply with that agreement, the new Government issued a law for salaries adjustments and promoted the constitution of tripartite sectorial committees, in order to concertate the fixation of minimum wages in more than thirty branches of economic activity. Other agreements adopted refer to legalization of both public and private workers' organizations; also to the strengthening of a labor relations system which, based on principles of the Constitution and on International standards ratified by the country, promote the collective bargaining, thus giving privileges to the concertation spirit; the derogation and "absolute nullity" of those labor and social security regulations issued by the Government since 18 December 1973; the salary policy and living and working conditions in the agriculture and cattle sectors; the elimination of every form of discrimination against women; the social security reforms, including unemployment insurance, family allowances, childhood and old age assistance; and consensus about productive reactivity, employment, and income, covering orientations about basic aspects, referred to the internal demand, fiscal policy, the performance of the financial system, the internal debt, the international trade and the external debt.

8. In the Workers/Employers Agreement (Acuerdo Obrero Patronal), under-signed in *Venezuela* in 1958, followed by the political agreement called Pact of the Fixed Point (Pacto de Punto Fijo), the conciliation procedure was promoted for the settlement of labor disputes, thus limiting the need of strikes. Termination of employment was also regulated, thus avoiding unnecessary dismissals.

With the said agreement it was possible to reduce conflicting tensions: in 1958–1959 only twenty-five legal and five illegal strikes were registered, at the time that 1,700 collective agreements were undersigned. That dialogue tradition was increased with the incorporation of workers' representatives to the board of directors of development entities, state enterprises, and autonomous institutions, arranged by one 1966 law. Later it was established by Decree (1981) that the National Costs, Prices, and Salaries Council (Consejo Nacional de Costos, Precios y Salarios), with a tripartite composition and in charge of the control of price raises, was to concert salary increases and cooperate with the fulfillment of objectives appointed in the VI National Plan. Bearing in mind those experiences gathered from the operation of that Council, the Congress approved the Law creating the National Cost, Prices, and Salaries Commission (Comisión Nacional de Costos, Precios y Salarios). Said law had the objective of securing productivity improvements and the basic and mass production of consumer goods and services; also to secure the balance of the general price levels with workers' income, accordingly with social justice principles and by a systematical concertation. The Committee was integrated by three representatives from the Executive Power (Ministers of Public Works, Labor, Agriculture and Breeding), one representative of the Venezuelan Workers Confederation (CTV), and one from the Chambers and Associations of Commerce and Production Federation (FEDECAMARAS).

The objectives of both, the Council and the Commission were not successfully attained. In the first case, the CTV decided to leave the Council and, in the second one FEDECAMARAS left the Commission.

A National Agreement for Concertation (Acuerdo Nacional para la Concertación), was signed on 1 July 1989, by CTV, FEDECAMARAS, and the Government. Essentially it is an "agreement to agree". After introducing a vision of the social economic situation of the country, all parties stated their faith in the democratic system and their firm will to preserve it and to improve it by concerted commitments. They indicated that basic objectives of concertation are the improvement of productivity and efficacy; the elimination of obstacles to the economic activity and of non-productive bureaucracy;

the governmental responsibility as to guarantee social welfare; the integration of new businessmen to the productive activity; the increase of motivation, discipline, and higher training capacity; the improvement of health levels for the community and the use of all possible means so as to reduce the conflictive effects of inflation, shortages, and deterioration of wages.

Parties agreed to establish a national concertation council integrated by representatives of the Executive Power, the CTV, and FEDECAMARAS. The council would have, as its main objectives, to facilitate consultations and cooperation for the parties and it would have internal rules and regulations, an executive secretariat and a follow-up and evaluation commission.

The Executive Power assumed several commitments in matters such as public deficit and budget, public investment; social programs to generate employment; family allotments, tax reforms, external debt, exchange policy. and commercial and industrial policies. At the same time, parties agreed to initiate negotiations to reach specific agreements in the following matters: increase of retirement pensions of IVSS; stabilization of the prices of goods and services; preventive programs of the National Council for Labor Health and Safety; unemployment insurance; assistance for peasants; credit capacity of the ICAP and BANDAGRO; creation of the Social Security Institute for Public Employees; extension of employment security measures; interests with preferential rates for certain kinds of housing; subsidies for agricultural and cattle activities; transformation of the Labor Ministry into a Ministry of Labor and Social Development, strengthening its institutional capacity to coordinate and participate in the issuing of the social economic policy; joint introduction of a bill transferring the INCE to the Labor Ministry; development of joint initiatives to improve educational, health, recreation, and welfare programs and to enlarge social security coverage.

Most analysts concur that this Agreement has not accomplished its objectives yet. Several reasons of economic and political nature have greatly complicated its operation. Nevertheless, they recognize its potentiality to possibly adopt specifc agreeements with one or more of above-mentioned topics.

Cases presented hereby, only resemble and bring up those concertation efforts which were conducted to adoption of pacts, some of them expressed through legislative texts. It is worth while recalling that concertation processes in Latin America have been much more than those recently mentioned. If they did not accomplish agreements in many opportunities, they produced some important effects like the adoption of labor legislation, especially in salary matters, and the sensitiveness of different social groups about the need to establish certain policies, programs and projects in subjects such as employment, salaries, productivity and social security.

We also should remember concertation experiences coming from operations of either bipartite or tripartite systems of cooperation, established in most Latin America countries. The said systems have general or specialized competence. Among the first group, we find national councils of work, national development councils, and State Councils that with different denominations are found in many countries of the region. Among those of specialized competence, stand out bodies for fixing minimum wages and councils for vocational training, safety and health and vocational rehabilitation. Recently, they are including those of employment and productivity.

Most of those systems belong to a consulting pattern and with that character they have participated in some processes of adopting concerted decisions.

Together with these systems of permanent or institutional character, there are others of a temporary nature which, with an *ad hoc* basis, are brought up to attend to certain matters, generally associated with the labor legislation reform. In those, they are looking for obtaining concerted proposals and agreements on specific subjects, as in the case, for example, of the National Tripartite Committee called in 1980 in Panama to propose reforms to the Labor Code.

Also, in Latin America it has been known for concerted experiences to continue in periodic calls for meetings of the social parties and the highest representatives of the public powers, especially the executive power, with the objective to revise sectorial, particular or national interest matters, and to adopt consensual decisions about them. That was the situation of *Venezuela* around 1980, when a High Level Committee was operating with the presence of the President, who participated with Ministers, Congress representatives, and high executive Government groups, holding monthly meetings with representatives from CTV and FEDECAMARAS to consider labor, social, and economic problems of common interest.

12.2 Latin American Perspectives

The Latin American experience shows that in spite of the insufficient presence of factors to facilitate the concertation, this has taken place in the region and has generated some pacts. This fact can prove that the main element leading to concertation is the conviction about its necessity. Strong stimulation makes the said social process active and it has become not only possible and needed but almost unavoidable.

The development, adjustment and change processes as well as political problems which Latin America confronts every day are of such magnitude that they allow us to forecast a bigger development of social concertation in coming years. Only the sharing effort will make it possible to reach a development in peace and with justice.

13 The Demise of Concerted Practices and Negotiated Economy in Sweden

Victor A. Pestoff

13.1 Introduction – The Idea of a Negotiated Economy and Concerted Practices

Negotiations are the subject of growing public attention in the Scandinavian countries. The academic discussion of the "negotiated economy" in the Scandinavian countries has gained in importance and scope in recent years. The concept was coined by an ambitious study of power and power relationships in Norway (Hernes 1978). This inspired further development of the concept (Nielsen and Pedersen 1988) as well as empirical studies in neighboring Scandinavian countries (Nielsen and Pedersen 1989). A wide range of applications in various fields proved fruitful, such as wage policy in Denmark (Pedersen 1989, 1990), consumer policy in Sweden (Pestoff 1988a, 1989a, 1990a) and negotiations about large investment projects in Norway (Berrefjord 1989, 1990). The Swedish Power Study pays tribute to the importance of this analysis for understanding and interpreting recent developments in Sweden (Pettersson 1990: ch. 8.3).

The negotiated economy is not a permanent institutional arrangement, but a process which is subject to constant change. A restructuring of the negotiated economy can be found in numerous policy areas in Sweden. Certain aspects of the negotiated economy have been subject to criticism, primarily by organized business. Some of its institutions have been curtailed or phased out in traditional policy areas, while certain of its features have taken root in new areas. This chapter examines the experience of Sweden in orchestrating the negotiated economy in three policy areas: industrial relations; consumer, agricultural, and food policy; and housing and rent negotiations, while industrial investments and building projects, which corroborate this development, are dealt with elsewhere (Pestoff 1990c).

The purpose of this chapter is to relate the concept of the negotiated economy to tripartite concertation (see Treu 1991). This will be done by focusing on the role of business in reorganizing and restructuring the Swedish negotiated economy in the 1990s. This intent is related to differences in the definition of the negotiated economy discussed below. Although business has not yet been subject to much systematic scrutiny, it is an important political actor in Sweden, perhaps *the* most important. In area after area it appears that Swedish business has embarked on a policy of radically changing established economic policies and political patterns in one of the most well-developed welfare states in Europe. Swedish business wants to substitute concerted economic/social policy practices with market forces and to replace the politics of compromise with the politics of confrontation.

The main business interest association, the Swedish Employers' Confederation (SAF), rightfully conceives of itself as "... the driving force in changing the system". Its adamant rejection of central collective bargaining initiated a reaction which brought down the Social Democratic minority government in February 1990. SAF recently spelled out a detailed plan for total privatization of the welfare state by the turn of the century. It announced a total withdrawal from the governing bodies of all public administration boards throughout Sweden, including those dealing with labor market policy. SAF repeatedly demands that all forms of industrial negotiations and regulations be replaced by market forces.

The importance attributed to negotiations in the Scandinavian countries should come as no surprise. Socio-economic bargaining or negotiations between divergent social and economic interests permeate these societies (Katzenstein 1985). Sweden has long been seen as "the middle way" and served as a symbol for "the politics of compromise" (Childs 1936, 1980). Major areas of social, economic, and political relations fall both outside the competitive sphere as well as that of authoritative decisions. Thus, they are governed by social barter and political exchange, rather than impersonal market signals, group or party competition, and bureaucratic decision-making.

According to Nielsen and Pedersen (1988, 1989, 1990), the concept of a mixed economy may be so broadly defined as to include almost all modern economic activity and it is therefore devoid of substantive content. Futhermore, they argue that the Scandinavian countries have developed from mixed economies into negotiated economies during the post-World War II period due to the unique institutional history and institutional arrangements they share.

The Norwegian Power Study provides no clear or concise definition of the concept of the negotiated economy (Hernes 1978). Berrefjord *et al.* (1982), however, analyze the development of the Norwegian economy during the 1960s and 1970s in terms of the negotiated economy. Berrefjord and Hernes (1989) update this analysis for the 1980s. They characterize the negotiated economy as the polar opposite of a free competition economy in several basic respects. The two are most pronounced in their contrasts along three dimensions: size of firm, degree of contact with authorities, and degree of inter-organizational penetration among competitors. The free competition model is characterized by small firms which only have sporadic contacts with authorities and which do not own nor participate in the management of each other. Large firms, which have numerous and frequent contacts with authorities and which either own significant financial stakes in each other and/or contribute to the management of each other by overlapping directorates, comprise the negotiated economy according to this analysis. Berrefjord and Hernes conclude that "... the negotiated economy is constantly undergoing development. It is not a state or a fixed structure, but a process – where large firms totally play the central role" (ibid., p. 189).

Nielsen and Pedersen (1988, 1990) define their concept of the negotiated economy as "... a structuring of society where an essential part of the allocation of resources is conducted through institutionalized negotiations between independent decision-making centers in state, organizations, and or corporations" (p. 7). Berrefjord (1989) and Pestoff (1989a) argue for the necessity of including reallocative and distributive aspects of the negotiated economy in the definition. Thus, Neilsen and Pedersen later modified their definition referring to "... those forms of allocation and (re)distribution which have been developed through the coordination of decision-making in autonomous centers in state, organizations, and corporations by institutional and discursive means" (1990: p. 14).

Nielsen and Pedersen also present an elaborate conceptual model of the negotiated economy, one which is highly institutionalized. They argue that the application of the instrument of negotiation in decision-making should not be seen as an isolated event. Thus, they conclude that it is impossible to understand the negotiated economy unless its overall structures and total processes are taken into account (ibid., p. 4).

Nielsen and Pedersen (1988, 1989, 1990) spell out numerous institutional features of the negotiated economy, including its structures and processes, its institutional history, and its institutional arrangements. In terms of its structures, they speak of five complementary institutions which provide the basis for its institutional arrangements, alongside negotiations as an instrument for decision-making. These are:

institutions for policy;
discourse;
campaigning;
negotiation; and
arbitration or sanction.

All five types, or at least their functional equivalent, are necessary for the negotiated economy. Existing institutions may, however, cover more than one function, according to Nielsen and Pedersen. However, when it comes to the institutional history of the negotiated economy, they revert to the specific referents of the labor market. Thus, they discuss four phases in the development of institutionalized class cooperation via historic agreements, which civilized class confrontation in the four Nordic countries. These four phases include:

juridification;
institutionalization of class relations;
integration of labor market organizations into the public administration; and
the innovation of coordinating this decentralized decision-making through discursive and institutional means.

Nielsen and Pedersen also provide institutional distinctions for the very processes of the negotiated economy. Foremost is the fostering of a socio-economic ideology as an institutional attempt to mobilize mutual understanding of the socio-economic situation, which provides an ideological framework for the machinery of the negotiated economy. The existence of a socio-economic ideology relies heavily upon the efforts of the institutional arrangements of the negotiated economy. Within it, the involved parties engage in institutionalized bargaining over the rules of the game or negotiation games. Finally, the substantive bargaining or negotiations take place around a negotiation table.

Treu addresses the need of adapting the definition of concerted action to encompass more than just a technique of labor relations. He argues that concerted practices are evident in areas and objects well beyond those considered by students of labor relations and industrial relations (op. cit.). Our discussion of changes in the Swedish negotiated economy during the 1980s bears witness to his perspective, in one of the most corporatist countries of Europe as well as to the similarity between his view of concerted practices and the concept of the negotiated economy.

Treu discusses the uneven impact of developments in industrial relations in Europe during the 1980s (ibid.). He highlights the diminishing importance of centralization, institutionalization, unions in the social and political relations of nation-states, and the increasing significance of the internationalization of the economy. The discussion below also looks at these factors.

There are numerous issues addressed herein in addition to the role of organized business in reorganizing and restructuring the negotiated economy in Sweden. These concern the general trend of this reorganization, whether it is an isolated event which is primarily confined to the arena of industrial relations and tripartite concertation or a broader social development which has an impact on numerous economic policies and political patterns. Also of interest here is whether the reorganization of the negotiated economy in Sweden is based upon a symmetrical balance of power and resources between organized business and its economic or political opponents, composed mainly of labor organizations and other popular movements closely affiliated with them.

13.2 Business and Politics in Sweden

Swedish business demonstrates a unique capacity for collective action compared with business in other industrial societies (Pestoff 1988b, 1989b). There are nearly 1,000 business interest associations (BIAs) in Sweden, compared to less than 100 trade unions. Swedish BIAs have several unique features compared with those found in other countries. These include a high degree of vertical integration and extreme centralization, both of which facilitate a unique degree of hierarchical coordination, manifest in "meta organizations", an unknown phenomenon in other polities (ibid.). Ownership is also important for membership, and the consumer cooperative sector is less organizationally developed than private business for promoting its collective interests (Pestoff 1988c).

The BIAs for private business collaborate extensively in politics. They have developed an elaborate and sophisticated strategy for influencing political decision-making in Sweden. SAF recently announced that it intended to unilaterally withdraw its representatives from the governing bodies of several hundred public authorities. It now emphasizes lobbying and opinion formation, as opposed to the more traditional channels provided by parliamentary *ad hoc* investigations, the *remiss* system, and lay representation of the governing bodies of public authorities. This strategy, which started as a defensive one in the early 1970s, had by the early 1980s become more offensive. Manipulation of public opinion and parliamentary lobbying are now seen as the key to political and economic influence in the future.

Thus, the Chairman of the Swedish Employers' Confederation (SAF), Ulf Laurin, made a pronouncement to his members, under the heading that "a new SAF was in the making" (*SAF tidn.* 16.02.90). He concluded his statement about SAF's future by noting that:

> ...The center of gravity in SAF's work has shifted to idea and opinion formation. It is ideas that change the world. (If) SAF can ... successfully propagate tomorrow's thoughts then its role will be larger than ever. SAF is the driving force in changing the system. – A new SAF is in the making (ibid.).

SAF and other BIAs for private business have developed an extensive network of joint committees, meta organizations, independent think-tanks, *ad hoc* campaign organizations, etc., for pursuing their political objectives. Numerous campaign and discourse institutions are prominent in this network.

For the last decade and a half SAF has devoted approximately 15% of its annual expenses to political activities. Now that SAF had disavowed centralized collective bargaining and that idea and opinion formation have become SAF's primary activity, this proportion can be expected to grow dramatically. In 1988 Swedish BIAs for private business spent nearly 200 M SEK (millions of Swedish crowns) for their political activities. SAF contributed more than three-fourths of this amount (Pestoff 1988b, 1989b, op. cit.). In comparison, all five of the established parliamentary parties combined had a similar amount at their disposal for political campaigning in the 1988 *Riksdag* elections (ibid.).

SAF's promotional campaign in the Fall of 1990 for Swedish membership in the European Community cost over 6 M SEK, a sum which was waved away as "small peanuts" by the director of SAF's public relations division (Beckman *et al.* 1991). Given its political ambitions, SAF will probably spend between 200 and 300 M SEK for idea and opinion formation in 1991. Ulf Laurin calculates expenses for SAF's information campaigns to 40 to 45 per cent of its total budget (SAF tidn., 17.05.91). The combined budgets of the established political parties will probably come to that amount in the 1991 Riksdag election. This has led some critics to equate SAF's activities with those normally associated with political parties (Vogel, *DN*, 12.01.91).

13.3 Reorganizing the Negotiated Economy in Selected Policy Areas

13.3.1 Industrial Relations

Centralized collective bargaining is the implicit core feature of the model proposed by Nielsen and Pedersen (1988, 1989, 1990). The core features of their model are most institutionalized in industrial relations of small, but highly developed economies of the northern European countries, although Katzenstein (1985) sees some similarities with other small European countries. The institutional history of the negotiated economy is synonymous with the development of the institutions of central collective bargaining, based on the historic compromises between the peak organizations of employers and trade unions in the four Nordic countries.

Elvander (1989) provides us with an overview for the 1970s and 1980s of variations in the development of collective bargaining in these four Nordic countries. Central collective bargaining is a basic feature of industrial relations in Sweden and of the "Swedish model". In its heyday the Swedish model relied primarily on bipartite patterns and agreements were negotiated between strong unions and a highly centralized employer organization. Government intervention became unnecessary after the 1938 Saltsjöbaden Basic Agreement.

Politics re-entered the scene with the radicalization of the late 1960s and early 1970s. A series of legislative proposals, known as the "Democratization of Working-Life" gained broad support in the *Riksdag* in the 1970s. This, however, changed one of the axioms of the Swedish model – that decisions were to be reached on the basis of consensus and compromise, rather than competition and confrontation. Decisions made under the former style of conflict resolution are subject to strict demands of unanimity, whereas legislative decision-making is subject to majoritarian rules. Consensus and compromise provided both the employers and unions with a veto over any changes (see Pestoff 1990b for more details).

SAF complained repeatedly that this legislative package changed the balance of power in the labor market and called for reinstating the old balance. In order to achieve this, labor's ability to extract benefits through political exchange had to be curtailed. If, as Pizzorno (1983) argues, labor underexploits its power in the labor market in order to achieve political influence, then it must be convinced to redirect its efforts back to the labor market.

Major labor market conflicts, after decades of labor peace, might help to refocus labor's attention on its "essential" responsibilities and functions. In 1977, under the first postwar non-socialist government, SAF planned to lock out 220,000 salaried employees for two weeks. In 1980 Sweden's largest labor market conflict broke out. Nearly three million workers were locked out by their employers or on strike for a few weeks in the Spring. The majority of the workers involved were employed in the private sector. The Chairman of SAF reassured his members on the eve of the lockout that this decision was "an investment for the future". Labor market conflicts have recurred periodically since then, though on a smaller scale.

Crouch (1990) analyzes the development of collective bargaining in several Western countries after 1968. Decentralizing collective bargaining, he argues, restores the initiative in industrial relations to management. This asserts the importance of the company level, where they dominate the balance of power, as opposed to the industrial or national level, where large unions operate in their preferred milieu (ibid.). In Sweden the employers embarked upon a policy of decentralizing collective bargaining in 1981, after initiating its centralization in the mid-1950s.

After more than ten years of struggle, centralized bargaining was finally laid to rest as a relic of the past in February 1990, through the systematic efforts of the Swedish Employers' Confederation. Their adamant refusal to discuss the reinstatement of centralized collective bargaining incidentally caused a major political crisis, which resulted in the only resignation of a Social Democratic government in the entire postwar period. It was also at that time that the Chairman of SAF announced that "a new SAF was in the making".

The Chairman of the Metal Workers' Union, Leif Blomberg, recently stated that much of the conflict on the labor market finds its origin in the fact that SAF has scuttled its collective bargaining division (*Dagens Nyheter*, 20.02.91). He continued:

> People (in SAF) who supported the "Swedish Model" have been replaced by spokesmen for the market. We have never been farther from the Saltsjöbaden Basic Agreement than

> now. SAF is emphasizing political opinion formation rather than taking responsibility for wage formation. ... Neo-liberals, who have the US and UK as their ideal, don't given a damn about wage differentials and unequality increasing at a catastrophic rate (ibid.).

He concluded that the trade union movement has been weakened by the lack of interlocutor for negotiating. The new role of the trade unions in the 1990s must be to emphasize opinion formation. The unions must become a countervailing power to SAF's political ambitions, according to him (ibid.).

Previously concerted practices were typical of most walks of Swedish industrial relations, not just of central collective bargaining. The interrelatedness of various segments of Swedish industrial relations has been analyzed in terms of generalized political exchange, in which each segment or policy area is conceived of as an independent meso game (Pestoff 1990b). There is a high degree of similarity in the central features of the various segments of Swedish industrial relations, as seen in collective bargaining, work environment regulation, codetermination, labor market insurance, the wage-earner funds, and lay representation on the governing boards of central public administrative agencies. The meso game in each of these areas or arenas is interrelated to that of the others. Each follows its own particular logic and rules of the game, but their outcomes are nevertheless all interdependent on each other (ibid.). A stalemate in one arena can easily spill over to the other. Negotiations were clearly the instrument of decision-making in Swedish industrial relations during several decades, rather than market signals or authoritative decisions.

Many, but not all, of the institutional features of the conceptual model of the negotiated economy, as spelled out by Nielsen and Pedersen, are, or at least were, present in Swedish industrial relations between the late 1930s and the late 1970s. Class cooperation was, however, replaced by class confrontation in Sweden, starting in the early 1980s. This was in line with the new strategy adopted by the dominant group in the Swedish Employers' Confederation, the Association of Engineering Employers, who organize most of the large Swedish multinational firms, such as Volvo, ABB, Electrolux, and Ericsson.

They were spurred on by the introduction of the wage-earner funds in 1983, which they adamantly opposed. They are now actively pushing for the deinstitutionalization of most aspects of Swedish industrial relations, in an effort to undermine labor's political position. Deinstitutionalization means that many of the general, and even some of the core, features of the model of the negotiated economy have disappeared, or will do so in the foreseeable future in Sweden. Thus, we find that Swedish industrial relations are being transformed into a labor market in the most literal sense.

The importance of the deinstitutionalization of Swedish industrial relations should not be underestimated, as they alone provide the core features of the full-fledged model of the negotiated economy. The decline in the importance of central collective bargaining and the deinstitutionalization of industrial relations imply an uncertain future for the negotiated economy in Sweden. Yet, it seems too early to conclude that the negotiated economy also ceased to exist with the final demise of the Swedish model in February 1990. We need to consider developments in other policy areas or arenas that might confirm or disavow this new pattern in Swedish concerted practices and the reorganization of the negotiated economy.

13.3.2 Consumer Policy

Swedish consumer policy has been analyzed in terms of the negotiated economy (Pestoff 1989a, 1990a). It has an institutional history and development of its own, starting at the beginning of the 1940s and running until present (Pestoff 1984, 1989a). It, too, is based on a bi- or tripartite configuration of principal actors, that is, consumers, producers, and the state. It attempts to shore up the organizationally weaker consumers and pit them as a countervailing power against the organizationally superior interests of business and commerce. It can be divided into five phases, including the present decentralization phase (Pestoff 1988a, 1989a, 1990a).

Some, but far from all, of the institutional features of the model of the negotiated economy were found here. In particular few, if any, of the structural requirements and institutional arrangements spelled out by Nielsen and Pedersen were observed. Those that existed were either primarily associated with the labor market bodies or they were public institutions designed to promote official Swedish consumer policy. Thus, the functions of the five complementary institutions for policy, discourse, campaign, negotiation, and arbitration or sanction were either undertaken by public institutions or they were absent.

The processes of the negotiated economy were only evident in a rudimentary fashion. There were few specific efforts to mobilize and promote a particular socio-economic ideology of bargained consumer policy in Sweden. The few existing efforts in this vein were mostly associated with parliamentary commissions on consumer policy between 1968 to 1971 and again 1982 to 1985. One of the "independent" think-tanks of private business did, however, back a major drive to deinstitutionalize consumer policy and replace it with the market in the late 1970s. It published several debate books which severally criticized official Swedish consumer policy, including *Mot en ny konsumentpolitik* (*Towards a New Consumer Policy*), Rydén (ed.), 1979; *I konsumenters intresse?* (*In the Interest of Consumers?*), Wikström (ed.), 1979; and *Konsumenten, politikerna and byråkratin* (*The Consumer, Politicians and the Bureaucracy*), Eliasson and Henning, 1981.

But, no discourse nor campaign institutions articulated the premises of Swedish consumers, because none exist. Businesses' efforts were only brought to a head and routed when the Social Democrats returned to power in the early 1980s. They initiated a new parliamentary investigation of consumer policy, which served to remove the debate from the public arena and confine it to the Parliamentary Committee on Consumer Affairs. The latter combined the functions attributed to discourse and campaign institutions with its policy functions, in an attempt to reach a negotiated compromise on the future of Swedish consumer policy.

Similar developments are seen in terms of agricultural and food policy as well as with regard to the use of price freezes. The same business-financed "independent" think-tank initiated a public debate about both of these types of regulation. Again, several debate books put the issues on the public agenda and generated enough interest and concern to result in major policy reformulations (Bolin *et al.* 1984). Consumers were, however, unable to express their concerns and interests, as they lack discourse and campaign institutions. The public authorities responsible for consumer policy must therefore deal directly with these business critics of negotiated consumer policy without the help or support of independent consumer organizations.

Similarly, the negotiation games and the round-table negotiations between organized business and consumers usually take place under the auspices of public consumer policy and in connection with the public agencies responsible for it. More important, many of the arenas for round-table negotiations instituted in the history of Swedish consumer policy have now ceased to function as bargaining arenas. Thus, several of the institutional arenas for bargaining, described in detail by Pestoff (1989a, 1990a), either no longer exist or have recently been radically curtailed. Not only has the Home Research Institute, which brought together consumers and producers in an effort to develop new home products between 1944 and 1957, disappeared. The annual food price negotiations between farmers and consumers, which took place between 1953 and 1990, will soon terminate. Sweden now plans to open her borders to imported foodstuffs, in an effort to adapt to the new GATT agreements anticipated in this area. Negotiated Swedish food prices will thus be replaced by world market prices.

Another area of importance for the negotiations which characterized Swedish consumer policy in the postwar period is that of price control and price freezes. They normally involved detailed negotiations between public authorities and individual firms or their representatives. The business community, through its discourse and campaign institutions, had criticized the policy of price freezes of distorting market signals for over a decade (Joung 1984). They achieved their objective at the end of the 1980s, when it was decided that the instrument of price freezes will no longer be employed. Once again we can note a return to the market.

Thus, many of the features and institutions associated with negotiated consumer policy in postwar Sweden are disappearing and being replaced by the market. It becomes necessary to question whether Swedish consumer policy can illustrate the negotiated economy in the future.

13.3.3 Housing

Sixty per cent of Sweden's population lives in single family dwellings, but this, however, represents less than half of the households. Many families with young children prefer living in villas, while older persons often live alone in apartments. Public housing makes up about one-quarter of the multiple-family dwellings, while cooperative housing provides accommodations for another 16%. Both landlords and renters are well organized and have negotiated with each other about rents and improvements of apartments for decades in Sweden.

The private landlords, cooperative housing, and the municipal housing companies each have their own negotiating organization for bargaining with tenants, who in turn are organized in the National Federation of Tenants' Associations. Private landlords usually belong to the Swedish Federation of Rental Property Owners, while municipal housing companies belong to the Swedish Association of Municipal Housing Companies. Rent negotiations have determined annual increases in rents, the overall level of rents, and the need for improvements in the standard of apartments since the end of World War II.

Rents were regulated for several decades after the end of World War II. Furthermore, the standard of newly built apartments was influenced by national building norms. Both the organized landlords and renters are represented in the policy institutions for housing policy in Sweden. Negotiations between the municipal housing authorities and the local and regional branches of the National Federation of Tenants' Associations sets the norm for annual rent increases, as rent laws prescribe that municipal housing firms should be price leaders as they cover a considerable proportion of the dwellings. General housing and building policy in Sweden is normally determined by parliamentary commissions.

The debate about housing is highly technical and the participants are therefore usually specialists. Some of the specialized institutions called for by Nielsen and Pedersen's conceptual model are found in this area. Policy institutions are normally parliamentary commissions. Discourse and campaign institutions are not specifically related to housing nor the building sector. Nor do we find a symmetrical relationship between the partners. Forces associated with private profit interests, which desire to return to the market, appear at present to dominate the debate.

Regional rent courts together with the national rent court provide a system of institutionalized arbitration and sanction, similar to that of the Labor Court and the Market Court in Sweden. These are bipartite bodies, with an equal number of members chosen among representatives of the landlords' and renters' organizations, plus a "neutral" legal council, who serves as chairman. The National Federation of Tenants' Associations represents private individuals, while the National Association of Retailers represents small shop owners as renters. Swedish Federation of Rental Property Owners, the building and tenant cooperatives and the Swedish Association of Municipal Housing Companies represent different categories of landlords, according to the needs of individual cases.

Turning to the processes of the negotiated economy once again, we find that only one actor seems more capable of actively participating in the development of a socio-economic ideology concerning housing. The same "independent" think-tanks of private business mentioned earlier play an important role in the debate about housing and rent policy. They recently published a debate book about "free rents", arguing that a return to the market would solve housing shortage problems (Meyerson *et al.* 1990). Another of private capital's discourse institutions, the New Welfare – a more aggressively neoliberal organ, also issued a report designed to stimulate the debate for a return to market forces in housing matters.

The National Federation of Tenants' Associations has issued its own debate book, which decries the lobby activities of interests promoting the liberalization of rent policy and adjustment of rents paid by private individuals for housing to market forces (Bergenstråle 1990). However, renters seem incapable of sustaining the debate or of mounting a full-scale campaign to protect the existing system of regulations and negotiations.

Implicit in such attempts to change the socio-economic ideology concerning rents and housing policy is a desire to eliminate negotiations as an instrument of decision-making. Once again it seems that the objective of the critics of the present system of negotiations is to deinstitutionalize it and return housing issues and rents to unbridled market forces. This in turn also implies the termination of negotiations as an institution for allocating and redistributing resources derived from rents for personal housing.

13.4 The Problems Facing the Negotiated Economy in Sweden

The degree of institutionalization called for by Nielsen and Pedersen's conceptual model, with both its structural and process-like aspects suggests a series of concentric circles, which have a hierarchical ordering, like a pyramid. Treu also refers to the hierarchical ordering of interests among tripartite actors in order to achieve a balanced pursuit of their common interests (op. cit.). Prior to the mid-1980s, central collective bargaining was usually coordinated in time with independent bargaining rounds concerning other common interests, such as food prices, rents, and, in times of inflation, even price stops. The reintroduction of market forces as the dominant criteria of decision-making concerning resource allocation and redistribution in each of these areas serves to isolate the bargaining arenas from each other.

The degree of institutionalization also appears to be related to the degree of repetition in round-table negotiations. The more often negotiations take place between any two actors, the higher the degree of institutionalization; and thus the more clearly most of the institutional features of the conceptual model will develop. Thus, it should come as no surprise that labor markets, with their special institutional histories and development involving more than half a century of collective bargaining, are the most institutionalized.

However, even in the least iterative and institutional areas, where negotiations only take place on an *ad hoc* basis and where most or all of the institutional requirements of the conceptual model are absent, there is still a tendency to copy some of the central features of the negotiated economy. Negotiations are sometimes employed as an instrument of decision-making concerning the allocation and redistribution of resources, rather than market signals or authoritative decisions.

There are a number of similarities between the areas in Sweden where negotiations are employed as an instrument of decision-making, yet none of them fit fully with the conceptual model provided by Nielsen and Pedersen. The labor market, consumer policy, and, perhaps, housing policy come closest. This in turn suggests that the negotiated economy, like generalized political exchange, can be conceived of as a series of independent arenas, where functionally interdependent actors are engaged in a semi-permanent struggle or meso games, although not necessarily for the final victory, but rather for the benefits stemming from a particular round of negotiations. Sometimes the same teams play in different games or in different arenas, although the better financed team may be able to change uniforms between games.

Berrefjord and Hernes (1989) see large firms as the single most important actor and force in developing the negotiated economy. Until recently Nielsen and Pedersen did not explicitly deal with the necessity of symmetry in terms of the institutional development of the different teams which play in various arenas or games of the generalized negotiated economy. Some semblance of parity in resources and similarity in development of the institutions can, however, be assumed for labor market organizations in most Nordic countries. But such assumptions are not always realistic in other areas where the negotiated economy has nevertheless taken root in these countries.

We noted that one of the actors in the Swedish negotiated economy appears often to be pushing for a return to the market, and is calling for measures which would deinstitutionalize the negotiation structures and processes which have been established in Sweden in the post-World War II tripartite concertation and the negotiated economy; this observation is also open to numerous interpretations.

The extent of this challenge depends upon the actions and reactions of other major social actors, like the trade unions and the nation-state. Do trade unions and the political elites have a clear understanding of the problems facing the negotiated economy and concerted practices? If so, do they have a strategy and the resources to promote the negotiated economy and concerted practices? The answers given to these questions may vary from one Nordic country to another.

Treu suggests that a new multi-level and multi-dimensional pattern of concertation may be in the interest both of capital and labor. This may prove more accurate in some countries than others. We feel that the degree of economic concentration and internationalization will be decisive in determining the future of the negotiated economy and concerted practices in the Nordic countries. Treu also argues that global competition will be governed by multinational companies, which will act as economic super-powers (op. cit.).

It is worth noting that there is a macro trend or general tendency for the nation-state to lose importance to other levels of decision-making, particularly for capital, though not necessarily to the same extent for labor. Both the regional and international levels appear to be gaining in importance at the expense of the nation-state. Swedish business is clearly a major actor in the trend toward internationalization. Swedish business is the most concentrated and probably one of the most internationally integrated of any European country (Pestoff and Ronit 1990). Swedish business bought more European firms during the first half of 1990 than businesses from all other countries of the world combined, and more than twice as much as American firms did during the same period.

The negotiated economy and concerted practices are national phenomena, most staunchly supported by the trade unions and Social Democrats in the Nordic countries. The economic integration and internationalization of the Nordic countries puts pressure on them to reduce public spending, which in turn curtails their national sovereignty. Variations in the rate of economic integration and internationalization should also be reflected in different rates of reorganization and restructuring in the negotiated economies and concerted practices of these countries.

Streeck (1989) and Schmitter and Streeck (1990) argue that organized labor lacks both the strategy and resources available to business for participating in decision-making in the European Communities. Nor are the institutions of the EC favorable to bi- or tripartite participation in decision-making. Lobbying by multinational firms and/or by the European branch organizations of organized business, without the participation of labor or consumers, seems to be a more realistic development, at least in the short term. Treu confirms this analysis, and speaks of regime or policy shopping by large multinational firms, that is, of choosing to invest in countries with less costly and more flexible social benefits (op. cit.). Streeck refers to this phenomenon as social dumping (op. cit.). Economic internationalization can thus include a political dimension which has implications for the balance of power at the national level.

Although Sweden is not (yet) a member of the EC, Swedish firms have been on the cutting edge of European intergration and they are helping to internationalize economic transactions. But in the process of doing so they are, of course, internationalizing themselves and Swedish politics as well. As the European level grows in importance both economically and politically, they quite naturally lose interest in developments, agreements, and negotiations at the national level. They naturally feel less constrained and concerned by political solutions and economic bargains at the national level. They are less committed to finding specific national formulas and more interested in finding flexible internationally applicable solutions that fit with a number of nation-states where they operate. To the extent that the negotiated economy is a specifically Scandinavian or Nordic phenomenon, it can therefore be expected to lose support and importance in the near future, as business options for more general market-orientated solutions to the problems they face in several countries.

It has, however, been argued from a macro-economic perspective that "structural competitiveness" requires a long-term strategic perspective (Jessop *et al.* 1990). Porter's (1990) comparative study of the competitive advantage of nations focuses on the multi-dimensional nature of competition between nations. It goes much farther than the relative price of the factors of production, or labor and social costs. He concludes that the presence of sophisticated and demanding customers in the home market, the existence of industrial clusters of internationally orientated firms, and an institutional structure appropriate for promoting competition are all necessary for providing a nation with the necessary structural competitiveness (ibid., Porter *et al.* 1991).

13.5 Conclusions

The negotiated economy and concerted practices face numerous problems in the Nordic countries. These problems concern centralization, institutionalization of concerted practices and the negotiated economy, and the role of trade unions and business interest organizations in the economic and social policies of these countries, as well as the internationalization and European integration of their economies. Reorganization and restructuring of concerted practices and the negotiated economy may entail rejuvenation in one country, yet it may spell out demise in another. Decentralization and deinstitutionalization are, of course, a matter of degree. The internationalization and integration of the national economies appear to be a decisive factor in determining the thrust and direction of this reorganization and restructuring. This in turn depends upon the role and importance of various large economic actors, in particular that of multinational firms.

Sweden is normally in the forefront of social and political developments due to its centralized collective bargaining, strong unions, active labor market policy, and well-articulated welfare state. However, in the 1990s she may well lead the retreat from concerted practices and the negotiated economy. Not much systematic attention has been given to Swedish business, its numerous multinational firms, and its unique business interest associations. This lack of attention perhaps made sense during the long period of Social Democratic hegemony, when concerted practices thrived and the negotiated economy took root. But today, at the beginning of the 1990s we are witnessing a new era in which the politics of compromise have been replaced by the politics of confrontation. In Sweden the reorganization and restructuring of concerted practices and the negotiated economy do not imply a rejuvenation, rather they demonstrate the demise of such practices and patterns and a return to the market.

This process can go much farther and proceed at a more rapid rate in Sweden than in the neighboring Nordic countries, due to the importance of Swedish multinational firms. The Swedish trade unions and the governing Social Democrats appear to be at a loss in terms of their analysis of the current situation, in terms of their stance toward the reorganization and restructuring of concerted practices and the negotiated economy, and, most important, in terms of developing a strategy and providing adequate resources to promote their own preferences on these matters. Thus, it might not be far fetched to suggest that Swedish employers appear to be inspired by their American counterparts. They are actively striving for "an organization free environment" and a "trade union free environment" by the turn of the century, and they may well be in the position to achieve it.

References

Beckman, Å. *et al.* (1991): *Från löneförhandling till EC-propaganda.* Student paper. Stockholm: Department of Journalism.

Bergenstråhle, S. (1990): *Bostaden & marknaden.* Stockholm: Hyresgästernas Riksförbund.

Berrefjord, O. (1982): *Rafnes-saken: forhandlingsøkonomien i aksjon.* Oslo: Universitetsforlaget.

Berrefjord, O. (1989): Økonomimotiverte beslutninger eller beslustmotiverte kalkyler? In: *Forhandlingsøkonomi i Norden.* Köpenhamn and Oslo: Jurist- og Økonomforbundets Forlag and Tano.

Berrefjord, O. (1990): *Semi-Public Projects and Corporate Behavior: A Negotiated Economy in Norway.* Washington DC: SASE Conference.

Berrefjord, O. *et al.* (1982): Økonomiske maktgrupperinger, kap. 5. In: *Maktutredningen – Slutrapport.* Oslo: NOU 1982:3.
Berrefjord, O. and G. Hernes (1989): Storforetak, marked og byråkrati. In: *Forhandlingsøkonomi i Norden.* Köpenhamn and Oslo: Jurist- og Økonomforbundets Forlag and Tano.
Bolin, O. *et al.* (1985): *Makten over maten.* Stockholm: SNS.
Childs, M. (1936): *Sweden: The Middle Way.* New Haven: Yale University Press.
Childs, M. (1980): *Sweden: The Middle Way on Trial,* New Haven and London: Yale University Press.
Crouch, C. (1990): Generalized Political Exchange in Industrial Relations in Europe During the Twentieth Century. In: *Governance and Generalized Exchange – Self-Organized Networks in Action,* Marin, B. (ed.). Frankfurt and Denver: Campus and Westview Press.
Eliasson, G. and R. Henning (1981): *Konsumenten, politikerna och byråkratin.* Stockholm: SNS.
Elvander, N. (1989): Inkomstpolitik i Norden. In: *Forhandlingsøkonomi i Norden.* Köpenhamn and Oslo: Jurist- og Økonomforbundets Forlag and Tano.
Hernes, G. (1978): *Forhandlingsøkonomi og blandningsadministrasjon,* Oslo: Universitetsforlaget.
Jessop, B., K. Nielsen, and O. K. Pedersen (1990): *Structural Competitiveness and Strategic Capacities: Scandinavia.* Conference paper. Cracow.
Joung, L. (1984): *Prisregleringen, företagen och förhandlingsekonomin.* Stockholm: SNS.
Katzenstein, P. (1985): *Small States in World Markets.* Ithaca and London: Cornell University Press.
Marin, B. (1985) (revised 1990): Generalized Political Exchange. In: *Generalized Political Exchange.* Frankfurt and Denver: Campus and Westview Press.
Meyerson, P. M. *et al.* (1990): *Makten över bostaden.* Stockholm: SNS.
Nielson, K. and O. K. Pedersen (1988): The Negotiated Economy: Ideal and History. *Scandinavian Political Studies,* 11 (2), 79–101.
Nielson, K. and O. K. Pedersen (1989): Forhandlingsøkonomi i Norden – en inledning. In: *Forlandlingsøkonomi i Norden.* Köpenhamn and Oslo: Jurist- og Økonomforbundets Forlag and Tano.
Nielsen, K. and O. K. Pedersen (1990a): *From the Mixed Economy to the Negotiated Economy in the Scandinavian Countries.* Washington DC: SASE Conference.
NOU (Norwegian Parliamentary Investigations) (1978, 33): *Om konsentrasjon og marknadsmakt.* Oslo: NOU.
NOU (Norwegian Parliamentary Investigations) (1982, 3): *Maktutredningen – Slutrapport,* Oslo: NOU.
Pedersen, O. K. (1989): Läreprocesser og forhandlingsspil, om löndannelse og forhandlingsökonomi i Danmark. In: *Forhandlingsøkonomi i Norden.* Köpenhamn and Oslo: Jurist- og Økonomforbundets Forlag and Tano.
Pederson, O. K. (1990): *Learning Processes and the Game of Negotiation. Wage Formation and Negotiated Economy in Denmark.* Washington DC: SASE Conference.
Pestoff, V. (1984): *Konsumentinflytande och konsumentorganisering – den svenska modellen.* Stockholm: Finansdept., Ds Fi 1985:15.
Pestoff, V. (1988a): Exit, Voice and Collective Action in Swedish Consumer Policy. *Journal of Consumer Policy,* 11, 1–27.
Pestoff, V. (1988b): *The Politics of Private Business, Co-operatives and Public Enterprise in a Corporate Democracy – the Case of Sweden.* Conference paper. Florence and Stockholm.
Pestoff, V. (1988c): Näringslivets strategiska marknadsföring av värderingar (The Strategic Marketing of Values by Business). In: *Kooperativ årsbok.* Strockholm: Föreningen kooperativa studier.
Pestoff, V. (1989a): Organisationernas medverkan och forhandlingar i svensk konsument-

politik. In: *Forlandlingsøkonomi i Norden*. Köenhamn and Oslo: Jurist- og Økonomforbundets Forlag and Tano. Och: *Ridskrift för Rättssociologi*, 6 (3/4), 1–45.
Pestoff, V. (1989b): *Näringslivsorgnaisationerna och politiken i Sverige*. Stockholm: TCO.
Pestoff, V. (1990a): *Organizing Consumers in a Negotiated Economy – Swedish Consumer Policy*. Washington DC: SASE Conference.
Pestoff, V. (1990b): Joint Regulation, Meso-Games and Political Exchange in Swedish Industrial Relations. In: *Governance and Generalized Exchange*, Marin, B. (ed.).
Pestoff, V. (1990c): *From the Market to Negotiations and Back Again? The Negotiated Economy in Sweden*. Conference paper. Cracow.
Pestoff, V. and K. Ronit (1990): *Changing Environments and European Integration: Accommodation by Organized Business in Denmark and Sweden*. Conference paper. Reykjavik.
Pettersson, O. *et al.* (1990): *Demokrati och Makt i Sverige* – Maktutrednings huvudrapport, SOU 1990 (44). Stockholm: Statsrådsberedningen.
Pizzorno, A. (1983): Political Exchange and Collective Identity in Industrial Conflicts. In: *The Resurgence of Class Conflict in Western Europe Since 1968*, Crouch, C. and A. Pizzorno (eds.). London: Macmillan.
Porter, M. (1990): *The Competitive Advantage of Nations*. New York: Free Press.
Porter, M. *et al.* (1991): *Advantage Sweden*. Stockholm: Noedstedt.
Ryden, B. (ed.) (1979): *Mot en ny konsumentpolitik*. Stockholm: SNS.
SAF tidningen (1991): "Ett nytt SAF håller på ta form" – Öppet brev i SAF tigningen, 16.05.1990.
Streeck, W. (1989): *The Social Dimension of the European Firm*. Discussion paper. Florence.
Schmitter, P. and W. Streeck (1990): *Organized Interests and the Europe of 1992*. Discussion paper. Florence.
Treu, T. (1992): Tripartite Social Policy-Making. An Overview. In Treu, T. (1991): *Participation in Public Policy-Making. The Role of Trade Unions and Employers' Association*. Berlin and New York: de Gruyter.
Vogel, J. (1991): Ovetneskaplig opinionsmätning. In: *Dagens Nyheter*, 12.01.1991.
Wikström, S. (ed.) (1979): *I konsumenternas intresse?* Stockholm: SNS.

14 Structural Adaptation of the Japanese Economy and Labor Market

Haruo Shimada

14.1 Introduction

For the last 15 years, the advanced economies of the world have been shaken by drastic and, at times, dramatic changes in economic conditions, which may be better described as "shocks" rather than mere changes, such as the two oil crises of the 1970s, the prolonged world-wide recession of the early 1980s, and the drastic realignment of exchange rates in the Fall of 1985.

The Japanese economy received perhaps the most forceful impact from these events among advanced nations. Although it is true that these changes always have positive as well as negative impacts, the Japanese economy had particular structural reasons to be especially vulnerable to the adverse effects of these changes, for example, uniquely high dependence on imported oil, very high dependence on exports to the United States, and so forth.

Nevertheless, among advanced economies the performance of the Japanese economy in surviving and overcoming these adversities has almost always been exceptionally good. The Japanese economy always seems to have adapted quickly and effectively. It appears that this successful adaptation was supported and promoted by the flexible structure of the economy and, perhaps most importantly, that of its labor market.

The purpose of this paper is to review the experience of the Japanese economy over the last 15 years in order to examine the critical phases of adaptation, identify the major factors which facilitated such adaptation, interpret the nature of Japanese-style adaptation, and to discuss remaining structural issues.

In Section 2, I will briefly review the macro-economic performance of several advanced economies over the last 15 years in order to compare it with the performance of Japan. Section 3 undertakes to describe in some detail the experience of the Japanese economy in adapting to the series of external shocks. In Section 4, I will discuss the nature of the Japanese model of structural adaptation. In Section 5, I will discuss some of the major structural problems currently faced by the Japanese economy and labor market. Finally, Section 6 offers concluding remarks.

14.2 Economic Fluctuations and the Effective Adaptation of the Japanese Economy: An International Comparison

Over the last 15 years, the advanced economies of the world have experienced fairly common major changes in economic conditions. Some of these changes were so acute that they may well be described as "shocks" rather than mere changes. These changes include the first and second oil crises of the 1970s, the large-scale recession of the early 1980s, and the drastic realignment of exchange rates in the mid-1980s.

Let us briefly review how several of the major economies responded to these critical changes in economic conditions. The purpose of this exercise is to see if the Japanese economy adapted more smoothly or quickly than other economies. To do so, we examine several principal macro-economic variables. Table 1 presents data for the last 15 years for Japan, the United States, the United Kingdom, Germany, France, and Italy.

First, to consider the economic growth: Over the last 15 years, these economies have experienced a more or less common pattern of economic fluctuations. Immediately after the first oil crisis of 1973, each of these economies suffered a deep economic recession. Indeed, most of them, including Japan, recorded negative growth either during 1974 or 1975, or both. After this sharp recession, most of these economies recovered rather well and enjoyed a decent pace of growth for a few years during the latter half of the 1970s.

The sustained recovery was, however, suddenly disturbed by the destructive impact of the second oil crisis of 1979. Under the acute inflationary impact, most economies were swamped in the trap of "stagflation", namely, price inflation and quantity depression. Growth rates declined markedly for many economies at the beginning of the 1980s. However, the extent of the decline varied across economies. While Japan and France experienced only minor slowdowns, the United Kingdom suffered substantial negative growth. This slowdown continued or even worsened during the early 1980s for many economies. During this phase of prolonged world-wide recession, Japan, again, was somewhat exceptional and enjoyed a higher pace of growth than other countries.

Toward the mid-1980s, many economies again started to enjoy the wave of world-wide recovery. But this recovery was disturbed by the drastic realignment of exchange rates, whereby the dollar was devalued against most other currencies. The dollar fell most sharply against the yen. This must have given a powerful negative jolt to the export-oriented structure of the Japanese economy. Indeed, the economy of Japan experienced a substantial slowdown in 1986. However, it did not last long. The economy started a vigorous recovery in 1987, and has been enjoying strong growth since. Other economies, including that of the United States, have been enjoying modest and more or less sustained growth over the same period.

Table 1: Macroeconomic Performance of Selected Countries, 1974–1988 [a, b, c]

	Japan						
	GNP	U	W	CPI	WPI	BP	EX
1974	−1.4	1.3	5.7	65.2	73.7	−1.0	292
1975	2.7	1.4	3.0	72.9	75.8	−0.1	296
1976	4.8	1.9	−1.7	79.7	79.7	0.7	296
1977	5.3	2.0	1.1	86.1	81.2	1.5	268
1978	5.2	2.0	1.9	89.4	79.1	1.7	210
1979	5.3	2.2	1.2	92.6	84.9	−0.9	219
1980	4.3	2.1	−1.8	100.0	100.0	−1.1	226
1981	3.7	2.0	1.7	104.9	101.4	0.5	220
1982	3.1	2.2	1.2	107.8	101.9	0.7	249
1983	3.2	2.4	1.0	109.7	101.2	1.8	237
1984	5.1	2.6	1.1	112.3	101.3	2.8	237
1985	4.9	2.7	0.2	114.5	100.5	3.6	238
1986	2.4	2.6	2.8	115.2	95.8	4.3	168
1987	4.3	2.8	1.0	115.3	92.8	3.6	144
1988	—	2.8	—	—	—	—	128

	United States						
	GNP	U	W	CPI	WPI	BP	EX
1974	−0.5	4.9	−2.0	59.8	54.6	0.1	1.00
1975	−1.3	5.6	0.0	65.3	65.1	1.2	1.00
1976	4.9	8.5	2.9	69.1	68.1	0.3	1.00
1977	4.7	7.7	2.0	73.6	72.2	−0.8	1.00
1978	5.3	7.1	1.0	79.2	77.9	−0.7	1.00
1979	2.5	6.1	−2.4	88.1	87.6	0.0	1.00
1980	−0.2	5.8	−4.4	100.0	100.0	0.0	1.00
1981	1.9	7.1	0.0	110.3	109.4	0.2	1.00
1982	−2.5	7.6	0.5	117.1	111.4	−0.3	1.00
1983	3.6	9.7	0.1	120.9	112.7	−1.4	1.00
1984	6.8	9.6	−0.2	126.1	115.4	−2.8	1.00
1985	3.0	7.5	0.2	130.6	114.9	−2.9	1.00
1986	2.9	7.2	0.2	133.0	111.5	−3.3	1.00
1987	2.9	7.0	−1.8	137.9	114.5	−3.4	1.00
1988	3.9	6.2	—	—	—	—	1.00

France

	GNP	U	W	CPI	WPI	BP	EX
1974	3.2	—	4.7	54.4	64.5	−1.5	4.81
1975	0.2	—	5.3	60.8	65.3	0.8	4.28
1976	5.2	—	5.0	66.7	71.0	−1.0	4.77
1977	—	—	4.0	72.9	77.0	−0.1	4.91
1978	3.3	—	3.0	79.5	81.4	1.5	4.51
1979	3.2	6.0	0.9	88.1	90.7	0.9	4.25
1980	1.6	6.7	2.3	100.0	100.0	−0.6	4.22
1981	1.2	7.9	1.5	113.4	111.7	−0.8	5.43
1982	2.5	8.2	1.8	126.8	124.4	−2.2	6.57
1983	0.7	9.0	2.9	139.0	135.3	−0.8	7.62
1984	1.4	10.2	−1.0	149.3	147.4	−0.2	8.73
1985	1.7	10.2	0.0	158.0	153.9	0.0	8.98
1986	2.1	10.5	1.4	162.2	149.5	0.4	6.92
1987	—	10.4	—	167.3	150.3	—	6.01
1988	—	—	—	—	—	—	5.95

Germany

	GNP	U	W	CPI	WPI	BP	EX
1974	0.2	2.6	4.1	77.4	78.7	2.7	2.58
1975	−1.4	4.7	2.3	82.0	82.3	1.0	2.46
1976	5.6	4.6	2.4	85.5	85.3	0.9	2.51
1977	2.7	4.5	3.7	88.6	87.7	0.8	2.32
1978	3.3	4.3	2.5	91.1	88.7	1.4	2.00
1979	4.0	3.8	1.2	94.7	92.9	0.8	1.83
1980	1.5	3.8	1.2	100.0	100.0	1.9	1.81
1981	0.0	5.5	−0.6	106.3	107.8	0.8	2.26
1982	−1.0	7.5	−0.1	111.9	114.1	0.5	2.42
1983	1.9	9.1	0.1	115.6	115.8	0.6	2.55
1984	3.3	9.1	−0.1	118.4	119.2	1.0	2.84
1985	2.0	9.3	2.3	121.0	121.8	2.5	2.94
1986	2.5	9.0	4.0	120.7	118.2	4.4	2.17
1987	1.7	8.9	—	121.0	115.6	4.0	1.79
1988	3.4	—	—	—	—	—	—

Italy

	GNP	U	W	CPI	WPI	BP	EX
1974	4.1	5.6	—	40.1	42.8	−4.4	650
1975	−3.6	6.1	—	46.9	46.5	−0.3	652
1976	5.9	7.0	—	54.8	57.1	−1.5	832
1977	1.9	7.2	—	64.1	66.5	1.1	882
1978	2.7	7.2	—	71.9	72.1	2.4	848
1979	4.9	7.7	4.0	82.5	83.3	1.7	830
1980	3.9	7.6	1.5	100.0	100.0	−2.4	856
1981	0.2	8.4	4.5	117.8	116.6	−2.3	1136
1982	−0.5	8.6	0.7	137.2	132.8	−1.6	1352
1983	−0.2	9.4	0.5	157.3	145.7	0.2	1518
1984	—	10.0	0.4	174.3	160.8	−0.8	1757
1985	2.9	10.3	0.5	190.3	172.6	−0.9	1909
1986	3.1	11.1	−0.3	201.4	171.1	0.4	1490
1987	—	12.0	1.6	211.0	175.6	−0.1	1296
1988	—	—	—	—	—	—	1301

United Kingdom

	GNP	U	W	CPI	WPI	BP	EX
1974	−1.3	2.6	5.0	41.1	40.9	−3.9	0.42
1975	−1.3	3.9	1.8	51.1	50.0	−1.4	0.45
1976	4.1	5.3	−3.3	59.6	58.6	−0.7	0.55
1977	0.1	5.7	−6.6	69.0	70.2	0.0	0.57
1978	3.9	5.7	6.1	74.7	76.7	0.7	0.52
1979	2.2	5.3	3.0	84.8	86.0	−0.3	0.47
1980	−2.3	6.8	−0.3	100.0	100.0	1.6	0.43
1981	0.4	9.4	−1.7	112.0	109.5	2.9	0.49
1982	1.1	10.9	0.4	121.6	118.0	1.5	0.57
1983	4.0	11.7	2.6	127.1	124.4	1.1	0.66
1984	2.5	11.7	1.9	133.5	132.1	0.3	0.75
1985	3.4	11.8	1.9	141.6	139.4	0.9	0.77
1986	3.6	11.8	3.4	146.4	145.7	0.0	0.68
1987	3.7	10.6	2.4	152.5	151.2	−0.7	0.61
1988	—	—	—	—	—	—	—

Notes: [a] Notations refer to:
GNP: Over-the-year per cent increase in real gross national product.
U: Unemployment rate.
W: Over-the-year per cent increase in the real wage rate.
CPI: Over-the-year per cent increase in the consumer price index.
WPI: Over-the-year per cent increase in the wholesale price index.
BP: Current account balance as a per cent of GNP.
[b] Real GNP was computed by using 1982 prices as the benchmark for the United States and 1980 prices as the benchmark for the other countries.
[c)] — designates unavailable data.

Sources: OECD, *Main Economic Indicators*, various issues, and relevant official data of each country. Much of the data were taken from the series compiled and edited by the Bank of Japan.

This brief comparison of growth performance suggests that, in spite of the serious impact of external shocks such as the oil crises and the realignment of exchange rates, the Japanese economy recovered quickly or maintained a good growth performance. This good performance was particularly pronounced in the wake of the second oil crisis of 1979 and in the wake of the 1985 Plaza Agreement. While the magnitude of the shocks were probably larger for Japan compared with other economies, its subsequent growth performance was almost always better.

Another important aspect of economic performance is price stability. Most of the economies shown in Table 1 shared a fairly common pattern of price fluctuations. That is, they suffered from very high rates of inflation, first in 1974 and second in 1980, both in the wake of the oil shocks. Inflation rates were much lower during the latter half of the 1970s and since around the 1980s. Among these economies, Germany, where inflation has been consistently kept at a relatively modest rate, is somewhat exceptional.

While there are some similar features to price fluctuations across these countries, the level and trend of inflation has varied considerably. The United Kingdom, France, and Italy have, at least until recently, suffered from relatively high inflation rates. The United States experienced high inflation until the mid-1980s when the rate became more modest. Germany has enjoyed more stable prices compared with other countries.

In the wake of the first oil crisis of the mid-1970s, Japan experienced one of the highest rates of inflation. However, the inflationary impact of the second oil crisis at the start of the 1980s was minimized; indeed, since the mid-1980s, Japan, taking advantage of the high exchange rate of the yen, has had, compared to most other countries, relatively stable prices.

Thus, it may be said that Japan, along with Germany, has managed to suppress inflation quite successfully in spite of the Japanese economy's high vulnerability to external shocks such as imported oil prices.

The third important variable is employment. Whether the economy can provide ample and stable employment opportunities to the population is the critical criterion to evaluate the effectiveness of economic policy. Whether the labor force is provided with a sufficient amount of such opportunities may be seen by examining the data on unemployment. Three different patterns of unemployment may be observed across these countries. One is the pattern which seems common to the European countries. Prior to the mid-1970s, their unemployment rates were rather low. Since then, the unemployment rate first increased markedly and since the early 1980s has tended to remain rather high. The United States experience has been quite different with the rate of unemployment exhibiting much bigger cyclical swings. Unemployment was high in the mid-1970s and the early 1980s, whereas it has been low during other phases of the business cycle.

The Japanese pattern is yet different. An outstanding feature of Japanese unemployment is its low level relative to other countries. Upon closer scrutiny, however, the level of unemployment has been increasing more or less secularly the last 15 years, perhaps reflecting some long-run structural change in the labor market. By the mid-1980s, the level had almost doubled, reaching the higher end of 2%. (In fact, in the Spring of 1987 the rate surpassed 3%.) Nevertheless, compared with other advanced economies, Japanese unemployment may be said to be quite low and stable. In other words, Japanese workers have been consistently provided with nearly full-employment conditions despite all the shocks and changes in external economic conditions.

This brief review of the macro-economic performance of several countries reveals that the economy of Japan has exhibited a rather successful pattern of overcoming and adapting to shocks or changes in external economic conditions. Despite the destructive inflationary shocks of the two oil crises, the prolonged world-wide recession of the early 1980s, and the drastic exchange rate realignment of the mid-1980s, it appears that the Japanese economy has usually managed to recover quickly from shocks, adapt to new external conditions, and has successfully restored stable prices and maintained full-employment conditions for workers. In this context, Japan certainly seems to exhibit one of the most successful models of adaptation to changes in environmental economic conditions.

14.3 A Review of the Experiences of the Japanese Economy in the Process of Adaptation

The process of adaptation of the economy may be described by the orbit of its performance as expressed by the quantity/price dimension. For example, the performance of the macroeconomy may be simplistically described by the combination of changes in aggregate output and the average price level. Figure 1 shows this orbit for changes in GNP and the GNP deflator.

Correspondingly, we may also depict an orbit for the labor market. Figure 2 shows labor market performance by the combination of changes in employment and wages.

Figure 1 indicates that the orbit makes a special move in each phase of economic fluctuations, reflecting the particular conditions of the phase. For instance, for several years in the mid-1970s, when the economy was hit by the first oil crisis, the orbit moved rapidly from the southeast to the northwest corners, and then moved downward rapidly. This reflects the fact that the Japanese economy suffered from acute stagflation in 1973–1974, but then quickly recovered, at least in the sense of restoring price stability.

In terms of movement in the labor market, this macro-economic change corresponds to a drastic increase in the wage rate in 1973, followed by a reduction in employment and subsequent reduction in the rate of wage

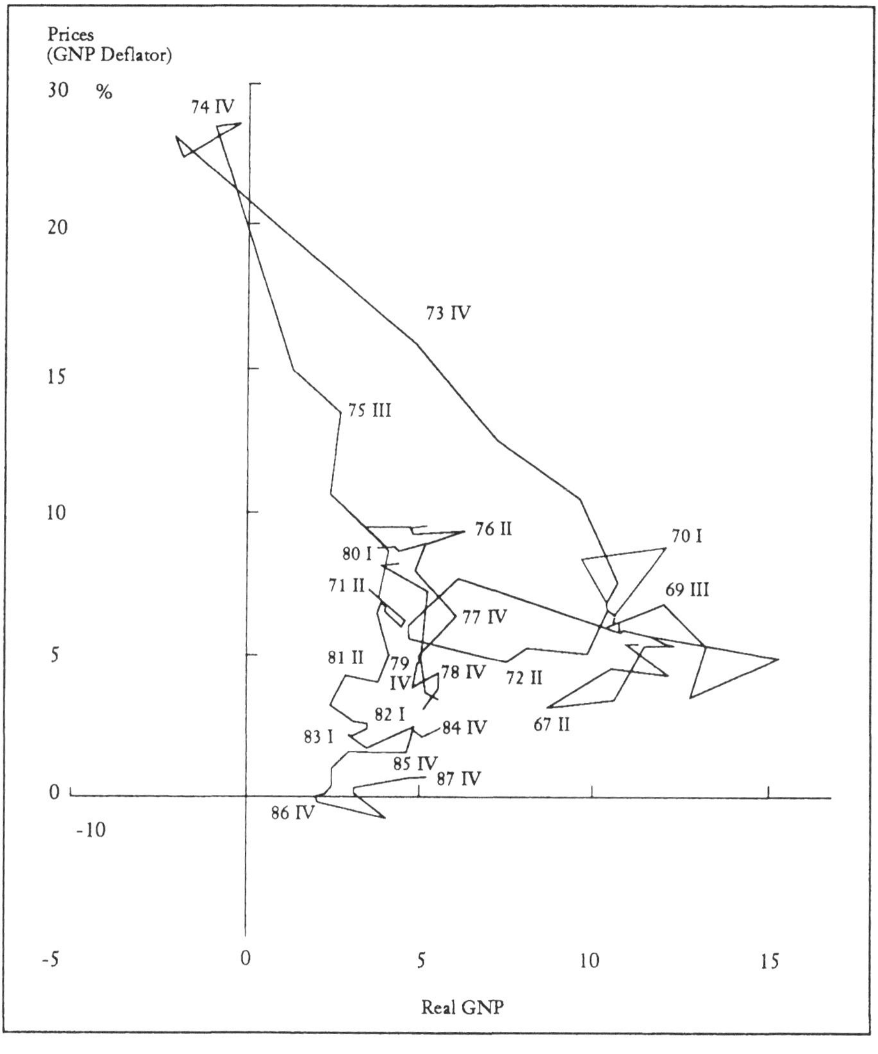

Figure 1: The Orbit of Rates of Changes of GNP and Prices:
The Case of the Japanese Economy

increase. In other words, sharp wage inflation was suppressed with a sizeable reduction of employment in the process of restoring stability in employment and wages.

The next interesting phase corresponds to the period when the Japanese economy was hit by the second oil crisis, around 1979 and 1980. This time the inflation rate accelerated but at a small margin with only a modest slowdown of the economy, and price stability was again restored quickly. In

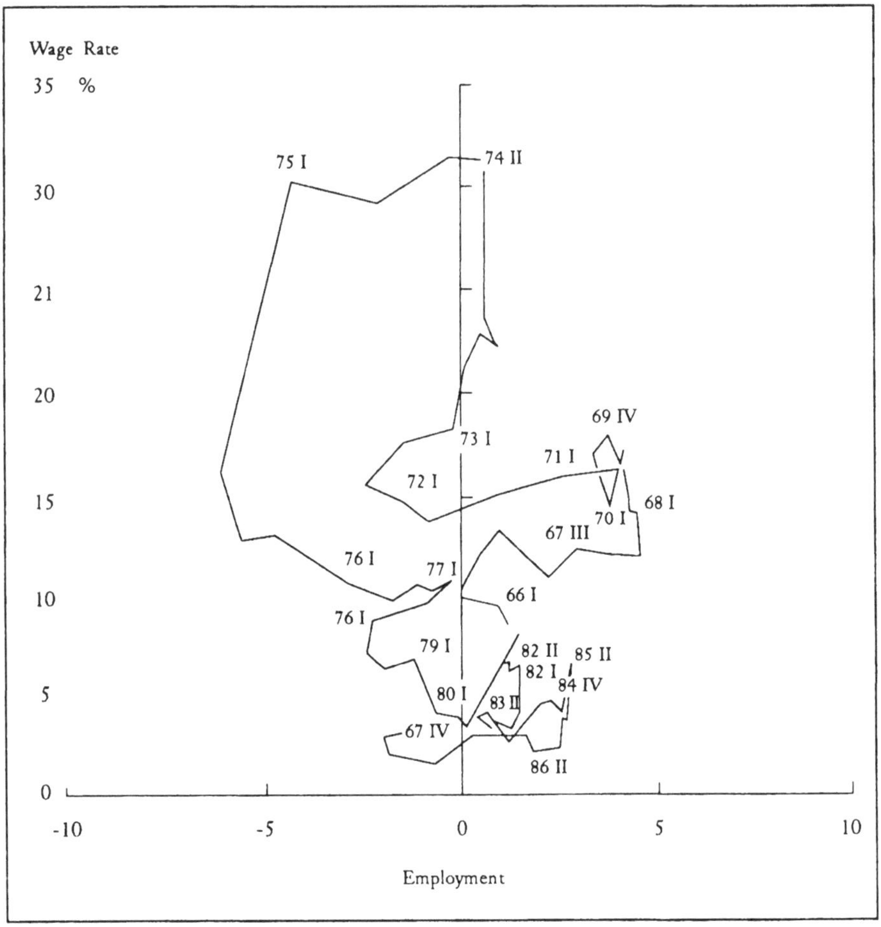

Figure 2: The Orbit of Rates of Changes of Employment and Wages: The Case of the Japanese Economy

the labor market, this change corresponds to only a modest increase in nominal wages and consistent improvement in employment conditions.

The third phase of interest is a few years during the early 1980s when the Japanese economy was caught in a prolonged recession, which stemmed from a deep recession in the United States in the early years of the Reagan Administration. Figure 1 shows that the economy clearly slowed down in 1981 and 1982, and then started to recover in 1983, while the rate of inflation has kept declining. In the labor market, as can be seen in Figure 2, the rate of increase of wages was further repressed during this phase while employment remained stable.

The fourth phase corresponds to the movement in the wake of the drastic realignment of exchange rates agreed to at the Plaza Meeting in 1985. Figure 1 exhibits a conspicuous downswing and a subsequent recovery of economic activity during the 1985–1987 period which has continued up to the present. Noteworthy is the fact that the rate of inflation has been suppressed down to near zero or has even been negative during this phase thanks to reduced import prices due to the increased value of the yen. Concerning the labor market, employment was reduced visibly during the down phase of the cycle, particularly in 1986, and the rate of wage increases has been kept at a low level.

After having briefly outlined the orbit of the performance of the economy and the labor market, let us look at the experience in four phases or sub-periods: (1) the first oil crisis, 1973–1978; (2) the second oil crisis, 1979–1980; (3) the Reagan recession and recovery, 1981–1984; and (4) the Endaka recession and recovery, 1985–1989.

14.3.1 The First Oil Crisis and the Adaptation Effort

The first oil crisis broke out in September 1973 when the oil producing countries decided on an oil embargo and then charged four times the price when they resumed exports. Since the Japanese economy had developed an industrial structure which was almost entirely dependent upon exported oil as the source of energy, the expected impact of quadrupled prices was seen as destructive or almost fatal.

It was anticipated that, as the economy used up its modest stock of reserved oil and began to rely increasingly on newly priced oil, the economy would be overwhelmed by a dramatic inflationary impact arising from very high energy costs. Such acute inflation would bring about a depressive effect on production, and it was expected, as a consequence, that the Japanese economy would be trapped in stagflation. Indeed, as anticipated under the impact of this oil shock, prices jumped up by a wide margin in 1974. Wholesale prices increased by 35% and consumer prices by 25% at their peak relative to prices of the previous year. As a consequence, production was disturbed, profits were squeezed, and investment was discouraged. In an attempt to maintain real wages, unions demanded wage increases of nearly 30% and were once accepted by management. However, as acute inflation proceeded still further unions had to further revise their demands upward, and eventually a 33% wage increase was granted to organized labor in the regularized Spring wage offensive of 1974.

Combating this acute inflation was seen as the prime target of policies and in the joint activities both by the government and business as well as labor leaders. The government launched severe austerity policies, particularly in terms of monetary policy. The government and the Bank of Japan pursued a tight money policy by strictly limiting new supply in order to siphon up excessive liquidity in the economy even at the expense of causing bankruptcy for some marginal firms. The financial circle, on the other hand, started to organize a special group of top executives from eight leading corporations in four major manufacturing industries in an attempt to set patterns for new wage policies.[1] Unions in the private sector also organized a special organization to promote policy activities more effectively.

Altogether, these efforts subsequently resulted in spawning a multitude of formal and informal organizations at various tiers of society, industry, and individual corporations ranging from a top-level tripartite consulting group to the Prime Minister to informal groups of workers organized at the workshop. These organizational networks have been highly instrumental for people, managers and workers alike, to share information and understanding about the state of the national economy as well as business conditions of individual companies. The author once called this organizational complex, which was organized more or less spontaneously rather than formally, the functional equivalent of the social partnership of neocorporatism. It served as vehicle when necessary to implement a *de facto* incomes policy largely through its informal information sharing functions rather than through the formal organization of a social contract as such.

In the sphere of corporate activities, serious efforts have been made to increase productivity. Perhaps the single most important strategy from the viewpoint of corporations' survival in an inflationary environment is to increase productivity. By increasing productivity, the company can reduce unit costs, which enables the company to lower the price of its product making the company more competitive. Strenuous efforts were made by Japanese corporations, particularly in export-oriented industries, to increase productivity by streamlining the production structure, saving energy consumption, developing new products, innovating production technologies, reshuffling and reducing the labor force, and so forth. As a result of such efforts, the labor productivity of Japanese manufacturing industry rose on the order of 10% per annum in the latter half of the 1970s.

Another side of the story was sizeable reductions in the workforce. This was called "employment adjustment".[2] As can be seen from Figure 2, Japanese manufacturing employment declined in the aggregate by 5% or so for a few years following the first oil crisis. Some industries were hit harder than others. The companies reduced their workforces, however, not in the

[1] The four manufacturing industries are steel, autos, shipbuilding, and electronics.

[2] Shimada, H. (1979): The Japanese Labour Market After the Oil Crisis. In: *Structural Determinants of Employment and Unemployment*, OECD, pp. 335–344. A more detailed exposition of employment adjustment may be found in Shimada, H. (1978): The Japanese Labor Market After the Oil Crisis: A Factual Report (I) and (II), *Keio Economic Studies*, 14 (1/2).

first instance, but as a final option after having mobilized all other measures to reduce the cost of production and employment, or even reducing the returns to investors and selling financial and other assets. The government partially supported efforts such as keeping a redundant workforce on the payroll by providing subsidies. Because of these efforts to avoid or minimize outright dismissals or layoffs, the employment adjustment process took much longer compared with other industrialized countries.[3] However, it is undeniable that the persistent effort of employment adjustment was at least partially responsible for the observed dramatic increases in productivity in the latter half of the 1970s.

Through these efforts, the Japanese economy was restored to a state of stable equilibrium rather quickly despite the fact that the impact of the first oil crisis was so massive that it was seen at the time to be almost fatal to the economy. Of particular importance among the various policies and efforts made during this phase were: extremely tight monetary policy which dampened inflationary expectations; a *de facto* incomes policy through information sharing; remarkable productivity improvement; and a sizeable employment adjustment.

14.3.2 The Second Oil Crisis and Recovery

The second oil crisis was no smaller than the first one if calculated in terms of Japan's increased aggregate payment to the oil producing countries relative to the size of the Japanese economy. However, the apparent consequences of this crisis seem much more modest and less disturbing than was the case of the first oil crisis (see Fugure 1 and Table 1). For example, the rate of inflation in 1980, one year after the oil crisis, was much less than just after the first oil crisis both in terms of the WPI and the CPI. Economic growth slowed down only marginally, and the volume of the reduction in employment was much smaller compared with the first oil crisis.

Why and how was the impact minimized in the aftermath of the second crisis? I would like to mention three reasons: (1) differences in the initial conditions; (2) learning by experience; and (3) a new industrial system was fostered. Let me discuss them briefly in turn.

The initial conditions of the Japanese economy prior to the second oil crisis were quite different from those of the first crisis.[4] Prior to the second oil crisis, the economy had excess supply capacity or a sizeable GNP gap. In contrast, in the case of the first oil crisis, the Japanese economy was already

[3] See, for example, Seike, A. (1982): Employment Changes and Analysis of Employment Adjustment Functions (in Japanese), *Keizai Bunseki* (*Economic Analysis*), (March), pp. 60–106.

[4] The difference in initial conditions has been stressed by Yoshitomi, M. (1981): *Nihon Keizai* (*Japanese Economy: A New Crisis of the World Economy and Japan*), Tokyo: Toyo Keizai.

overheated from a sustained period of accelerated growth and prevalent inflationary expectations. In the second crisis, the Japanese economy had been cooled enough by tight monetary policy and, as a result of substantial productivity improvement and continued moderate growth, had sufficient supply capacity. Given such conditions, it was not surprising that the economy was able to absorb the inflationary impact of the oil crisis more flexibly than occurred during the first oil crisis.

Learning effects should also not be underestimated, however. After going through the painful experience of struggling with rampant inflation and its depressive effects on production and employment, corporations and workers developed new schemes of cooperation such as information sharing networks, new production systems, and so forth.[5] On the basis of these new schemes, they reacted quite differently when hit by the oil shock. A notable example was the way in which employers and workers reacted when they engaged in wage negotiations. They were already fully aware of the lesson that simple-minded nominal wage increases just to keep up with inflation would only prolong the unproductive adjustment period. Instead, they chose to restrain nominal wage increases to somewhat lower than price increases and this helped to absorb the inflationary impact of the oil crisis more quickly than would have occurred otherwise.

Some of the efforts made during the learning process have had a persistent and long-lasting effect in the sense of developing new systems and new patterns of behavior. These long-lasting effects may be described as the spontaneous formation of a new industrial system. From the number of elements of such a new system, I would like to mention the following examples. One is the development of a more efficient system of production. A noteworthy example was the rapid diffusion of the so-called "Toyota System" during the latter half of the 1970s, not only among auto-makers but also more widely among various types of fabricating manufacturing industries.[6] The critical advantage of the Toyota system is its extraordinary efficiency in material and inventory handling to minimize the costs of production and distribution. Another is the development of energy-saving technologies. The new energy-saving technologies were applied not only to production machineries and facilities, but also consumer goods, and contributed greatly to altering the propensity to consume energy of the Japanese industrial and economic structure.

The third example that I would like to emphasize is the reinforcement of

[5] The development of information-sharing networking during this period is described in Shimada, H. (1983): Wage Determination and Information Sharing: An Alternative Approach to Incomes Policy? *The Journal of Industrial Relations* (June), 177–200.

[6] See Ohno, T. (1978): *Toyota Seisan Hoshiki* (*Toyota Production System*), Tokyo: Diamond Publishing Company; Monden, Y. (1989): *Toyota Production System: A Practical Approach to Production Management*, Atlanta: Industrial Engineering and Management Press.

what I call the "industrial culture" of Japanese corporations and industrial relations.[7] The joint experience of managers and workers in each corporation to work hard together in an attempt to overcome the hardships brought about by the oil crises reinforced the common belief and the confidence in close management/worker cooperation. This "culture", which had been cultivated earlier and was reinforced through the joint experience of overcoming the crises, has a profound meaning in the sense of molding common values, in the way of thinking, and in the peculiar behavioral patterns in the Japanese corporate community. It has had, in my judgement, significant implications for the nature of Japanese industrial relations and for the patterns of responses of Japanese management and workers in the subsequent phases of economic changes.

14.3.3 The "Reagan" Recession and Recovery

The Reagan administration appealed to the public when they stated that they would bring about more viable economic growth by applying the so-called "Reaganomics" approach. Their scenario was to encourage savings by reducing income taxes and to stimulate investment. For the first few years of the administration, the scenario did not work, and the United States economy drifted into a deep and prolonged recession. Because other economies were dependent upon the US economy through trade and other relationships, this recession affected them as well. Since the Japanese economy is closely tied with that of the United States, Japan was deeply affected by the recession.

The United States and Japanese economic relationship during this period developed into a peculiar and problematical interdependence. While the Reagan administration cut taxes sizeably, it was unable to reduce expenditures, particularly defense expenditures, as much as they wished. As a result, the fiscal deficit grew rapidly. Deficient revenue had to be supplemented by other sources. Since both the government and private sector were short of savings, the source of funds had to be sought overseas. On the side of Japan, the government had been suffering from a fiscal deficit for some years, and the prime policy target was to squeeze the deficit. Because of this policy constraint, the government did not want to engage in expansionary policy to increase public investment. The excess savings of the Japanese private sector, particularly the household sector, which was not offset by domestic investment, therefore found its way to increase Japanese exports particularly to the United States, whose currency was kept at an unduly high value. Trade surpluses accumulated in Japan were then recycled to the United States under

[7] The concept of "industrial culture" is presented in Shimada, H. (1990): Japan's Industrial Culture and Labor–Management Relations, Paper prepared for the Japanese Political Economy Conference (forthcoming from the University of California Press in Volume III of the project).

high US interest rates, partially to finance the US government's fiscal deficit. In other words, the US and Japanese economies were closely intermingled via highly lopsided trade and capital flow relationships.

Under the prolonged recession, unemployment kept steadily increasing in Japan, even though its level is relatively low compared with other countries. Since domestic investment opportunities were limited, exports tended to increase. Increased exports to other countries which were also suffering from stagnant economic conditions triggered, not surprisingly, trade conflicts. With the increased pressure of trade conflicts, Japanese corporations started to shift their resources increasingly from direct exports to foreign investments. After having completed massive employment reductions in the late 1970s to restore competitive balance, many corporations started to develop new corporate strategies for R&D and the diversification of corporate activities.

Around the beginning of 1983, the US economy started a vigorous recovery from the recession. The recovery of the US economy, quite ironically, deepened the distorted relationship with the Japanese economy. Exports from Japan increased even further to satisfy increasing US domestic demand. The US economy now suffered from serious dual deficits – fiscal and trade. In spite of huge trade deficits, the value of the dollar was kept unduly high partly because of the high interest rate policy, and partly because of speculative factors. This situation continued up to the shocking realignment of exchange rates which followed the Plaza Agreement of 1985.

14.3.4 The "Endaka" Recession and Recovery

Immediately after the announcement of the Plaza Agreement, the value of the dollar dropped sharply against most other currencies. The rate of adjustment was perhaps the largest against the Japanese yen. Within ten months after the Plaza Meeting, the yen was revalued from 250 yen per dollar to 150 yen, a change of some 60%.

This sharp increase in the value of the yen was perceived as a fatal shock to the Japanese economy, whose growth had been heavily relying on increases in exports. Export-oriented companies tried to struggle against this adverse impact in an attempt to preserve their past pace of exports. They tried to do so by means of squeezing production costs, cutting into profits, restraining wage increases, etc. Indeed, exports from Japan did not decline as much as anticipated. In fact, despite the large increase in the value of the yen, the nominal value of exports even tended to increase for some time. While this phenomenon, known as the J-curve effect, is often observed, part of the observed persistent increase in exports under the rising trend in the value of the yen may well have reflected the desperate efforts of export-oriented companies and industries. Under these circumstances, the Japanese trade surplus kept rising for some time through 1986 and reached the historically high level of 4.6% of GNP.

However, after a while, many export-oriented Japanese companies realized that their efforts were in vain. In spite of their strenuous efforts, it became increasingly evident that maintaining the past pace of exports was difficult and, in fact, not even economical in the face of the drastically increased value of the yen. Painfully realizing the changed trade environment, alert companies started to shift their emphasis from exports to production for the domestic market. Their strategy for shifting to the domestic market was facilitated by two major boosts: One was the high value of the yen, and the other was the drastically increased price of land. The increased value of the yen meant that Japanese industries were able to benefit from cheaper prices of imported materials, particularly oil and raw industrial materials. According to an estimate made by the Economic Planning Agency, the Japanese economy benefited from as much as a 25 trillion yen windfall saving during the three years from the Fall of 1985 due to the increased value of the yen. On the other hand, the increased value of urban land helped many corporations, which had some land in urban areas, to finance their investments to shift to the domestic market by borrowing from banks. Banks were willing to give loans to land-rich companies, even though their main activities were not going well, because the increased price of land meant to the banks a high collateral value. Increased land values also stimulated the consumption of land-rich persons through the so-called "wealth effect". In other words, in addition to the quick and flexible transformation of corporate strategies and activities, supplies to and demand from the domestic market were stimulated to some extent by these factors.

In early 1987, when the Japanese labor market recorded the postwar peak unemployment, reflecting the lagged effect of the previous recessions, investment for fixed capital was already vigorously increasing. This investment increase was soon followed by sizeable consumption increases, which together led to a marked increase in aggregate demand. Consequently, production and employment increased, which then again increased aggregate demand. In other words, a virtuous circle of economic growth was triggered from early 1987 which was centered around domestic demand, and it grew increasingly powerful in subsequent years.

While the Japanese economy managed to realize a "miraculous" recovery from the "Endaka" shock in this way, in the process some serious issues of structural distortions were left. Let me briefly mention three of them: (1) an increased gap between adjusted and non-adjusted sectors to the increased value of the yen; (2) an excessive concentration of resources and economic activities in the Tokyo metropolitan area *vis-à-vis* other areas; and (3) excessively long working hours for the high nominal incomes of Japanese workers.

The first problem is reflected in the wide gap between the nominal value of the yen and its domestic purchasing power.[8] This wide gap was created largely because the domestic prices of many consumer goods and services did not decline as much as fast as the increase in the value of the yen. The sluggishness in the decline of domestic consumer prices reflects the fact that some of the industries which produce goods and services such as agricultural produce, construction, distribution, and many personal services did not improve their labor productivity, and also that some of the industries are highly protected and regulated. High domestic prices, which suppresses the domestic purchasing power of the yen, keep the real standard of living of Japanese workers much lower than their nominal income.

The second problem distorts the allocation of employment opportunities in the direction of concentrating them in Tokyo and in the areas which are directly and closely related to Tokyo. In contrast, rural and countryside areas are provided with deficient demand. Since the Japanese labor force has been, for some inevitable reasons to be discussed later, losing its regional and occupational mobility over the long term, this phenomenon of an excessive concentration of economic activities in Tokyo is likely to weaken the structural adaptability of the Japanese labor market.

The third problem reflects, in part, the fact that Japanese workers have to work relatively longer hours than their Western counterparts because of much higher domestic prices, and, in part, the fact that both employers and workers have not come to the stage of realizing the high value of free time.[9] While the length of working hours of an average Japanese worker seems to be abnormally long for his rather high nominal income, this apparent gap is considerably dwarfed once it is contrasted against real income as measured in terms of domestic consumer prices rather than in terms of nominal dollar income. In other words, Japanese workers may work much longer hours than workers of other advanced nations partly because of the unique value associated with working itself, but they are also in fact obliged to work long hours because of high domestic prices which erodes their real standard of living.

14.4 Flexible Adaptation and Structural Rigidity

Reviewing the experience of the adaptation of the Japanese economy to changes in external conditions over the last two decades reveals a curious, mixed picture. In terms of macro performance, the economy seems to have adapted quite flexibly. However, when you scrutinize the structure and

8 While the exchange rate of the yen and its purchasing power parity relative to the dollar were in equilibrium in 1985, the gap has increased rapidly since then. As of 1987, for example, the gap is 145 yen per dollar for the exchange rate compared with 214 yen per dollar in terms of purchasing power parity.

9 Japanese manufacturing workers work more than 2,100 hours per year, which is about 200 hours more than their United States and British counterparts, and as much as 500 hours more than their German and French counterparts.

institutions of the Japanese economy in adapting to external changes, the responses seem to be more rigid than flexible. On the other hand, micro agents such as corporation seem to be quite flexible. Let us examine and evaluate the complex nature of the Japanese model of adaptability.

14.4.1 The Apparent Flexible Adaptability of the Aggregate Economy

At the national level, the Japanese economy seems to have exhibited quite flexible responses to external changes. In terms of aggregate performance, it has managed to maintain a decent pace of growth, nearly full employment, and price stability. The economy seems to have shown a remarkable capacity of suppressing the government's fiscal deficits and trade surpluses, both of which were once regarded as approaching dangerous levels.[10] The fact that Japanese unemployment has been consistently at a much lower level compared with other industrialized economies seems to imply that the labor market adapts better than other countries to structural changes in the sense of minimizing frictional unemployment.

However, once you begin to scrutinize more carefully the specific factors involved in the adjustment process, you may feel skeptical about the legitimacy of making such a general statement as the "flexible adaptability of the Japanese economy". The large part of the recent reduction of the government's fiscal deficit stemmed from voluminous increases in tax revenues due to unexpected increases in land prices. Had this not happened, it would have probably taken much longer before the fiscal balance would have been restored.

The rapid reduction in the trade surplus in recent years was due to a large extent to increased imports from the newly industrialized economies, and to some extent to the slow growth of exports due to the high value of the yen. Imports of manufactured goods have been penetrating the Japanese market in spite of restrictive regulations and *de facto* protective trade practices.[11] In fact, as we will see later, protective practices and regulations restrain the free inflow of cheaper foreign products and commodities, and consequently prevent Japanese consumers from fully enjoying the merit of the high value of the yen.[12] One of the reasons that Japanese workers work much longer hours than European or American workers with comparable industrial productivity lies in the fact that Japanese workers suffer from very high living costs when evaluated at the current exchange rate. This implies that the Japanese commodity market is in effect quite rigid and somewhat closed.

[10] In 1986, Japan's current account surplus reached a level of 4.6% of GNP.
[11] During the 1986–1988 period, the proportion of manufactured goods in total Japanese imports rose from about 30% to more than 50%.
[12] This is reflected by the large gap between the nominal value of their income measured in terms of the exchange rate and the real domestic purchasing power of their income as measured by purchasing power parity.

Moreover, quite ironically, the fact that the economy has had a consistently low unemployment rate may not suggest flexible adaptability as such, but rather the fact that there exists a large segment of rigid and low productivity industries. The economy as a whole can enjoy a low unemployment rate perhaps because this low productivity sector absorbed a large part of the labor force which could not be employed in the sector of highly efficient export-oriented industries. In other words, despite a seemingly flexible adaptability, the economy's internal structure and institutions are not that flexible or adaptable.

14.4.2 The Rigid and Less Productive Segment of Domestic Industries

There exists within the Japanese economy, as in other economies, a segment of industries which are quite rigid and of low productivity. These industries include some portions of the construction industry, distribution, agriculture and personal, services.

These industries have some common and critical features. Most of them produce non-tradeable goods and services and, therefore, are less likely to be exposed to the competitive stimulus of the external world. Most of them are run by small units of family businesses and, consequently, do not enjoy economies of scale. Most small family businesses are not capable or even interested in rationalizing and modernizing their management in order to enhance efficiency and competitiveness. These industries employ a large number of workers: some 15 million are employed in the distribution industry; 10 million in services; 5 million are in construction; 4 million in agriculture, and so on. By contrast, manufacturing as a whole employs 13 million. These industries have strong political influence by organizing their own pressure groups to protect their interests.[13]

Given this, it is difficult to expect rapid and flexible adaptability among these industries. These industries are currently regarded as being of low productivity and of charging extraordinarily high prices to consumers, when evaluated in terms of current exchange rates. However, just four years ago, when the exchange rate of the yen was nearly half of its current level, their labor productivity in nominal terms was not necessarily particularly low. This is because the nominal wage rate of Japanese workers was then much lower than now in dollar terms. The issue, therefore, is not so much absolute productivity differentials as much as changes in productivity over time. In other words, the real challenge is whether and how fast these industries can improve their labor productivity to cope with current exchange rates. The

[13] Too rapid changes forced by external pressures may well stimulate resentment among these interest groups and may well weaken the political basis of the ruling Liberal Democratic Party, as witnessed by the recent political development in Japan concerning the 1989 Upper House election.

fact that the manufacturing sector, particularly its leading segment, has somehow managed to increase productivity substantially over the last several years and, thereby, made themselves internationally competitive at current exchange rates suggests that the challenge is more real than imaginary.

At the same time, however, one needs to bear in mind that this large sector of low labor productivity does absorb well over two-thirds of the Japanese labor force thanks to its low productivity. If the sector increases its productivity by a wide margin, it is conceptually expected that a large proportion of its workforce would lose employment opportunities.

14.4.3 Flexible Adaptability of the Corporate Sector

Japanese corporations have been highly flexible in adapting to changes in external conditions. They adapted to high energy costs by developing energy-saving technologies. They adapted to slower economic growth and uncertain demand prospects by diversifying their corporate activities. They adapted to the increased value of the yen or increased costs by increasing productivity. They adapted to acute inflation both by increasing productivity and by fostering new schemes of wage moderation and labor/management cooperation. Indeed, this flexible and effective adaptation of Japanese corporations has been the most instrumental and critical factor making for the quite successful adaptability of the economy to external shocks and structural changes as a whole over the last 15 years.

Let us identify once again some of the important features of the adaptability of Japanese corporations. One example is their rapid productivity improvement. In the latter half of the 1970s, Japanese corporations sought to vigorously increase productivity by streamlining the production structure, innovating production technology, reshuffling and reallocating the labor force, etc., and consequently did attain remarkable productivity improvements, restoring not only their own international competitiveness, but also that of the Japanese economy. Similar efforts have been made more recently in the attempt to adapt to the new *Endaka* (the high value of the yen) environment. Japanese export-oriented industries have successfully increased their productivity to cope with an exchange rate of 120 yen per dollar.

Another example of adaptability may be found in the process of employment adjustment. While Japanese corporations minimize outright dismissals or layoffs in response to reduced demand, they eventually reduce employment burdens without much friction. To do so, they try to mobilize many possible measures for reducing costs or increasing revenues before resorting to reductions in employment. In case companies do have to adjust employment, they still try to transfer workers across workshops, plants, or even different companies to minimize layoffs. In order to make such transfers effective, corporations usually rotate workers among different job assignments either for a short or a long period. In other words, the flexible reallocation of the workforce serves both the purpose of training and minimizing intra-organizational mismatches. Japanese corporations adjust their workforce in this way by carefully reducing labor costs, spending sufficient time in the process to minimize the frictional costs of adjustment.

The third example is structural adaptation by diversifying or modifying the mix of corporate activities. The corporate strategy of diversifying business activities has become increasingly popular since the early 1980s when changes in technologies and the demand for products and services started being perceived as becoming more rapid and unpredictable. Under the slogan of corporate "restructuring", many corporations developed new corporate activities, including financial engineering and foreign direct investment, as well as stressing R&D and the fostering of corporate networks.

Government has provided policy assistance in many forms such as assisting and subsidizing R&D, advising and assisting structural adjustment, and by providing information, facilities, and subsidies to protect employment security, etc. Much of the government's policies worked effectively when applied to assist, encourage, or control corporate activities.

14.5 Remaining Structural Issues

While the Japanese economy has exhibited, in terms of macro-economic performance, successful adaptation to changes in external conditions, in the process there emerged some serious structural problems which have important implications for the economy in general and for the labor market in particular. Let us briefly review three issues: the land issue; industrial restructuring and the issue of hollowing out of the manufacturing sector; and structural change and employment issues.

14.5.1 The Land Issue and the Tokyo Problem

For a few years from the mid-1980s, land prices in major urban areas, particularly in and around Tokyo, increased drastically. For instance, over three years beginning in 1986, land prices in the residential district of Tokyo increased by nearly 170% and prices of apartments in the Tokyo area increased by more than 200%.[14] This abnormal phenomenon, which might be termed "stock inflation", occurred for several reasons.

One reason is the concentration of multiple functions in Tokyo such as the center of economic activities, monetary transactions, government administration, international exchanges, education, and so forth. This extraordinary

[14] For the three years from 1986 through 1988, the average official price of residential land in Tokyo increased by 167%, and the average market price of apartment houses rose by 205%.

functional concentration naturally promoted the concentration of economic resources and opportunities in Tokyo, and consequently generated an enormous demand for office and other space for industrial and commercial activities. A second reason is a monetary phenomenon. Because the rate of interest was kept at a historically low level around the mid-1980s, and also because the sharp decline of the value of the dollar since the mid-1980s discouraged Japan's investment into United States financial assets, a large amount of accumulated funds was directed either toward buying urban land or corporate stocks, which were both perceived as yielding relatively high returns. The third reason is insufficient investment in enriching the urban infrastructure in terms of supplying necessary housing spaces and transportation capacity to meet the increased demand generated by rapid economic growth. The fourth reason is inadequate tax policy. Property taxes are kept at so low a level that landowners are not pressed to sell their land, and what makes the problem worse is the rather high tax imposed on gains from selling land which discourages landowners from selling their land. Moreover, the rate of inheritance taxes imposed on land assets is in effect much lower than that on other financial assets so that people try to hold on to their land as an inheritable asset rather than selling it as a commodity. All these features of the tax system add up to discourage landowners from selling, and thereby contributes to intensifying the shortage of land supply.

This dramatic increase in land prices during the latter half of the 1980s has had some mixed and important effects on the Japanese economy and labor market. On the other hand, it has resulted in some favorable macro-economic effects: As mentioned earlier, it helped corporations to increase investments making use of their increased value of assets, it stimulated private consumption as a result of the wealth effect, and increased tax revenues accrued from the increased value of fixed assets helping to reduce the governmental fiscal deficit, and so forth. However, on the other hand, it seems to also have some serious distorting effects on the economy: It may well discourage the work incentives of ordinary workers who failed to take advantage of this drastic increase in land prices to increase their wealth, it may also discourage the incentives of people to save because many people will realize that they would not be able to purchase their own houses in major urban areas by saving part of their incomes, it may also effect the start-up of small venture businesses because of the extremely high costs of running offices and plants in the Tokyo area, and it clearly distorts the possibility of enriching the urban infrastructure for public purposes.

While the increase in land prices in the Tokyo area certainly reflects a more than proportionate increase in the intensity of economic activities centered around Tokyo, this tendency gives rise to some distorting effects on the labor market in the sense that it aggravates regional mismatches between labor demand and supply. Labor demand has markedly increased in and around the Tokyo area in recent years while the distribution of labor supply has not matched this changed distribution of demand. This appears to increase mismatches, and the fact that mismatches remain at a high level seems to imply that the Japanese labor market is rather rigid in responding to structural change. I will return to this topic later.

14.5.2 Industrial Restructuring and the Issue of "Hollowing" Out

The increased value of the yen since the Plaza Agreement in 1985 has had a substantial impact on the trade and industrial structure of the Japanese economy and, hence, on the structure of employment.

Under the high value of the yen, imports, particularly of manufactured goods, have increased markedly. Over the three years from 1985, the proportion of manufactured goods in total Japanese imports increased from some 30% to more than 50%. Many of the imports come from the newly industrialized economies such as Korea, Taiwan, Hong Kong, etc. This is a natural change which reflects the change in relative prices, namely, much cheaper prices of imports and much higher domestic costs of production due to the value of the yen.

Another side of the coin is increases in foreign direct investments. The increased value of the yen, and consequent cost differentials between Japan and other areas, naturally promotes the outflow of capital from Japan. Foreign direct investment has been increasing rapidly since 1986. While much of the investment has so far been in the area of financial assets and real estate, investment in services and manufacturing industries has also been steadily increasing. Despite this increase, Japan's foreign direct investment is still in an early stage. The proportion of manufacturing output produced outside of Japan through foreign direct investment is still only of the order of 5%, which is much less than (say) the 15–20% of Western European countries such as Germany.

Japan's foreign direct investment in manufacturing had, in its early stages, been promoted as a remedy to mitigate trade conflicts. That is, export oriented-industries were solicited to make investments in production facilities in the markets where they sell their products. However, after the mid-1980s, such investment has been further promoted by the high value of the yen. This factor, coupled with the aforementioned factor that Japan is not yet a completely mature country in terms of foreign investment, means that it is likely that Japan's foreign direct investment will increase much more in the long run. This trend and prospect, however, gives rise to a concern that the Japanese industrial base and employment structure may be "hollowed" as a result of increased foreign direct investment.

If things are interpreted in a static sense, it is plausible that the industrial and employment base could be hollowed out by substantial increases in capital outflows for manufacturing investment outside of Japan. The critical question is whether new industrial activities will be created to replace previously existing activities which have declined as a result of such outflows of capital. In the case of the Japanese economy over the last several years, it is more the case that new industrial activities have been created to fill the gap rather than simply suffering from the hollowing out of the industrial base. While a substantial part of the productive capacity of the Japanese electronics and automobile industries has been transferred to North America and other areas, and a large share of the domestic market for industrial commodities such as electric appliances has come from the NIEs, Japanese industries have simultaneously shifted their foci to new areas and activities such as new products, high-tech frontiers, R&D activities, and the international networking of corporations. This large-scale shfit of industrial activities is supported technologically by the increased strength of electronics, particularly of the IC technologies of Japanese industry.

This shift of industrial activities aggravates the shortage of human resources in areas of computer and electronics specialists on the one hand, while leaving aged workers relatively redundant on the other hand. Nevertheless, this shift of industry is generally vouched by the long-run change in the nature of the Japanese labor force in the direction of higher educational attainment and stronger preferences for high value-added and communications-related jobs. The fact that Japanese industry was able to take full advantage of the epochal development of information technology and internalize it for industrial and commercial uses while the economy was beginning to experience a massive increase in foreign direct investment was, perhaps, instrumental for the economy in minimizing the demerits of industrial hollowing out.

14.5.3 Structural Change and Employment Issues

Recently, particularly over the last year, Japanese industries have been increasingly suffering from labor shortages. With recovery and the subsequent expansion of the Japanese economy from mid-1987, labor demand has been increasing vigorously in Tokyo and areas directly linked with Tokyo by highways, or other transportation and communication systems. This disproportionate increase in demand centered around Tokyo reflects the disporportionate concentration of economic resources and opportunities in Tokyo, as I discussed earlier.

This uneven distribution of labor demand is reflected in regional differentials in the balance of supply and demand. Indices of such balances like unemployment rates or ratios of job openings to job applicants vary considerably across regions. Tokyo and other major urban industrial areas record demand/supply balances twice as tight as rural areas such as Hokkaido,

Shikiku, Kyushu, etc.[15] However, even for these rural labor markets the indices have been recently improving. This reflects the fact that much of the mobile and marginal labor force in these areas has been attracted and absorbed by the enormous demand centered around Tokyo.

Another feature of recent labor shortages is that it is largely a phenomenon of youth. The job openings to applicants ratios for other age groups indicate that neither middle-age nor older workers are in short supply. In addition, the current shortage of youth is expected to intensify in the future due to the predicted demographical-related decline in the youth population in the 1990s as well as because of reduced average working hours per worker in the future. Moreover, young workers seem to be increasingly selective in choosing their jobs partly because of their higher level of education and partly because of the general increase in wealth which increases the minimum supply price of labor. Faced with a severe shortage of young people, particularly in the areas of manual work and unskilled service jobs, employers in some segments of some industries are increasingly attracted to employing illegal foreign unskilled workers.[16]

These features of the current labor shortage seem to suggest that there are some serious structural and institutional problems which aggravate the issue. One problem is the regional immobility of the labor force. Thus, the shortage of labor is intensified partly because the actual or potential labor force in rural areas has not been mobilized to work in urban areas where demand has been increasing. There are several structural reasons behind this lack of mobility: family size has been declining for several decades and migration out of prefectural boundaries has secularly declined since 1970; the aging labor force makes occupational mobility increasingly difficult; families have accumulated a certain amount of assets and wealth which has increased the minimum supply price of labor; and greatly increased housing prices in the Greater Tokyo area has made migration to Tokyo difficult.

Under these circumstances, a sensible approach to minimize mismatches of demand and supply is to reallocate the distribution of demand. In other words, appropriate policy measures should be taken to encourage the relocation of industries and corporations to areas where potential labor supplies are available. To solicit such relocation, both the central and local governments should, working with the private sector, take appropriate measures to enrich the infrastructure so that operating in rural areas is just as profitable as operating in the Tokyo area. In my judgement, policy measures to relax

[15] Even in a year of booming demand such as 1989, there are large regional differentials. This is exemplified, for example, by the 3.2% unemployment rate in Hokkaido compared with a rate of 1.3% in the North Kanto district, and by an effective job openings to job applicants ratio of 0.7 in Hokkaido compared with 2.2 in North Kanto.

[16] Although no reliable estimates of illegal foreign workers in Japan are available, the sharp increase in the number of illegal workers who were identified or arrested suggests that the number has been rapidly increasing in recent years.

domestic aviation regulations and to reform telecommunication prices could be effective in triggering such relocation.

Another problem is the institutional rigidity of traditional Japanese employment practices. Japanese companies who wish to increase their workforce seek to recruit young workers. This practice was institutionalized during the postwar growth period when young workers were in abundant supply. Most Japanese companies are still bound by this practice and still seek new recruits from an increasingly scarce pool of young workers. This practice tends to aggravate the shortage of labor.

To circumvent this problem, what companies can do is to reorganize their employment systems to make more effective use, both in terms of hiring and training, of the middle-age workforce. This might involve overhauling not only conventional human resource management policies, but also corporate organizational policies. If Japanese companies are not able to reform their internal institutions to meet new environmental conditions, they will suffer more severely in the near future from the shortage of young people.

14.6 Implications for Tripartism

In the previous section, we have seen that the Japanese economy and labor market are suffering from several agonizing problems and consequently are faced with important policy challenges, particularly in the current phase of major structural change. These issues include, most notably, land and housing problems for urban workers and consequent deterioration of their substantive living conditions, changes in industrial structure and consequent changes in the nature and opportunities of employment, and mismatches between labor force and employment opportunities.

These issues provide policy agenda and tasks for each major actor within the society. The government, which is chiefly responsible for legal and institutional systems which govern and regulate allocation of resources, must be responsible for formulating an adequate legal system and policy measures to protect basic living conditions of workers such as their housing. Management is required to adapt their corporations flexibly to changed external conditions such as relative prices and social expections. To be more specific, changes in export and import prices, and increased demand of workers and people at large for shorter working hours and better quality of working life. Unions are hoped to act more forcefully and effectively to improve working and living conditons of their members. In the policy arena, they are encouraged to exert more powerful pressure to enact necessary legal measures to solve urban land problems and improve housing conditions for workers. In the sphere of labor/management relations within industry and corporations, they are requested to act more forcefully to protect working conditions of their members, most notably shortening working hours.

Many of these issues, however, cannot be solved easily or handled effectively by each actor alone. The government alone cannot amend or formulate laws. It needs political approval at the legislature, and this in turn requires popular support of the society. Management and organized labor are critical actors which can either foster or undermine support for government proposals. Management also needs support from the government and labor to adapt their corporations effectively to changed environmental conditions and social expectations. Corporate investment plans for innovation and restructuring are affected sensitively to interest rates, depreciations rules, tax prescriptions, and macro-economic conditions, many of which are decided or influenced by the government. Labor cooperation is critical for management to improve productivity and quality of their production and services. Labor unions cannot achieve their goals of improving living and working conditions of members, may they be improvement of housing or working hours, without understanding and reasonable cooperation of the government and management.

What makes the process of tackling these policy objectives more difficult or even disturbs is the almost innate organizational biases which are deeply rooted in the behavior of these actors. The Japanese government cannot make strategic decisions effectively on the basis of broad perspective. This is because of the highly segmentalized nature of its bureaucracy among different ministries and offices. Since each ministry and office is so rigidly and closely tied to its own demarcation, the government as a whole cannot easily take a broad view to make a strategic decision for the benefit of the population at large. Japanese corporations alike are driven so strongly by mutual competition that they often compete too fiercely among themselves even to such an extent to defeat the purpose of competition. For example, many companies compete fiercely not to lose their market shares even at the expense of increasing marginal costs such as in the areas of distribution, labor cost, and international trade conflicts. Labor unions also suffer from similar weakness. Japanese labor unions are good partners as well as reasonable bargainers for management within each enterprise. Because of this nature, their visions are often confined narrowly within the realm of individual enterprise and fail to see a broad societal world and to act effectively to promote social and institutional reforms.

To supplement such organizational biases and behavioral weakness, the spirit of tripartism is called for. Policy objectives, which cannot be attained easily by each actor alone or even disturbed when attempted by isolated actions of actors, could well be pursued and realized by fostering mutual understanding and organizing joint actions in the spirit of tripartism.

In fact, the spirit of tripartism has been penetrated broadly in the Japanese industrial society and indeed practiced quite widely at various levels of decision-making. At the level of each company, the system of joint consultation is widely prevalent. Although this is bipartism, the spirit of sharing information and fostering mutual understanding at this micro level of operation has been highly instrumental to support and enhance the spirit of tripartism at higher echelons and broader arenas of industrial society.

At the levels of industry and region, tripartite systems of representation are organized in a variety of forms. Interests of labor, management, and the general public are represented in such systems to facilitate mutual understanding and effective actions. In industry-level tripartite organizations, such as committees and special task forces, representatives of management, labor, and public interest work together to identify issues, analyze the situation, and discuss feasible options that they can jointly tackle. Industrial restructuring and improvement of working conditions such as shortening cf working hours are some of the focused agenda. In regional or local tripartite organizations, issues of improving housing conditions, protection of natural environment, regional economic development, and promoting local identities, etc., are often discussed. And at the level of national tripartite organizations, which are often organized by the initiative of the national government, issues of tax reform, regional development, housing, industrial restructing, and improvement of working conditions are discussed from a broader national and international perspective.

The spirit and system of tripartism, whereby relevant information is shared and common understanding of issues are fostered to pave the way for constructive negotiation, seems to be highly necessary for modern industrial societies to tackle complicated policy issues effectively, especially in the era of rapid structural change.

Notes on Contributors

Dr. Alan Brown, B.Com. (Hons), M.Com., Ph.D. is Associate Professor of Management in the Faculty of Business at the Edith Cowan University, Perth, Western Australia. He holds Honours and Masters degrees in Commerce and a doctorate in industrial relations from the University of Western Australia. Alan held the position of President of the Industrial Relations Society of Western Australia between 1988 and 1990. He has presented papers at local and international conferences and published in the areas of industrial relations and Total Quality Management. Alan is also active in consulting in the areas of general management, industrial relations, and Total Quality Management.

Renato Brunetta is Professor of Labor Economics at the II University of Rome (Tor Vergata). He has published numerous papers on the labor market, and the volumes *Economia del lavoro e equilibri, conflitto e piena occupazione* and *Microeconomia del lavoro*. He is the editor of *Report 89: Labour and Employment Policies in Italy* and the journals *Economia & Lavoro* and *Labour*.

Gian Primo Cella is Professor of Economic Sociology and Vice-President at the University of Brescia. Member of the Editorial Board at *Stato e mercato* and *Giornale di diritto del lavoro e di relazioni industriali*. Recent publications: (with T. Treu) *Relazioni industriali*, Bologna 1990: Il Mulino, and *National Trade Union Movements*, in Blanpain, R. (ed.), *Comparative Labour Law and Industrial Relations in Industrialised Market Economics*, Deventer 1990: Kluwer; *La solidarietà possibile*, Roma 1989: Edizioni Lavoro.

Carlo Dell'Aringa is Professor of Economics and Director of the Center of Labor Economics at the Catholic University of Milan. He has published several papers and books in the field of wage determination and income policies. With R. Brunetta he has recently edited the book: *Labour Relations and Economic Performance* for the International Economic Association.

Kevin P. O'Kelly is a consultant with the Irish Productivity Centre and a lecturer in industrial relations at the National College of Industrial Relations. He has worked as a researcher on developments in European industrial relations systems with the European Foundation for the Improvement of Living and Working Conditions. From 1977 to 1981 he was Political Adviser to the Irish Minister for Labor. He has a B.A. degree from the National University of Ireland and a postgraduate degree from the University of Dublin, Trinity College. He is a former Chairman of the Irish Association for Industrial Relations, an affiliated organization of the IIRA.

Manuela Samek Lodovici is Senior Researcher at Istituto per la Ricerca Sociale of Milan and teaches Labor Economics at the Catholic University of Milan. Her work is on industrial relations and labor policies.

Daniel J.B. Mitchell is Professor at the Anderson Graduate School of Management, University of California, Los Angeles, and Director of the Institute of Industrial Relations, UCLA, Los Angeles, California 90024, USA.

Emilio Morgado is an Official of the International Labor Organization. He has been the ILO Regional Adviser on Labor Law and Relations, then Director of the ILO Office for Central America and actually he is the Director of the Inter-American Center of Labor Administration (CIAT-ILO), a specialized and decentralized regional technical service of the ILO. He is a lawyer and Professor of Labor Law at the University of Chile. He is also one of the fifty members of the Iberoamerican Academy of Labor Law and Social Security and Doctor Honoris Causa of the University of Bordeaux.

Serafino Negrelli is Researcher of Economic Sociology at the University of Brescia. He is author of many researches on industrial relations at the enterprise or micro level. His contributions include "Management Strategy: Towards New Forms of Regulation?" (1988), in Hyman, R. and W. Streeck (eds.), *New Technology and Industrial Relations*, Oxford: Basil Blackwell; and "Industrial Relations in Italy" (1990, with E. Santi), in Baglioni, G. and C. Crouch (eds.), *European Industrial Relations: the Challenge of Flexibility*, London: Sage. His last book: *La società dentro l'impresa* (1991).

Victor A. Pesto is a member of the Department of Business Administration at the University of Stockholm, Sweden.

Haruo Shimada is Professor of Economics at the Keio University in Tokyo, Japan.

Hans Slomp (*1945), Assistant Professor of Comparative Politics and Labor Relations, University of Nijmegen. Publications on European labor relations, including a number of articles on Holland and Belgium, a monograph, *Arbeidsverhoudingen in België* (Utrecht: Het Spectrum, 1984), and more recently *Labor Relations in Europe, A History of Issues and Developments*, Westport CT: Greenwood Press, 1990.

Wolfgang Streeck is Professor of Sociology and Industrial Relations, University of Wisconsin–Madison. Diploma in Sociology (Frankfurt); M.Phil. (Columbia); Dr.Phil. (Frankfurt); habil. (Bielefeld). Senior Research Fellow, Wissenschaftszentrum Berlin (–1988). Visiting Professor, European University Institute, Florence (1983–1984); Leverhulme Visiting Professor in European Industrial Relations, University of Warwick (1985); Visiting Professor, Center for Advanced Studies in the Social Sciences, Madrid (1988). Publications on trade unions, business associations, industrial relations, politics in West Germany, and advanced industrial societies. Most recent articles and books (selection): "More Uncertainties: West German Unions Facing 1992", *Industrial Relations* (1991); *Beyond Keynesianism: The Socio-Economics of Production and Employment* (co-edited with Egon Matzner), London: Edward Elgar, 1991; "On the Institutional Conditions of Diversified Quality Production", in Matzner, E. and W. Streeck (eds.), *Beyond Keynesianism: The Socio-Economics of Production and Employment*; "Status and Contract as Basic Categories of a Sociological Theory of Industrial Relations", in Sugarman, D. and G. Teubner (eds.), 1990: *Regulating Corporate Groups in Europe*, Baden-Baden: Nomos, pp. 105–145; "Successful Adjustment to Turbulent Markets: The Automobile Industry", in Katzenstein, Peter (ed.), 1989: *Industry and Politics in West Germany: Towards the Third Republic*, Ithaca and London: Cornell University Press, pp. 113–156; and *New Technology and Industrial Relations*, co-editor with Richard Hyman, Oxford: Basil Blackwell, 1988.

Tiziano Treu is Professor of Labor Law at the Catholic University of Milan and President of the Italian section of IIRA (International Industrial Relations Association), Member of the Executive Committee of IIRA. Recent publications: Italian monograph of *International Encyclopaedia for Labour Law and Industrial Relations*, Kluwer, Deventer (Netherlands) 1991; *Labour Relations in the Public Service* (ed.), ILO.

Leonello Tronti is Professor of Labor Economics at the "Gabriele D'Annunzio" University at Teramo. He has published numerous papers on the labor market. He is co-editor of the volumes *Welfare State e redistribuzione* and *Report 89: Labour and Employment Policies in Italy*. He is research coordinator at the Fondazione G. Brodolini.

Mahmood A. Zaidi is Professor at the Industrial Relations Center, University of Minnesota and Director of the International Program Development, Carlson School of Management, University of Minnesota, 271 19th Avenue South, Minneapolis, Minnesota 55455, USA.

Francisco Zapata, 1943, is a Chilean sociologist. Author of *El Conflicto Sindical en América Latina*, El Colegio de México, 1986; *Ideologia y politica en América Latina*, El Colegio de México, 1990. Has published articles in *Sociologie du travail* (France), *Journal of Latin American Studies* (UK), and *Estudios Sociologicos* (México).

Bei Fragen zur Produktsicherheit wenden Sie sich bitte an:
If you have any questions regarding product safety,
please contact:

Walter de Gruyter GmbH
Genthiner Straße 13
10785 Berlin
productsafety@degruyterbrill.com